STEVENAGE

Frontispiece: Painting of St Nicholas' church by Ronald Maddox, PRI, Hon RWF, Hon RBA, one of a series commissioned by the Stevenage Development Corporation c1962. Reproduced by permission of the artist.

STEVENAGE

a history from Roman times to the present day

MARGARET ASHBY
AND DON HILLS

STEVENAGE BOROUGH COUNCIL

Other publications by Margaret Ashby

The Book of the River Lea, Barracuda, 1991. ISBN 0–86023–495–9. (Out of print).
The Book of Stevenage, Barracuda, 1982 (Out of print).
Elizabeth Poston, composer: her life at Rooks Nest, Stevenage, November 2005, Friends of the Forster Country, ISBN 0–9550669–0–5
Forster Country, Flaunden Press, 1991. ISBN 0–951–8242–01 (Available from bookshops or direct from the author)
The Hellard Almshouses and other Stevenage Charities, Hertfordshire Record Society, November 2005. ISBN 0 9547561–2–6
A Hertfordshire Christmas, 2nd edition, Tempus, November 2005. 0–7524–3679–1
A New History of Holy Trinity church, Stevenage, 2006.
St Nicholas' church; recent research 1 (editor), Friends of St Nicholas' Trust,1999.
Six Hills Nursery, Stevenage, Stevenage Museum, 1998
Stevenage, history and guide, Tempus, 2e, 2002. ISBN 0–7524–2464–5.
Stevenage Past, Phillimore, 1995. ISBN 0–85033–970–7.
Stevenage Streets, Tempus, 2004. 0–7524–3369–5.
Stevenage Voices, Tempus, 1999. 0–7524–1593–x.
Voices of Benslow Music Trust, Tempus, 2000. 0–7524–2048–8.
Historic Buildings of Stevenage (with Alan Cudmore and Colin Killick) The Stevenage Society, 2008. ISBN 978–0–9512073–2–1

Videos and DVDs – available from Stevenage Museum

Elizabeth Poston at Rooks Nest (October 2005). ISBN 0–9550669–1–3
Country Town
The Day War Broke Out
Two Mediaeval Churches
Wartime Voices

First published in 2010 on behalf of the authors by
Scotforth Books, Lancaster
www.scotforthbooks.com
www.carnegiepublishing.com

ISBN 13: 978-1-904244-61-5

Printed in the UK by Jellyfish Solutions Ltd

Acknowledgements

WE ACKNOWLEDGE WITH GRATEFUL THANKS the help in researching this book given us by so many people, especially; Richard Arnold, Ian and Patricia Aspinall, Melvyn Barnsley, Grahame Bowles, Margaret and Ken Bowyer, Peter Brown, Peter Conchie, Alan Cudmore, Marion De La Haye, Geoffrey Dennis, Michael Downing, Marilyn Emerson, Roy Findley, Alan Fuller, Claire Game, Ray Gorbing, Gwynneth Grimwood, Colin Haigh, Brian Hall, John Hepworth, Andrew and Tony Hills, Steven Hodges, Richard Holton, Clifford Ireton, Stella Kestin, Colin Killick, Adrian Knight, Alex Lang, Hilda Lawrence, Mike Leverton, Valerie Lines, Evelyn Lord, Aaron McDonald, Pauline Maryan, Volker Mathes, Gary Moyle, Ann Parnell, June Pitcher, Connie Rees, Christine Saint-Leitner, Arthur Scarrow, Alistair Scott, Hilary Spiers, Mary Spicer, Claire Sutton, Fred and Vi Udell, John and Sue Vincent, Ron Walker, Jo Ward, Owen Welch, Philip Westmacott, Adam Wood, Chris Woodard, Hertfordshire Archives and Local Studies staff, Stevenage Borough Council staff, Stevenage Central Library staff, Stevenage Museum staff.

Sadly, several people whose help we gratefully acknowledge died during the time that this book was being written, including Bill Lawrence, Eddie Messent, Hedy Pocock, Huw Rees, Alf Stokes and, most recently, Betty Game, in whose name a trust is being set up to help people living in Stevenage who need financial help to study with the Open University.

We have quoted from Jack Balchin's excellent book, *First New Town,* published by the Stevenage Development Corporation in 1980. Despite making every effort to do so, we have been unable to trace any members of his family who may have inherited the copyright.

Quotations from *Howards End* and *Two Cheers for Democracy* by E M Forster are used with permission from the Provost and Scholars of King's College, Cambridge and The Society of Authors as the literary representative of the Estate of E M Forster.

Despite making every effort to do so, we have been unable to identify the copyright holders of *Stevenage; a sociological study of a new town* by Harold Orlans.

Quotations from *The Comet* newspaper are used with permission from the editor, Darren Isted.

Barnett Street Plan of Stevenage used with permission of G I Barnett & Son, Ltd.

Contents

Abbreviations used in the text

ALMO – Arms Length Management Organisation
ARIBA – Associate of the Royal Institute of British Architects
AUBTW – Amalgamated Union of Building Trades Workers
BA – Bachelor of Arts
BAC – British Aircraft Corporation
BAe – British Aerospace
BBC – British Broadcasting Corporation
BEAMS – Built Environment Advisory and Management Service Hertfordshire Buildings Preservation Trust
CASE – Campaign Against Stevenage Expansion
CAUSE – Campaign Against Unnecessary Stevenage Expansion
CB – Companion, Order of the Bath
CBE – Commander, Order of the British Empire
CCTV – Closed circuit television
Cllr – Councillor
DSIR – Department of Scientific and Industrial Research
EADS – European Aeronautic Defence and Space company
ESA – Educational Supply Association
ESRO – European Space Research Association
FA – Football Association
FC – Football Club
FGS – Fellow, Geological Society
FLS – Fellow, Linnaean Society
Fr – Father
FRAS – Fellow, Royal Astronomical Society
FRIBA – Fellow of the Royal Institute of British Architects
HALS – Hertfordshire Archives and Local Studies (at County Hall, Hertford)
HCC – Hertfordshire County Council
ICI – Imperial Chemical Industries
ILEA – Inner London Education Authority

IRA – Irish Republican Army
ITV – Independent Television
JP – Justice of the Peace
KBE – Knight Commander, Order of the British Empire
KCMG – Knight Commander, Order of St Michael and St George
LCC – London County Council
LSVT – Large Scale Voluntary Transfer Scheme
MA – Master of Arts
MBDA – Matra BAe Dynamics Alenia
MBE – Member, Order of the British Empire
MC – Military Cross
MP – Member of Parliament
NAPGC – National Association of Public Golf Courses
NHDC – North Herts District Council
NUGMW – National Union of General and Municipal Workers
OBE – Officer, Order of the British Empire
OP – Order of Preachers
PhD – Doctor of Philosophy
RAF – Royal Air Force
RE – Royal Engineers
Revd – Reverend
RN – Royal Navy
RSPCA – Royal Society for the Prevention of Cruelty to Animals
SCLC – Stevenage Conservation Liaison Committee
SDC – Stevenage Development Corporation
SDP – Social Democratic Party
SITEC – Stevenage Information Technology Centre
SIWSSO – Stevenage Interworks Sports and Social Organisation
SMAC – Shephall Manor Action Committee
SOE – Special Operations Executive
SUDC – Stevenage Urban District Council
UCATT – Union of Construction, Allied Trades and Technicians
UN – United Nations
UNISON – Public service trade union formed in 1993
USA – United States of America
WVS – Women's Voluntary Service (WRVS from 1966 – Women's Royal Voluntary Service)
YMCA – Young Men's Christian Association
YTS – Youth Training Scheme

Foreword

ON THE NIGHT I was elected as Member of Parliament for Hitchin, I remember driving to the top of the hill on the A1 just south of Stevenage and looking at the lights spread out below me in the night sky. I was delighted and astounded at winning the constituency in the very close 1964 General Election which brought Labour to power after thirteen years of Conservative governments. I was also awed by my new responsibilities for the large constituency of Hitchin, a constituency that covered most of north Hertfordshire.

It was a very varied constituency, with four substantial towns and many villages. In the north there was Royston, at the edge of East Anglia, rolling country where racehorses galloped across Therfield Heath, where you could still find remnants of the camps in which once prisoners of war from the long campaigns against Napoleon Bonaparte at the beginning of the nineteenth century had been held. A few miles south was the fine old market town of Hitchin, after which the constituency was named, and the lively garden city of Letchworth, home to many voluntary organisations engaged in everything from Morris dancing to overseas aid.

And then there was Stevenage, once a village supplying travellers on the long journey north from London, in the middle of a transformation into the first of Britain's post-war New Towns. In the years between the wars, new housing had been provided by private developers mainly by building suburbs around existing towns. Many of these suburbs were dormitories for commuters and their families, with few facilities for shopping or entertainment. After the second world war, however, a more imaginative generation of planners and architects led by Patrick Abercrombie came up with the idea of "green belts" around towns so that they could no longer spread randomly into the surrounding countryside, with people who needed rehousing instead being offered houses in new towns beyond the Green Belt. These new towns would be much more self-contained than the pre-war suburbs. There would be industries and offices to provide jobs, schools, shops and churches to meet the needs of their citizens, and hopefully the construction of the civic loyalty and community spirit among them. Stevenage was to be the first pioneer in this great social experiment.

So I had a special relationship with Stevenage. The town and I would grow up together over the next fifteen years, learning from experience. There would be difficult times, some of them reflecting what was happening nationally, like industrial unrest or recession, others connected specifically with the rapid growth of the town, like the considerable tensions between the Stevenage Development Corporation and the town's own elected Urban District Council. And there would be mistakes, like the long delay in providing the public services the rapidly growing town needed.

The first generation of builders and pioneers of Stevenage New Town is now passing away. This was the generation that constructed the early neighbourhoods in Bedwell, Broadwater and Shephall, started some of the imaginative civic schemes like the Youth Trust that culminated in the youth centre of Bowes-Lyon House, and saved Fairlands Valley, making Stevenage a green town long before that was fashionable. It wasn't easy. The birth and infancy of the New Town was attended by controversy, and there were many stand-offs between the Corporation and the Council, a Council that had seen most of its powers overlaid by an unelected Corporation which could sometimes be high-handed. In the early years, the Corporation too often failed to consult either the Council or the people of Stevenage, some of whom became highly antagonistic to any plans for expansion. But all of us learned from our mistakes, and that it is essential to work together. By the 1970s, that was happening. The Corporation contributed to the building of community centres and accepted important proposals from the Council, like the construction of a centre that combined the arts and sports, a radical idea at the time. It managed to handle pressures from Whitehall for greater housing density to save public money without sacrificing the green quality of the town. The Council had its own representatives on the Corporation board, leading to much better mutual understanding. At Corey's Mill, a handsome modern hospital, the town's most aching need, was finally opened in 1972.

That first generation of New Towners came mainly from London – and from some of the most overcrowded and deprived boroughs of north London. As children and young people, many had endured dreadful housing and attended grim schools. The streets were their playground. Stevenage seemed too many of them a paradise. But mistakes in its planning brought problems in their wake.

One was the delay in providing services like schools, health centres, and sports facilities. Another was the lack of provision for the older generation, the grandparents who could be a source of care and support for their sons and daughters trying to establish themselves in a new setting. Both mistakes were corrected, but only after a decade or so. What did emerge, however, were natural leaders, men and women prepared to take responsibility for their fellow-citizens as well as themselves.

Among the most outstanding was Phillip Ireton, a native of Hertfordshire, with a genius for planning born of his admiration for the garden city of Letchworth, a self-taught authority on local government who became chairman both of Stevenage Council and Hertfordshire County Council and was later awarded the CBE. He was the first person to be made a Freeman of Stevenage. Another was Brian Hall, who led the Council for many years, a gifted and determined man who steered his way through the difficult rocks and sandbars of Whitehall changes of mind about Stevenage expansion. Every change of Minister, let along changes of government, would once again raise the question of the town's future. The boldest attempt finally to settle the issue was the Council's proposal for a private bill under which the assets of Stevenage would pass to the town council and become the basis for self-financed future development. The idea of a town that belonged to itself, municipalised rather than nationalised, was a brilliant one. But it was too far ahead of its time to commend itself to the government, and failed to get through Parliament.

There were many others who made an outstanding contribution to Stevenage: Alf Luhman, the first new town resident to become chairman of the Urban District Council, Michael Cotter, Hilda Lawrence and Peter Metcalfe, who served both on the Council and on the Corporation's board, building the essential bridges between the two; Bill Lawrence, who devoted himself to realising the dream of a sports and arts centre worthy of the first New Town and many many others. From the Corporation sides there was a corresponding emergence of sympathetic leaders, from "Sedge" McDougall, General Manager of Stevenage Development Council, with whom I worked closely in the 1960s, to Evelyn Denington, the chairman who did most to strengthen links with the elected council, not least because she herself had been an outstanding figure in local government in London.

Britain in very bad at appreciating and publicising its own contemporary achievements. We have the National Trust and English Heritage to remind us of the triumphs of the past, lovely countryside and graceful mansions, well-tended gardens and beautiful cathedrals and churches. But few celebrate the successes of the present age. We rightly admire the rebuilding and preservation of Europe's loveliest cities, from Paris to Barcelona, but say little of our own. Yet the New Towns experiment has proved itself a bold response to the rehousing of hundreds of thousands of people from the cities without the despoiling of the countryside in a densely populated country. Of course it hasn't been without problems. That is the nature of life itself. As in Britain the composition of Stevenage's population today is different and more cosmopolitan .A significant number of residents commute to London each day, but the town-though not without problems is a good place to live, bearing witness to the firm foundations laid down in the New Town Act of 1946.

The story celebrated in this excellent book, with its carefully researched detail and its determination to tell the story of Stevenage accurately and truthfully, deserves its important place in out modern history. Those whose work and devotion culminated in the first New Town, now for over thirty years the Borough of Stevenage of which I, too, am proud to be a Freeman, deserve our thanks and our appreciation.

Shirley Williams

CHAPTER ONE
From early settlement to market town

IN THE YEAR 100 AD, travellers making their way north along the Roman road, which later became known as the Great North Road, would have come upon some impressive earthworks 30 miles from Londinium. This place was the burial ground for a wealthy Romano-British family who farmed land to the east of the road, near Humley (or Whomerley) Wood. Only an important family could afford to build on this scale. Eventually there were six burial mounds, now known as the Six Hills, and until recently they were the chief known evidence of a Roman presence in the district which has become Stevenage. The travellers, gazing admiringly at the work in progress, could not know that the Six Hills would still be standing nearly 2,000 years later.

Most of the area which is now called Hertfordshire had been ruled from the beginning of the first century AD by the British Catuvellauni tribe, but in the north of the county the Trinovantes were also a powerful force. Chieftains from the two tribes battled for supremacy until the Catuvellauni were triumphant. They in their turn were vanquished by the conquering Roman armies of 43 AD.

An essential element in the Roman strategy for subduing the native British population, and enabling trade to flourish, was the construction of roads, some new but most based on existing tracks. Two of these were particularly important for the future Stevenage. One, the road from Verulamium (St Albans) to Baldock via Wheathampstead, Coleman Green, Fishers Green and Coreys Mill, was in use for over 1,500 years but today remains only as a series of footpaths. The other, from Londinium (London) to Eboricum (York) was not yet fully completed as a continuous road, but it grew in importance over the centuries,

Hornbeams in Whomerley – correctly pronounced 'Humley' – Wood. (Margaret Ashby)

Drawing of the Six Hills, 1724. (Stevenage Museum)

The Six Hills early twentieth century, looking north along the A1, the Great North Road towards Stevenage. (reproduced from an original Frith & Co. postcard held at Stevenage Museum P0074)

becoming known eventually as the Great North Road, the A1. This road influenced the history and development of Stevenage for nearly 2,000 years: its importance cannot be over-emphasised. Without it there would have been no Stevenage.

During the Roman occupation there were significant Romano-British settlements at Baldock, Welwyn and Braughing; a villa of perhaps 680 acres at Great Wymondley; and the great Roman city of Verulamium 15 miles to the south-west. There were also many small, often isolated farmsteads although communication between them improved as roads were upgraded thanks to Roman engineering skills. In particular, the north–south roads through Hertfordshire were increasing in importance. Whether the native British inhabitants of the area lived in peaceful co-existence with their conquerors or in resentful subjection is not known, or to what extent they were involved in the events of 60 AD. In that year Boudicca, Queen of the Iceni tribe based in Essex, lead a great rebellion against the Romans who had committed gross acts of brutality against her people. Seeking vengeance, she led an army of 120,000, who burnt Colchester, London and St Albans. Members of the Trinovanti tribe who had joined her took vengeance on the Catuvellauni as they marched through the countryside. If any of these attacks took place in the Stevenage district it must have been a frightening time for the occupants of those little farmsteads near Humley (Whomerley) Wood, Great Collens Wood, Sish Lane and others whose remains have not yet been found.

Archaeological dig at Boxfield Farm housing development site. (Stevenage Museum).

For centuries, only the fragmentary evidence of such objects as pottery, iron work, bone tools and cremation remains had been found to point to the existence of local Romano-British farmers. However, between 1986 and 1990, archaeologists began excavating the site of one farm, at Boxfield in Chells. They were able to establish that this farm had existed in some form before the Roman invasion in 43 AD. Its occupants grew wheat, kept cattle and ensured a supply of water by first digging a well and then, a century later, converting it to a series of ponds. They also used coins for trading and at least one individual, or perhaps a group, hoarded them in a large pottery vase, which was buried in the ground for safe-keeping. By 263 AD a total of 2,579 coins had been accumulated, mostly dated between 163 and 193 AD. Then some disaster must have occurred

Chells coin hoard.
(Stevenage Museum 0590)

– perhaps a serious fire – and the coin hoard was never retrieved. It stayed there, undiscovered, until found in 1986 by the archaeologists who had been called in when a few coins were seen lying on the surface of the newly turned earth. They were particularly intrigued to find that one of the coins was minted during the brief reign of Emperor Pacatian in 249 AD. It is the first and so far, the only, coin of Pacatian that has been discovered in England.

The Roman armies left Britain in 410 AD, as Germanic tribes of Angles, Saxons and Jutes over-ran the country. The next four centuries are known as the Dark Ages because there are very few contemporary records of events and very little in the way of archaeological remains from that time, thus it is hidden in intellectual darkness. It is believed that the area which later became the county of Hertfordshire was one in which Celtic British language and customs survived longer than in many others. In his book, *Britons and Saxons; the Chiltern regions 400–700,* K Rutherford Davies suggests that, 'the inhabitants of this region still spoke British ... as late as about 600 AD or even afterwards'. One oft-quoted piece of evidence for this is of local interest. The river into which the tiny Stevenage Brook flows is the Beane, a Celtic name originating c600 AD as 'Beneficcan'. This and other place-names indicate a considerable British presence here for centuries after the Roman Conquest and during the subsequent invasions.

As wave after wave of Germanic tribes arrived, roads, towns and cities built by the Romans fell into ruin, but farming continued, as did trade. The Jutes settled mainly in Kent and the Angles, who gave us the English language, in East Anglia, but it was the Saxons who became dominant and divided England into kingdoms. At this time the county of Hertfordshire did not exist as a separate entity but was part of the East Saxon territory of Essex, which itself was later taken over by the kingdom of Mercia. During the sixth century, Saxon communities settled in parts of what became north Hertfordshire, including a site east of the Six Hills. Here, as Stevenage New Town was being built 1900 years later, traces of an early Saxon hut were discovered in the garden of 444, Broadwater Crescent. It was excavated in 1960–61 by Irene Traill, Assistant Curator at Stevenage Museum, who described it in detail. It is still unclear whether the building was an isolated dwelling or part of a large settlement, or even if it was a dwelling at all, but perhaps some kind of meeting place.

Information about life in the Stevenage area for several centuries after the Romans left Britain is almost non-existent. Yet it was in this period that the original settlement, which was to become our town, was built on the hill where

St Nicholas' church still stands. By about 500 AD, the Saxon village of Stithenaece or Stigenace had been established, half a mile above the Roman road. Because most Saxon buildings were of wood, the majority have vanished without trace, but it is probable that a simple wooden hut was built to serve as a church, which in succeeding centuries was enlarged and rebuilt. The name 'Stevenage' is clearly of Saxon origin: its spelling has varied over the centuries, the earliest recorded being 'Stithenace' in 1062. In 1902, the historian E V Methold traced many of the spellings known at that time and published this list, to which many variants could be added;

> Estevenach, Stephen-Edge, Stigenace, Steavenidg, Stevenege, Stigenhaga, Steavenidge, Stevenage, Stigenhage, Steevenage, Stevenhaugh, Stigenhant, Stevenach, Stevenhaught, Stithaye, Stevenache, Stevenidge, Stigehauht, Stevenedge, Stevenig, Styvenage.

Whatever the spelling, the most likely meaning of the name is probably 'At the strong oak'. During the sixth century other Saxon settlements existed in the Stevenage district, including those at Chells, Box and Woolenwick. Some incoming Saxon farmers took over fields previously cultivated by their Romano-British predecessors; others either created new farms or increased the area of the existing farmland by clearing woods for grazing and arable crops. The woodland itself was important, to produce timber for building and many other purposes, and the Saxons were skilled in such techniques as pollarding, coppicing, close planting and charcoal burning. As for water, the villagers of Stigenace had a plentiful supply from the many springs in the chalky soil.

The Saxon form of local government included a system known as Frankpledge, in which a village or other area was divided into tithings. These were groups of ten householders and their families who were pledged to obey the laws and customs of the village and to answer for each other's good conduct. Each male over the age of twelve was obliged to be in a tithing. For matters of wider importance, a moot, or court, was held. In parallel with the development of civil law, arrangements were being made for governing the Church in England. In 597, Pope Gregory had sent his emissary, Augustine, to England to convert the Saxons to Christianity. In due course the country was divided into dioceses, each under the jurisdiction of a bishop. The dioceses

St Nicholas' church. (Margaret Ashby)

themselves were subdivided into parishes, each with a priest to minister to the people there. The parish of Stevenage became part of the enormous diocese of Lincoln, which stretched from the Humber to the Thames.

Saxon England did not survive undisturbed. During the ninth and tenth centuries more invaders arrived, Danes, or Vikings, from Scandinavia. In 878 the English King, Alfred, defeated them in battle and then imposed the Treaty of Wedmore, by which a boundary was drawn between land which would be subject to Danish law and that which would be subject to English law. The boundary line was defined as along the River Thames, from its mouth as far as its confluence with the River Lea, then along the Lea to its source. Land to the east of this line, that is East Anglia, Lincolnshire and most of Yorkshire, would be part of the Danelaw. As a result, Stevenage was in an unenviable position, just inside the Danelaw but in border territory and likely to be fought over. People living in the little Saxon village must have been in a constant state of alert, if not complete fear, as the Danes broke the treaty and fighting broke out again.

There is no written record of battles, or of Danish settlements, in the Stevenage district. One small piece of evidence is the place-name Gunnell's (or Gunhilda's) Wood but nothing at all is known of this woman, Gunhilda. However, there was for centuries a belief that Danes had fought in battle in or near Stevenage and that the Six Hills were the tombs of Danish warriors. A lane called Danestrete is believed to have existed in the middle ages and there are several places in east Hertfordshire, one of which is very near Stevenage, called Dane End. However, according to the English Place-Name Society, they 'have nothing to do with the Danes' but are corruptions of the Old English word 'dene' meaning 'small valley' or 'dingle'. Nevertheless, the belief persisted in Stevenage that there had been a strong Danish presence here.

In the years 912–13, King Edward the Elder, son of Alfred the Great, built two fortresses on the River Lea, at a place which became the town of Hertford. It also became the county town, as the county of Essex was divided and the western part made a county in its own right, with the name of 'Hertfordshire'. Its purpose was to protect the strategically important town of Hertford.

By the end of the tenth century the final piece of the Saxon local government system was in place, the division of counties into hundreds. Not all hundreds were of the same size, but each had within its bounds 100 families, or 100 hides. A hide was either approximately 120 acres or sufficient land to support one family. Hundred courts were held outdoors, very often at a wide open space beside a road. Stevenage was in the Broadwater Hundred, which got its name from the place where the Stevenage Brook tended to overflow, at the point where the Roman road forked for Hertford or London. The importance of this historic place, which gave its name to a hundred stretching from Hatfield in the

Stevenage Bury c1800. (Stevenage Museum P4503)

south to Baldock in the north, has diminished over the centuries, but Broadwater Hundred courts were still being held up to the 1930s although by then they took place indoors, in Stevenage town hall.

The first known written record of the existence of Stevenage occurred in 1062 when King Edward the Confessor gave the manor (estate) of Stithenace to the Abbot and convent of Westminster. This meant that the Abbot, as Lord of the Manor, was entitled to the produce from the manor farm, or demesne, and to rents from tenants, fines from the manor court and other taxes and tolls. At this date, Westminster Abbey was being built as a new foundation, started in 1050 and completed in 1065. By their labour in the fields, the people of Saxon Stevenage were directly supporting this great new abbey and also beginning the link with London which would forever influence the future development of their village.

At the time of the Norman Conquest in 1066, Stevenage was well-established on its hill-top site. By then it almost certainly had its wooden church, with the manor house or Bury nearby, where the representative of the Abbot of Westminster held court. The surrounding fields were ploughed by oxen, pigs were kept in the woodland and there was pasture for the livestock. It was a large village of eight hides, compared with the more common five-hide village, as *Domesday Book*, compiled in 1086, describes:

> The Abbot holds Stevenage himself. It answers for 8 hides.
>
> Land for 10 ploughs. In lordship 4 hides; 2 ploughs there.
>
> 16 villagers with 8 smallholders have 7 ploughs; an eighth possible. 4 slaves.
>
> Pasture for livestock; woodland, 50 pigs.

The total value is and was £12; before 1066 £13.

This manor lay and lies in the lordship of St Peter's church [ie Westminster Abbey].

The other *Domesday Book* entries relating to Stevenage are those for; Woolenwick, held by Robert Gernon and Peter of Valognes; Chells, held by Geoffrey of Bec and Peter of Valognes; Box, held by Peter of Valognes and William of Eu. The village of Shephall, some three miles distant from Stevenage, was held by the abbot of St Albans and the Archbishop of Canterbury.

For many centuries *Domesday Book* was unavailable to all but the wealthy and those who could read Latin, but in the 1970s paperback county editions, in English, were being produced by the publisher Phillimore. The first general editor was John Morris, who lived at Shackleton Spring, in the new town of Stevenage during the 1950s and '60s.

During the following two centuries, Stevenage appears to have prospered and its population increased. Farmsteads grew up some distance from the main village and became manors in their own right. One of the earliest recorded was the manor of Homleys or Homeleys: Ivor de Homlie held land in 1275 and it was probably his descendants who built the moated and fortified manor house in Homley [Whomerley] Wood in the thirteenth century. Closely associated with Homeleys was the neighbouring manor of Halfhyde. By the fifteenth century both were for a time held by the wealthy Chertsey family of Broxbourne. The manor of Bromesend probably took its name from the Brome family but it too came into the possession of the Chertseys. Another wealthy family who held land in Stevenage was the Broks. Somewhat confusingly, another manor was

Stevenage Fair. (Margaret Ashby)

Middle Row, site of Stevenage's mediaeval market place. (Margaret Ashby)

thought to have been in the south-west part of Stevenage called Cannix, Canwykes or Broxbournes and was named after John de Broxbourne.

Meanwhile, dwellers in the main village, probably encouraged by the Abbot of Westminster, were beginning to see advantages in moving closer to the Roman road half a mile below their settlement. They realised that the constant stream of travellers moving through needed food, drink, perhaps somewhere to spend the night, to rest their horses and to stock up with provisions. Some also brought with them goods that the villagers wanted to buy. So, gradually, the majority of the population moved down to the road, at the point where it forked to Baldock or Hitchin.

The thirteenth century was a time when many towns were seeking permission to hold markets. One Abbot of Westminster at this period, Richard de Ware, was very keen to see Stevenage become a market town and he even envisaged it developing into a borough. It was probably he who, in the early 1200s, requested King Edward I to allow him to hold a market here. For many centuries it has been understood that the market began in 1281, the year that Edward I granted the Abbot of Westminster a charter to hold a fair and a market in his manor of Stevenage, some 23 years after the important market at Hitchin. However in 2005 Dr Samantha Letters published research which shows that Stevenage market began in 1223, some 45 years before that of Hitchin. Thus the grant of Edward I can be taken as confirming an existing market and establishing a new fair.

By about 1300, Stevenage High Street would have begun to take on the shape still familiar today. Houses, almost entirely of wood or lath-and-plaster, would have spread along the North Road from about Rectory Lane down to the Burymead. At this point, near the track that was later to be planted as The Avenue, there may have been a rudimentary civic building of some kind, opposite the triangular space that would later become the Bowling Green. Houses would have continued southwards from the top of the Bowling Green on both sides of the road, the space between forming a wide market place. A market cross was erected near where the NatWest Bank stands today and dealers would bring their wares and set up their stalls and booths. As the years passed, some stallholders managed to keep their traditional sites and positions and eventually erect permanent dwellings there: the result was Middle Row, a commercial thoroughfare. Stevenage was no longer a village off the beaten track but a prosperous mediaeval market town.

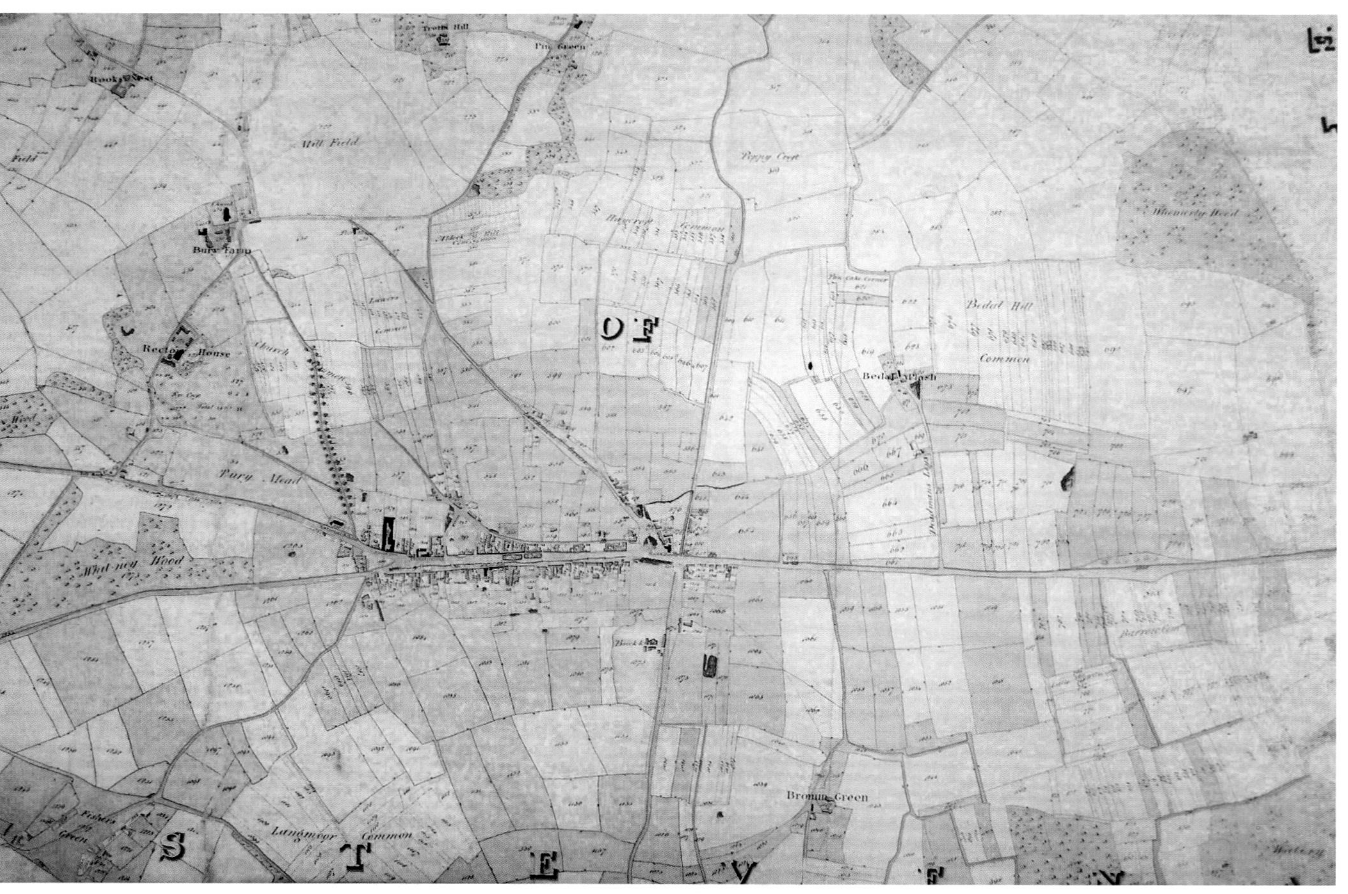

Section of the 1834 Stevenage Tithe Map. Watercourses and ponds are marked in blue. (HALS; DSA4/99/2)

CHAPTER TWO
The middle ages to the Victorian era

EVEN THOUGH THE TOWNSPEOPLE were moving away from their original settlement, they continued to improve and extend the church they had left behind. During the Norman period they completely rebuilt the original wooden church. Sometime after 1100 they built the tower in three stages, using flints gathered from the surrounding fields. Then they replaced the wooden nave and chancel with stone, only to rebuild them and add a side aisle a century later (1200–1300). In about 1330 yet again the chancel was replaced and in the same period the aisles were widened and the tower itself was embellished with the addition of a spire. The mediaeval wall-painting which adorned the north wall cannot now be discerned, but there are still traces of colour on the carved tracery of the screen. It is quite clear that, although by the middle ages, most people lived at least half a mile from their church, it continued to be the main focus of their lives, the most important building in the town.

Next to the church stood the Bury, or manor house, the centre of local government for the town. Here the Abbot of Westminster's representative, or tenant, lived and here were held the manorial courts, which sat three times a year. At each court, the steward of the Westminster estates would normally preside, with the heads of tithings as jurors. Although the Normans had brought with them the feudal system by which the country was governed from 1066 to the late fifteenth century, the former Saxon custom of tithing continued. From the age of 12 boys were required to join a tithing and if they failed to do so would be taken before the manor court. Other offences dealt with at the court included poaching game, allowing ditches to become blocked, allowing livestock to stray on to growing crops, selling weak beer or giving short measure. Fines levied at the court produced a useful income for the Lord of the Manor.

During the middle ages a number of Stevenage people were making money by offering food and drink to passing travellers, but this was a sideline to their major occupation of agriculture. Arable crops were grown in large open fields and cultivated by the villagers who were tenants of the manor. Part of the land, known as demesne, or home farm, was kept for the Lord of the Manor; the rest was divided into strips and shared among the villagers by an annual ballot which was intended to ensure that everyone took turns with both good and poor soil. In addition, in return for their strips, they were required to work on the demesne land for a set number of days each year and to transport produce from Stevenage to Westminster Abbey.

Rents and payments were paid in kind rather than cash, or in a combination of the two. For example, in 1315 Annabel Geffray paid rent of 16d (7p) in cash payment for her homestead and 28 acres of land, plus a bushel of wheat at Michaelmas (29 September), 2 hens at Christmas, and 15 eggs at Easter. More important was her rent in service. She, or someone on her behalf, was required to plough 12 acres per year upon the demesne, harrow 4 acres and in addition undertake reaping and other work throughout the year. Manorial servants were also paid in kind. The swineherd received 3 quarters of flour. Cash was paid for some work on the manor farm, for example, the carpenter was paid 3d (1½p) for making a new door for the sheepfold, using three boards which had cost 1½d (½p).

Well before 1273 the Lord of the Manor had a windmill, in Churchfield, near the church and Bury. In that year it was repaired with a new millstone, repair of the iron spindle of the millstone, steel for the billows and tallow to grease the moving parts, at a total cost of 17s 9d (89p). Another 7s 9d (39p) was spent on 24 yards of canvas for the sails.

A misericord seat at St Nicholas' Church. (Margaret Ashby)

The former Falcon Inn, behind and over Lloyds chemist shop, next to the former saddlery and the Red Lion Inn. (Margaret Ashby)

Instruments of punishment included stocks, a pillory and a ducking stool. These were provided by the Lord of the Manor. In the year 1310 the king had a prison in Stevenage, but nothing more is known about it other than that a man named Andrew Baron, accused of theft, had sought sanctuary in the church and was dragged from there and thrown into prison by 'certain malefactors'.

On a more cheerful note, in his *History of Stevenage*, Robert Trow-Smith quotes from the 1312 annual report to the Abbot of Westminster which contains evidence that a school existed at Stevenage in that year. The details of the clothing of one pupil, William le Rous, reads very much like a modern school uniform list: blue tunic and hood, 2 caps, shirts, stockings and 2 pairs of shoes. In the middle ages classes were often held in church porches and it is possible that this was the case here, but it is perhaps more likely that William's school was a building on or near the Bury Mead where, two and a half centuries later, Alleynes' Grammar School was founded.

A survey made in 1315 for the Abbot of Westminster recorded details of land holdings in his manor of Stevenage. Twelve local men, or jurors, were sworn in to make an honest survey. They listed 140 heads of households, which approximated to a population of at least 700 people, possibly even as many as 1,000 including all the outlying manors and greens.

Years later, in 1349, the Black Death reached Stevenage, brought by travellers fleeing from London along the Roman road. Inevitably the resulting deaths had a serious effect on the town but it did recover in due course, unlike Chesfield and Box, which joined the ranks of 'deserted villages' where only remnants survive.

The fifteenth century saw many changes in Stevenage. Men who were previously tied to their villages were travelling in search of work, for which they would now usually be paid in cash rather than kind. Wealthy merchants from London were moving into surrounding rural counties, including Hertfordshire, and buying themselves country estates. This happened at Stevenage, when men such as John Sylam, a pewterer, and John Hemmings, a barber, bought land here. William Reeve acquired land in various parts of the parish and also got himself licensed to enclose parts of the waste, that is, land not yet used for agriculture.

By this time buildings in the High Street, then known as Stevenage Street and later as Fore Street, had reached at least as far south as the Falcon Inn, beyond which was the manorial waste. A document of 1460 refers to the Falcon as being built on the 'hope' an Old English word meaning 'a piece of enclosed land in the midst of waste land'. The former Falcon, now 84a, High Street, is currently occupied by the Maharajah Indian Restaurant behind Lloyd's chemist's shop. The 1460 document is particularly interesting in that the signatories were associated with the Guild, or Brotherhood, of the Holy Trinity, a religious organisation that existed to do good works for the town. During the fifteenth century, members of the Guild were working towards setting up almshouses for homeless or needy people but progress was slow until the Reverend Stephen Hellard arrived as Rector of Stevenage in 1472. He encouraged the Guild members to acquire land and income for a charitable foundation and by 1501 had built a messuage (house and garden) in Dead Lane, better known today as Church Lane. His will, dated 20 December 1501, describes his bequest, 'I have a messuage ... newly built lying in a lane called Dead Lane, nigh unto Stanmor ... which house I have built for the habitation of three poor folk without any rent therefore to be paid ... .'

Hellard died in 1506 and the Almshouses Trust came into operation at once. It has continued unbroken until today, although the house was rebuilt following the disastrous Stevenage Fire of 1807. It is unlikely that the Guild or Brotherhood of the Holy Trinity ever became rich or powerful but it certainly carried out good works, had its own priest and also a Guild House on or near the Bury Mead, which later became incorporated into Alleyne's Grammar School. It is thought that the original school room (now the Headmaster's study) could be that building, but other possibilities are 1, High Street, formerly the Headmaster's House, and even 3, High Street, formerly known as 'The Ancient House'.

The unsettled period of religious strife following Henry VIII's dissolution of the monasteries must have been a difficult time for Stevenage. In 1540 the monastery at Westminster was dissolved and dispossessed of its land and property including the manor of Stevenage. However, the town's link with Westminster was to continue for a while longer, as the king decided to form a new Bishopric of Westminster, and Stevenage became one of its possessions. The new administration took its responsibilities towards law and order seriously. In 1542 instructions were sent that the town's stocks should be repaired and a new ducking stool and pillory should be made. However, in other respects it appears that the Bishopric was concerned more about raising money by renting out its lands than in caring for the people within its manor. This change of approach had been happening for some time, and now continued. As early as 1509 the Stevenage yeoman farmer Edward Kympton had been renting all the Westminster Abbey demesne at Stevenage.

When Edward VI succeeded Henry VIII in 1547 he renounced the Roman Catholic faith for good and finally declared England a Protestant country, sending commissioners to remove religious ornaments from churches and crush any signs of former belief. It appears that the Stevenage churchwardens took care to hide most of the ceremonial articles belonging to St Nicholas' church before they could be removed. Finding little of interest in the church building, the commissioners seized land and property belonging to the Guild of the Holy Trinity and this was subsequently granted to a Sir George Howarde, in recognition of unspecified 'services rendered'.

It was Edward VI who, in 1550, broke the town's 500-year association with Westminster and gave Stevenage to the newly-created Bishopric of London. So it remained for the next 300 years, apart from one short break in the seventeenth century. This bishop also showed little apparent interest in the affairs of his manor. In 1598 he leased the right to collect fines and tolls payable to the manor courts to Rowland Lytton, of Knebworth, whose family had been acquiring property in the Stevenage district for many years. By 1610 they had bought the whole estate of Half Hyde and six years later they also owned the manor of Cannix. They played their part in society, becoming Justices of the Peace and, in later centuries, Members of Parliament.

On the death of Edward VI in 1553, his half-sister Mary came to the throne and set about restoring the old religion: persecution of Protestants now replaced persecution of Roman Catholics. Among all the upheavals of Mary's reign there was one piece of legislation that was to endure for nearly 300 years. This was the 1555 Highways Act which required parishioners to appoint annually a surveyor of the highways, who could raise local rates for the upkeep of roads. He also was responsible for supervising 'statute labour' whereby local people had to give four days (later increased to six) of unpaid labour to repair roads in their parish. As the centuries passed and road traffic increased this Act became increasingly burdensome, particularly to a town such as Stevenage on a main road from London to the North.

Queen Mary died in 1558, as did Thomas Alleyne, the beloved Rector of Stevenage who had helped so many people through the difficult years of reformation and counter-reformation, offering practical as well as spiritual help to his flock. No doubt he survived the various religious persecutions by keeping quiet and apparently conforming to the prevailing faith, although it is thought that he was sympathetic to the Protestant cause. In his will he left most of his considerable landed property to the Master, Fellows and Scholars of Trinity

The original school house of Alleyne's Grammar School showing timber framing. (Stevenage Museum P11218)

Alleyne's Grammar School early twentieth century. The old school house on the left is now faced with brick. (Stevenage Museum P4403)

College, Cambridge, for the founding of three free grammar schools; one at Uttoxeter in his home county of Staffordshire, another at Stone in the same county and a third at Stevenage, where Alleyne's Grammar School (now called the Thomas Alleyne School) has the distinction of being the second oldest school in the county of Hertfordshire.

There is confusion over what happened to the Guild, or Brotherhood, House but it may eventually have been bought, along with land formerly belonging to the Guild, by a Stevenage yeoman farmer, Edward Wilshere. He seems to have been a philanthropist, or perhaps he had been a member of the Brotherhood and still lived according to its precepts. In 1562, he left the former Brotherhood House, together with land and £37 raised by subscription, to be a school for the elementary education of small children. For a while the two foundations worked together, Alleyne's paying for a schoolmaster and Wilshere's providing a building, but very soon there were disagreements. Eventually matters reached such a point that, by order of King Charles I, the spokespersons for the two sides were made to attend an inquisition held at Hertford in 1632, where complaints related to charitable foundations of all kinds were being dealt with. The judgement, put very simply, was that the Grammar School master could use the building for his pupils but must also teach the little children. The full details are inscribed on a board hung in St Nicholas' church.

Many wills and inventories (lists, with valuations, of personal belongings of deceased persons), survive from the sixteenth and seventeenth centuries and from them much can be learned about life in Stevenage during those days. For instance, it is clear from the number of deaths and the references in wills to 'this plague time' that Stevenage suffered a severe outbreak of smallpox in 1544. Among those who died was John Dyllie, one of the many husbandmen (tenant farmers) in the town, whose brief will, made during his illness, instructed that 'I give and bequeath to my wife all my goods, none excepted.' There were wealthy men such as John Huckell, a fuller, who died in 1554 leaving 7 acres of land called Gleviscroft at Woolenwick Green, together with other land and income to the trustees of the Hellard Almshouses. Others, such as the tailor John Bozyer, who died in 1608, had only their clothes or household furnishings to leave. His will included mention of a mattress, a bolster, a little kettle, a pair of sheets, his best hat, cloak and doublet and some pewter platters.

Assize court records are also valuable sources of information for social historians. From these documents it is evident that theft was one of the commonest crimes, particularly sheep-stealing and the theft of clothes and household items. There were also cases of law-breaking by bakers and other traders who had not

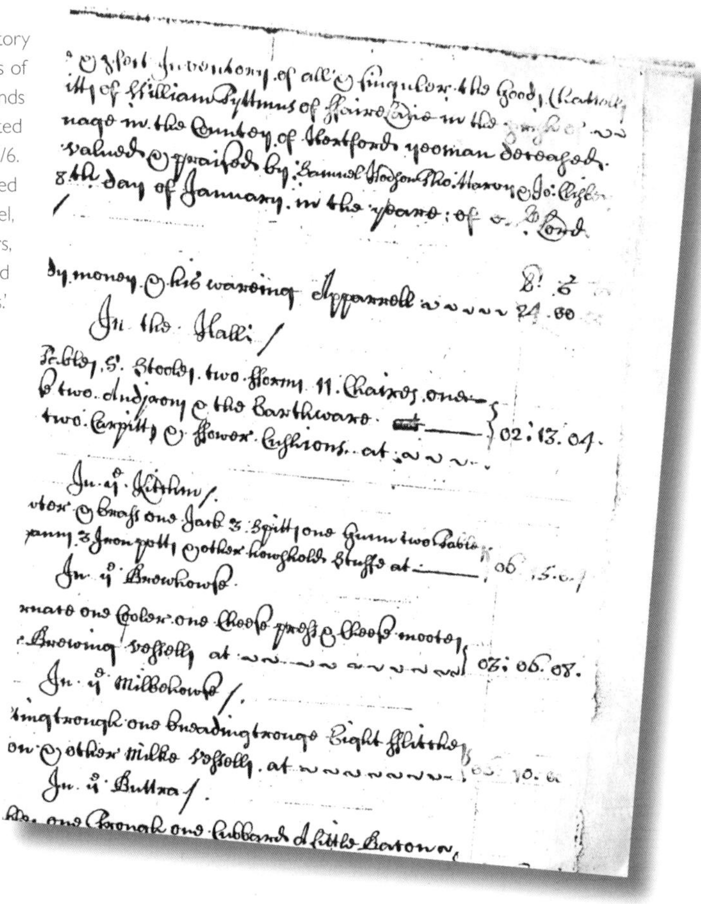

Extract from the inventory of goods and chattels of William Tyttmus of Fairlands Farm, yeoman, dated 28 January 1685/6. Among the items listed are 'wearing apparel, two forms, 11 chairs, two carpets and three iron pots.'

served the requisite seven-year apprenticeship, or who had ignored regulations relating to monopolies, or committed other offences against civil laws. The Assize courts, were held at Hertford or St Albans and cases were heard by Justices of the Peace. In parallel to these, the ancient manor courts continued, still held at the Bury beside St Nicholas' church, in what was once the centre of the village of Stevenage. These courts dealt only with customs and rights relating to land held by the Lord of the Manor.

During the reign of Queen Elizabeth I, Stevenage prospered, no doubt helped by the proximity of Knebworth, where the Queen's loyal servant, Sir Rowland Lytton, was Lord Lieutenant of Hertfordshire and Essex. She stayed at Knebworth more than once, most notably in 1588, the year of the Spanish Armada. Yet, in spite of the general well-being, there were in the town many people who were poor, homeless and unable, for various reasons, to find work. The problem of the poor was a national one and in 1601 an Act codifying previous legislation was passed, the first of a series of Acts known as the Poor Law. These required parishes to establish an Overseer of the Poor who could raise taxes to pay for his office and also allowed them to set up workhouses. The mechanism by which such laws were carried out was the Vestry meeting. This originated as a committee concerned purely with Church affairs, which met in the vestry or robing room of a church but by the end of the sixteenth century most towns and villages in the country were run by a Vestry meeting which elected the constable, carried out the Poor Law and undertook other responsibilities in the town. The Stevenage Vestry has been in existence since at least 1575, which is the date of the first book of minutes and accounts. Meetings were held in various places in the town, but most frequently at the White Lion, in the centre of the High Street facing the market square, the commercial heart of the town.

The road from London to the north was becoming increasingly important to the economy of Stevenage, as travellers stopped in the town for food, drink and a bed for the night. The High Street today is lined with buildings which once were, or still are, inns and hostelries. By the seventeenth century the High Street had extended to the south of its junction with Sish Lane. As well as inns, there were farmhouses which fronted on to the High Street, with yards and fields behind. Most of the buildings were timber-framed, but those that survived the hazard of fire were in later centuries faced with brick. Amongst the more substantial buildings were many small dwellings of lath-and-plaster, some of which were also workshops for tailors, bakers, shoemakers and other craftsmen.

When Cromwell's men marched through Stevenage in 1647 they saw much that is still standing today. The building most popularly associated with this event was 25, High Street, the Cromwell Hotel. There is an enduring belief that

The Cromwell Hotel, originally a farmhouse which may have belonged to John Thurloe, Oliver Cromwell's Secretary of State. (Margaret Ashby)

Cromwell gave it to his Secretary of State and chief of intelligence, John Thurloe, although no documentary evidence has ever been found to support this. The original property was a farm, but its fields have long been buried under modern roads and the farmhouse itself, the present hotel, much rebuilt over the years.

There is no doubt, however, about the presence in Stevenage of the great diarist, Samuel Pepys. He travelled through here a number of times in the years 1661 to 1668 and stayed at the town's famous coaching inn, the Swan (later called the Grange). It was at the Swan, on 15 October 1664, that Pepys noted in his diary the helpful discovery 'I find … that eating after I come to my inn, without drinking, doth keep me from being stomach-sick; which drink doth presently make me.'

By 1700 Stevenage had acquired a reputation as a great market for cattle, driven down on the hoof from the North to London. Drovers and dealers frequented the town and butchers were becoming numerous, not only in the High Street but also in the roads off it. There were many slaughterhouses operating cheek by jowl with dwelling houses. Scott's Slaughter House was situated at the High Street end of Letchmore Road, on the manorial waste, opposite a large pond. It is a substantial timber-framed hall house, with two cross wings, dating from about 1600, currently known as Tudor House.

In 1722 an Act of Parliament permitted parishes to set up workhouses, or poorhouses, to deal with the many homeless and destitute people in the country who had no means of subsistence. The Stevenage Vestry responded quickly to the Act and at their meeting on 9 May that year they negotiated with Henry Trigg, of the Old Castle Inn (now NatWest Bank), to rent his barn for use as the parish workhouse. An annual rent of £1 10s (£1.50) was agreed but, before anything could be put into practice, Henry Trigg died. In his will he left

Henry Trigg's coffin in the rafters of the barn behind the former Old Castle Inn. (Stevenage Museum P239)

The Gas House, formerly the Workhouse, 1940s. (Stevenage Museum P5113)

instructions that his body should be placed in its coffin on the rafters of his barn, possibly to avoid the depredations of grave-robbers who at that time were digging up newly-buried bodies and selling them to medical students. Although the bones have long-since disappeared, Trigg's coffin remains in the rafters of the barn to this day.

As for the workhouse, a substitute building, site unknown, was provided by George Crouch and used from 1724 to 1773, during which time numbers increased and larger premises were sought. Eventually the Vestry was able to acquire Scott's Slaughterhouse, which was to serve as the Stevenage parish workhouse for the next 62 years. Not to be confused with the Workhouse were the Pest houses, which served as the town's isolation hospital for people suffering from smallpox which was all too common and highly infectious. They were situated on high ground on the west side of Weston Road, now the site of Mount Pleasant Flats, opposite Mill Field (on which Headingley, Trafford, and Trent Closes were later built).

The eighteenth-century increase in coach travel and in trade generally was making heavy demands on the country's roads. The system of 'statute labour' which had prevailed for 200 years was now completely inadequate to cope with repairs, let alone improvements, and stories abounded of horses unable to pull coaches out of deep ruts and passengers falling into muddy water, some even drowning. The solution reached was the establishment of turnpike trusts, by which private individuals invested money to enable major roads to be properly drained and surfaced, and hoped to recoup their outlay by charging tolls to road users. Each turnpike trust was set up by a separate Act of Parliament. The Stevenage and Biggleswade Turnpike Trust was established in June 1720 to improve the 13-mile stretch of the Great North Road from Stevenage to Biggleswade, from the Swan Inn at the north end of Stevenage High Street to the Spread Eagle Inn on the south side of Biggleswade. Milestones were erected as the roads were turnpiked, and three still remain along the Stevenage section; one to the south of Jack's Hill, another to the south of Graveley and the third south of Rectory Lane. Toll-houses were set up at the Stevenage turnpike, situated just north of the junction with Rectory Lane, another at Graveley to catch those who tried to dodge the first one.

The Welwyn Turnpike Trust, established in May 1726, was responsible for the roads from Lemsford Mill through Welwyn and Stevenage to Corey's Mill, and from Welwyn through Codicote to Hitchin. The Act laid down that two-thirds of the Trust's income, was to be expended in repairing the road from Welwyn to Corey's Mill (7½ miles). Thus, rather confusingly, it was the Welwyn Trust which maintained Stevenage High Street as far as the Swan Inn. At first the Trust was forbidden to erect a toll-gate north of Welwyn but an Act of 1831 permitted three gates, one of which was at Broadwater. Subsequently this was moved nearer Stevenage, to Monksbottom at Monk's Wood.

Competition between stage-coach companies grew fierce as both roads and the design of the coaches improved. The first regular stage-coach service to Stevenage was John Shrimpton's *The Perseverance* which left the Greyhound Inn at Smithfield 'at 3 of the clock precisely' every Tuesday morning, going through Hatfield, Welwyn, Stevenage, Hitchin, Arlesey, Henlow, Southill, Old Warden and Cardington to Bedford. Stevenage was usually the first overnight halt, where passengers stayed at one of the inns and horses were changed. The road through Stevenage was part of the primary route to the north, known as the Great North Road. This was the era of highwaymen, such as Dick Turpin and the local James Whitney, who probably took his surname from Whitney Wood. They were glamorous in story books but terrifying in real life and cause of ever-present anxiety in the world of travel and business. Legend has it that Dick Turpin used to frequent the Swan Inn (later renamed the Grange) whence he could make his escape by the secret passage which still exists.

Fear of fire was something that haunted most people and with good reason, Stevenage was ravaged by fire many times. In 1763 the Vestry approved the purchase of a fire engine, with a treadle-operated water pump, which was helpful against small fires, but useless in the face of the Great Fire of Stevenage which broke out in a wheelwright's shop at the corner of Walkern Road and the High Street on 10 July 1807. More than forty – mostly wooden – houses were burnt down, together with outhouses, maltings, straw and haystacks. Another casualty was the 300-year-old Hellard Almshouses building, which was completely destroyed. However, the Vestry, meeting on 3 September, agreed to pay Thomas Muncey and Parish Austin £270 to rebuild them, which they did in less than a year.

Another major fire occurred in 1829, starting in the yard of the White Hart at the south end of the High Street. The inn, its stables, all its horses and ten nearby houses were destroyed. Following this second disaster, the Vestry bought a new and up-to-date fire engine and had a fire-engine house built on to the Almshouses in Church Lane. Meanwhile, the task of rebuilding the High Street was ongoing. Wooden houses were being replaced by brick and many of the older, timber-framed buildings which had survived the fire, mostly those on the west side, were being given brick facings and their thatched roofs replaced with tiles or slates. Although many of its oldest buildings remained, the outward appearance of the High Street was changed for ever.

Change was to continue at an ever-increasing rate for the rest of the century, bringing with it new responsibilities for the Vestry as the role of local government

The Avenue, by Sidney Massie c1860, showing the trees planted by Nicholas Cholwell in 1756. (Stevenage Museum 4298s)

The White Lion was frequently used for vestry meetings. (Stevenage Museum).

expanded. Traditionally, the Church of England, in the person of the rector, had been the leading figure in the parish and that was to continue for many years. At the beginning of the century the Church was among those pressing for improvements in the provision of education. For most children of poor families in the Stevenage district, their only exposure to learning was in one of the small 'dame schools' that were run in private houses, often combined with a straw plait school, where the priority was to teach children to make and sell straw plait rather than to become literate, although some children were well-taught. In 1834, a new Church of England school, St Nicholas' School, built under the auspices of the National Society, opened on the Bury Mead across The Avenue from Alleyne's Grammar School. The building cost £709 3s 11d, most of which was raised by local subscription. At last there was provision for all children, girls as well as boys, to receive a basic education, even though attendance was not yet compulsory. That came about with the 1870 Education Act, after which the St Nicholas' School was greatly increased in size to accommodate both infants and boys and girls up to the age of 10.

Poverty continued to be a problem. The 1834 Poor Law Amendment Act abolished the previous system of parish workhouses and set up Poor Law Unions made up of a number of parishes with one central workhouse. Stevenage was in the Hitchin Union, where a substantial brick workhouse was built near the lavender fields to serve the surrounding towns and villages. A charitable home of a very different kind was opened in 1865 after a long struggle to raise funds by Charles Dickens and his friend and fellow-writer Edward Bulwer-Lytton. This was the Guild of Literature and Arts, built on the London road near Six Hills and intended to provide homes and security for struggling writers and artists. It was an imposing Gothic building but unfortunately not appreciated by the struggling ones, who were disinclined to be 'buried alive at Stevenage', and the scheme failed. Dickens knew Stevenage quite well. To the annoyance of many, in his short story *Tom Tiddler's Ground*, he famously described the High Street as 'drowsy in the dullest degree'.

The unpopular system of repairing roads by statute labour was abolished in 1835, when parishes were permitted to levy a highway rate and employ workmen to maintain their roads. Subsequently the turnpike trusts were rendered redundant by the 1862 Highways Act which required groups of parishes to set up local highways boards and to employ a paid district surveyor. The turnpike trusts had been successful in improving the country's roads but they had never managed to become profitable and the continuing expense of maintenance was becoming too much for them. In 1868 the Stevenage and Biggleswade Trust ceased operations and responsibility for the Hertfordshire stretches of road which it previously administered was taken over by the Hitchin District Highway Board. The Welwyn Trust continued until 1877, by which time Stevenage had set up its Local Board of Health and took responsibility for the former turnpike road through the town.

In any case, road transport was going into a decline as steam railways took over. Stevenage station, serving the Great Northern Railway Company, was opened in 1850. Later that year Queen Victoria herself made the journey along the new line from Kings' Cross to Peterborough, passing through Stevenage and Hitchin, where the station was decorated with straw plait, evidence of the importance of this cottage craft to the local economy. Stevenage station was sited at the former Julian's Farm and a new road was built linking it to the High Street. Named Railway Street, this road later acquired an unsavoury reputation and was renamed Orchard Road. Nevertheless, in 1871, a most important and much-appreciated new building was opened there. This was the town hall, which became not only the meeting place for local official and administrative bodies but also the natural venue for concerts and other entertainments,

Stevenage Station, opened in 1850. (Stevenage Museum P8025)

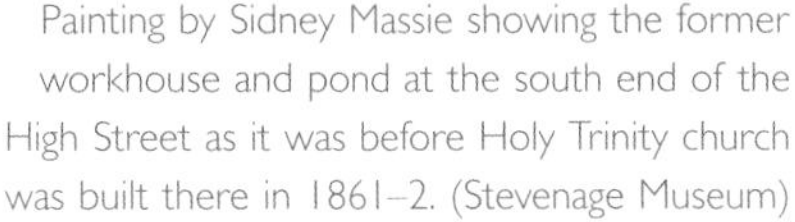

Painting by Sidney Massie showing the former workhouse and pond at the south end of the High Street as it was before Holy Trinity church was built there in 1861–2. (Stevenage Museum)

Holy Trinity church, 1862. It was extended to over twice its size in 1882. (Stevenage Museum)

lectures, societies and public meetings of all kinds. From June 1872 it became the venue for the Saturday straw plait market, which previously occupied the open square bounded by the High Street, Holy Trinity church (built in 1861–62), Southend Farm and Church Lane.

The latter part of the nineteenth century saw many local government reforms. Boards of Health were set up to succeed the vestries. In Stevenage the new system, established in 1873, may not have been immediately noticeable, since the rector, the Revd William Jowitt, who had of course run the Vestry meetings, now chaired the Board of Health. However, one result of the Board's work was welcomed, in that, from 1885, the town had its first supply of piped water from a borehole at Rooks Nest. This was not accessible to everyone and wells or pumps continued in use far into the next century, but it was a promising start.

Twenty years after they were set up, Boards of Health were replaced, in 1894, by Urban District Councils. They were run by elected councillors who could levy rates and pay staff to deal with a range of responsibilities, especially public health. The first chairman of the Stevenage Urban District Council was the rector, the Revd William Jowitt. In 1899, following the Local Government Act of the previous year, the Hertfordshire County Council was established. Among other duties, it took over responsibility for the county's roads.

Change was happening in the Church of England too. Dioceses were being reorganised and new ones established. The parish of Stevenage was no longer part of the large Diocese of Lincoln, having been transferred in 1845 to the Diocese of Rochester,

The Reverend William Jowitt, Rector of Stevenage 1874–1912. (Stevenage Museum)

New Town Post Office, Fishers Green, early twentieth century. (Mrs R. Sanders)

then in 1877 to the new Diocese of St Albans. The reorganisation also affected another centuries-old institution, that of the Lord of the Manor. Since 1550, apart from the break of 11 years in the Civil War, the Bishop of London had been Lord of the Manor of Stevenage. In 1868 that role, although considerably reduced over the centuries, was taken over by the Ecclesiastical Commissioners, whose successors, the Church Commissioners, retain the title of Lords of the Manor of Stevenage today.

As the century drew to a close, Stevenage was beginning, in a small way, to emerge from its rural past. The railway made the town attractive to commuters who came to live in the pleasant country town and travel daily to London. Many of the wealthier incomers built substantial houses in Hitchin Road and North Road and along London Road as far as Six Hills. The young E M Forster, who came with his widowed mother to live at Rooks Nest in 1883, considered the latter to be 'ugly new houses'.

The first factory in Stevenage worthy of the name was also opened in 1883 in Fishers Green Road opposite the station. It was the Educational Supply Association (ESA) which manufactured school furniture and was to become the town's major employer. Nearby, a cluster of new roads grew up, with brick-built houses for working people. Some, such as Bournemouth and Southsea Roads were named after seaside towns: Jubilee Road commemorated Queen Victoria's Golden Jubilee in 1887. Together, they housed a new community, away from the main population in and around the High Street. They had their own Post Office and football team and were given the semi-official name 'New Town'.

CHAPTER THREE
1900 to 1945

STEVENAGE ENTERED THE TWENTIETH CENTURY as a reasonably prosperous small town, no longer quite so heavily dependent on agriculture. Its population of 3,958 included increasing numbers of commuters and also of factory workers employed at the ESA. Despite the decline in road transport since the coming of the railway, Stevenage inns and public houses continued to supply refreshment, but now their customers tended to arrive by bicycle, as Stevenage was a popular destination for cycle rides from London, or by the new-fangled motor cars for those who could afford them.

In the early years of the century the face of the High Street changed, as shopkeepers and businessmen succumbed to the fashion for replacing existing small windows with full-length plate-glass. The Council received a steady stream of applications for planning permission to 'bring out' frontages and the results can be seen today. Another change was to follow, as motor car ownership increased and High Street businesses applied first for permission to store petrol, then to install petrol pumps (manually operated by turning a handle) where the many passing motorists could refuel. By 1920 the High Street abounded in places where petrol could be obtained, including Shelford & Crowe Ltd, G E Harper and the Stevenage Motor Company Ltd who, in that year submitted a plan showing the position of a proposed petrol pump and tank in front of their garage at the south end of the town.

The increasing volume of traffic was problem enough for the formerly peaceful country town, where pedestrians, children and animals were accustomed to wandering casually across the road, but when all speed limits were abolished under the Road Traffic Act 1930 the situation became intolerable. The Council wrote to the Minister of Transport and the Chief Constable of

Stevenage Great Northern Railway station forecourt, Julians Road, c1910. (Mrs D. Stewart)

Hertfordshire, saying that they 'view with grave alarm the very large number of road accidents which are taking place owing to fast and reckless driving and urge the Police to exercise greater vigilance ... and that the Council are strongly of the opinion that the time has arrived for the restoration of a reasonable speed limit (say 20 miles per hour) through all populous districts ...'

The town itself was in an agricultural setting of gently undulating fields and woodlands, as it had been for hundreds of years. The surrounding greens and hamlets, although within the Stevenage Urban District, had their own small communities of farmhouses and cottages: Fishers Green, Symonds Green, Broomin Green, Norton Green, Chells, Rooks Nest and Pin Green. Outside the Stevenage boundary, but adjacent to the southern outskirts of the town were the tiny hamlet of Broadwater and the village of Shephall; to the east, the larger village of Aston and to the north, Graveley with Chesfield: these were administered by Hitchin Rural District Council.

Comparatively modern, substantial houses, built since the railway came, lined the main roads into Stevenage; Hitchin Road, North Road and London Road. They provided employment for domestic servants and trade for the High Street shops. Many of their residents supported the two Anglican churches, St Nicholas' and Holy Trinity, took leading roles in the affairs of the town and were generous with their time and money in aid of charitable causes.

At the other extreme there were pockets of real poverty, in parts of Back (Church) Lane, in some of the cottages at Fishers Green and Norton Green and in isolated cottages such as Six Bottles in Sish Lane. Many cottages lacked the basic amenities of sanitation and clean water. Children of the poor were leaving school at 13 with very little education and limited horizons. There was a desire on the part of many in the ruling classes to improve the lot of their less fortunate neighbours but others were against anything that would upset the status quo. The Stevenage Urban District Council, led by its chairman, Rector Jowitt, made great efforts to provide services that would today be considered essential, but they could not cope with everyone who needed help. Out of sight, in the

Hitchin Union Workhouse, were the really destitute people of Stevenage who were unable through poverty or old age to look after themselves. Their numbers were swollen in bad times by the many tramps who passed along the roads of Hertfordshire looking for work or, failing that, a bed for the night.

Outbreaks of infectious disease were an ever-present danger at the beginning of the century, but the determined efforts being made to improve sanitation and standards of hygiene were eventually successful in overcoming the worst of them. A case of typhoid at a cottage on Letchmore Green was reported by the Medical Officer in March 1903 and a notice served on Miss Bates, owner of the premises, to provide two additional water closets and to have a separate one for each house. As late as 1910 Hitchin Rural District Council agreed to retain the Smallpox Hospital near Hitchin and accept cases from Stevenage provided that Stevenage Council contributed towards the upkeep of the building.

In such a rural area poaching was commonplace, but not all poachers achieved the notoriety of the Fox twins. They were born in 1857, in a rented cottage in Symonds Green, where their father, Henry, farmed 10 acres of land and their mother augmented the family income by making straw-plait. Henry Fox was also a Baptist preacher at the Ebenezer Chapel, which was opened in the newly-built Albert Street the same year as his sons were born. He named the twins Albert Ebenezer and Ebenezer Albert, perhaps hoping that the religious association would influence their future lives. In this he was disappointed, but the similar names, coupled with their identical appearance, did help in their poaching careers. They made a point of never poaching together, so that, if one was caught he could claim mistaken identity.

The Fox twins had another claim to fame, in that they took part in a series of experiments on the use of fingerprints in identifying criminals. With their help, and that of other identical twins, Sir Edward Henry had established that

Pond at corner of Walkern Road and Church Lane, c1912.

The Fox Twins. (Stevenage Museum P330)

every human being has a unique fingerprint. He published a book entitled *Classification and Uses of Fingerprints* in 1900 and, on his appointment as Assistant Commissioner of the Metropolitan Police in 1901, introduced his system at New Scotland Yard. The first criminal conviction based on the evidence of fingerprints was obtained in 1902.

Another modern development, the provision of a telephone service for Stevenage, was initially opposed by the Stevenage Urban District Council. There had been great hostility when telegraph posts had been planted all along the Great North Road, including of course the High Street, in 1883, one man even threatening to take an axe and chop them down. Now that a local telephone service was proposed, necessitating additional posts and overhead wires, strong feelings were aroused against it. Only about thirty people, mostly businessmen, were in favour. The Council tried to persuade them to change their minds, but the Postmaster General prevailed and in 1906 the first 28 subscribers were connected. The number '1' was reserved for the public telephone in the Post Office and number '2' went to the old-established firm of W Austin & Sons, builders and undertakers.

This was the Edwardian age, to be recalled for years after with nostalgia for garden parties and elegance, when the British Empire was at its peak, when everyone knew his place in society. In fact, it was a time of unrest, with periods of unemployment and hardship. Voting in parliamentary elections was restricted by law to men over 21 who were householders or tenants but there was increasing political awareness, as both men and women agitated for the universal right to vote, although women made the headlines and had the most unpleasantness to face from opponents. The Hitchin, Stevenage and District Women's Suffrage Society, set up in 1909, held meetings at various places in the district and was often met with hostility or even physical attack. The cultured and erudite local MP, Julius Bertram, who lived at Sishes, was an implacable enemy but support came from the Lyttons of Knebworth. Lady Constance Lytton joined the Women's Social and Political Union, was imprisoned and ruined her health for the cause.

There is evidence that the middle classes of Stevenage were concerned about the condition of the poor and other social issues. On 15 February 1910 the first of a series of lectures on various branches of social reform was given by Sidney Webb, who explained the Minority Report of the Poor Law Commission. The meeting was chaired by the Earl of Lytton and the town hall was almost full. The Stevenage Popular Lecture Society also engaged speakers on a wide range of other topics, including: Madame Bertha Moore on 'Sir Arthur Sullivan and his Music', with vocal illustrations (accompanist, Miss Kathleen Wurr); Mr Richard Kerr, FGS, FRAS on 'Wireless Telegraphy', illustrated with experiments, and Mr W Percival Westell, FLS on 'Common Objects of the Countryside', illustrated by lime-light views.

A few years earlier a young man had given a talk at the town hall, deputising for another speaker. He was Edward Morgan Forster, who had lived with his mother at Rooks Nest House from 1883 to 1893. Since then he had become a successful writer and in 1910 his 'condition of England' novel *Howards End* was published, to great acclaim. Based largely on his memories of life in Stevenage, the story explores contemporary but enduring themes, such as the relationships between rich and poor, commerce and the arts, the heart and the head. It also contains some very vivid evocations of Stevenage itself at the beginning of the twentieth century; for example, chapter three includes this description of a motor car journey from the station at the top of Julians Road to the High Street:

> They drew up opposite a draper's. Without replying, he turned round in his seat, and contemplated the cloud of dust that they had raised in their passage through the village. It was settling again, but not all into the road from which he had taken it. Some of it had percolated through the open windows, some had whitened the roses and gooseberries of the wayside gardens, while a certain proportion had entered the lungs of the villagers. 'I wonder when they'll learn wisdom and tar the roads,' was his comment.

In reality, the Stevenage Urban District Council was well aware of the condition of their roads. At a meeting on 26 March 1900, Cllr Graham proposed the motion, seconded by Cllr Clarke and carried, 'That the continued dirty condition of our roads and paths being highly detrimental to the best interests of the town, the Council do resolve itself into a committee to consider the matter and make arrangements to remedy the nuisance'.

At this period in its history Stevenage, in common with most other small towns in England, lacked services that are considered essential today. The majority of roads were un-metalled cart-tracks. On the other hand, in such a rural area, with its small hamlets and isolated farms, footpaths (field paths) and bridle-ways were extremely important means of communication for residents, but often regarded as a nuisance by landowners. When, in March 1902, Charles Poyntz-Stewart proposed to close a footpath across his Trotts Hill estate, the Council formed a sub-committee of several councillors to discuss the matter with him. No doubt feeling somewhat overwhelmed at the strength of the response, he wrote a firm letter saying that he was prepared to meet no more than two councillors.

Most members of the Stevenage Urban District Council described themselves as Independent, meaning that they did not represent any political party. However few, if any, would have been sympathetic to the newly emerging Labour Party. The Council met every month in the town hall, in Orchard Road, under Rector Jowitt's chairmanship, with W O Times as clerk. A major preoccupation at this time was the need to provide an adequate sewerage system and to ensure that houses were connected to it. Oversight of these matters was the responsibility of John Gillespie, the SUDC's surveyor, whose duties included the inspection of new buildings and superintendence of the sewage farm, combined with the roles of water engineer and surveyor. For this he was paid £60 per year in comparison with Mr Times, whose salary was increased to £100 per year from 1 April 1900.

The surveyor's work in connection with the town's sewage farm, which was sited in the field named Roaring Meg, on the London Road near Broadwater, was not without its difficulties. The land belonged to Colonel Heathcote of Shephalbury. He was concerned about the bridle path that crossed the sewage farm and requested representatives from the Council to discuss it with him 'on the spot' in the spring of 1900. Eventually, in December of that year, agreement was reached that the Council would give up the existing right of way in exchange for a new one. Then, in January 1901, Colonel Heathcote was back on the warpath, this time to give formal notice to the Assessment Committee of his objection to their scheduling the sewage farm as agricultural land. This time he was unsuccessful and the Council's ruling was upheld.

There was a steady stream of applications for connection to the main sewer from the owners of private houses, shops and other premises, but also many failures to comply with orders to do so. For example, on 30 July 1900 the Council resolved to give notice to Messrs Fordham to connect the new urinal at the Coach and Horses with the main sewer. Resolutions in the following year included: notices to Mrs Pearman to connect her cottages in Sish Lane, occupied by the Salvation Army, George Ireton, George Woods ... and George Newberry with the main sewer; to Mrs E Shelford to connect her two cottages in Sish Lane, occupied by Thomas Chance and Levi Field, to the main sewer; resolution to take proceedings before magistrates against Mr Josiah Blow in the event of his failing to connect his two cottages in Alleyns Road with the main sewer. Occasionally even plans for new houses omitted this essential amenity. In 1901 a planning application submitted by William Austin, for Mr H Burrows, for a house at the Four Want Way (junction of Weston, Walkern and Letchmore Roads) was refused because no drainage was shown on the plan.

The word 'nuisance' had a particular connotation at this time: it usually referred to refuse of an insanitary or offensive nature which could be hazardous to public health. The Council had powers to enforce its removal but sometimes there was a long battle before those responsible complied. This was so in the saga of butcher Harry O'Clee's offal. A letter from Mr A B Champness, in January 1909, stated that Mr O'Clee had ignored a notice served on him by the Council to abate the nuisance caused by the deposit of offal in a field. On 27 April 1910 Mr Pallett, SUDC Vice Chairman, reported that he had seen Mrs O'Clee who stated that Mr O'Clee had no intention of removing the offal. On 29 August it was further reported that the offal deposited by Mr O'Clee on land in his occupation in Brick Kiln Lane had still not been removed. The matter was deferred until the next meeting, when further proceedings would be taken. Eventually, on 26 September 1910, a communication was received from Mr O'Clee, regretting that he could not remove the offal, but he had treated it carefully and covered it. The Council decided to consider this satisfactory.

Progress was being made in the provision of education for Stevenage children following the 1902 Education Act which gave local education authorities powers to provide elementary and secondary schools. In 1910 the newly-built Letchmore Road Elementary School for Boys was opened by Hertfordshire County Council. It took boys aged from seven to fourteen although, until 1918, the official school leaving age was still thirteen. There was no new provision for girls, who continued to share with the infants at St Nicholas' School on Bury Mead, but at least they now had more room. 1910 was also the year when road names had to be erected and houses numbered. This apparently sensible requirement was not without its opponents: one lady in Hitchin Road wrote objecting strongly to her house being numbered 13.

In 1911 the Council approved plans for a new fire station on the corner of Basils Road and Church Lane, to replace the nineteenth-century fire engine house attached to the Hellard Almshouses. At the same time they decided to convert the old building into a public bath-house, where people lacking such a facility in their own homes could wash themselves. On 29 July 1912 the Water Engineer submitted a plan and specification. The estimate for the supply and installation of baths and a geyser amounted to £65 plus £35 for alterations to the building. The Council approved the proposed conversion in principle at a cost not exceeding £100 and also resolved to adopt the Baths and Wash Houses Act. The slipper baths, as they were known, proved very popular: two future Labour Councillors, Philip Ireton and Fred Newberry, were among those who used them in their young days. However, some patrons were inclined to wallow for too long and in 1914 it was 'proposed that printed notices be posted at the Bath House calling attention to extra charge for using a bath longer than half an hour'.

The 1914 Housing Act had underlined the need for more and better housing for the working classes. Stevenage Council was well ahead with plans for Council housing which included building on sites in Walkern Road, Haycroft Lane and Hellards Road but within a few months England was at war with Germany and all projects of this kind ground to a halt. In March 1915, the Council received a circular from the Local Government Board on the Organisation of Labour and Borrowing by Local Authorities, instructing them 'to avoid inception of all new works except such as are of pressing necessity either for reasons of public health or on account of war requirements'.

During the First World War, 1914–1918, the population of Stevenage was swollen by an influx of mainly Belgian refugees and of troops stationed in and around the town. Some were billeted in the Parish Room in Basils Road, others camped in the fields. Public facilities such as the slipper baths were greatly

The Hellard Almshouses, Church Lane, with the bath house on the right. (Stevenage Museum P3486)

Middle Row. (Stevenage Museum P5337)

Unveiling the Stevenage war memorial in 1921. (Stevenage Museum).

appreciated but struggled to meet demand. Soldiers marched through the High Street, sometimes halting there for the night. Often they had nowhere to sleep and were forced to spend the night in the open unless some kind person gave them shelter. The landlady of the Buckingham Palace public house was one who took pity on the men trying to sleep outside in Middle Row and invited them indoors where they slept on chairs or the floor, before marching off again early the next morning. Local residents set up working parties to make bandages and comforts for soldiers stationed overseas. The Grange School (formerly the Swan Inn) was one centre for a group which made dressings for the wounded.

Food and materials became increasingly scarce, as the nation's resources were channelled into the war effort. In spite of obvious inequities in the availability of food, rationing was not introduced until 25 February 1918. The Stevenage Food Control Committee, chaired by Mr B H Reginald Daltry, went hastily into action, preparing handwritten food and meat rationing cards with the aid of volunteers.

One building project which was allowed to continue was the completion, in 1916, of the new police station and court house in Stanmore Road, to replace the existing one adjacent to the town hall, which in its turn had replaced the first Stevenage Police Station in North Road. Two of the labourers who worked on the site were the Fox twins, appearing amused to have their photographs taken there. Later, they were among the first to be incarcerated in the cells.

When the war ended, there were further horrors facing the country. Of those men who did return from the fighting, many were wounded or suffering from what was then known as 'shell-shock' but is nowadays called 'post-traumatic stress syndrome'. Food and coal were still in short supply, as were jobs. In an attempt to provide a means of livelihood for at least some of the men, the Hertfordshire County Council bought or rented land to provide smallholdings which ex-servicemen could apply for. One Stevenage applicant was Driver J W Wilson, RE, of 123, Letchmore Road, on whose behalf the Council agreed, at their meeting on 30 December 1918, to write to the County Council. Examples of the former HCC smallholdings remaining today can be seen on the outskirts of Baldock, along the A505 to Royston and on the minor road to Bygrave.

The Stevenage Council did their best to help the returning soldiers. On 24 February 1919, having received a letter from Mr L Bray, expressing his readiness to accept the post of horse-keeper/ploughman at a wage of £2 per week or slightly less if a house were found for him, they resolved to engage him at £2 per week. The unfortunate man suffered from malaria as a result of his wartime posting and was frequently absent from work. Inevitably, as the surveyor explained at the Council meeting on 26 April the following year, this caused 'great inconvenience'. Although there was sympathy for the surveyor's problem, he was instructed 'to make the most satisfactory re-arrangement of work to meet the difficulty'.

As for the women who had worked to keep industry and agriculture going for the previous four years, they found themselves out of work as the men returned to take over. For the rest of their lives thousands of war widows struggled to make ends meet on inadequate pensions in a social climate where, despite being granted the right to vote in 1918 at the age of 30 and in 1929 at 21, the idea of married women working, let alone receiving equal pay, was frowned upon.

The year 1919 must have been one of the most unpleasant in the twentieth century. The war was over, but even as the government and local authorities struggled to cope with its aftermath, another blow fell in the form of the worldwide 'Spanish' influenza epidemic which, in Britain alone, killed some 228,000 people, more than those who had died in the fighting. In Stevenage, the Council met on 25 November 1919 to consider the Public Health (Influenza) regulations. These required that where the public were admitted to a place of public entertainment as defined in the order, the entertainment should not be carried on for more than three consecutive hours, that there should be an interval of at least 30 minutes between two successive entertainments and that during the interval the building should be effectively and thoroughly ventilated. To add to the gloom, at the same meeting the Medical Officer reported that there was a measles epidemic and the two elementary schools – St Nicholas', on Bury Mead, and the Letchmore Road Boys' School – were being closed for six weeks.

Meanwhile, the town was seeking to honour the memory of those who had died fighting for their country. After a series of public meetings, it was decided to erect a war memorial on the Bowling Green, subject to the agreement of the Ecclesiastical Commissioners, Lords of the Manor of Stevenage. The Commissioners gave their consent provided that the memorial did not occupy a greater area than 24 feet x 24 feet (7.3 m x 7.3 m) and that it did not prejudice the use of the Green as open space. The memorial, paid for by public subscription, was unveiled in 1921, commemorating 125 Stevenage men who died with the inscription: *In honour and in grateful remembrance of the men of Stevenage who gave their lives for king and Country in the Great War 1914 – 1918. Their names liveth for ever more.*

Gradually, the outlook became less bleak. The Council was able to begin preparations for the long-promised new houses for the working classes although, over the next few years, periodic shortages of labour and materials prevented work from going ahead as swiftly as planned. Despite difficulties, houses eventually did get built and by the end of 1920 the Council was able to decide that rents for the twenty new houses in Haycroft Lane would be 8s 0d (40p) per week including rates. The class of tenants to be provided for would consist of 'labourers and like persons'. In 1921 the first Council houses were let in Hellards Road. Progress was being made in other respects, too. A Maternity and Child Welfare Centre was proposed for Stevenage. On 25 October 1920, in response to a letter from the Hertfordshire County Council, Mrs Clark, Mrs James, Mrs Nye and Miss A Villiers were appointed as representatives of the Council on the local sub-committee. The Clinic, as it became known, was established next to the Cromwell Hotel, at 27, High Street and eventually also provided a school dentist's surgery, with a district nurse's flat upstairs.

By 1924 the housing situation had become critical. The Council did not have its own direct labour force and all building was carried out by private firms, such as R H Field, of Letchmore Road, who built many of the Council houses in Stevenage between the two World Wars. He and other contractors bought land from the Council at a price set by the District Valuer. However, at this time, although the Council owned a suitable site in Walkern Road, the price had gone beyond the reach of local builders. At its meeting on 28 January 1924, the Council was urged by Cllrs Leonard and Lawrance '... in view of the urgent need for houses a deputation be appointed to interview the Minister of Health with a view to the District Valuer's price of the Council's land being reduced and that failing building being undertaken by private enterprise the Council will consider whether they should themselves proceed to build'. So great was the need for houses that the dentist, F S Higgins, sent in a proposal to convert the old army huts at the rear of 3, High Street into a dwelling house.

At this difficult period for the country William Jowitt, KC, only son of the former Stevenage rector, entered politics. His legal career had already been highly successful and he was recognised as having one of the finest legal minds of the time. Holding strong radical views, he supported what would today be called the left of the Liberal Party and stood as Liberal candidate for the Hartlepools. Somewhat unexpectedly he was elected, but at the General Election in 1924 he lost his seat. In the 1929 election he stood again as a Liberal and was elected MP for Preston.

At this election Britain's second Labour Government was returned to power, with Ramsey MacDonald as Prime Minister. Realising that he had very few legal experts among his MPs, MacDonald asked Jowitt to join the Labour Government as Attorney General. Jowitt agreed, stating that he believed there was now more chance of achieving the radical aims he had always striven for through a Labour Government than through continued membership of the Liberal Party. He resigned as Liberal MP, stood again and was re-elected as Labour MP for Preston with a majority of 6,400. In 1931, following the collapse of the Labour Government, a National Government was formed. MacDonald continued as Prime Minister with a Cabinet of Conservative, Liberal and Labour MPs. Shortly afterwards the Labour Party repudiated this coalition, and when Jowitt agreed to continue as Attorney General he was expelled from the Labour Party. He lost his seat at the next election.

Those in government, be it central or local, were faced with many and diverse problems at this time: ongoing treaty negotiations after the end of the First World War; unemployment, highlighted by the General Strike of 1926; Britain's near bankrupt economic state and the Great Depression following the Wall Street Crash of 1929.

All these national problems were mirrored to a greater or lesser extent in Stevenage. While it could not be called a commuter town at this time, there were commuters among its residents, some of whom had been attracted here by the convenience of a short journey to London on the Great Northern Railway. So it was with considerable annoyance that, in December 1919, they complained of the inadequacies of the service. Their voice was heard and the Council resolved 'to call the serious attention of the Great Northern Railway Company to the grave deterioration in the railway service between London and Stevenage which is now worse than the wartime train service and fails to provide for the needs of residents in the town, many of whom travel daily to London … trains fewer in number and less convenient than heretofore, are very unpunctual and that it is not unusual for a journey which used to take some 50 minutes to now take 75 minutes … Council are of the opinion that it is unreasonable that workers whose office hours are 9.30 to 6 should have to leave Stevenage at 7.40 and not get back until 8.17 pm or later'.

Over the years the Council had had many disagreements with the railway company over matters such as footbridges (or the lack of) and poor upkeep of roads, footpaths and other features for which they were responsible, but assurances were now received that special attention would be given to the service from Stevenage to London. Life for commuters did improve from 1923 when at last the long-delayed 'Hertford loop' reached Stevenage. This line, with terminus at Moorgate, made it possible for residents to travel directly into the City of London. Twenty years later, it was to have a decisive influence on the town's future.

The 1930s was the era of the Great Depression, a time of unemployment, poverty and hardship for many, overshadowed by the threat of another war. Yet a surprising amount was being achieved in the country as a whole in terms of improving people's lives. The government's house-building programme was succeeding; there was help, admittedly on a limited scale, for the unemployed; the school leaving age had been raised to 14; women had at last been given the same voting rights as men and there were plans nationally and locally for more improvements. In Stevenage, the 1935 celebrations to mark the Silver Jubilee of the reign of King George V and Queen Mary had prompted an extension to the town's beloved Avenue. It had been planted with lime and horse-chestnut trees in two sections; the first by Rector Nicholas Cholwell in 1756, the second (High Street end) by Enclosures Commissioner John Bailey Denton in 1857. Now the third section, leading from St Nicholas' church, was realigned and planted with money given by the people of Stevenage and named the Jubilee Avenue.

At the same time there were exciting – and sometimes controversial – plans for a King George V playing field, to be created adjacent to the Stevenage Cricket Club ground in London Road. Land off Sish Lane was given by a former chairman of the Council, the benevolent J Marsden Popple, who lived at Daneshill, London Road, next to Clarence Elliott's famous Six Hills Nursery. It was Clarence Elliott who discovered a hardy fuschia growing in their garden and christened it 'Mrs Popple', a name still well-known in gardening circles. Good progress was made on the playing field, although the Council's original intention to build a swimming pool had to be abandoned for the time being. On 7 June 1937 a letter was received from the National Playing Fields Association saying that a coloured drawing of the layout of the proposed King George V Field would be on exhibition at 66, Portland Place, London, during an exhibition relating to Health, Sport and Fitness. There was also good news with regard to a grant from the King George's Fields Foundation.

For several years the Council had been hoping that a new school could be built in the town for both girls and boys aged 11 to 14. At first it was thought that the Church of England, who had raised the money for St Nicholas' School, could do the same for the new school. After long deliberations they decided that this would not be possible. Then, on 31 October 1938, came the good news that 'Hertfordshire County Council intended to provide a County Public Elementary School to accommodate about 320 senior mixed children on the site acquired off Walkern Road. The Clerk was instructed to write thanking HCC and hoping that the work would start as soon as possible'. Unfortunately, once again war deferred progress, although the playing field did go ahead.

In 1937 the young Philip Ireton was elected as one of the town's first Labour councillors. He was keenly aware of the importance of planning. The nearby example of Letchworth Garden City inspired him to hope for something similar at Stevenage and, as a member of the Town and Country Planning Association, he attended conferences and was often aware of new developments before his fellow councillors. Under the terms of the 1932 Town and Country Planning Act, Stevenage Urban District Council was preparing its own development plan, showing a natural evolution from the existing town. It proposed an industrial area, schools, public open space, housing to accommodate an eventual population of 30,000, allotments and several private open spaces. The latter was a strategy by which agreement was reached between landowners and the local authority to leave specific pieces of land undeveloped, but not necessarily open to the public. One example of this in the Stevenage plan was land between The Avenue and Rectory Lane belonging to Michael Tetley.

After a great deal of hard work the Stevenage plan was completed and given the official seal of approval on 26 September 1938 ready to submit to the Ministry of Health on the next stage of its progress. Then the Council turned its attention to the ominous signs of war. Evacuees from London arrived by the trainload and had to be found accommodation. Once again Stevenage was filled with troops, some billeted in the area, others passing through. The Women's Voluntary Service, under the leadership of Mrs Helen Inns, of Springfield House, set up a canteen in the Old Castle Inn for passing service men and kept it going non-stop for the whole of the war. It gained a reputation as one of the best in the country. The town hall came into its own, as the centre of local life, where boy scouts manned an information post, dances and social events were held almost every night and the British Restaurant provided cheap meals in the day.

Watercolour of the Old Castle Inn, by Mabel Culley, 1940–45. During the Second World War it was used as a forces canteen run by Helen Inns. The picture shows soldiers entering the building. (Stevenage Museum P2621)

Life was tough in wartime Stevenage, where 41 families lost sons, husbands, fathers and brothers. Life in London, for many people, was terrible. One woman who had first hand experience of the blitz was a young housing manager named Mary Tabor. At the end of 1940 she was working in a school turned into a rest centre in Camberwell, rehousing bombed-out people from four districts. Stevenage residents, listening nervously to the sound of German bombers passing overhead, could see the red glow of fires burning in London, 30 miles away. The blitz began on 7 September 1940 and continued until 10 May 1941. London was bombed for 57 consecutive nights and, by the end of May 1941, some 22,000 people had been killed, 1,400,000 bombed out of their homes and over a million houses destroyed or damaged. Hornsey, a north London borough later to become closely associated with Stevenage, was very heavily bombed, 80 per cent of its houses being damaged. Stevenage firemen were called on to help brigades in London, Bedford and other towns. Most people who were not conscripted to fight had to serve locally as Air Raid Precautions officers or in the Home Guard or other unpaid service.

In the closing stages of the war in Europe, pilotless V1 flying bombs (known as doodlebugs) and V2 rockets enabled Germany to attack London again. 8,938 civilians were killed in London and the South East. Stevenage was fortunate in that several V1 and V2 rockets fell harmlessly in the countryside outside the town, but Camberwell was on the line of the V1 bombs and from her top flat in Camberwell Grove, Mary Tabor would listen for the familiar drone, wondering if it would cut out and the rocket fall in Camberwell, which would mean more people to be rehoused.

Many local women were called up to work in factories, such as the ESA in Stevenage or in the industrial area in Letchworth. The George W King engineering factory, the Vincent HRD motorcycle works, and the smaller engineering firms of Wickham French and W H Sanders were also engaged on war work. A number of young women from Ireland were recruited to work at the the ESA. They lodged with Stevenage families and in 1944 the government built them a warden-supervised social centre in Pound Avenue. Furniture for the centre, which was named the Lytton Club, was provided with money donated by the Women of America organisation. Some of the girls married local men and made their homes in the town but the majority returned to Ireland when the war ended.

One of Britain's revolutionary 'weapons' was the high speed, twin-engine de Havilland Mosquito aircraft – the 'wooden wonder'. Wings for the aircraft were made at the ESA factory in Fairview Road which, before the war, had produced school furniture. The work done there was of such a high standard that the government built a second factory for the company in nearby Fishers Green Road.

Stevenage Firemen, 1940s. (John Allen)

Stevenage Home Guard parade with John Appleton's Bentley converted to an armoured car during the Second World War. (Stevenage Museum P2650)

Even during the darkest days of the Second World War, when the outcome was far from clear, men of faith and vision were turning their attention to actions that would need to be taken at home in the aftermath of the six-year long conflict and the material damage suffered in Britain's principle cities – especially London. In 1944, while the country's political and military leaders were planning the campaign that would lead to victory in Europe, academics were planning for the future that would follow the end of the war.

Among them was Professor Patrick Abercrombie, an eminent town planner, who concerned himself with the London situation and the opportunity now offered to halt its sprawling suburban development by the creation of a protected, constraining Green Belt. In his Greater London Plan, published in 1944, he suggested that, beyond the Green Belt, an outer-country ring be designated with eight self-contained 'satellite towns' to which people and employment would decamp from inner London. He named ten possible sites, all approximately 30 miles from London and located in a ring around the capital. One of them was the north Hertfordshire town of Stevenage – an ideal location because of its main rail and road links with London and its south and west sloping land for residential development. At the time that Abercrombie had carried out his research into the suitability of Stevenage for the purpose, its population was in the region of 6,000. Under his plan, it would be increased ten fold to 60,000.

At a meeting of the SUDC on 26 July 1943, Philip Ireton, reporting on the County Planning Conference held in London on 29 June, expressed the view that the public should be made aware of the government's intentions regarding the Uthwatt and Scott Reports. These were concerned respectively with the use of rural land and the future of the countryside in relation to town and country planning, both of which had implications for the future of Stevenage. He also suggested that the Council's Planning Scheme should be reviewed, particularly in relation to industrial development and, further, that the Council should appoint a post-war development committee. No-one seconded his proposal but the chairman, J A Marsden Popple, said that the points he had raised would be borne in mind.

The Council had many other, more obviously pressing matters to deal with. Stevenage was doing all it could to support troops passing through or camped in the town. Most recently it had agreed to allow the use of its new tennis courts, on Tuesday and Sunday evenings, to soldiers stationed at Aston House. But a military presence in the town was not without its drawbacks, as army vehicles churned up roads and caused other damage, including wrecking the St Nicholas' School playground. The Council wrote to the Commandant of the War Office staging camp, asking for it to be repaired, one of many similar letters that had to be written.

A special meeting of the Council was held on 25 January 1944, attended by Mr G N C Swift, deputy clerk of the Hertfordshire County Council, and Miss Adburgham, assistant to the Hertfordshire County Council planning consultant, Mr W R Davidge. Mr Popple, as chairman, reviewed the principal features of the SUDC scheme, referring to possible amendments, consultations with public utility undertakings, the railway company, the chamber of trade and others. Mr Swift said that all towns should have the authority to lay out estates and be given sufficient power to do the work properly. He stressed the importance of future highways, special motor roads (ie motorways), provision of amenities including open spaces, amusements, educational facilities, a civic centre, welfare services and hospital accommodation.

Miss Adburgham spoke of the importance of preparing a 'town plan', as well as the statutory plan, and the preparation of an ownership map. The town plan should deal with such matters as view points, footpaths, springs, trees, special buildings and open spaces. She also mentioned tree-planting, green belts and housing sites and the need to pay attention to architectural design. The discussion which followed focussed on amendments to the Stevenage scheme and the introduction of new industry. Mr Swift suggested that a variety of industries was desirable, to avoid excessive unemployment. There was talk of transferring some industry from London, but no detailed proposals as yet. He thought that Stevenage was fortunate in its electricity and gas supplies and it also seemed to be well provided with water. Its sewage disposal was satisfactory. Perhaps some councillors, well aware of the hard work that they and their predecessors had put into ensuring that their town was supplied with electricity, gas and water, felt a twinge of annoyance at the use of the word 'fortunate'. This no doubt was balanced by the slightly generous comment of 'satisfactory' for the sewage farm.

As to future population, the Stevenage surveyor estimated that the Council's planning scheme provided for an ultimate figure of 34,000. Mr Swift commented that Stevenage was exceptionally well placed for future development. He referred to the Bressey report which recommended a by-pass for the town and also for an east–west route through the district, adding that if these roads were to be proceeded with they would be shown on Professor Abercrombie's plan for London.

At the Council meeting on 31 January 1944 Philip Ireton again proposed that 'a special committee' to be known as the Development Committee be set up. This time, seconded by J H Reeves, he was successful. The first members were; Ireton, Reeves, A E Locke, R H Walker and the chairman. Subsequently the Council agreed to apply for membership of the Town and Country Planning Association at an annual subscription of £2 2s 0d (£2.10), plus 15s 0d (75p) each to send two representatives to attend the National Conference in London in December 1944. By that time the Council had received from the Ministry of

Town and Country Planning three copies of an advance edition of Professor Patrick Abercrombie's Greater London Plan together with tickets to allow three representatives of the Council to view a private exhibition of original maps and plans. They immediately asked for more tickets 'in view of the important place occupied by Stevenage in the Greater London Plan so that all members could view the exhibition'. Whether they were successful is not recorded but on 9 January 1945 a proposal by Ireton, seconded by Reeves, 'that the proposal [under the Greater London Plan] to site a satellite town at Stevenage be approved in principle subject to reservations with regard to financial provisions and any necessary boundary revisions' was carried.

Among the many other matters on the Council's agenda in the spring of 1945 was the loss of their clerk, Arthur Primett. They eventually appointed Geoffrey V Berry, of Rishton, Lancashire, first as Acting Clerk then, from 1 June 1945,

Stevenage Urban District Council Planning Scheme, 1942. (HALS CP3/1/24)

as Clerk and Chief Financial Officer at a salary of £550 per annum plus cost of living bonus. He could not have arrived at a more crucial time in the history of Stevenage. Meanwhile, there was routine business to be dealt with: the death of the Council's mare, 'Peggy' and payment to A J Gates, slaughterer, for her disposal; a Stevenage District Education Committee, a North Herts Further Education Committee and a Stevenage Library Committee to be set up, all under the auspices of the Hertfordshire County Council. The Council was also moving rapidly to provide dwellings for those residents who had been waiting since before the war for housing, whose numbers would soon be increased by the return of service men and women. Even before the official end of the war, they had authorised an advertisement for tenders to develop a site in Sish Lane for 20 temporary bungalows – known popularly as 'prefabs' – and later in the year started procedures for the compulsory purchase of more land for housing between Sish Lane and Haycroft Road.

When the war finally came to an end the Council looked forward with some confidence to the future. Much-needed new houses for local people were on the way. The Council's development plan for an enlarged Stevenage with new industry to provide jobs, had been completed in 1942, but necessarily shelved during the war. Now it could be acted upon. Most excitingly, Stevenage seemed poised to become one of London's 'satellite' towns, with financial support from the government and the prospect of working with the Ministry of Town and Country Planning.

BUSES FROM THE NORTH STAR

Before the Second World War a bus service between Stevenage and Hitchin was operated by the family-run North Star Bus Company, of Stevenage. The small company took its name from the North Star public house, number 12, High Street, where it first kept its passenger vehicles. There were two single-deck buses, one driven by Albert Candler, senior, the other by his son, also Albert. Their conductress was Albert's fiancee, who was the daughter of the licensee of The New Found Out public house in Stevenage Road, Hitchin.

In the early 1930s one of the Candlers would drive his bus from Stevenage to Hitchin to pick up passengers waiting to go to Stevenage. On the return journey he would stop briefly at the New Found Out to pick up his conductress, who would then collect the fares from the Stevenage-bound passengers. At about the same time, the other bus would leave Stevenage for Hitchin. The two buses would meet at Little Wymondley where the conductress would transfer to the other bus to collect the fares from the Hitchin-bound passengers.

CHAPTER FOUR
The road to Silkingrad

THE END OF THE WAR in Europe brought huge relief to an exhausted Britain, but life would not be easy for a very long time to come. The overwhelming Labour victory at the General Election in July 1945 encouraged many to hope for a better world: others were filled with alarm. This seemed justified the following month when American President Harry S Truman ended the Lend-Lease agreement which had allowed Britain to import food from the United States with deferred payment. Then, in September, a seven-week dock strike began.

Stevenage was part of the Hitchin Constituency, or Division as it was then called, which traditionally elected Independent MPs with Conservative leanings. It was a shock for many – and a triumph for others – when the Labour candidate, Philip Asterley-Jones, was elected MP for Hitchin. The news that Clement Attlee, the new Prime Minister, had appointed William Jowitt as his Lord Chancellor, with the title Baron Jowitt of Stevenage, was greeted with mixed reactions. There was local pride but also, especially among those of similar social standing, a feeling that he had betrayed his class. Whatever their politics, no-one could deny that, over the next six years, Jowitt earned the epithet 'the most overworked Lord Chancellor in history', as he dealt with an exceptional amount of new legislation, including much work to assist the progress of the New Towns Act through parliament.

The year 1946 opened in an atmosphere of uncertainty. Nationally, Britain was facing a period of austerity worse even than that which had prevailed during the war. At the same time the government was committed to the introduction of a welfare state in what amounted to a revolutionary programme of social reform. Stevenage found itself swept into the forefront of change. The Council minutes, increasingly lengthy, are evidence of the great range of activities for which the councillors had responsibility. Of immediate concern were buildings which had been requisitioned for various purposes during the war, some of which now needed repairs or alterations to make them fit for habitation. One of these was The Warren, in London Road, which the Council were hoping could be converted into flats to help ease the housing shortage in the town. Meanwhile preparations were moving ahead for the building of long-awaited council housing on land between upper Sish Lane and the top of Haycroft Road and discussions were taking place with the Hertfordshire County Council to build a junior school at the top of Pound Avenue. In all these matters, as with requests for permission to erect new buildings, the Council, as the local planning authority, had power within the existing law to grant or refuse applications.

It was something of a shock, therefore, when in February 1946 an application by the Stevenage firm of Geo. W King Ltd to build three pairs of semi-detached houses for its employees was refused by the Town Planning Officer on the grounds that it might prejudice the future development of the proposed satellite town. This was just one of the many instances of lack of prior communication from the Ministry of Town and Country Planning which were now occurring. Another was the number of notices now being sent out to landowners 'concerning the acquisition of their land'. All this was taking place when the new town was legally still only a proposal. At its meeting on 26 February the Council resolved

Aerial view of Geo. W King factory, 1939. (Stevenage Museum P09301)

to seek an immediate interview with the Ministry 'in view of the important principles raised in this case' and decided to send a deputation to the Minister, Lewis Silkin.

A special Council meeting was held on 25 April, at which Messrs Beaufoy, Elliott, and Stephenson, representing the Ministry of Town and Country Planning, and Messrs Ridgeway and Thomas, representing the North Herts Joint Planning Committee, were in attendance. A plan was displayed and Mr Beaufoy expressed the hope that he and his colleagues would be able to give as much information as the Council wished and that any complaints regarding lack of co-operation in the past would be remedied. Questions were asked and answered and the Ministry officials assured the Council that the plan in its present form was provisional and that further consultations would take place with the Council and the North Herts Joint Planning Committee before the final layout was decided. Subsequently the Council asked that a plan similar to that displayed at the meeting should be sent to them for public display. The answer came that 'a plan, but not necessarily one similar to that on display at the meeting' would be sent for display. A series of maps showing the stages of development of the new town was also offered, so that a public exhibition could be set up. The Council then arranged with the North Metropolitan Power Company (known as the 'Northmet') to house the display in their showroom, at 38, High Street.

By this time many residents, especially the 179 who had already been told that their land would be compulsorily purchased or their houses destroyed, were in a state of high anxiety. The lack of reliable information was disturbing even those who looked forward to the promised houses and jobs. Almost overnight, as it seemed to Geoffrey V Berry, Clerk to the Council, the Stevenage Residents' Protection Association was formed and very soon had over 1,000 members and a fighting fund. The ensuing publicity was enormous and, said Berry, 'Stevenage became not the place where a new town of some 15,000 houses was to be built, but where houses were to be pulled down and gardens destroyed.' At this time of acute housing shortage everywhere, including Stevenage, it had never occurred to any resident that perfectly good houses would be knocked down. The main local newspaper, the *Hertfordshire Express*, was deluged with letters, the majority against the new town proposal although some were in favour. Many were concerned with injustices relating to compulsory purchase. Stevenage was soon hitting the headlines as the national press took up the story. Inevitably it soon became politicised along party lines, distorting valid arguments.

Although the new town idea was in many ways a part of the garden city movement, there was one important difference. Whereas the garden cities were privately funded, the new towns would be built using public money and their houses and flats would not be available for purchase but for rent only. This

Elizabeth Poston in the 1930s

posed immediate problems for local people whose homes were to be demolished. They would be paid compensation at the 1939 valuation plus 30 per cent but, as one of many letters on this subject to the *Hertfordshire Express* explained, this would be inadequate. 'Let us assume that a house at 1939 values was worth £700 and the land £150. Under the proposed scheme of compensation ... the owner will receive £700 + 30% (or £910), plus £150 for the land – total £1,060. The present cost of building such a house is about £1,500, plus land £150 – total £1,650. This represents a net loss of £590. The unfortunate man is then told he must pay his own removal expenses.'

Alternatively, the dispossessed householder could invest his compensation payment and accept the offer of a property rented to him by the Stevenage Development Corporation. This aroused enormous resentment, as expressed forcefully at one meeting by George Hearn, of Corey's Mount, speaking for the Residents' Protection Association. Referring to the proposal to buy out freehold owners and institute a leasehold system as the most wicked thing he had ever experienced in his 60 years of public life, he said, 'You are coolly asked to bargain your birthright for a mess of pottage – and what a mess!'

The injustice of this situation was recognised by Silkin who, in June 1946 proposed an amendment to the New Towns Bill then going through Parliament, so that 'accommodation should be offered to persons displaced suitable to the reasonable requirements of those persons'. This is typical of the type of language used in official and public communications by the Ministry of Town and Country Planning which antagonised and frightened people in Stevenage. Europe at that time was full of 'displaced persons' as a result of six years of war. To be referred to as a 'displaced person' in your home town was, to say the least, upsetting.

One of the most active members of the Residents' Protection Association was the composer, Elizabeth Poston, at Rooks Nest. She persuaded E M Forster to lend his support, which he did rather reluctantly as a lifelong Labour supporter. The dilemma he expressed in a BBC broadcast, entitled *The Challenge of Our Time*, must have struck a chord with many of his listeners. He said,

> In a time of upheaval like the present, this collision of principles, this split in one's loyalties, is always occurring. It has just occurred in my own life. I was brought up as a boy in one of the home counties, in a district which I still

> think the loveliest in England ... Life went on there as usual until this spring. Then someone who was applying for a permit to lay a water pipe was casually informed that it would not be granted since the whole area had been commandeered. Commandeered for what? Had not the war ended? Appropriate officials of the Ministry of Town and Country Planning now arrived from London and announced that a satellite town for sixty thousand people is to be built. The people now living and working there are doomed ...
>
> "Well," says the voice of planning and progress, "why this sentimentality? People must have houses." They must, and I think of working-class friends in North London who have to bring up four children in two rooms and many are even worse off than that. But I cannot equate the problem. It is a collision of loyalties ... I wonder what compensation there is in the world of the spirit for the destruction of the life here, the life of tradition.

After the broadcast Forster was taken to task by the Ministry of Town and Country Planning for implying that Stevenage people had been given no warning of the scheme for a new town when, in fact all the legally-required notices had been displayed. He replied in a letter dated 28 May 1946 that '... correctness is not enough. In this age of changes drastically affecting the ordinary man, it is the duty of officials not merely to advertise their plans but to bring them home to him in an appropriate form. They ought, in other words, to make a more profound and a more respectful study of local psychology than appears to have obtained in the present instance.'

The question of the proposed new town was now overshadowing all other concerns. Council minutes for 29 April included only the briefest mentions of matters which might normally excite much more interest, including; the victory celebrations planned for 8 June; the Prime Minister's letter on the world food shortage, the importance of maintaining food production and preventing waste; the establishment of a North Herts Further Education Committee. Instead, a great deal of time was spent in drawing up proposals for amendments to the plan for a new town. In this respect the Council's main aim was to avoid the destruction of houses in London Road, Bedwell Lane and Fairview Road. They were also concerned about the plan to site the industrial area to the west of the town, which they believed would mean that smoke and other pollutants would be blown by the

The town hall in Orchard Road. (Stevenage Museum P1703)

prevailing wind into residential areas. At a time when the majority of homes were heated with open coal fires and the word 'industry' conjured up images of smog and soot-blackened buildings, it was difficult to have confidence in the planners' assurances that the new town industry would be smokeless. Another concern was the route of the A1(M), which the Council was anxious should be moved further to the west, to reduce to an absolute minimum its encroachment on Watery Grove, an important woodland wildlife site.

At last Lewis Silkin, the Minister for Town and Country Planning, agreed to come to Stevenage on Monday 6 May 1946 and to address a public meeting at the town hall. The Council issued a press statement and invited people to send in questions which could be raised with the Minister. In addition, all those who had been sent notices about the acquisition of their land, together with the owners of property in Fairview Road and 'New Town' (the roads off Fishers Green Road, near the station), whose houses were threatened with demolition, were invited to choose representatives who would be given priority of admission to the public meeting.

Mr Silkin spent much of Wednesday 6 May in the town – a little longer than he had expected or intended. Having held discussions with Urban and County Council representatives in the morning, he made a tour of the town in the afternoon. Wherever he went he was greeted with the sight of hostile posters and notices, leaving him in no doubt about the strong feelings held by many. Surrounded by a crowd of officials, local residents, national and local press reporters and cameramen, the Minister walked along Fairview Road, a pleasant modern street of owner-occupied semi-detached houses which was marked in the Master Plan for demolition to make way for factories. He stopped to have a word with one owner-occupier who was standing at his front gate. 'We can build you another house,' the Minister told him. 'Yes, you can build me another house but –', he asked, pointing to a mature tree in his garden, 'can you build me another tree like that?' The Minister made no reply.

In the evening, Lewis Silkin spoke from the stage to a packed public meeting in the town hall. Long before the doors opened, a queue of residents had formed, stretching from Orchard Road around the corner and into the High Street. So large was the crowd that the hall was soon filled to capacity and there were as many standing outside as were seated inside. Proceedings were relayed to them over a loudspeaker mounted on a car roof. The meeting started good-humouredly enough but soon turned hostile. Gripping the lapels of his jacket, Silkin spoke of wanting to carry out in Stevenage a 'daring exercise in town planning'. This was greeted with boos and jeers. 'It is no good you jeering, it is going to be done,' he retorted angrily. Later he told the meeting, 'The project will go forward because it must go forward. It will do so more surely, more smoothly and more successfully with your help and co-operation.' Prophetically, he added, 'Stevenage

The crowd waiting outside the town hall where Lewis Silkin was speaking, on 6 May, 1946. (Stevenage Museum P2636)

Lewis Silkin speaking at the public meeting in the town hall, Orchard Road on 6 May 1946. (Stevenage Museum P2635)

will, in a short time become world famous. People from all over the world will come to Stevenage to see how we in this country are building for the new way of life.' In answer to a question from the floor, he said, 'Local authorities will be consulted all the way through. But we have a duty to perform and I am not going to be deterred from that duty. Whilst I will consult as far as possible all the local authorities affected, at the end, if people become fractious and unreasonable, I shall have to carry out my duty.'

Some Stevenage people carried out what they evidently considered to be their duty. When the Minister left the meeting he discovered that his car had been immobilised, its tyres deflated and sand poured into the petrol tank.

The outcome of Silkin's visit to Stevenage was not, as had been hoped, to calm fears and arouse support for the new town proposal, but rather the opposite. The Residents' Protection Association was incensed and on 9 May they formally requested the Council to support their demand for a public inquiry. Paragraph 3 of the first schedule to the New Towns Bill stated; 'If any objection is duly made to the proposed order and is not withdrawn, the Minister shall, before making the order, cause a local public inquiry to be held with respect thereto, and shall consider the report of the person by whom the inquiry was held'. On 27 May the Council received a letter from the Ministry of Town and Country Planning explaining that a local inquiry was now obligatory but that the Minister could not comply with the Council's request that nothing further should be done until after the inquiry, in view of the large amount of preliminary work to be carried out.

Meanwhile, under pressure from many voters, the Council was arranging a referendum. There was no support for this from the government, but Cllr Arthur Howard guaranteed to pay the costs of a referendum up to £60. Voting took place on 18 May when the public were asked chose between three options;

1– Entirely against the New Town
2– In favour of the Council's amended proposals
3– In favour of the Ministry of Town and Country Planning scheme.

Only 52 per cent of the population voted. Whether the other 48 per cent had succumbed to feelings of powerlessness, whether they realised that the referendum carried no weight in law, or whether they were put off by the wording of the questions is not known, but the result was a small majority for those against the scheme in any form. A letter from 'G S' of Hitchin, published in the *Hertfordshire Express* for May 1946 made the point that 'The fact that 47.6 per cent of the votes were in favour of the scheme, or a modification of it, and 47.8 per cent did not vote at all, shows that the vociferous disapproval that has been expressed is greatly out of proportion to the feeling, even in the town itself.'

Nor did the protesters receive much support from their Labour MP, Philip Asterley Jones. In reply to a letter from Mr A Russell, one of his constituents, he wrote, 'I cannot agree that the question is one in which the present population of Stevenage should have the last word ... I may be the member for Hitchin, but I am a Member of Parliament, and parliament is concerned with the welfare of the whole nation.' However, speaking in the House of Commons in support of the New Towns Bill, he did express criticism of the way the Minister of Town and Country Planning had handled matters, saying,

> Many of the events which took place at the [public] meeting at Stevenage on Monday evening of last week were in my view due to the fact that there had not been enough preparation of the ground beforehand. It would have been better had the Minister gone to Stevenage not last Monday, but two months ago,

> before the notices were served on the people inviting them to sell their property by agreement. No great damage has been done, but at all stages in the development of this great new town – as I hope it will be – the fullest possible disclosure must be made to everybody concerned.

This was a confusing time. One great fear of local people was that the old town would be destroyed or at least changed out of all recognition. Time and again there came spoken reassurances that 'the Old Town will not be touched' but these words could not be found in print after the visiting politician or official had left. Then there came the question of what exactly was understood by the words 'the Old Town' and 'will not be touched' which left an aftermath of bitterness.

Preparations for the public inquiry now took up much of the Council's time, although even as they were preparing for it, they were also responding to requests from the Ministry of Town and Country Planning. In reply to a letter dated 2 July 1946 they agreed to send the Minister a list of names to serve on the proposed New Town Advisory Committee, 'it being understood that this action is without prejudice to the outcome of the inquiry'. The following nominations were submitted: Councillors W E Conlin, A G Howard, P T Ireton and R A V White, together with Mr J Appleton or Mr D M King, representing Stevenage and District Industrial Employers' Group; Mr S Ellis for the Stevenage Trades Council, Mr C Day for the Stevenage Chamber of Trades, Mr G L Hearn for the Stevenage Residents' Protection Association and Mr C Richardson for the National Farmers' Union, Hitchin Branch. They engaged Mr E G Culpin, their former Town Planning Adviser and a resident of Stevenage as their expert witness and appointed Cllr R A V White to be ready to speak also if called upon.

Despite the big question mark hanging over the town, its life went on superficially undisturbed during the summer of 1946. The Victory celebrations were held on 8 June as planned. Later in the summer, in a welcome return to the type of traditional entertainment that had been impossible during the six years of war, the Tetleys held a grand fete at their home, The Priory in Rectory Lane, a happy, peaceful occasion bathed in sunshine. Michael Tetley and his wife were among the leading opponents of the proposed new town and were particularly anxious that the land (now known as Priory Field) between their house in Rectory Lane and The Avenue should be protected. To this end they offered to give it either to the Urban District Council or the Development Corporation after their deaths, if it could be kept undeveloped in their lifetimes.

By 1 August the New Towns Bill had passed through all its parliamentary stages and become law as the New Towns Act 1946. Paragraph 1(1) stated; 'if the Minister is satisfied, after consultation with any local authorities who appear to him to be concerned, that it is expedient in the national interest that any area of land should be developed as a new town by a corporation established under this Act, he may make an order designating that area as the site of the proposed new town.' Silkin lost no time in responding to the sweeping powers the Act conveyed upon him and two days later he was able to issue the draft Stevenage New Town Designation Order.

In September came the news that the Minister of Town and Country Planning had accepted only one of the Council's nominees for the New Town Advisory Committee, Philip Ireton, who had also been nominated by the Hertfordshire County Council. The Council at once wrote to demand more representation and requesting that their chairman, W E Conlin, should be appointed. They were unsuccessful. Then a list of proposed Advisory Committee members arrived with no background information, meaning little or nothing to the Council, who asked for more detail.

This was supplied with a covering letter from Mr Silkin in which he said,

> I have in mind that the appointments (which will be subject to the provisions of the second Schedule to the New Towns Act) should in the first instance be for three years ... I consider it most important that the people appointed should have enthusiasm for the project and sufficient time to give it and that they should in no sense regard themselves as *representatives* of a particular locality or interest, but rather as Corporation members having *special knowledge* of that particular locality or interest.

The Minister's proposed New Town Advisory Committee members were;

Chairman: Mr Clough Williams-Ellis, MC, JP, ARIBA; architect; Chairman of the Council for the Preservation of Rural Wales; Member of the Town Planning Institute; Fellow of the Institute of Landscape Architects; owns and is designing and building Portmeirion in North Wales.

Vice-chairman: Dr Monica Felton, PhD; Member of the Herts County Council (by which her name was put forward to the Minister); formerly Member of the LCC for SW St Pancras, 1937–46; Chairman of the LCC Supplies Committee, 1939–41; Member of the Housing and Town Planning Committees; served in the Ministry of Supply, 1941–42; clerk, House of Commons, 1942–43; lecturer to HM Forces and for London University Tutorial Classes Committee; Governor of the London School of Economics.

Mr J D Campbell Allen, BA, 1st Class Honours Mechanical Science Tripos, Cambridge; was Director of Building and Financial Operations in the John Lewis Partnership, 1932–46; Member of the London Diocesan Re-organisation Committee.

Mr Hinley Atkinson; until recently was on the staff of the Labour Party where he was responsible for its organisation in the County of London and the Greater London Area; was a member of the Ministry of Information London Regional Committee from its inception.

Councillor Frank Corbett, JP; Mayor of Wood Green (one of the authorities intending to 'export' population and industry to Stevenage); Alderman of the Middlesex County Council; Chairman of the Wood Green Divisional Executive of the Middlesex County Education Committee; Chief of the Legal Department of the National Union of Railwaymen; Member of the Trades Union Congress Committee on Industrial Diseases.

Alderman W J Grimshaw, JP; Member of the Hornsey Borough Council (one of the authorities intending to 'export' population and industry to Stevenage) since 1927, represents the council on the housing, Education and Health Committees of the Association of Municipal Corporations; Member of the Middlesex County Council; Chairman of the Non-County Boroughs Association.

Councillor P T Ireton, JP; Member of the Stevenage Urban District Council and Chairman of its Town Planning Committee for some years; Member of the Herts. County Council; railway clerk.

Mrs Elizabeth McAllister, MA (Editor of *Town and Country Planning*); formerly Public Relations Officer to the Town and Country Planning Association; joint author (with Gilbert McAllister) of *Town and Country Planning – the Prelude to Post War Reconstruction,* 1941 and joint author (with Gilbert McAllister) of *Homes, Towns and Countryside,* 1945.

When the list was made public at a meeting on 3 October, there was animated discussion. Mr J P L Skeggs said that only two of the eight persons named had any practical experience whatever of town planning or anything that went with it – water, sewerage, building and so on. He noted that the chairman had designed and built Portmeirion. 'If Stevenage is going to be anything like Portmeirion,' he said, 'God help Stevenage!'

Not everyone agreed with him. Cllr J F Mackay pointed out that members of the Corporation would have technical experts to advise them, just as the Council did. He did think that there should be two representatives from Stevenage but was otherwise satisfied with the proposed Corporation. Cllr A G Howard moved 'That this Council, bearing in mind the magnitude of the project and the finance involved, is of the opinion that the persons proposed by the Minister for membership of the Development Corporation have not, in the majority of cases, the qualifications and practical experience to inspire confidence in the success of the undertaking.' The resolution was carried, with Councillors Mackay and Ibbetson voting against and Councillor Ireton abstaining.

Meanwhile the Council's many other duties had to to be carried out. It was over a year since the war had ended but the world food shortage and the country's grave economic situation meant that for many people life was a constant struggle. At the Council meeting on 30 September it was reported that a committee consisting of Mrs Margetts, Revd L F Higgs and Mr A E Coulson had 'distributed gifts of food from [South] Africa and Australia and that more than 400 aged and needy persons had benefited in this district'. The Council also had the duty of sending to the Ministry of Food nominations for membership of the town's Food Control Committee, which included representatives from consumers, the Co-operative Society, dairymen, grocers, butchers, bakers and trades unions.

Even cursory attention to the wording of the New Towns Act, with its unpromising provision for a public inquiry, might have convinced objectors that the fight was lost before it began. However, encouraged by the national press, now firmly divided along party lines, they went on with the public inquiry, which was held at the town hall on 7 and 8 October 1946. Reporting on it later, the Clerk to the Council, Geoffrey V Berry wrote, 'The inquiry was held by an inspector of the Ministry. The Inspector opened the proceedings with a short factual statement dealing only with the general necessity of setting up New Towns. No other official or witness appeared on behalf of the Minister and there was no cross examination. The Residents' Protection Association, the National Farmers Union and the Council were represented by counsel and engaged expert witnesses. The Metropolitan Water Board, the Lee Conservancy and the Lee Catchment Board also lodged objections from their own particular point of view.' Despite objections, the Order was confirmed on 11 November and the government made a Statutory Order establishing a Stevenage Development Corporation on 5 December.

The action was regarded in some local circles as nothing less than a communist-style act of dictatorship. One snowy morning shortly afterwards, staff of Stevenage's Victorian railway station could hardly believe their eyes when they arrived for duty. A 14-foot long sign above the station entrance proclaimed 'Silkingrad'. The same name also appeared on all the name boards on the 'up' and 'down' platforms. Years later, Jack Franklin, a member of a well-known local farming family admitted to his role in the matter. A wartime RAF pilot, he told an interviewer that, following his and his bride's release from the Forces, he had bought 'a nice little Georgian cottage', called White Cottage, in London Road, and moved in. About three weeks later he had received a letter from the Development Corporation telling him that the property was required and he must agree to sell it to them or have it bought by compulsory purchase. 'I was very mad about it,' he said. His friend Clarence Elliott, an authority on alpine plants, who was to lose his famous Six Hills Nursery, was also 'very irate'. It was he who had coined the name 'Silkingrad'. With a few friends they made hardboard signs to be erected at the railway station at night. 'Whilst putting them up we were interrupted by the local 'Bobby'. We told him that there was a brace of pheasants in the back of the van if he would like them. And that was that!' To get maximum publicity, they tipped off the press. 'Within about four hours it had even got as far as the American Press. The Residents' Protection Association received donations from all over the world. People who had once lived in Stevenage – even people as far away as New Zealand – sent us money.'

The objectors refused to accept the result of the public inquiry. In December 1946 the Residents' Protection Association and the Hitchin branch of the National Farmers' Union, led by William Vernon Franklin, farmer, of Rooks Nest Farm, George Leonard Hearn, of Coreys Mount, Chairman of the Stevenage Residents' Protection Association, and Michael Robert Tetley, landowner, of The Priory, Rectory Lane, took an action in the High Court, asking for the Designation Order to be quashed on the grounds that the Minister had displayed clear bias leading to a denial of natural justice. Their argument was that his statements at the 6 May public meeting, when he had expressed his determination to go on with the Stevenage new town project whether people liked it or not, proved that he was quite unable to discharge his duty under the New Towns Act of considering fairly the objections raised at the October public inquiry.

'Silkingrad'. (Stevenage Museum P9316)

As 1946 ended, the Council were still hoping that the Ministry of Town and Country Planning would accept their suggestions for amending the plan so as to avoid destroying houses. They had also written to the Minister, requesting a conference with him in London for consultation on the membership of the Development Corporation. But the priority for most people at this time was the cold weather, the lack of food and coal and the approach of a second peacetime Christmas.

The opening of 1947 was even more depressing than the previous year. A transport strike meant that troops might have to be called in to move supplies. On 22 January the government announced that the meat ration would be reduced again. Some of the heaviest snowfalls in living memory occurred and the weather was bitterly cold. By 28 January most of the country was brought to a standstill by the freezing temperatures and there were widespread power cuts. Coal was piled up at the pits but could not be delivered because roads and railway lines were blocked with snow. The 'big freeze' continued to the end of February and the possibility of re-introducing coal rationing was discussed. Many factories introduced short-time working and over four million workers were laid off.

On 20 February the Appeal under the New Towns Act was heard at the High Court before Mr Justice Henn Collins, who upheld the appeal by Messrs Franklin, Hearn and Tetley and ordered that the Stevenage New Town (Designation) Order, 1946 be quashed. The objectors had satisfied him that the Minister had not acted with an open mind and that had involved a denial of natural justice. 'Stevenage Order Quashed' and similar headlines appeared on the front of most national newspapers next day, surrounded by captions such as 'Freeze-up may last till March', 'Frost Causes Explosion', 'London Last to Switch On'. The papers also carried news from other proposed new towns such as Crawley and Hemel Hempstead where, said the *Daily Mail*, 'New Hopes Rise' for their own campaigns, inspired by the success of the Stevenage objectors. Not everyone was pleased by the result. Interviewed by the press, Philip Ireton, of Fairview Road, whose own house was scheduled for demolition, said that he thought the decision was a tragedy for Stevenage.

The objectors' jubilation was short-lived. The Minister appealed against the judgement at a hearing in the Court of Appeal on 24 March before Lords Justices Oaksey, Morton and Tucker who found in favour of the Minister. They ruled that even if the Minister had shown bias at the May public meeting before the New Towns Act had been passed, it had not been proven that he had remained biased afterwards while fulfilling his duties with regard to the October public inquiry.

Meanwhile, other local affairs had to be dealt with. On 24 February, nearly two years after the war had ended, Mr J D Marshall, surveyor to the Stevenage

Aerial view of Stevenage, 1947. (Stevenage Museum)

Urban District Council, was able to report that replacements for about 24 trees in The Avenue which had been 'damaged by the military' could be purchased and planted in the autumn. The snow remained until March, but when the thaw came the result was devastating flooding in many towns and parts of the countryside. At the Council meeting on 31 March, the clerk was authorised to receive donations to the Lord Mayor's National Flood Distress Fund. At the same meeting, on a more optimistic note, it was reported that the first twenty new Council houses in Ellis Avenue were complete and footpaths were about to be laid.

On 15 April, Mr W E Conlin stood down as chairman of the Council and, after a contest between Major A G Howard and Mr J Mackay, Major Howard was elected with Mr R A V White as vice-chairman. Among other matters, over the summer months the Council were still objecting to the route of the proposed A1 by-pass and still being frustrated in their attempt to convert the Warren into badly-needed flats. In June there came a request from the Hertfordshire County Council to allow schoolchildren to have meals in the British Restaurant in the town hall during the summer months. This was agreed for a trial period.

Despite the ruling against them in the Court of Appeal in March, the Residents' Protection Association would not give up. They gathered new strength – and more money – in one last do or die action and took their case to the highest court in the land, the House of Lords, on 24 July 1947. Law Lords Thankerton, Porter, Uthwatt, Du Parq and Norman did not accept that questions of Ministerial bias or denial of natural justice were relevant. They ruled it mistaken to think of the Minister acting in a judicial or quasi-judicial capacity against which bias might be alleged. The Minister's role was simply an administrative one – and on those grounds his decision to confirm the Designation Order was upheld and the objectors' case was dismissed.

On the national scene, things were getting worse. Although, in June, the United States Secretary of State, George Marshall, had outlined a plan to help European nations recover from the ravages of war, the British government announced in August yet another package of austerity measures. This was forced upon them by economic circumstances and meant further reductions in rations. These even included, on 30 September, a warning to women to avoid the fashion for longer skirts in order to save cloth.

The new town was no longer a proposal, but a fact. On 25 July 1947, Clough Williams-Ellis, chairman of the Development Corporation, announced that work on the new town could now begin. He said that long-term development plans had not been completed but, as a start, 100 aluminium prefabricated houses would be erected for workers, and during 1948 400 aluminium prefabricated houses, 200 permanent flats, and 200 permanent houses would be put up. Some key posts had been filled including those of general manager and finance, estate and legal officers. Charles Madge, of Mass Observation, had been appointed Social Development Officer. It would probably be two to three years before any real development would be seen, but already over 1,200 firms had applied for sites in the new town, which was far more than the was space available. The final cost of the development was expected to be about £30,000,000.

12, High Street, formerly the North Star public house. (Stevenage Museum)

CHAPTER FIVE
The first master plan

THE NEW TOWNS ACT of 1946 was undoubtedly one of the most significant pieces of government legislation in the post-war years. New towns were a bold experiment in social planning but there was no certainty of success and in Stevenage, two years on, little seemed to be happening. Aston House, where the first Development Corporation staff were now installed, was at the extreme southern boundary of the designated area. Furthermore, its occupation during the war for top secret work by the Special Operations Executive meant that it had not played a part in local life for over six years, so that it was to a certain extent out of sight and out of mind. The only people for whom the new town was a reality were those whose property was being requisitioned.

As usual, people were more concerned with the problems of their own lives, such as a major outbreak of chicken pox in January 1948. At that time diseases such as measles, mumps, whooping cough and chicken pox were unavoidable in childhood. There were no vaccinations or cures and the only way of halting the spread of infectious disease was to isolate the patient at home for periods of from three to six weeks. Those unfortunate enough to develop scarlet fever and other more serious infectious illnesses were despatched to the isolation hospital at Hertford, where they were not allowed visitors from the outside world, including their parents, for many weeks.

Then, in July 1950, came the announcement that British troops would be sent to support the United Nations forces in Korea. Conscription was still in place and families who had so recently given thanks for the arrival of peace now lived once again under the shadow of death. As this new war progressed, names of the dead were eventually published in long lists in the daily press. The

Korean War dragged on for another two years: meanwhile, in London, thousands of people made homeless by the Second World War were still waiting for houses.

In 1946, the Stevenage Urban District Council had accepted the new town cuckoo in its nest. However, the relationship between the two authorities steadily declined into animosity. The Corporation was larger, it had the ear of the Minister, access to more money and better qualified officers who commanded higher salaries than Council staff. The position was summed up by Harold Orlans in his book, *Stevenage: a Sociological Study of a New Town*. He wrote; 'The Council's legal rights under the New Towns Act were rather ambiguous. The Minister [of Town and Country Planning] could not legally undertake certain actions such as issuing a New Town designation order, appointing Corporation members or approving Corporation development plans until after consultation with the local authority within whose district the land is situated, and with any other local authority who appear to him to be concerned. But after the Town and Country Planning Act 1947, the County and not the Stevenage Council became the local planning authority. It remained for the Minister to determine if the Stevenage Council was "concerned" in a particular instance. Thus he did not feel obliged to consult the Council before making his second series of appointments to the Corporation in January 1950.'

The Stevenage Development Corporation did not get off to a good start. Clough Williams-Ellis, its first chairman, resigned in October 1947. It has been suggested that, as an architect rather than an administrator, he felt out of his

Aston House. (Stevenage Museum PP508)

New Urban District Council houses on the north side of Sish Lane. (Stevenage Museum P10563)

depth. He was succeeded from 1947 to 1948 by Sir Thomas Gardiner, a distinguished civil servant who had been Permanent Secretary at the Ministry of Home Security during the war. As he began his term of office Britain's economic situation and the austerity measures announced by the government meant that work on all the new towns was brought to a halt.

The Urban District Council was also constrained by the austerity measures. As the local authority it was responsible for enforcing the stringent rules which governed most aspects of life in the town. So desperate was the shortage of materials nationally that people were not permitted to carry out repairs or renovations to their private property without a licence. The Stevenage Council had the added restriction that all its planning decisions, even to the smallest detail, had to be submitted to the Ministry of Town and Country Planning for approval. For example, when Mr F Ashwell requested permission to have a burst boiler removed and a new one fitted at his house at 132 Fairview Road, the application had first to be considered by the Council's Town Planning and Development Committee (who resolved to approve it), and then to be passed to the Ministry of Town and Country Planning in London.

Equally strict rules applied to temporary planning permissions, one of which concerned Miss F Lawrence, Headteacher of St Nicholas' School, Burymead. A tiny room off a cloakroom had been temporarily converted for her to use as an office, including the installation of a telephone. She now requested that this arrangement be allowed to continue and the Council recommended that it should do so for 18 months. Another request was from Mr G G Ivory, who wished to continue using a chicken shed in Bedwell Lane. Again, the Council agreed, subject to approval by the Ministry of Town and Country Planning.

However, an application from Mr F Appleyard for alterations to Chells Farm and Chells Farm Cottage was outside the designated area and the Council had great satisfaction in approving the plans and informing the Ministry that in this case, they were empowered to make the final decision.

In other respects the Council was making good progress. It was building much-needed houses for Stevenage residents, many of whom were living in sub-standard accommodation, extremely overcrowded and often with no bath or indoor lavatory. By January 1948 the brickwork of the Rowan Crescent houses was almost complete. There had been a delay in obtaining hot water fittings but supplies were now available and the Council's Housing Interviewing Sub-Committee had interviewed 96 applicants for the 24 dwellings. The Greydells Road estate was behind schedule, partly because work on concreting the road was not finished. However, the Minister of Town and Country Planning was now prepared to sanction the building of 12 houses on this road, on condition that a satisfactory price could be negotiated with the builders, Messrs Willmott of Hitchin.

At last, thanks to the Council's determination The Warren, in London Road, was being converted. It would contain; a two-bedroom flat, to be let to a family with children over the age of 12; five one-bedroom flats to go to families without children, at rents from £1 3s 0d (£1.15) for flats whose tenants would be required to share a bathroom and WC, to £1 5s 0d (£1.25) per week for those with their own facilities. Equally satisfactory was a message from the Ministry of Works confirming that refrigerators for the temporary bungalows (prefabs) at Sish Close would be fitted shortly. At a time when few people owned a refrigerator, this was luxury indeed. Also in January came a very pleasing report from the Rent Collector: there were no arrears of rent.

The Council had serious concerns about the quality of the water being supplied to the town from the pumping station at Broomin Green. Looking to the future, informal discussions were taking place between the Council, the Corporation and the Water Board about the supply of water for the new town. The Council was also anxious to extend its sewage disposal works at Roaring Meg, beside the London Road, and had drawn up a scheme in consultation with the Corporation, who agreed that they would help financially subject, of course, to the approval of the Minister of Town and Country Planning and consent from the Treasury.

There was continuing pressure on the public to save salvage (in modern terms, to recycle), which a council employee collected in a trailer attached to the dustcart. There were also pig bins which were used to collect food scraps for pig farmers. Food rationing remained in force and this had wide-reaching affects. For instance beekeepers, of whom there were many in rural Stevenage, keeping a few hives in their back gardens, had to be registered in order to obtain the essential supplies of sugar. At the appropriate time this was collected from Cllr Charles Day at his house in Walkern Road. Sweet rationing ended in April

1949, but as children raced in excitement to the shops they found the familiar barren shelves and empty sweet jars. It took some time for supplies to find their way to the town.

Meanwhile, two major Hertfordshire County Council building projects were progressing well. A new junior school was built at Primrose Hill, between Sish Lane and Pound Avenue. Having been vaguely referred to as 'the Sish Lane school' since plans for it were discussed in 1945, it was finally given the inappropriate name of Fairlands. At that time Sish Lane was a rural by-way leading to Fairlands Farm. Even so, a little thought might have resulted in a less confusing name, given that Fairlands Way and Fairlands Valley would soon appear on the map.

The other new school under construction was one of the first of the secondary modern schools to be built in Hertfordshire following the 1944 Education Act which promised secondary education for all and raised the school leaving age to 15. It was to be named the Barclay School, in memory of Henry Noble Barclay who had died in 1939, a member of the philanthropical Barclay family of Whitney Wood. The school would take both girls and boys from the age of 11 years. Until it was built, girls over 11 who did not go on to the Hitchin Girls' Grammar School had to remain at St Nicholas' School on the Burymead. This 1832 building was desperately overcrowded and some classes were being held at the Grange (former Swan Inn) in the High Street, which was then owned by the County Council. Dedicated teachers struggled with very limited accommodation and resources to give all pupils an education suited to their age.

The site chosen for the Barclay School was less than 200 yards from St Nicholas', on land between The Avenue and Walkern Road. Its playing fields were adjacent to those of Alleyne's Grammar School, separated only by a footpath from Church Lane to The Avenue. The architects of this ultra-modern building, with its full-length glass windows, were Messrs Yorke, Rosenberg and Mardell. As a finishing touch, 'Family Group', a sculpture by Henry Moore, was installed by the main entrance door in 1950. The work had originally been commissioned by Impington Village College, Cambridgeshire, but they had cancelled it because of lack of funds. Now, thanks to the persuasive powers of John Newsom, Hertfordshire County Education Officer, the County Council had paid for the sculpture to be completed.

The erection of two new schools, taken together with the new council houses being built in Old Stevenage, became associated in people's minds with the arrival of the new town, even though almost nothing had as yet been built by the Development Corporation. The different responsibilities of the Stevenage Urban District Council and the Stevenage Development Corporation were far from clear to residents, particularly when the similar initials, SUDC and SDC were used. As for the Hertfordshire County Council and where it fitted in, that was often incomprehensible. All was made worse because there seemed no connection between the various authorities: they appeared to work in parallel. Many people gave up trying to make sense of it all and referred to the whole lot as the mysterious, all-powerful 'They'.

As for the two Stevenage authorities themselves, there was irritation on both sides. The Corporation, forbidden by the government to undertake any building work, was apparently doing nothing, while the Council, with fewer and less well-paid staff, managed cheaply and efficiently to build nearly 200 Council houses by the end of 1950. During the same period the Corporation built 28. The reason for this was explained by Jack Balchin in his book *First New Town*. Not only had the government limited to 75 the number of construction workers who might be recruited to Stevenage in 1948, but had also refused the Corporation a licence to import timber houses from Finland, and instructed it to link up with certain north-east London boroughs only – a restriction that had to be abandoned later.

A report in *The Times* newspaper for 15 January 1948 may have given a little encouragement to the frustrated Corporation. In a speech he made at Letchworth, Herbert Morrison, Lord President of the Council, announced that the government had decided that the new town of Stevenage would be given preference in considering sites for new scientific establishments in the London region.

This was important because a number of research stations would have to move from their present sites, which they had outgrown. He could not say what actual research would be located at Stevenage, or when it would come, but Stevenage would be one of the important scientific centres of the future.

If there was little new town building work going on at this time, there was an enormous amount of theoretical discussion and planning on paper. One major topic of debate concerned housing densities. Strong opinions were aired by such people as F J Osborn who, as an advocate of the garden city movement, urged a density of 12 houses, or approximately 48 persons, per acre, while A Trystan Edwards, an influential architect and an admirer of Georgian terraced houses, recommended a density of 25 houses or 100 persons per acre. Among the comparisons being made were the figures of 136 persons per acre which the London County Council used for rehousing people in central London and the current figure of approximately 15 persons per acre in the built-up parts of Old Stevenage. Among those who favoured higher density housing were the farmers, largely supported by the County Council, who feared the loss of agricultural land.

When the Stevenage Development Corporation was established in December 1946, it had worked to the draft Plan drawn up early the same year by a team of professional officers at the Ministry of Town and Country Planning. Foremost among them were architects Gordon Stephenson, the Ministry's Chief Technical

Officer, and Peter Shepherd, both of whom had assisted Professor Patrick Abercrombie in preparing his Greater London Plan, and Eric Claxton, a civil engineer on loan from Surrey County Council. During the first year of its existence the Corporation had the benefit of Stephenson, on secondment from the Ministry, as its first architect/planner, with Shepherd as his deputy and the equally innovative Claxton as acting Chief Engineer. He was later to become deputy Chief Engineer and then Chief Engineer, remaining with the Corporation for the next 26 years.

In drawing up the draft plan, account had been taken of the natural features and physical barriers existing in the proposed new town designated area which encompassed 6,070 acres of land – 3,378 acres in the Stevenage Urban District, 1,664 acres that would be taken from the adjoining Hitchin Rural District, and 1,028 acres from the adjoining Hertford Rural District.

To the north of the proposed designated area was a ridge, running east/west, that was a natural drainage area boundary, to the south there was the Hertford loop railway line, to the east the Beane valley and to the west the main London/ Edinburgh railway line and, beyond that, the line of a proposed Stevenage by-pass road. It therefore made sense to locate the proposed new industrial area of 600 acres between the railway and the proposed by-pass and the new town centre on the eastern side of the railway tracks, just to the south of the old town's High Street, with six residential neighbourhoods, each of approximately 10,000 population, in a fan-like configuration to the north, east and south of the town centre. As one of the six neighbourhoods, the old town of some 6,000 residents would be expanded to approximately 10,000.

The residential neighbourhoods would be separated from one another by east/west principal roads, with attendant cycle-ways, linking them to the town centre and industrial area or by swathes of open space, including a large park, a 'lung' (Fairlands Valley) running north/south through the centre of the town. Each neighbourhood would have a main shopping centre, sub-centres, primary and secondary schools, community centre and playing fields and would be divided into three estates, each of approximately 3,000 people, with its own sub-centre within easy walking distance of primary schools, community centre, pubs, children's playgrounds and doctors' and dentists' surgeries. Existing woodlands would be retained.

The plan provided for 13 acres of open space per 1,000 people living at a density of 30 people, or 8 dwellings, per acre, excluding incidental open space within the housing estates and generous space reserved for school playgrounds and playing fields. This would result in 19 acres of open space per 1,000 population – a high figure indeed and one that was greatly eroded in the years that followed, during which several amendments to the 1946 Master Plan were made.

The Development Corporation's chairman from October 1948 was the Revd Charles Jenkinson, whose appointment was widely welcomed. He was leader of Leeds City Council and had also been chairman of its housing committee, where he had directed a successful slum clearance scheme. A Socialist, he had served with Silkin on the Labour Party's wartime reconstruction sub-committee. In his book, *Our Housing Objectives*, published in 1943, he had shown understanding of the need for balance in such matters as the flats versus housing debate. As chairman of the Stevenage Development Corporation he made a good start in beginning to resolve some of the conflicts between the Corporation and the Council. Jack Balchin records that it was Charles Jenkinson who had suggested the words 'Consider thy purpose' as the Corporation's motto.

It was under Jenkinson's chairmanship that the long awaited revision of the original Master Plan was completed. Although the Urban District Council had strong objections to certain of its provisions, neither the exhibition of the plan, nor the subsequent public inquiry caused very much of a stir. There was still some bitterness and disillusionment but the fire had gone out of the opposition and there was no repetition of the angry scenes of three years before.

The revised plan was submitted to the Minister of Town and Country Planning, as *The Times* newspaper for Saturday 27 August 1949 reported:

> Mr Charles Madge, Social Development Officer to the Stevenage Development Corporation, said yesterday that the master plan for the new town at Stevenage was submitted to the Minister of Town and Country Planning last week. It had been with the technical department of the Ministry since March.
>
> The plan is to be exhibited to Stevenage residents and a public inquiry will be held for the hearing of objections. Stevenage Urban District Council has already objected to the proposed site for the new town's centre, thus preventing the Development Corporation from proceeding with the construction of a loop-road giving access to housing sites. It is hoped to start work on two other roads within two months.
>
> The first buildings to be erected, for which the Corporation expects to let the contract by the end of October, will be 217 workers' flats. The largest block of about 72 dwellings will be seven storeys high. The ground floor will contain laundries, stores, perambulator garages and workshops, and there will be lifts to give access to the flats.

The public inquiry was held on 18 October and reported in *The Times* the next day:

> Plans for the new town at Stevenage, which include the provision of a helicopter landing pitch, an art gallery and museum, with the possibility of an

> airport at a later date, were discussed at a Public Inquiry at Stevenage Town Hall yesterday.
>
> The Inquiry, which was ordered by Mr Silkin, was to enable people of Stevenage and interested local authorities to hear about the master plan for the development of the existing town ...
>
> Mr G V Berry, Clerk of the Urban District Council, said the Council's objections to the master plan were that the town centre should be situated some distance to the east of that shown on the plan and that the industrial area should not be concentrated in one area but subdivided.
>
> Mr J D Marshall, surveyor to the Council, gave evidence upon these two points and said that an alternative suggestion would mean that not one house would have to be demolished. He produced the Council's alternative plan for the development of the town, which recommended the division of the industrial area and certain alterations to the town centre.
>
> Mr Slessor said it was not the Corporation's intention to demolish property until it was absolutely necessary.
>
> Mr C Holliday, the chief architect, said that in the next eight years it would be necessary to demolish four houses and it was likely to be well over ten years before the remaining houses in Fairview Road would have to be demolished.

In February 1950 the plan received the approval of the Minister, who commented that he considered the provision of open space to be unduly generous, the new town centre, as then proposed, to be too large, and that Fairview Road should not be redeveloped for industry until and unless warranted.

A summary of the plan was published in a well-designed booklet entitled *The New Town of Stevenage*. Its introduction explained clearly the stages through which each aspect of the Corporation's work had to pass:

> Both in the planning stages and in the realisation of the Plan, the Corporation has constantly to consult a great number of authorities, official and otherwise. To take some obvious examples, the County Council, being the Local Education Authority and the Local Health Authority, will build and administer schools and health centres. The County Agricultural Executive Committee is responsible for seeing that farmland is turned over for building with the minimum loss of food production. The Board of Trade, through its Regional Office at Cambridge, is responsible for deciding whether or not a given industrial firm should be allowed to come to Stevenage, and only when this approval has been given can the Development Corporation usefully start

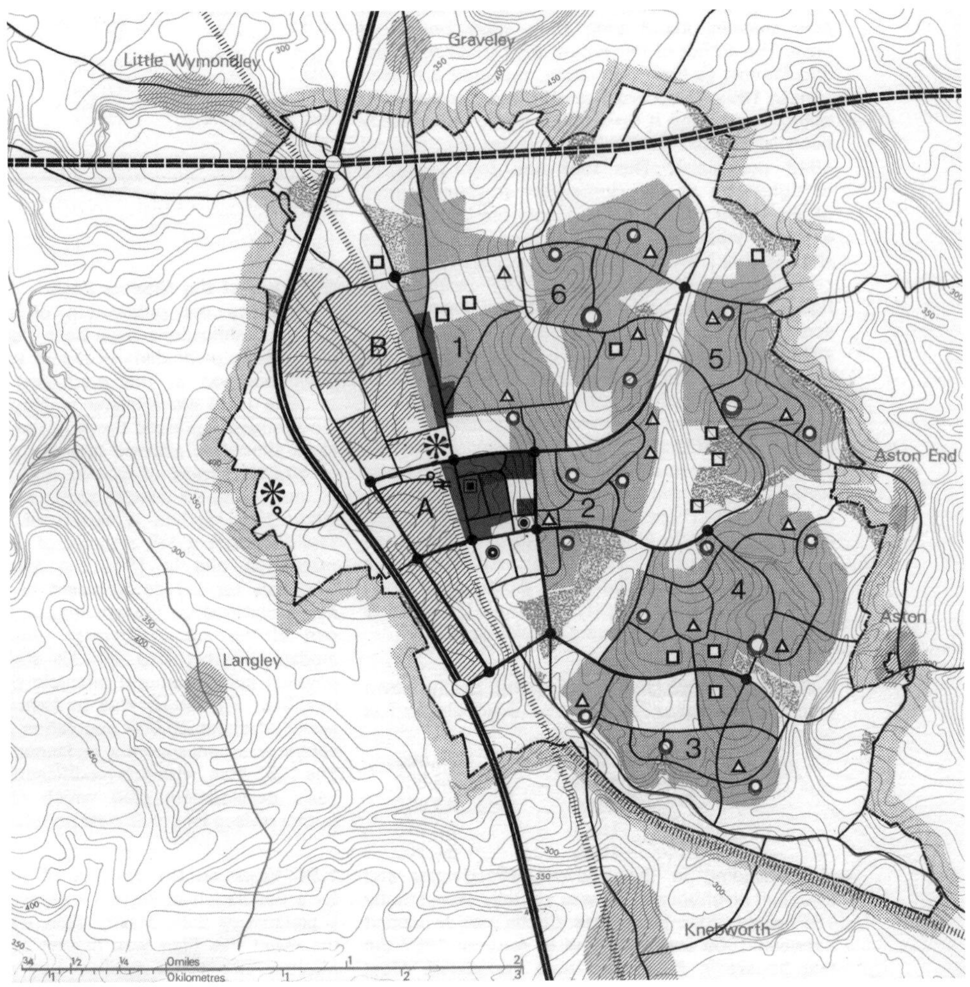

The 1949 Master Plan. (HALS HCP3/1/24)

negotiations with the firm as to site, buildings, terms of lease, etc. The Ministry of Health, must similarly approve the design of any house which the Corporation wishes to build, in order that they can apply for housing subsidy. Finally, any detailed proposal for development, such as a residential neighbourhood, must, like the Master Plan, pass through various stages of consideration and approval by the planning authorities at all levels, starting with the Stevenage Urban District Council, and ending with the Ministry of Town and Country Planning. Meantime, none of these processes escapes the watchdogs of the Treasury, and the whole development is subject to National resources of labour and material.

The new town was expected to be completed within 20 years, at which time the Corporation would own over 6,000 acres of designated area, plus a great number of shops, factories, houses and other assets. All these would provide considerable revenue which it was hoped would justify the new town as a national financial investment as well as giving great social and economic advantages. Finally, when its purpose had been achieved, the Development Corporation would be dissolved and the administration of the whole town would probably be handed over to the Stevenage Urban District Council. To that end, it is clearly of great importance that the local Council should retain its prestige and should grow in importance with the growth of the town and that Council and Corporation should work together in the closest harmony.

That day seemed a long way off, however.

The 1955 Master Plan. (HALS: HCP 3/1/25)

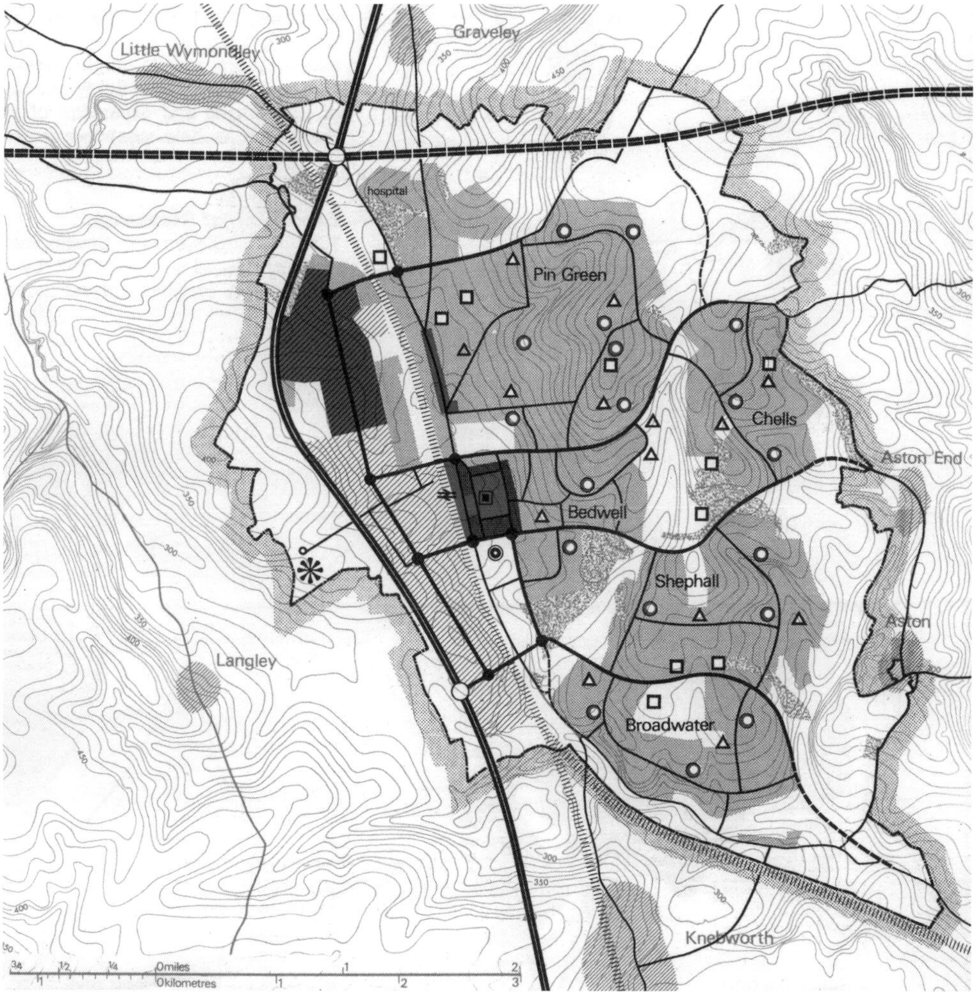

The layout of the designated area was shown as an overlay of an Ordnance Survey map of the Stevenage district. It was accompanied by explanatory text and illustrations, including photographs showing street after street of dense housing in London, unrelieved by community buildings or open spaces, the type of building that the town and country planning movement was pledged to do away with, that the new town would replace.

In the Stevenage plan, great faith was placed in the neighbourhood concept;

> The present town of Stevenage is itself to be the nucleus of the first neighbourhood of the new town. There will be added ... five other neighbourhoods which will be called by the names of existing hamlets and farms: Bedwell, Broadwater, Shephall, Chells and Pin Green. On average about ten thousand people will live in each of these neighbourhoods. Each will have its own local shops and schools and playgrounds, there will be houses and flats of different types and sizes ... and gardens will vary in size to cater for different tastes. Arid stretches of brick and asphalt will be avoided. There will be trees to punctuate the buildings, grass commons between houses, views of open country at the turn of the road.'

The Designated Area consists of 6,100 acres. On the Plan this is shown as including:

Residential Areas	1,753	acres
Industrial Area	448	"
Town Centre	100	"
Neighbourhood centres and subcentres	164	"
School sites	334	"
Public open space	666	"
Woodland	252	"
Farmland and related uses	1,679	"
Railway, land, road reservations & other uses	704	"

The intended final population is 60,000 people.
The Gross Residential Acreage is 2,000 acres.
The Gross Residential Density will therefore be 30 persons per acre.
The Net Residential Acreage is 1,753 acres.
The Net Residential Density will therefore be 34 persons per acre.

The planners were aware that their idealism had its critics and they themselves realised the inherent contradictions in their aims when they asked,

> Can towns be built in which all kinds of people can live and work together happily and productively, towns with plenty of shops and cinemas, health

> centres and schools, but in a setting where the trees and fields of the countryside are never far away? Those associated with New Town projects believe the answer is 'Yes'.

With the garden city ideal of *Rus in Urbe* (the country in the town) very much in mind, the plan gave assurances that the 6,000 acres would not all be built over;

> The woods and copses will be preserved, so will the vast majority of single trees and many of the existing hedge-lines. Fairlands Valley ... will remain open space. Other green spaces will be retained as town parks, while there will be a broad belt of farmland separating Stevenage from any other village or town. The north Hertfordshire landscape is a rolling landscape of peculiar charm, with spacious fields, tall ashes and elms. Not only will the new town dwellers be able to take their country walks through it but by the skill of the landscape architect something of the character of the local countryside will pervade the whole of the town itself.

The plan made many promises, the majority of which have subsequently been fulfilled, but the botanic gardens, the new town hall, the helicopter pad and other admirable ideas never got beyond wishful thinking.

The Development Corporation set up a display in its rented High Street premises, which it used as a Housing Office. Somewhat alarming to old-town residents was an attractive frieze-type exhibit showing the whole length of the High Street, with a black-and-white photograph and a water colour drawing of every building. The drawings were colour-coded to indicate the use and condition of each. Alarm bells rang again. What had this to do with the building of a new town? Was the promise that 'the Old Town will not be touched' an empty one? In fact, the display and the publication of *The New Town of Stevenage* was intended to inform and persuade possible immigrants from London of the attractions of life in the new town. The boroughs linked specifically with Stevenage for this purpose were Hornsey and Wood Green. In addition, Tottenham, Edmonton and Enfield were linked jointly with Stevenage and Harlow, while Hendon was linked with Stevenage and Hemel Hempstead. However, industry from any part of Greater London could also move to Stevenage, subject to approval from the Board of Trade and could, if they wished, bring with them employees from any part of London. The intention was that, as far as possible, people would both live and work in Stevenage, thereby fulfilling another of the theorists' dreams, that new towns should be complete in themselves.

In addition to the display the Corporation published its *Four Year Development Programme, 1949–52.* Dated 16 June 1949, it was introduced by General A C Duff, General Manager, who made the point that the programme could only be carried out if no further restrictions were imposed and assuming that the necessary labour would be forthcoming as and when required.

The programme proposed that the first building would begin in July 1949 with four cottages and six garages in Shephall Lane. In October 1949 work would begin on the Stony Hall site in Sish Lane and also on three small sites in the old town. There would be more building in 1950; hostels in Sish Lane for 320 building workers; a phased development of houses, flats and shops in the Bedwell neighbourhood; and six staff houses at the Whitehall Water Works, near Watton-at-Stone. It was anticipated that in 1951 the Shephall Lane, Old Town, and Stony Hall sites and much of the Bedwell neighbourhood would be complete and occupied and the population increased by 4,060 persons. In the spring of 1952, it was hoped, work would begin on 400 dwellings in the Broadwater neighbourhood, 800 in Shephall neighbourhood and a start would be made on the town centre, giving a total population increase by the end of the four-year programme of 6,888 persons. In the event, the planned developments fell way behind schedule.

One of the most controversial topics relating to the Master Plan was the question of flats. In rural areas such as Stevenage blocks of flats were unknown. Such flats as did exist were few and far between and were apartments over shops, or rooms in large houses. The idea of blocks of flats brought with it the connotation of inner city poverty. As Orlans pointed out, not only the existing population of Stevenage but also those likely to move here from London, preferred houses. Of 1,056 mainly working class applicants for housing in the new town, 86 per cent said they would prefer a house, 8 per cent said they would prefer a flat to nothing and 6 per cent said they would prefer a flat.

The dividing line between Old Stevenage and the new town was Sish Lane, a country lane mainly with farmland and fields on both sides. It was on the south side of Sish Lane that the first new housing estates were built by the Corporation. A contract was let for 22 flats in four blocks, 144 houses and six shops with maisonettes above. Arrangements were made for the Urban District Council to widen and improve Sish Lane with a major contribution from the Corporation towards the cost of the works. For building workers who did not travel daily between London and Stevenage, the Corporation provided hostels in Sish Lane, Bedwell and in Aston.

Given the strong antipathy to flats it was, to say the least, unfortunate that the first substantial building project by the Development Corporation, the Stony Hall site in Sish Lane, was not only adjacent to one of the old town's most ancient lanes, but also consisted largely of blocks of flats of non-traditional materials and design. As a concession to the protests which greeted these plans, the Corporation decided to make them attractive to middle-class tenants and to charge higher rents than would apply to other new-town dwellings; thus

Stevenage Development Corporation Office at number 114, High Street. (Stevenage Museum P11092)

hoping to rebuke the criticism that they were 'building the slums of the future'. The flats were named after notable figures in the history of Old Stevenage: the seven-storey block was called Chauncy House, after Henry Chauncy, first historian of Hertfordshire. Other blocks were named after the former rector, William Jowitt; the notable sculptor, Harry Bates and former MP, Julius Bertram. The fact that the flats internally were of a very high standard did little to alleviate the pain that was felt by local people as they watched their fields and hedgerows being torn up for what the Council Chairman, Major Arthur Howard, described as 'a barracks', an alien feature in the landscape.

Yet another debate was being joined with great enthusiasm by the many theorists who thought they knew how others should live. 'Social engineering' was much in the minds of planners. Sociology, at that time a comparatively new science, was fixated on the question of class and of the possibility of breaking down the divisions between classes by techniques of town planning. Idealists promoted visions of manual workers and professionals living side by side and argued over the number of better class houses that should be incorporated into lower class streets. It seems now, over sixty years on, that these discussions served only to reinforce the existence of class divisions.

In August 1949 Charles Jenkinson died, to universal regret. His loss dealt a blow to the improved relations between the Development Corporation, the Council and other bodies. But in his short time as Chairman he had achieved a great deal, including publication of the 1949 Master Plan.

At last, in 1951, the Development Corporation was able to complete and let its first houses. Ironically, they were not in the designated Master Plan area, but

Chauncy House. (Stevenage Museum P399)

infilled roads in the old town. At this time, government restrictions were preventing the Corporation from developing the necessary new roads on which to build houses, or the infrastructure to support them. One solution was to buy up sites in existing roads in the old town and this the Corporation decided to do. As Jack Balchin was to explain 30 years later, 'This enraged some local people that, with some 6,000 acres to build on, the Corporation should be exercising its statutory muscle to filch the few sites still available to Old Town people and local builders.'

In all, 36 houses were built in the old town. The Corporation was only allowed to allocate them to people on the housing lists of Hornsey, Wood Green, Tottenham, Edmonton, Enfield or Hendon, with particular preference in these early days for key workers or professional people who were needed to help build or provide services for the town. Thus, teachers such as D Neville Wood and architects such as Leslie Aked were among the first residents in the eight new houses at the top of Pound Avenue, while in Walkern Road the Blagg family moved into number 88. Their son, Peter, was the first 'new town' boy to be enrolled at the Barclay School and to mark this the teacher entered his name in red on the register.

CHAPTER SIX
First neighbourhoods

THE STONY HALL ESTATE, being adjacent to the built-up part of the old town and its infra-structure, was the first new town development to be started, closely followed by work on the Bedwell neighbourhood. The new road system as shown on the Master Plan was mainly the projected north–south A1 by-pass, with east/west roads both linking and dividing neighbourhoods, each of which had its own shops, schools and community buildings. So the architects had to start with an area within the main roads, to design dwellings for a population of about 10,000 people. The Chief Architect and Planner from 1947 to 1957 was Clifford Holliday, who was succeeded for two years by D Reay. He was followed by Leonard Vincent until 1962, when he became Consultant Planner for the remaining 18 years of the Corporation's existence. Leslie Aked became Chief Architect from 1962 until his untimely death in 1968, when his deputy of 16 years, Brian Alford, took over.

Ray Gorbing began work as a Corporation architect on 1 January 1950. He was based at Aston House, where Irish workers were also installed, living at first in a variety of sheds and tents. When he arrived he was shown the Master Plan and, with a small team of qualified architects, including Cynthia Wood, one of very few women in this profession, he began working on the Bedwell layout, travelling to the various building sites on his bicycle. He and his colleagues had to work within a given housing density and a budget cost. This was not always easy. For example, they might design an area of brick houses only to be told, when building started, that bricks were now in short supply. Also, as time went on, the Ministry continually increased housing densities in order to get more people out of London, so that it was difficult to keep to the original plan. This happened in Bedwell where plans had to be amended even while building was going on. The architects sometimes worked all night to change a plan, after which they were involved in difficult discussions with builders about costs.

Most houses were of a simple three-bedroom design, with coal fires for heating. There was a preponderance of terraced houses because of the pressure on architects to conform to high density requirements. They were also cheaper to rent. There would be 300 to 400 houses in a contract, designed by young architects who were unused to contracts of that size. One small error would be multiplied by hundreds, with the result that some builders made their fortunes.

In terms of design, architects were given a reasonably free hand but were constrained by the budget and strict rules about the area to be occupied by each building. All plans had to be submitted to the Ministry of Town and Country Planning by the architect in person, who had to talk through the proposals and possibly be asked to make alterations. It was also necessary to confer with the Stevenage Urban District Council.

The Development Corporation's architects planned neighbourhood shops and social amenities, but not schools, which were the responsibility of the Hertfordshire County Council. Main roads also came under the County Council's remit, but side roads were planned jointly by Development Corporation architects and engineers and those of the Stevenage Urban District Council. Despite strained relations between the two authorities at management level, working relationships between the two sets of staff were generally very good.

It was unfortunate that, just as building work was getting into its stride, the Corporation received unwelcome publicity in the press. Following the death of Charles Jenkinson in 1949, Silkin, apparently without any consultation, appointed the left-wing intellectual Dr Monica Felton as chairman of the Board of the Stevenage Development Corporation. She had been a member of the Stevenage Board two years previously, before her promotion to the position of chairman of the Peterlee Development Corporation. She held strong political views and was an ardent supporter of Marxist ideologies. A number of young intellectuals had similar opinions at this time, but very few put them into practice. In 1951, Dr Felton accepted an invitation to go to Korea, but failed to ask permission of Hugh Dalton, the Minister of Planning and Local Government. She went on to Moscow, where she was heard to criticise the British government and the actions of British forces in Korea. Her promised return flight to London was delayed and she missed an important meeting at the House of Commons. Balchin describes the horror with which news of her adventure was received, 'Then the news broke about the Moscow speech and a thunderstruck Corporation faced public criticism from all sides ... MPs and others called for her dismissal, indeed impeachment, and attacked the Minister for retaining such an outrageous person as chairman of a government-appointed body.'

The Corporation passed a motion condemning their chairman and she was immediately dismissed by Dalton. Inevitably the episode aroused the dormant political animosity towards the new town, which still existed both nationally and locally. Furthermore, the Corporation was now regarded with deep disfavour by civil servants and others at the Ministry. However, in due course, a new chairman was found in Sir Thomas Bennett, KBE, FRIBA, who was an architect, a man of energy and drive but also, according to Balchin, one who preferred not to argue with the Ministry's directives, even in the interests of the Corporation he chaired. He had many other commitments, including the chairmanship of another Development Corporation, that of Crawley in Sussex. At the same time, there were other changes of Board membership, including the appointment of Major Arthur Howard, previously chairman of the Urban District Council, giving Stevenage a second local Board member, with Philip Ireton, but of a different political persuasion.

At last the numbers of houses completed began steadily to increase, from a mere 16 in 1951, to 420 in 1952, 720 in 1953, 862 in 1954 and 1,257 in 1955. This was still far short of the original four-year programme, but nevertheless progress was now being made. The Corporation was subject to frequent criticism because it was an unelected body and therefore undemocratic, but there is no denying the fact that, once its early difficulties were overcome, it was extremely efficient. The Board met monthly behind closed doors, only its general manager and chief officers being in attendance to submit development proposals for approval or otherwise. Board members were of varying political persuasions and the way they worked together as a team for the good of the new town and its residents was to be admired. Unlike locally-elected members of the Council, they did not have to worry about pleasing political parties; there were no members of the public looking over their shoulder during their deliberations, no-one to whom they had to present themselves at regular intervals for re-election.

In 1951 tenants moved into the first Development Corporation house to be completed in the new town 'proper', in Broadview, on the Stony Hall estate. They were Bob Sulzbach, a former sergeant in the United States 8th Army Air Force stationed in England, and his English wife, Thelma. Bob had obtained a position in the Corporation's architects' department in 1950 and thus qualified for housing. Also arriving in Stevenage in 1951, and overjoyed to see the new development, was Mary Tabor, who had been working since 1945 as a housing officer in Holborn, where she and her colleagues faced such 'appalling lists' from an ever-growing stream of applicants that she despaired of ever finding enough houses. It gave her enormous pleasure, when she came to Stevenage, to be able to offer a choice to people, many of whom had been waiting for eight years.

The Sulzbach family outside their new home. (Stevenage Museum P6523)

As the newcomers arrived, members of the old-town churches organised teams of visitors to welcome them. At Christmas, carol singers from the churches trudged through the dark, snowy landscape across once-familiar fields to reach the first occupied premises. Some were unnerved by the height of Chauncy House and rather than venture up to the narrow walkway at each floor, preferred to wait outside, singing appropriately 'See amid the winter snow'. The Church of England wasted no time in building a new church for the Bedwell neighbourhood, which was dedicated by the Bishop of St Albans in December 1953. Unusually for that time, it was designed to be a dual-purpose building, capable of being used as either a hall or a church and was provided with cloakrooms, a kitchen and community rooms. Over the next few years more new churches were built for all the main Christian denominations.

On 1 July 1952 Harold MacMillan, then Minister of Housing and Local Government, came to Stevenage to lay a commemorative stone in the first factory built by the Development Corporation. The building was to be occupied by the Bay Tree Press and was expected to be completed in six months, by which time many of the firm's London staff would have moved to Stevenage. In an introductory speech, Sir Thomas Bennett, chairman of the Development Corporation, explained that firms could either build their own factories on land allocated to them, or occupy factories built by the Corporation. He also pointed out that housing development was currently in advance of industrial development: more than 1,500 houses were under construction and 736 were occupied. However, the de Havilland company was about to start another factory and other firms would soon be arriving.

The Minister said that the new towns had their growing pains but, in Stevenage as in others, he found great determination among all concerned to make the experiment a success. He was gratified to see that the most modern methods had been used in the building of this factory, making a saving in the use of steel. After the stone had been put in place, Miss J A Reynolds, chairman of Messrs Samson Clark and Co. Limited, of the Bay Tree Press, planted a bay tree.

Mud was something with which the early settlers were only too familiar as they found themselves surrounded by it. For young wives and mothers among early Bedwell neighbourhood residents it was a tiresome hazard in inclement weather. They had to make a long trek, often pushing a pram, across fields to the nearest shops in the old town High Street. It meant taking off their shoes before going indoors, to avoid dirtying the clean floors of their new houses and in dry summer weather, when there was no mud, there was dust to contend with.

As much as the newcomers loved their new homes, not everything was perfect. Earwig infestation and weather-boarding that let in the rain were among their problems, as well as a lack of facilities such as shops, buses, post boxes, meeting places for social events, telephone kiosks and children's nurseries. In London, they had turned to 'the borough' in connection with most things. In Stevenage they were confused as to who was responsible for what because they had to deal with three authorities – the Development Corporation, the Urban District Council and the County Council, each of which had its own separate and distinct areas of responsibility. The solution came about when groups of residents began to join together to make their voices heard. As numbers grew, these informal groups developed into tenants' associations, each with a chairman and secretary, to whom newcomers could take their questions and complaints and which in turn could make representations to the relevant authority, speaking on behalf of everyone.

The first tenants' associations met in one another's houses. As membership grew, they met in building workers' canteens and hostels and later in schools. Then, with a tenants' association in each new area, it became necessary to form an 'umbrella' organisation, the Stevenage Residents' Federation, on which each association was represented, to speak with greater force. It was to be expected that the provision of amenities would lag behind the building of houses. Shopkeepers, bus companies and others could hardly be expected to invest a great deal of money until there was sufficient custom to make it economically worthwhile, but the newcomers, who had been used to having everything practically on their doorstep in London, began to campaign for the earlier-than-planned provision of necessary facilities and services. The Federation could not be ignored; it was a formidable body.

In March 1953 the first issue of the New Town Residents' Federation newspaper was published. Titled the *Stevenage Echo*, it was an excellent production, well-written and well-designed, which maintained a very high standard throughout the five years of its life. The first editor was Jack Hawkins, whose vision and enthusiasm made it a success with no financial backing apart from that of the residents themselves and from advertisements. George Braithewaite was treasurer and later became advertising manager also. The chairman of the Federation, Jack Pickering, wrote an introduction in which he assured residents that 'The Federation is doing its best to make things easier for the whole town in the way of shops, schools, roads, etc with a fair amount of success. So don't despair, things are certainly looking brighter, especially now that the Twin Foxes will be opening shortly.'

Under the Labour Government's 1949 Licensing Act, the development corporations were responsible for building and managing licensed premises in new towns, on behalf of the Home Secretary. The Stevenage Development Corporation went through the due legal processes and set up the mandatory advisory committee, which proposed that the first new public house should be built at the shopping sub-centre in the Monks Wood estate in Bedwell neighbourhood. There were already 23 long established pubs in the old town, but it was reasonably felt that they were too far away and that new ones should be provided for the new residents.

In 1951, the Corporation's architects designed the proposed new Monks Wood pub and construction began. Tenders were invited on the basis of occupation as a free house on a 14-year lease. However, before the pub was completed, the incoming Conservative Government repealed Part 1 of the 1949 Licensing Act, leaving a newly-built but unoccupied pub in the hands of the Corporation, which promptly offered it on tender as either a free or a tied house. The best tender, for a 99 year lease, was submitted by a consortium of three breweries.

One of the two local newspapers, the *Hertfordshire Express*, ran a readers' competition to find a name for the new pub. The winning entry, submitted by local historian Harold Roberts, was 'The Twin Foxes', after the town's notorious identical twins, Albert Ebenezer and Ebenezer Albert Fox, whose happy hunting grounds had included Monks Wood. In 1953, the Twin Foxes public house finally opened.

Memorable nationally, 1953 began with disastrous floods in East Anglia, when storms battered the coast, causing the deaths of at least 280 people and

The Twin Foxes public house. (Stevenage Museum P3974)

making thousands of others homeless. Throughout the country, the public gave money to help the flood victims and in Stevenage both old and new towns ran fund-raising appeals. The Whomerley Wood Tenants' Association took part in a social at the Lytton Club, in Pound Avenue, Old Stevenage, in aid of the National Flood Relief Fund which achieved a total of £21 5s 0d (£21.25) and this was just one of many.

More happily, 1953 was also coronation year and throughout the town there was more fund-raising to pay for the celebrations and special events for children. Huw Rees, of 26, Stony Croft, reported 'A good time was had by all at the social in the Sish Lane canteen. Provision of pram parking space much appreciated. £3 10s 0d (£3.50) was raised for the coronation celebrations.'

The weather on coronation day, 2 June 1953, was cold, wet and dismal, but most activities went ahead as planned, not all being held on the day itself as some had taken place the previous weekend. The *Echo* reports included:

> **Whomerley Wood:** At 2pm on Saturday 30 May, fancy dressed children were wending their way down Abbots Grove, to be judged by Mrs Brennan of Rockingham Way. Owing to the inclement weather the remainder of the party was held in St Andrew's church hall by kind permission of the Revd E J Harper. Before tea Ian Stott and Gaye Westwood were crowned king and queen of the celebrations, the Rev. Harper said grace, then it was a case of

St Andrew's church. (Stevenage Museum P4177)

every man for himself as the kiddies tucked into the excellent fare provided. Then there was entertainment, a sing song led by Mrs Brennan at the accordion, a film show by Major Ferguson of Knebworth, a lucky dip for each child, and a Punch and Judy show by the local puppet master. The two-tier coronation cake was made by Mrs Taylor. All the tables were bedecked with flowers presented by Mrs Humphries and these were given to the church committee afterwards.

Ramsdell; Owing to bad weather on 2 June, the party was held in St Andrew's church hall instead of the street. There was a tea party, a sing song, then a magnificent parcel for each child including a coronation mug.

Vintners Avenue: In spite of the weather, events went with a swing at Homestead Social Centre on June 2, with fancy dress, a Punch and Judy show by Mr Wallace of Holly Copse, community singing, competitions and games for children and grownups. During the whole afternoon Mr M Aitken and Mr A Marshall, dressed as clowns, added to the jollifications by entertaining the children.

Bedwell north: Enjoyed a fine day and events were a complete success on the ESA sports field. For the fancy dress show three independent judges, Messrs B Savage, L Grey and B Cook eventually chose Rosemary Margot and Judy Conlon as the winners. The wheelbarrow race was won by W Reeves and John Ashmore.

Stony Hall A party was held in in the Sish Lane canteen on 30 May. There was slapstick entertainment by Messrs Luhman, Clarey and Foster and a fancy dress competition judged by Mrs E Longford [wife of the Revd E Longford, curate at St Nicholas and Holy Trinity] The afternoon closed with *God Save the Queen* and three cheers and was followed by a social for adults in the evening. Shopkeepers and others gave donations for a raffle which raised £4 for Whitney Wood old people's home TV fund.

Finding suitable venues for social gatherings was not easy in the early days. The old town hall in Orchard Road was, of course, open to all and was heavily booked for dances, meetings, parties and other events, but it could not cater for the needs of a rapidly-increasing population, nor was it easy for people from the new areas to reach. The Master Plan did promise a new and bigger town hall to serve the whole town but it has never materialised.

Strictly speaking, provision of community centres was the responsibility of the County Council, but for many reasons they were unable or reluctant to do so and the Development Corporation stepped in, to build centres first in Bedwell then in Shephall. Before that, the Corporation arranged with its major building contractors for workers' canteens to be made available for evening meetings and weekend social events. It was unavoidable that the building workers who used the huts in the day should take dirt into them, on their boots. Although the organisers of Saturday night dances in a canteen in Bedwell did their best to sweep the floors clean, dirt remained firmly embedded in the cracks between the boards. When the dancers took to the floor, clouds of dust arose and in the end they could hardly see across the room. On another occasion, a tenants' association meeting in a builders' hut in Broadwater was lit by Tilley lamps.

In the early summer of 1953, a group of Stevenage tenants visited Harlow New Town which they found to be one year ahead of Stevenage, with its town centre started and neighbourhood shops flourishing. The visitors were particularly interested in the Harlow Community Centre 'housed in a fine old mansion' and also the children's playground. They saw that 'having a building for community activities had made all the difference to Harlow, allowing many groups, ranging from country dancing to gardening, to grow and flourish' and they realised how imperative was the need for a similar building in Stevenage. In response to this, the Development Corporation decided to offer the Bedwell Community Association Field View, former home of the Mason family. It was one of the houses in Bedwell Lane which they had obtained by compulsory purchase and would, in due course, demolish.

The Association found that Field View is in excellent condition apart from minor damage to windows and crockery by irresponsible youths. It has many rooms, suitable for a wide range of activities.' Possibly they, like many old town residents, wondered why it need be destroyed at all. From the point of view of Bedwell residents, although the building itself was very suitable, it was not in a good position. To get to it from the new neighbourhood would be an ideal walk on a fine summer's day, but not so good in wet, cold weather. However, the Bedwell Community Association agreed to take it over from the Development Corporation until their own community centre was built in Bedwell Crescent. The first wardens were Mr and Mrs Copping, who arrived in August 1954 from a flat in Wood Green. Their accommodation was on the first floor and three rooms downstairs were hired out at 3s and 5s (15p and 25p) per evening. Clubs for boys and girls were formed and run very successfully by enthusiastic volunteers.

In the next spring, Field View was demolished and the The Plash, former home of Clarence Elliott and his family, became the new temporary community centre.

Some campaigns were supported throughout the town, not just in the new neighbourhoods. Hospital provision in north Hertfordshire was already barely adequate in 1946, before any new town building began. There were two hospitals at Hitchin, the Herts. and Beds. in Bedford Road, including a maternity wing, and the Lister, in Oughton Head Way, consisting of prefabricated buildings surrounding the former Hitchin Union Workhouse, that had been erected in 1941 as a temporary hospital for Second World War casualties. At a time when very few people had cars, patients and visitors from Stevenage and the outlying villages faced a long walk uphill from their bus stops in St Mary's Square. Visiting hours were from 7 to 7.30 in the evenings, and on Tuesday and Sunday afternoons only. This was the main hospital provision for all the towns and villages of north Hertfordshire, thus it was hardly surprising that one of the first causes promoted in the *Echo* was the need for improved health care. An early editorial asked,

> What hospitals are being built to cater for the rapidly expanding New Town population – a population chiefly comprised of young families, with three times the national average maternity rate? Not one! 'We have not enough beds to cope with the people who live here,' said Dr Eberlie, Chairman of the Medical Committee. A hospital takes about five years to build. May we suggest to the medical authorities that a prognosis of public need – even though it is now four years late – and some immediate remedial treatment would be preferable to a diagnosis and a hasty emergency operation.

The campaign gathered momentum. In November 1953, the *Echo* reported the Ministry of Health's new policy of 'All Confinements at Home'. This hardly worried the old town, where home births were the norm, but it came as a shock to ex-Londoners. 'I couldn't understand why they built this town, and encouraged all these people to come, with no hospital,' said one. 'We had to have our babies at home. In London they would have been born in hospital.' She added that the midwifery service was excellent. However, the *Echo* pointed out, the policy brought special problems to new towns like Stevenage, where rent took much of the wages, there were no relatives nearby and there was no money for home help, although the County Home Help Service would give special consideration to appeals in cases of hardship. For the midwives themselves life had its problems: one had to attend five births in one day. Stella Kestin recalled,

> We kept on appointing extra midwives. They needed houses and the Corporation offered us one in what became Valley Way, which was just acres of mud with houses popping up. I remember one of the other midwives saying, 'You can't possibly ask a midwife to live right out there.' But gradually the mud dried out and the roads came and she did quite well out there.

Sir Thomas Bennett resigned from the chairmanship of the Corporation Board in May 1953, to be succeeded by Sir Roydon Dash. Before he left, Sir Thomas had addressed a large audience on 26 May, at a meeting in the Barclay School on the subject of the new town's progress. According to the *Echo* report, he made an admirable speech, but failed to strike the right note with his audience. They gained the impression that the new town was a 'financial success' but that the Development Corporation was 'more concerned with … a proper financial return on their expenditure than with the perquisites of families living in communities.' The report then listed the concerns which it felt the Corporation should address; 'hospital facilities sadly overworked … telephone system creaking with increase in demand … need for increased transport has been aired but there is no sign of improvement … density of traffic on the Great North Road is cause for concern … shopping facilities are seriously behind schedule … within a month or so residents will be moving into Roebuck houses. Shops haven't started yet and if they take as long to build as the block in Stony Hall our new neighbours will have 18 months of shopping in the High Street.' In fact, it was pointless to expect the Corporation to do much about the first four of these problems because they were the responsibility of other authorities, but the Federation had perhaps hoped for more support.

Not everyone was dissatisfied, as one letter to the editor shows;

Dear Sir,

After hearing so many complaints about the New Town I really think it is time somebody gave it a word of praise. I have been here now since November and have never once wished I was back in London.

Here I feel that I am part of a community, not just another pebble on the beach. It is fascinating to see the progress being made; the houses going up, the trees and grass being planted. I would like also to mention that my house is my pride and joy and when I hear all these petty complaints, it seems that some people don't know when they are well off.

J D Baker.

With so many city dwellers engulfing a rural community, culture clashes were inevitable. As Mrs Lily Glazebrook explained, 'You see there was a difference in their culture: we were country born, we knew the ways of the country and then the people from London came down and they thought that we were simple people. In those days you could tell where people came from, even different villages because people lived in such close communities ... and we certainly could tell people by their accent from London'.

Growing crops were not always recognised for what they were and and the following notice was published in the press: 'To help local farmers in the Fairlands Valley, will all residents keep to the footpaths and bye-ways when passing through the farm lands.' Then there was the question of dogs. Some residents were allowing them to run wild and were told, 'People looked forward to being able to have a dog in the new town but must be responsible for control.' The problem was exacerbated by the design of some housing areas where there were no individual front gardens but a shared grassed area which was maintained by Corporation staff. This looked good on paper but was totally impractical in real life and after determined campaigning the Corporation were persuaded to erect fences and allow residents to cultivate their front gardens.

At times other, more serious unpleasantness occurred, such as 'the increasing number of cases of drunkenness and disorderly conduct reported in the local press lately ... the majority seem to concern men from the Monks Wood Hostel ... these hooligans ... seem to be bent on their own so-called pleasure regardless of the misery they are causing to respectable citizens'

On a more positive note, there had been a minor victory in that London Transport, the local bus operator, had agreed to run an extra bus from Hitchin to Stevenage at 10.58 pm on Saturday evenings, about half an hour later than the present last bus and the 716 Green Line coach route was also under review. Both old and new town residents fought for better bus services; those in the old town being particularly irritated because, by the time buses reached the High Street, they were often full.

The White Cottage, London Road. (Stevenage Museum P11931)

John Morris, extreme right, at Westmill Museum, 1958. (Stevenage Museum)

There was cause for celebration on 26 June 1954. Stevenage became the first new town to have a museum, opened at White Cottage, London Road, by Cllr Philip Ireton and the General Manager of Stevenage Development Corporation, Major-General Alan Duff. It started in small way, opening only from 2.15 to 7.30 pm every Wednesday and Saturday. The founders, including Dr John Morris, who held the chair in ancient history at London University, were full of enthusiasm for the future, announcing that 'Anyone, child or adult can come and bring anything of interest. The museum will not be simply full of things in glass cases. It will have a meetings room where photographers, artists, naturalists, and others can meet, it will offer workrooms for interested groups and exhibitions of local art and industry. Its success or failure will be what Stevenage people make of it.' The official opening was attended by 235 people from both old and new towns, and in its various locations, it has continued to attract town-wide support ever since.

At the end of 1954 the Museum was justly proud of its new exhibition, Roman Bedwell, which included exhibits lent by the London Guildhall Museum and a display of the evidence of an early farm, probably Romano British, which John Morris had located on the east side of Colestrete. An Association of Friends of Stevenage Museum was formed and that, too, is still in existence as the Stevenage Society for Local History, with a vigorous town-wide membership. Early in its existence, the Society took the brave decision to publish a history of Stevenage and commissioned Robert Trow-Smith, a respected agricultural historian then living in Weston, to write it. This excellent book was published in 1958 and remains the standard work on pre-twentieth century Stevenage.

The Congregational church had been active since the earliest days of the new town, having applied for and been allocated a site in the Bedwell area on the 1946 Master Plan. The congregation met in the Homestead Moat Community Centre until September 1954, when the Congregational church in Cutty's Lane was opened. For the first year Miss Pat Ashton, a student from St Paul's House, Liverpool, training centre for women Congregational ministers, served as resident Leader of Stevenage Congregational Church under the supervision of the minister for Knebworth. On 1 January 1955, her place was taken by the Revd Ernest Wimpress, who was to stay for 37 years, making an invaluable contribution to the life of Stevenage.

As 1954 closed, although there was considerable satisfaction for what had been achieved, there was also increasing frustration at delays. Work on the town centre had not even started. There was a tendency to blame the Corporation for all disappointments and to compare the Stevenage Corporation unfavourably with that of Harlow and other new towns. The January 1954 issue of *Town and Country Planning*, in an article entitled *New Towns in 1953*, concluded that most new towns had similar problems, one of the most serious defects being the absence of places for meetings and recreation. The article noted that industrial development in Stevenage was 'now expanding vigorously' but with consequent heavy demands on housing. The writer also commented that in Stevenage 'home gardens are a striking feature' and that a competition for a silver cup was planned.

For those living in the town, however, there could be no doubt that the lack of hospitals, schools and the A1 by-pass were uppermost in their list of concerns. Campaigners rose to the challenge and prepared for battle. On 22 June 1954, Sir Roydon Dash, Chairman of the Development Corporation chaired a public meeting to report on the progress of the new town. During question time, there was an impassioned plea for Sir Roydon to approach the Ministry of Transport about the A1 by-pass. He explained that this was not the Corporation's responsibility, but the speaker insisted that the Corporation could and should press for the by-pass. At the same meeting, Huw Rees' suggestion that the time was now ripe for residents in new Stevenage as well as old to be appointed to the Corporation Board was well received in the body of the hall.

In November 1954, the *Stevenage Echo* included a gentle reminder to residents:

> Remember,
> Remember,
> 26 November
> By-Pass meeting

Despite an evening of very rough weather, the meeting held at the town hall and chaired by Cllr Philip Ireton was very well attended by a cross-section of people from the whole of the town. Mr Hardy, the Corporation chief engineer, said that the by-pass was an integral part of the plan of the new town. Other comments, faithfully reported by the *Stevenage Echo*, included;

> Make sure Hertfordshire gets its fair share from the national exchequer. (Peter Benenson, prospective Labour Party candidate).
>
> Should the Stevenage by-pass take priority? In my own view it has a very high priority. (Colonel ffolliott, Hertfordshire County Surveyor).
>
> The Group is in favour of the by-pass and consider it an essential feature necessary for the efficiency of transport, both passenger and freight, and for the safety of the inhabitants of the town. (Harry King, Secretary of Stevenage Industrial Employers' Group).
>
> It will make shopping easier on Saturday morning as well as being a good thing from the road safety point of view. (L J Longhurst, chairman of Stevenage Chamber of Trade).
>
> The number of accidents on the Great North Road at Stevenage has doubled during the past four years. (Cllr Ken Ellis).
>
> The only way to get a high place in the queue for a by-pass is to shout as loud as we can. Never Let up. (Mr Sykes of British Road Federation).

The meeting was reminded that there had been

> two fatal accidents in three days. A by-pass had been planned for Stevenage before the New Town began, because main road traffic was judged too heavy for old Stevenage to bear. Government planners decided to put a new town here on the assumption that a bye-pass would exist before the town grew to any great size. Now Stevenage is more than twice its old size and growing faster than ever before. Local traffic had more than doubled, national through traffic was ever greater. The Ministry of Transport had not yet decided to build the by-pass. Write to your MP.

The *Echo* reported that the audience

> became thoroughly enthusiastic ... when they chose a deputation of seven to go to Westminster with a petition for a by-pass ... The first to be chosen was Mrs Kathleen Newman, who has been an ardent and almost superhumanly active member of the campaign committee. She was supported by Messrs Peter Benenson, Mr Munden, Mervyn Pritchard, Mr Longhurst, Harry King.

As if to underline the importance of the meeting, yet another death occurred on the Great North road, even as the speeches were being made. The *Echo* reported;

> John F Riley of 63, Shephall View was killed when returning from work at St Albans at 7.30 on the evening of Friday 26 November. He was knocked from his motor bike by a car travelling in the same (northward) direction which ran into him. The accident happened just as he was turning into Elder Way. The night was stormy and very dark. Its is probable that two other cars travelling south also ran over him. At the inquest there was evidence that the motor bike was lit by cycle battery lamps, the rear one of which was not working. There are two junction signs near the turning but the nearest lamp is 180 yards [165 m] north of it and nearest lamp in Elder Way 28 yards [26 m] back from the scene of the accident.

The deputation from Stevenage was well-prepared and had clear objectives for their meeting at Westminster on 17 December. They wanted, firstly, to secure a definite agreement that Stevenage would have a by-pass and secondly that there would be immediate improvements to the Great North Road through Stevenage. Their leader, Mrs Newman, insisted that they would not go back with only 'faint promises of sympathy.' In this she was successful, the deputation being granted one and a half hours of discussion with the Minister's representative, Mr Molson, the outcome of which was a definite assurance that Stevenage was now in the queue for a by-pass, since the government had recently announced a doubling of the yearly allocation for expenditure on roads, from £15 million to at least £30 million.

The demand for immediate improvements in the Great North Road was also met. Within days, representatives from the Ministry of Transport, the Hertfordshire County Council, the Urban District Council and the Development Corporation met at Elder Way and discussed possible improvements, the Ministry representative being instructed to report back directly to the Minister himself.

Encouraging though these promises were, still more tragedies were taking place. The industrial area was separated from the residential neighbourhoods by the Great North Road, which workers had to cross, on foot or bicycle, twice a day. It was a nightmare for all concerned and when, in February 1955, another death occurred, workers and supporters staged marches, one with a coffin, along the Great North Road. The Corporation then moved rapidly into action and organised a Bailey bridge to carry cyclists over the road and, later, a pedestrian subway, at its junction with Six Hills Way. Even so, work did not begin on the by-pass until 30 May 1960 and then it was not opened until July 1962. Some of the most delighted residents were those living in the old town where, for years, simply crossing from one side of the High Street to another had been a very hazardous act.

Another matter of concern to both new and old towns was the lack of schools. Although Broom Barns, Bedwell and Roebuck primary schools were open by the end of 1954, there was now a shortage of secondary school places, particularly of grammar school places for girls. This had always been so, but of course the coming of the new town exacerbated the problem. Here was another cause for the *Echo* to report,

> The Hertfordshire County Council Education Committee recommends the building of a [Girls'] Grammar School in Stevenage in the 1955–56 building programme. Without such a school it was calculated that only 6.7% of our children would have Grammar School tuition in a few years time. Assuming that the Ministry sanction the school it could hardly be ready before late 1957 or more probably 1958. What is to happen in the meantime? Plans have been made to enlarge Alleyne's Grammar School and for it temporarily to take girls but not a brick has been laid so far and any extra accommodation will not be ready for at least a year. By next summer there will be five full primary schools operating in Stevenage and probably an extra one at Peartree, six in all. Compare this with the [one] that used to feed Alleyne's.

The other ongoing campaign, for better hospital and health service provision, was doomed to a much longer wait. Although an outpatients' clinic was provided in the town centre, it was nearly 20 more years before the new hospital was opened.

Erecting the Bailey bridge across the A1 in 1955. (Stevenage Museum P3706)

COMMUNITY CENTRES

Although responsibility for the provision of community centres rested with the County Council and, to a lesser degree, with the Urban District Council, both of which received the rates income from the town, it soon became clear that if such centres were to materialise, then the Development Corporation would have to go it alone and come up with the necessary funds.

In early 1953, the Corporation had provided a site in Homestead Moat for the construction of a temporary social centre for residents of the Bedwell area who were also provided with the materials to put it up themselves. It became well used by a number of local organisations, including church Sunday schools, Corporation tenant interviews, a chess club, the women's co-operative group, dance classes, the County Council welfare clinic, Labour Party meetings and an athletics club. Two of the moving spirits behind the project were Basil Wratten, an officer in the Corporation's Estates Department, and his wife, Maureen.

The Corporation was permitted to provide tenants' meeting rooms only, so it had to persuade the Ministry to allow it to build community centres, using the argument that provision of a particular community centre would make it unnecessary to provide the three tenants' meeting rooms that would otherwise be needed. The first community centre built by the Corporation was the Broadhall Centre (later retitled the Shephall Centre) in Shephall Village in 1956. It was originally meant to cater for residents of both the Broadwater and adjoining Shephall neighbourhoods. The Bedwell Community Centre was built the following year. One centre that the Corporation did not have to build was Springfield House, in the High Street, which was left to the town under the will of Jeremiah Inns and eventually became the Old Stevenage Community Centre. As the town developed, further centres were provided by the Corporation at Broadwater, Chells, Pin Green and St Nicholas, and by the Borough Council at Symonds Green. The centres at Pin Green and Symonds Green incorporated ecumenical church accommodation, shared by different denominations for religious worship.

Once built, the centres were leased to local community associations, which were given grants by the Council for furniture and equipment.

CHAPTER SEVEN
Shephall Village

STEVENAGE, IN 1946, was a country town surrounded by the villages of Knebworth, Shephall, Aston, Walkern, Graveley, Little Wymondley and the hamlet of Todds Green, most of which lost small areas of their land to the designated development area. Shephall, however, was entirely swallowed up, losing its separate identity and becoming a mere neighbourhood of the greater Stevenage.

The earliest versions of the name 'Shephall' are 'Sepehale' in the St Albans Abbey rolls for 1077–93 and 'Escepehale' in *Domesday Book* of 1086, which the English Place-Names Society translates as 'A corner of land where sheep are pastured.' An alternative meaning, supported in some quarters, is 'ash-tree slope'. However, another piece of evidence which gives weight to the first meaning is that of the name 'Fairlands' which has its origin in the Scandinavian word 'faar' meaning 'sheep'. Fair Lane, leading from Shephall village into the fields beyond and Fairlands Farm (now Fairlands Valley) all make it most likely that the name 'Shephall' does indeed mean 'a sheep pasture.'

Although geographically so close, the history of Shephall was in many respects quite separate from that of Stevenage. *Domesday Book* records that Shephall was five hides in extent, a size typical of many villages in this part of England. Before the Norman Conquest, it appears that the whole manor of Shephall was held by St Albans Abbey, but after 1066 two hides (about 240 acres) were transferred to Stigand, Archbishop of Canterbury, and farmed by his tenant, Aelfric. By the time *Domesday Book* was compiled, in 1086, this land was still in the lordship of of the Archbishops of Canterbury, although another tenant, named Ansketal, was farming it. This part of the village had sufficient arable land for five plough teams, meadow for half a plough team and woodland

St Mary's church, Shephall. (Margaret Ashby)

to support 20 pigs. The other three hides were held by the Abbot of St Albans, whose servants farmed one and a half hides on his behalf. The remaining land was let out to tenants. There was enough arable land here for five plough teams, but the eight villagers who are mentioned had just three between them. In addition, there was meadow land, pasture for livestock and woodland to support ten pigs. Two cottagers and one slave are also recorded.

At the time of the Domesday survey, Shephall was in Broadwater Hundred, but shortly afterwards the Abbot of St Albans, who had somehow acquired the two hides of Shephall land formerly held by the Archbishop of Canterbury, managed to transfer it to Cashio Hundred, with his many other holdings. This meant that the local government of the village was thereafter administered from St Albans, unlike that of Stevenage and all the neighbouring villages, which were in Broadwater Hundred. This arrangement was particularly ironic, given that the tiny hamlet of Broadwater was adjacent to Shephall and part of it (the Hertford Road and land to the east of it) was in Shephall parish. The site of the Roebuck Inn, the Great North Road and land to the west, was in Knebworth parish. So, for centuries, Shephall people must have been aware of the Broadwater Hundred courts taking place on their doorstep, while their own centre of administration was fifteen miles away at St Albans.

In its early years, Shephall was also closely associated with its neighbour, Aston, a village which, according to *Domesday Book*, was then larger and more prosperous than both Shephall and Stevenage. At some time in the early twelfth century a small church was built at Shephall as a daughter of the larger church at Aston, which probably also supplied a priest. Aston at this time was briefly held by Reading Abbey and it appears that the little church at Shephall was included in that holding. Sometime later, an agreement was reached between the Prior of Reading Abbey and the Abbot of St Albans to transfer the Shephall church to the jurisdiction of St Albans. This is recorded in a document dated to 1151–54, which describes the visit of Prior Hugh of Reading to St Albans, where he renounced his claim to the church at Shephall. As far as is known, the first vicar was Robert Goderich, who died in 1351, but records are incomplete and there may have been earlier incumbents. Although nothing now remains of the first church building, Shephall does possess a remarkable survival from the twelfth century, the oldest church bell in Hertfordshire. It hangs in the bell turret of St Mary's church and is still rung for services today.

During the middle ages the abbots of St Albans leased the manor of Shephall to a succession of tenants, including Adam the cellarer and an unnamed kitchener in the twelfth century and Geoffrey de Homele in the early fourteenth century. In 1349 the Black Death reached the neighbourhood, killing many of the inhabitants so that afterwards the depopulated countryside was not properly farmed for many years. Some small villages were wiped out altogether and appear today on the map as 'deserted villages'. This happened at Chesfield, near Graveley, and probably also to Chells and Box, on the outskirts of Stevenage. But Shephall survived, so there is a possibility that it escaped the plague altogether thanks to its secluded situation off the main road.

Life was hard for most people during the rest of the century and was made worse by King Richard II's imposition of a poll-tax in 1377. Shephall was doubly unfortunate in that the Abbot of St Albans at this time was the harsh and greedy Thomas de la Mare. Peasants were very much at the mercy of their lords, but in 1381, in what became known as the Peasants' Revolt, men from Kent and Essex marched on London. A similar uprising took place against the Abbot of St Albans, in which the men of Shephall joined, to demand a charter of liberties. The Abbot gave in, but the rebels' initial success was short-lived as Richard II came in force to St Albans, annulled all the charters and forced the men of Hertfordshire to swear allegiance to him.

The end of the fourteenth century brought the promise of better times when a kinder Abbot, John, was installed at St Albans. He seemed to have the welfare of his people at heart but unfortunately he made a disastrous choice of tenant for the manor of Shephall when he leased it for life to a Robert Brome. This man let the village go to waste and caused a great deal of trouble for Abbot John before he managed to eject him, retrieve his manor and restock it. Part of the rebuilding work that was done at this time may have included the restoration of the church of St Mary. The carved chancel screen dates from this period and the chancel roof from the early fifteenth century, slightly earlier than the nave roof. One intriguing feature is a stone high up in the south wall of the chancel which has an inscription possibly of Saxon origin.

During the middle ages land changed hands frequently and men who were trying to build up large holdings locally often held land in both Shephall and Stevenage. Among these were members of the de Broc family. They described themselves in the thirteenth century as 'Lords of Shephall' and two hundred years later a charter of 1443 refers to 'all the lands called Bromes Lands in Shephall and Stevenage'.

The big change to the traditional way of life came in 1536, when King Henry VIII began dissolving the monasteries which for centuries had been central to town and country alike, providing employment, care of the sick and education as well as religious services. The dissolution process went on for several years as monastic lands and properties were taken over by the monarch and sold or granted to new landlords. St Albans abbey was not dissolved until 1539 and the time of waiting and uncertainty must have been difficult for the people of Shephall, wondering who their new lord would be and who would be living at the manor. In fact, the change was not as great as they feared. At the time of the dissolution George Nodes was farming the Shephall Manor land as tenant. He was a royal servant who had worked his way up from a Yeoman of the Guard to become Sergeant of the Buckhounds, which was a prestigious post held for life. In 1542 he was allowed to buy the manor of Shephall, together with some land in Aston which had previously belonged to the Abbot of St Albans. George had no legitimate children and on his death the manor came to his nephew, Charles Nodes and through him to successive generations of the Nodes family. One of George's two illegitimate daughters was Joan, who married Thomas Chapman. Their second son, George, became the playwright and translator of Homer, immortalised in Keats' poem, *On First Looking into Chapman's Homer.*

The Nodes remained Lords of the Manor of Shephall until the early nineteenth century. During those 300 years the family steadily increased their landholdings in Hertfordshire and Bedfordshire and amassed considerable wealth. The George Nodes who inherited the manor in 1664 inherited also the manors of Holwell and Langford, together with other land and property. According to his memorial tablet in St Mary's church he was 'a tender husband, a careful father and a diligent peacemaker'.

The Nodes were resident Lords of the Manor, living in the original small manor house known as Shephalbury, a long, low building with some twelve rooms and additional domestic offices. The only other substantial buildings were the Vicarage, later known as the Rectory and the church itself. Otherwise the village consisted of estate workers' cottages, the Bury Farmhouse and, beside the cottages on the green, the Red Lion Inn. Some way from the centre of the village, but still part of the parish of Shephall although a separate manor, was Half Hyde farm and, in the extreme south, Broom Barns farm.

In small villages such as Shephall the Lord of the Manor and the rector or vicar were very clearly the leading citizens. They did not always agree, as happened during John Rudd's incumbency of Shephall between 1595 and 1640. At the back of the Parish Register, which he kept in meticulous order, Rudd recorded accounts of two disputes with George Nodes. The first concerned a boundary fence around the Rectory and the second the rebuilding of the Rectory itself. In both cases George Nodes accused him of encroaching on his land, but with no justification according to the detailed description in the Parish Register.

John Rudd was a memorable priest. Having spent several years in Cambridge, where he was often in trouble with the University over points of doctrine in his sermons, he arrived in Shephall in 1595. Preaching was his great enthusiasm, as is shown in a report from the churchwardens to the archdeacon in 1603, 'Our minister, John Rudd, preacheth at the least every Sabbath twice, in the forenoon for the most part ... in the afternoon referring all his exercises unto catechizing ...' As sermons in those days could last for an hour or even longer, the parishioners of Shephall certainly had value for money.

In his will John Rudd left instructions for the monument which is now fixed to the east wall of the north aisle in St Mary's church. It should depict him as the shepherd of his flock, carrying a lamb over his shoulders but unfortunately, when it was restored in modern times the artist mistook the faded image of a lamb for long grey hair. John Rudd's will included a bequest of money for bread to be distributed to the poor. The Nodes and others also made charitable bequests over the centuries, but the bread charity is one which survived into the twentieth century, supported by additional gifts in the wills of Thomas Chapman of Stevenage, in 1666 and Thomas Threader, a farmer of Shephall, in 1768.

There were sorrows and disappointments in the lives of the Nodes, as well as success and wealth. Often mothers died in childbirth and children in infancy. Some couples died childless, so that entailed estates passed to nephews and in the end, to daughters. This happened to the John Nodes who died in 1761. His marriage to Katherine Vaslet, in 1739, had begun with high hopes. No less an artist than William Hogarth had visited Shephalbury that year to paint Katherine's portrait. She and John had three sons and three daughters but none of the sons lived long after his death, no other male heirs could be found and so, eventually, the Shephall estate was divided between his daughters, Margaret Mary, wife of Richard Price; Sarah, wife of Robert Jacques and Catherine, unmarried. In the early nineteenth century various portions of the estate changed hands, eventually coming to the Heathcote family, who were to be Lords of the Manor of Shephall for the next one hundred years.

Shephalbury was occupied by Samuel Heathcote Unwin Heathcote from 1818 and in 1838 he inherited the estate. A man of strong and sometimes

Shephalbury. (Stevenage Museum P383)

eccentric views, he became well-known in the district. One of his obsessions was a dislike of railways and he tried, by various means, to prevent the Great Northern Railway line from coming through the county. He died in 1862 and was succeeded by his son, Unwin Unwin Heathcote, who immediately set about building a magnificent new manor house, to replace the original long, low building. He chose as architect the highly-regarded T Roger Smith, and spared no expense on the ornate neo-Gothic mansion, which was completed in 1864. It was built of red bricks made on the estate, with Staffordshire tiles for the roof and materials of the finest quality throughout the interior. The former manor house was demolished and a rose garden planted on the site. Another new building was going up at the same time, a new village school to take the place of the cramped cottage which had served this purpose previously. The villagers had raised £358 which, with £25 from the Diocesan Board of Education and £20 from the National Society, covered the cost of the building. Unwin Heathcote gave land for the site and pledged money for the running costs.

Unwin Unwin Heathcote died in 1893, to be succeeded by Colonel Alfred Unwin Heathcote, the last of the family to live at Shephalbury. He died in 1912. Later, during the First World War, Shephalbury was let to Colonel Woods, a kindly man who made regular visits to the school and sometimes invited the children to tea. The rector at this time, from 1916 to 1928, was the Revd

Alexander Macrae, a good and conscientious man, who cared deeply for his parishioners. His entries in the Shephall Charities minute book are models of how minutes should be taken and his beautiful handwriting makes them a pleasure to read.

In 1926 Shephalbury was rented to David Augustus Bevan, and from 1929 to 1937, to Lieutenant Colonel Morgan Grenville Gavin. However, the Heathcotes retained their interest in village affairs, as in 1935 when Miss Evelyn Heathcote attended a tea to celebrate the Silver Jubilee of King George V and Queen Mary and helped to plant the Jubilee Oak on the green. In 1939 came the final break with tradition when Michael Heathcote sold the property to William Harriman Moss. Almost immediately the Second World War broke out, during which the mansion housed 32 children aged from two to five years, who were evacuated there by the Waifs and Strays Society with the co-operation of the Moss family. When they left it became a convalescent home for Polish officers and, after the war, a school for Polish children.

For Stevenage residents, Shephall, with its picture-postcard village green, was the culmination of a pleasant footpath walk. One route led from Sish Lane, across a meadow of grasses, buttercups, ox-eye daisies and meadow saxifrage, where cattle drank at a small pond, and overhead the air was alive with skylarks, swallows and martins. The path continued through a spinney into cornfields bright with poppies and cornflowers, to Pancake Corner at the top of Bedwell Lane. Here was Bedwell Plash, a spring which fed a boggy pool. Overlooking it were some old, black, weather-boarded barns once typical of this part of

Shephall Green. (Stevenage Museum 0075)

Hertfordshire, and opposite, in a house of the same name, lived Clarence Elliott, owner of the Six Hills Nursery. At this point the path turned sharp left and eventually reached Humley (Whomerley) Wood which was effectively part of the boundary of Stevenage Urban District: Monks Wood, which adjoined it, was in Shephall parish. In spring, the woodland floor was thickly carpeted with a succession of primroses, wood anemones and bluebells, but inevitably a gamekeeper with a shotgun would appear and firmly direct walkers along the path round the edge. The final part of the walk was along the narrow Fair Lane, though the arable fields of Fairlands Farm and into the tiny village of Shephall. The ancient church of St Mary, the Rectory, the Red Lion inn and a few cottages clustered round the green, where gracious elm trees gave welcome shade. Situated a little distance away were the manor house and grounds, carefully screened from view by tall hedges.

For local government purposes Shephall had only limited control over its own affairs. The Parish Council could deal with allotments, charities and other very local matters but in all other respects, including planning, the village was governed by the Hitchin Rural District Council, on which it was represented. Following the 1932 Town and Country Planning Act, the Hitchin Rural District Council drew up a planning scheme which involved very considerable development at Shephall and Knebworth and could have provided the basis for one of the satellite towns currently being discussed by those responsible for the future rehousing of Londoners. The scheme was later criticised as being an example of the dreaded 'ribbon development'. Councillor Philip Ireton suggested that Stevenage would be a better location because it had access to two railway lines, the Great Northern main line and the loop line to Hertford. This was the deciding factor.

Development of the Shephall neighbourhood began in 1953. The old village around the green, although preserved and protected, was closely surrounded by new buildings and divided from its manor house and grounds by Broadhall Way. People were expected to move into the new houses in the summer and the Residents' Federation were vocal on their behalf, pointing out in the July 1953 issue of the *Stevenage Echo*, that,

> The first tenants will take possession in Roebuck area within a few weeks and the first shops will not be completed for at least 12 months ... The Corporation vaguely propose 'temporary shops'. The Federation has warned of these problems several times but with no result. For example, on 13 September 1952 the Federation was told that Bedwell shops 'should start soon, possibly within the next two months.' Bedwell is still waiting for shops to be started. Stevenage Development Corporation admits that the situation regarding shops in Bedwell and Roebuck is very unsatisfactory. That, my dear readers, is the understatement of the year.

Shephall village Green, showing the well. (Stevenage Museum P8240)

However, the new tenants managed quite well. Grace Drackford explained in *The History Makers*, that she and her neighbours moved into their newly-built houses within a few weeks of each other and were very much on their own, with no social amenities. They all became very friendly, helping each other out, taking cups of tea to new arrivals and sharing tasks such as baby sitting. They were so pleased to have houses of their own that they made light of problems. In the very early days these new residents had to walk, with their babies in prams, to the shops in the old town. Otherwise there were mobile shops in vans, which were greatly appreciated until, after a few months, temporary shops were opened in St Margaret's.

There were by this time several active building sites, from Bedwell through to Broadwater and Shephall. Conditions for the workmen were often grim, as Fred Udell explained in *The History Makers*. He described the unheated shed which served as a canteen and the callous attitude of the contractors who expected work to continue in pouring rain. Worst of all was the lack of toilets, as a result of which the woods, which had once been protected by their owners and loved by local people for their beauty and tranquillity, were now fouled by the unfortunate building workers.

In May 1954, the *Echo* published a letter from W Kenneth Shaw, Secretary of Bedwell Community Association, drawing attention to the tragic abuse of Whomerley Wood;

> Dear Sir,
>
> At this month's meeting of the Council of the Association the question was raised of the serious misuse and despoiling of parts of the Whomerley Wood Green Belt. It was reported that the woods are being used:

> a) As a source of cheap fuel involving the damaging and chopping down of branches of growing trees.
> b) As a lavatory for workmen.
> c) As a source of free plants for the garden (such as primroses plucked by the roots) and
> d) As a convenient rubbish dump involving the fouling of the once pleasant stream running through the woods.
>
> It would appear that the main culprits in this instance are not the much maligned children of the New Town but adults from all parts of Stevenage old and new and it is surely a matter of very grave concern to all Stevenage residents that a part of the very precious unspoiled woodlands which will one day be a means of much pleasure and recreation to the town population should be maltreated in this abominable manner ... We hope for increased police surveillance, or action by Corporation but finally responsibility rests on every one of us.

Walking in Whomerley – correctly pronounced 'Humley' – Wood. (Margaret Ashby)

As the town developed, land values rose, the cost of building houses increased and at the same time inflation was rising, causing building costs to go up dramatically. As a result, the Ministry instructed the Development Corporation to build at a higher density than the 9 to 10 houses per acre which had been the norm at Bedwell. The required density for Broadwater and Shephall was around 12 to 13 houses per acre, with smaller gardens. Inevitably, in order to house more people at no greater cost, high rise flats began to make their appearance. At the other end of the scale, the Corporation was concerned that their efforts to achieve a more balanced community in Stevenage by encouraging people in higher income groups into the town had not yet been achieved. To this end they decided to build 10 larger houses for sale, either freehold or leasehold, in Shephall Park.

With so many people now moving into the new areas, the need for a community centre became urgent. In November 1953 the Development Corporation put forward plans for a community building for Shephall, but it was immediately rejected as not big enough. Residents

Broadhall Community Centre.
(Stevenage Museum P6901)

The original 'Our Mutual Friend' public house in London Road, opposite the Guild of Literature and Arts house at Six Hills, which Charles Dickens and Edward Bulwer Lytton raised money to build.
(Stevenage Museum P7858)

The new 'Our Mutual Friend' in Broadwater Crescent, replacing the original which was demolished.

felt that a hall sufficient to hold 300 people was needed and the in the following December the Corporation produced a revised plan. Three years later, in August 1956, the first community centre in Stevenage, the Broadhall Centre, was opened by Dame Evelyn Sharp, OBE, Permanent Secretary to the Ministry of Housing and Local Government. The *Echo* reported that, 'A shy child with an impish face, Jane McKay aged 5, daughter of a Broadhall Association Committee member, presented Dame Evelyn with a bouquet of red roses.'

January 1958 saw the end of an era in Shephall, as Mr and Mrs Alfred Lake retired after thirty years as licensees of the Old Red Lion on the village green. The Winter 1958 issue of *Purpose* reported that the Lakes had gone to live at Meppershall, near Shefford, adding 'In the past ten years they have seen the

Private housing by Taylor Woodrow at Ridlins, Shephall, 1960. (Stevenage Museum P3755)

character of the countryside around them change almost beyond recognition. *Purpose* extends on behalf of its readers every good wish to them both for many happy years to come.'

Also in 1958, the housing scheme at Loves Wood, designed by Messrs Clifford Culpin and Partners, was completed. As it was so near St Mary' church and rectory, the new roads here were mostly named after former rectors of the parish of Shephall. One exception was Breakspear, named after Nicholas Breakspear, a former scholar of the monastic school at St Albans abbey, who, as Hadrian IV, became the only English pope. As a new Roman Catholic church was planned for the site bounded by this street, Hydean Way and Shephall Way, it seemed an appropriate name.

Shephall village, population about 250 in 1946, became Shephall neighbourhood, with a population that would grow to ten times that by the end of the century. Apart from the church and cottages on the green, nothing remains of the old Shephall, although the manor house, Shephalbury, now the headquarters of the Coptic church in England, is well cared for and the remaining grounds have become a public park. The only reminders of the people who once lived there and the fields they tended are in the name-plates on modern roads but, thanks to Mary Spicer, the Shephall story has been preserved in her book, *Tyme Out of Mind.*

The village of Aston, close neighbour of Shephall, did not fall within the New Town Master Plan, but it did lose part of its land which was taken into the designated area. Life in the village was greatly affected by the development which was going on so near at hand. Des Turner, author of *Aston: Jack Pallett's Memories and the Village History,* wrote,

> Gradually the beautiful open countryside on Aston's western and northern flanks disappeared within the encroachment of Stevenage New Town, though fortunately the Aston House parkland was selected as the town's golf centre. New developments also took place within Aston's shrinking boundaries. As the elderly inhabitants died their cottages were sold off and updated. The population almost doubled.'

The decision to make the seventeenth century Aston House the headquarters of the Stevenage Development Corporation was not popular, especially, as Brian Bostock, editor of *Aston in Your Pocket,* commented, 'In 1959 Queen Elizabeth II visited the house when she came to study the town's master plan but sadly, when the Development Corporation had no further use for the house, they demolished it.'

ROARING MEG AND WHITE HALL

In pre-new town days, Stevenage's sewage disposal and treatment works was at Roaring Meg, on the London Road, a field which was within Shephall parish. The works were totally incapable of coping with the greatly increased population of the town and sewage was pumped to a new regional sewage disposal and treatment works at Rye Meads, 14 miles to the south, near Hoddesdon. When the Roaring Meg site was filled in it became an incidental open space and was used by residents for a variety of unofficial purposes – as a place for archery practice, dog training, a practice golf-driving range, kite flying and bird-watching, to name but a few.

Also in pre-new town days, Stevenage's water supply came from the Urban District Council's pumping stations at Broomin Green (in the present Gunnels Wood Industrial Area) and on the Weston Road at Rooks Nest. It was obvious that a new water supply system would be needed with the development of the new town. So a major new pumping station was built at White Hall, south of the village of Aston. From the bore holes, 350 feet deep in the chalk there, the water was pumped by a rising main to a new underground reservoir, holding four million gallons, at Pin Green, highest point of land in Stevenage at 450 feet above sea level. From the reservoir, water was pumped up into an 85 ft high water tower holding half-a-million gallons, from whence it was gravity fed to domestic and other properties in the town. The Pin Green facility was opened in 1952.

CHAPTER EIGHT
The town centre

THE 1949 MASTER PLAN had promised a new town centre for Stevenage, where there would be 'big shops and ... cinemas and theatres, the new town hall and other public and cultural buildings, including the principal Anglican church.' However, the project had been bedevilled by disagreement and progress was very slow. From the beginning the Urban District Council, the County Council and others had objected to the proposed location of the new town centre, suggesting that it should be further to the east, nearer the new housing areas. Although the Minister of Town and Country Planning had approved the site, he considered the area too large and plans had to be re-drawn. He was also concerned about the the viability of the new shops in the early days, before there was a sufficient body of new residents to justify their existence and expressed the fear that people would continue shopping in the old town High Street. Balchin quotes a somewhat unethical letter from the Ministry, dated 19 June, 1951,

> The essential complement of your proposals for the new town centre of Stevenage is, of course, your policy of reducing the status and competition of the old centre ... we feel that further definitive study must be given to the problem, so that effective action can be taken to this end as the phased development of the new centre proceeds.

The town centre plan was drawn up by a team of three, the Corporation's Chief Architect Clifford Holliday, with his predecessor, Gordon Stephenson and Clarence Stein, the American architect who had designed the town of Radburn, New Jersey, where houses and traffic were segregated. There were arguments about many aspects of the plan, including height of buildings, car

Aerial view of Town Centre, late 1970s. (Stevenage Museum PP851)

parking and, dominating the whole debate, whether or not the town centre should be traffic-free, for pedestrians only. The architects, although still with some doubts, decided that it should. The original team members then moved on and Donald Reay became Chief Architect and Planner. He continued working on the plan and submitted it to the Board, who agreed it on 7 October 1952 and instructed that detailed planning should continue.

Meanwhile, the Dr Felton episode had erupted and Sir Thomas Bennett had taken over as chairman of the Board. At a special meeting on 19 December 1952, he asked for alternative plans to be drawn up. One of his reasons was the evident dislike of the idea of a pedestrian centre by many of the big stores, upon whom the success of the town centre would depend. At that time it was assumed that most people would arrive at the town centre by foot, bicycle or bus and the importance of having bus stops close to the shops was emphasised.

The next stage of the saga occurred when Sir Thomas Bennett resigned and his place was taken by Sir Roydon Dash, who was less rigid in his opposition to the pedestrian plan. By this time, too, more Board members had changed their views and were in favour of it. In July 1953 the Board agreed to look at it again. However, following advice from spokesmen from the commercial world, they voted by a small majority at their meeting on 15 August to keep the vehicular scheme. News of the decision was made public and new residents were generally pleased that at last things seemed to be moving on. They decided to press the County Council to build its projected new central library as early as possible and at a meeting on 19 November 1953, discussed with Miss Lorna Paulin, County Librarian, the possibility of providing mobile or temporary libraries in the new areas. The small library in Orchard Road had hardly been sufficient for the old town and was now struggling to cope with the new influx.

Then there was another change of direction. The Urban District Council, whose two members on the Corporation Board, Philip Ireton, a Labour member and Major Arthur Howard, a Conservative, were both now in favour of the pedestrian scheme, decided to try to find a way of reversing the last decision. In the end it was agreed that the Stevenage Residents' Federation should organise a meeting at which the public could, for the first time, have their say. The meeting, advertised under the heading 'What kind of Town Centre do You want?' was held at the town hall, in Old Stevenage on 15 January 1954 and the result was overwhelming support for the pedestrian option from those who attended. It has to be said that many people, especially in the old town, did not have strong views either way. One problem which resulted from the pedestrian-only design is the view from St George's Way, which shows only the uninspiring backs of shops and other buildings.

Meanwhile, officials at the Ministry of Town and Country Planning were being required by the Treasury to cut down on spending and to this end they were asking for the area of the town centre to be reduced, together with other alterations. The Board authorised Leonard Vincent, its deputy chief architect, and Eric Claxton, deputy chief engineer, to produce an amended plan, which they did by April 1954. A small group of members and officers of the Corporation who went to look at the pedestrian shopping centre in Lijnbaan, near Rotterdam, and later the Vallingby centre in Stockholm, returned full of enthusiasm, particularly as shopkeepers in these centres had expressed their support for the scheme. In December that year, the Ministry gave its approval and work could begin.

Leonard Vincent had taken over as Chief Architect and Planning Officer in 1954 and he now worked on the outline plan for the town centre as a whole, with others in his department producing detailed designs for the southern section, which would be started first. In order to build the new

Leonard Vincent, CBE. (John Vincent)

town centre, the large detached houses in London Road and Bedwell Lane were gradually demolished. Ray Gorbing, who was appointed to design the first phase, found that the large garden where the Town Square was to be built contained a number of mature trees and wherever possible these were retained. Only two were moved, one a full-grown walnut and the other a catalpa, both of which were re-planted in the square.

By March 1955 the Corporation had let contracts for the roads around the town centre and work had begun. The first major contract went to Harry Neal Ltd and the two main sub-contracts to Franki-Pile Co. Ltd for pile driving and foundations, and to Eagan's for reinforced concrete frames. The first stage of the town centre to be built would include national multiple stores, department stores, banks and shops. However, the years of argument and indecision had held up progress to such an extent that it was thought unlikely that the town centre shops could start trading before 1958. The ever-increasing population would have to continue managing without main shopping facilities. The only thing that the Corporation could do was to invite mobile shops to operate in the new neighbourhoods, which by then included Monks Wood and Roebuck, and to persuade the London Transport Bus company to increase its services to the old town.

Once work had started on the site, the Corporation ran a competition for street names for the town centre, with a closing date of 18 June, 1955. The plans were displayed at number 114, High Street, the temporary location for the Corporation Estate Office and the place to which many prospective new residents first came to find out about life in Stevenage. Most arrived by train and walked down the High Street from the station in Julians Road, no doubt wondering where the expected new houses were.

Unsurprisingly, the town centre development was not without its problems. The sub-soil of the site which had been chosen for the town centre was extremely porous, so that concrete piles had to be driven down to about 70 feet (21 m) before foundations could be laid. In some places this was not successful, as piles were simply disappearing into the soft earth and at one point a hidden underground spring suddenly gushed up alarmingly. Eventually vast quantities of anhydrous cement were pumped in to form a solid, impermeable base. There was also great difficulty in obtaining piles. The original plan had been to have them cast in a plant in the Midlands, but the mid 1950s were years of strikes and international crises. Transporting 70-feet-long, solid concrete piles across country, during a petrol shortage was out of the question. The solution decided upon was to cast them on site and this was done. Tragically, one man lost his life there, when he was crushed against a wall.

In 1957 there was a shortage of building materials; copper was unobtainable, lead was in short supply and very expensive. As a result, there were times when felt had to be used for roofing and flashings, giving an inferior finish and, of course, being less durable. As for the architects, their department was understaffed to cope with such a major and complex project. Again, they often worked all night to produce a small amendment to a plan, in order to avoid laying-off men or machinery. They were grateful for the goodwill and understanding of the contractor Harry Neal Ltd who was much more co-operative than some of the earlier housing contractors. Fortunately the multiple store clients were also very understanding, making for a 'happy contract'.

Although good progress was now being made, there was disappointment for residents in July 1956 when it was announced that the new central library had been 'shelved'. Philip Ireton took up the matter with the County Council, pointing out that the existing service of a mobile library was quite inadequate for a town the size of Stevenage. As a result, a new, large trailer library was provided, which could be towed to a site, plugged into an external power point and allowed to stay there all day. It was an improvement on the previous fleeting visits but still unsatisfactory. The town's readers were not the only ones to be upset. The news came as a blow to the Hospital Campaign Committee, which had been led to expect that the County Council would provide a building big enough to house both the library and a hospital out-patients centre.

The first meeting of the Hospital Campaign Committee, held in St Andrew's Church Hall, Bedwell, on 19 April 1956 had been well supported. Harry Luxton, Chairman of the Federation's Health Committee and agent for the local constituency Labour Party, had read out a long list of people and organisations supporting the campaign and commented that everybody was interested

Mobile clinic. (Stevenage Museum P3981)

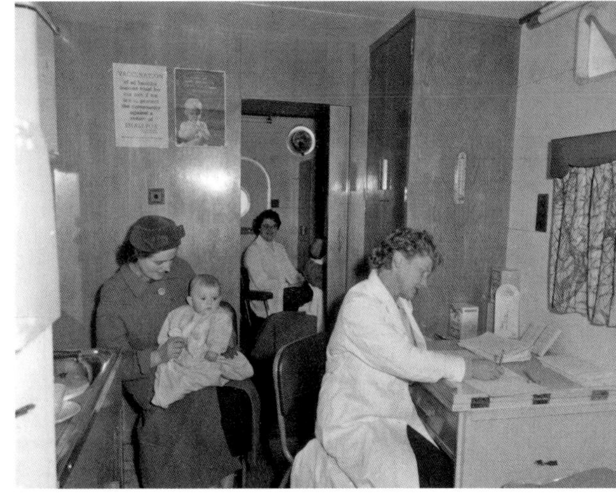
Interior of mobile clinic. (Stevenage Museum P3983)

in having a hospital in Stevenage – except the officials in Whitehall. Cllr Mrs Renee Short, the guest speaker, had said that Stevenage was not included in the hospital building programme for the next three years and she thought that Stevenage might have to wait perhaps ten years. At a campaign meeting on 2 July, Dr M Trosser stated that there was a delay of two years for tonsils and adenoids operations in Hitchin and six months delay for priority cases. Those cases assigned to Paddington Green Hospital in London had to wait only six to nine weeks. He also referred to the 'almost non-existent' psychiatry service in the district. The Three Counties Hospital at Arlesey was the nearest but very difficult to reach by public transport.

The campaign was being well-supported by donations from the public and a petition was circulating, which it was hoped to present to the Minister of Health. A campaign stall set up in the old town market place, 'attracted hundreds of signatories, about 75% of whom were from the old town and nearby villages. Over 3,000 signatures had been counted by July 2 and the majority were then yet to be called in.' Martin Maddan, Conservative MP for the Hitchin Division, agreed to support the Campaign and, on 24 July, at the House of Commons, he met the Stevenage deputation, consisting of Harry Luxton, Dr Deneys Swayne of Stevenage, Dr Allan of Knebworth, Ernest Wimpress representing the churches, Cllr Kathleen Newman, Hilda Lawrence (Secretary), Mick Cotter (Chairman) and Winifred Fowler. They were presented to Mr Turton, Minister of Health and gave him the hospital petition, with 5,912 signatures. The meeting was followed by tea on the terrace and they returned home feeling optimistic, but there was still no date for building the hospital.

Stevenage was beginning to attract attention from all over the world. On 15 and 20 July 1956, industrialists and trade unionists from Canada, Nigeria, South Africa, New Zealand, India, Australia, Ceylon, Singapore, Northern Rhodesia, British Guiana and the British Isles visited Stevenage under the aegis of the Duke of Edinburgh's Study Conference on Human Problems of Industrial Communities. They met about twenty people from Stevenage, covering a wide range of interests, including medicine, welfare, teaching, industry and local government. Social Clubs and the Residents' Federation were represented.

Among other questions, the visitors asked about hospital facilities, whether there were too many churches, the place of married women in industry, the incidence of juvenile delinquency and if there were any particular grouses against industry. The Revd D L Howells, priest-in-charge of St Mary's, Shephall, said that church attendance was if anything higher in Stevenage than in other areas and that, though the number of churches in the town might appear excessive now, it would not be when the population target was fully realised. Tom Hampson, the Corporation's Social Relations Officer, pointed out that cinema circuits, theatre companies and the large multiple stores would not come to the town at this comparatively early stage of its development. Somewhat strangely, in answer to a question about social activities, there seems to have been an assumption that these were poorly attended, a lack of support which could be put down to the attractions of television, then still a new and exciting medium, and gardening, which was from the early days a highly popular activity. This contrasts with earlier reports of well-supported social events, despite the shortage of suitable accommodation.

On 30 August came the news that new town residents had been fearing. Sir Roydon Dash, chairman of the Corporation Board, and his deputy, Sir Arthur Rucker, announced at a meeting at Aston House that rent increases would come into effect on 1 October. There was to be a rent rebate scheme to help the least well-off, but he admitted that it was very limited. He also said that all the new towns, jointly, had put every possible argument to the Ministry to avoid the increase.

The Residents' Federation believed that one reason for the increase was to pay for mistakes made by the Corporation in some of their building projects. They were not taken unaware by the announcement and had already, on 1 August, sent a deputation consisting of Mr Luxton, Michael Cotter, Mr Morgans and Ken Douglas, to the House of Commons, where they had asked their MP, Martin Maddan, at short notice to meet them. He was unable to do so because of a previous engagement. After a disappointing afternoon, they eventually found a sympathetic ear, that of E Redhead, MP for Walthamstow, who undertook to write immediately to the Rt Hon Duncan Sandys, Minister of Housing and Local Government, making the point that the increase in rents might well seriously discourage people from living in new towns. The Federation emphasised their desire to be constructive and to be able to make alternative proposals, but to do this they needed to see full details of the Corporation's housing accounts which, they said, should be publicly available in the same way as those of the elected local authority.

In the September 1956 issue of the *Stevenage Echo*, Hilda Lawrence, a prominent member of the Residents' Federation, wrote:

> I read an article in a daily paper which said that a man, wife and child could live on £12 0s 0d per week, provided that he did not pay more than £1 10s 0d [£1.50] for rent. Here the average working class of Stevenage is dreading 1 October. Our rent will not be £1 4s 0d [£1.20] but an average of £2 6s 0d [£2.30] a week. We have had an increase imposed upon us of 3s 8d [18p] plus a 1s 9d [9p] rate per week. When our husbands came to work in Stevenage they were forced to take a decrease in pay. The reason for this, we are told, is that Stevenage is outside the London area, therefore 'country' rates are paid. Does this mean that the commodities produced here are sold at a lower prices?

Examples:

	London	Stevenage
Shoulder of lamb (English)	2s 6d per lb	3s 6d per lb
Tin corned beef	2s 9d	3s 0d
Cooked shoulder of ham	4s 8d	8s 0d
Butter	from 3s 0d	from 3s 4d
Typhoo tea	6s 4d	6s 8d
Runner beans	10d	1s 2d
Mandarin oranges	tin 1s 0d	tin 1s 4d
Peaches	2s 0d	2s 2d
Apricots	1s 3d	1s 9d

The Residents' Federation had many questions, such as why the rents of Corporation houses were so much higher than those of Council houses. They pointed out that the answer was doubly important because eventually the Urban District Council would take over from the Development Corporation. Harry Luxton, Mrs Hilda Lawrence, Cllr Alf Luhman and Mr K Douglas compiled 'a list of conditions causing hardship to new town tenants, emphasising provincial rates of pay, hire purchase burdens, fear of redundancy in a town where most workers relied on overtime earnings to carry them from week to week.' Other new towns, including Basildon, were also facing higher rents and it was decided to invite them to join in deputations to the Ministry.

On Friday 14 October 1956, a march against rent increases took place in Stevenage. Demonstrations of this kind were very uncommon in the country as a whole at this time, let alone in rural Hertfordshire. Protesters with banners marched along the High Street and London Road, resulting in the disruption

Demonstrators against new town rent increases gathering in the old town. (Stevenage Museum PP213)

of traffic all around. Afterwards, there were angry letters in the local press, one from the old town coach proprietor, Albert Candler, who was taking '36 hard-working Stevenage ladies to a London theatre'. They had paid for their tickets, and didn't want to be late for the outing, which they had been looking forward to for months. When the coach was brough to a standstill, some irresponsible people put their children in front of it and one man deliberately damaged the coach by scraping his bicycle along it. Mr Candler said that he was sorry if they had a grievance but it was not the fault of the coach party and there was nothing they could do about it anyway. Another letter from one of the organisers said that the traffic chaos was the fault of the police who had directed them to take a route that was bound to cause disruption. They had planned another route, but were refused permission to use it after objections from a 'middle class street'. He added that he was proud of the marchers.

Before a landlord could impose a rent increase, notification of the date and amount of the increase had to be sent to tenants, in writing. The Residents' Federation urged all new town tenants to seal their letter boxes so that the notification could not be delivered, which many did. However, the Corporation reasoned correctly that when tenants realised that they were sealing their letter boxes against the delivery of everything, including letters from family members and friends, they would quickly unseal them. That is exactly what happened. The notices were then delivered and the increase went ahead.

In November 1956 a deputation went to the House of Commons, hoping that their grievances could be aired through the Conservative MP for Hitchin constituency (which included Stevenage), Martin Maddan. They felt that the visit was valuable, but gained the impression that their MP was not wholly committed to their cause. The Urban District Council called a public meeting at which there was a unanimous vote for a public inquiry to 'call upon the government to examine fully the financial structure of the new towns in order to prevent further large sums of money being demanded from the rate-payers.' This was supported by the Amalgamated Engineering Union, the Amalgamated Society of Woodworkers, the Stevenage Trades Council, the National Union of Sheet Metal Workers and Braziers, Bedwell Ward Labour Party, and its women's section, the National Assembly of Women, Old Stevenage Labour Party, Broadwater Friends' and Neighbours' Club, St Andrew's church, the Union of Postal Workers, Shephall Labour Party, NUGMW (Gas Workers) together with the delegates from various Residents' Associations throughout the town. The Revd G Heath, of St Andrew's church, Bedwell, said, 'It is in the grand tradition of John Ball ... that the priest should march with his flock to voice the woes and strive to right the wrongs of his flock.'

Not everyone was in favour of the proposal. Tom Hampson, Social Relations Officer for the Stevenage Development Corporation, representing the Stevenage

Nature Wardens, and Geoffrey Hughes, a member of the Corporation Board, representing Stevenage Conservative Central Committee, voted against it. There were also many residents, mainly in the old town, who did not get involved in the protest campaign, being largely unaffected by the rent rises.

The Corporation itself had grave concerns about the high rents, which it expressed in several of its Annual Reports. It tried, also, to explain to residents why Corporation rents were higher than Council house rents. The reasons included the fact that Corporation houses were built at post-war costs and there was no existing stock of older houses to provide another source of income. Also, the Urban District Council could subsidise rents from their income from rates, whereas the Corporation had no such resource.

In the end, the government held firm and refused to alter its policy on rent and rates, but the rent rebate scheme was widened in 1958 to include more people and eventually the Minister of Housing and Local Government did make grants to new town development corporations to enable them to keep rent increases to a reasonable level.

Both nationally and internationally 1956 had been a turbulent year. British troops were fighting to maintain order in those colonies which still existed, most notably at this time in Cyprus. In June came the beginning of the 'Suez Crisis' and the year ended with the ill-fated Hungarian uprising which was severely crushed by Soviet Russia. Many Hungarians were killed, but over 100,000 escaped and, on Friday 23 November, some of them ended up in Stevenage. They were housed initially at the Monks Wood Hostel: help of all kinds was given by people throughout the town, including the Women's Voluntary Service (WVS), Bedwell Community Association, tradesmen who gave fruit, cigarettes, free cinema seats, Stevenage Town Football club which offered free facilities for training, and many others. By good fortune the Corporation had on its staff a Mr Sachs, who was himself Hungarian, and he was able to help the Ministry of Labour with their interviews.

The town centre development was now making steady progress. In July 1957 came the good news that the Hertfordshire County Council had approved the purchase of a site for a new central library and health centre from the Stevenage Development Corporation. This was to be in Southgate, a name which caused much confusion in the Post Office before the days of postcodes, when mail intended for Stevenage library ended up in Southgate, north London.

Stevenage often featured in the media, especially when new industry or government departments decided to move to the new town. Residents became slightly blasé when reports such as this, dated On 21 October 1957 appeared in *The Times*; 'The Department of Scientific and Industrial Research, has announced that the fuel research station at Greenwich which was set up in 1917, will be replaced by a new research station at Stevenage, estimated to cost about £750,000.

Work on the site had already started.' There was much greater excitement on 23 May 1958, when Francis Cammaerts, former Special Operations Executive [SOE] agent, hero of the French Resistance and currently headmaster of Alleyne's Grammar School, appeared on the immensely popular television show, 'This is your life', chaired by Eamonn Andrews. The head boy, David Harding, also took part, greatly impressing his fellow-pupils. Most Stevenage residents were previously unaware of Cammaerts' distinguished career, not least because of his own reticence and modesty, but many boys who were his pupils at Alleyne's were inspired by his wide-ranging knowledge and his enthusiasm for learning.

At least one other person living in Stevenage at this time had been involved in secret work during the Second World War. Elizabeth Poston, composer and musicologist, best known for her work on Christmas carols, had been employed throughout the war by the BBC. She was given responsibility for a scheme, devised by Churchill, which involved sending and receiving coded messages in music to occupied countries in Europe via gramophone records. It was work demanding intense concentration and precision, as a mistake could result in the discovery and deaths of agents overseas. She and Francis Cammaerts had much in common but, having signed the Official Secrets Act, neither was prepared to reveal details of their wartime activities. Both contributed immensely to the local community; Francis Cammaerts through his promotion of educational travel and exchange visits, and Elizabeth Poston by supporting music education through the Rural Music Schools movement and the formation of voluntary organisations such as the Stevenage Music Society.

On 22 May 1958, a conference was held at the Ministry of Housing and Local Government offices in Whitehall, where details of the new town centre were at last made public. *The Times* reported that Sir Roydon Dash told the audience that Stevenage now had a population of 30,000 and would be fully developed with twice that number in about six or seven years' time. He expected that the first stage of the centre would be completed early in the autumn.

R S McDougall, the Corporation's General Manager and former Hertfordshire County Treasurer, said that Stevenage was fortunate in having a few large industries of worldwide repute already established. Soon a by-pass would be built to the west of the railway and a new railway station would be constructed opposite the new town centre. The Great North Road would then cease to be the through road and the old town of Stevenage would become a neighbourhood shopping district. The new town centre would be less than a quarter of a mile from the industrial area. In some ways it was a planner's dream. Care had been taken to preserve the trees. There would be free parking space for 3,000 cars.

Leonard Vincent said there were one or two other places in Europe with similar pedestrian shopping centres, but Stevenage was the first in England to 'go the whole hog' in this respect.

Leonard Vincent (fifth from left) and colleagues. (Stevenage Museum 0562)

Town centre shops. (Stevenage Museum PP1184)

The Co-op in the Town Square in 1958. (Stevenage Museum P6537)

They had decided that the right solution to the problem was to compress the shopping population which, with the people of outlying villages, might total 120,000, into a canopied area. The canopies over the shops would give complete protection to pedestrians in wet weather. The new town centre occupied a site of 55 acres, about half of which would be the central shopping, bounded by four traffic roads. The shops would face inwards on to pedestrian ways.

The first phase of the town centre was finished in June 1958 and that month the first of the new shops opened. This was the Co-operative Department Store, complete with a large and attractive mural. Other multiple stores followed in July. Alan Cudmore was with the Development Corporation from 1957 and its chief commercial surveyor from 1978. In *Stevenage Voices,* he explains the Corporation's system of leasing commercial properties:

> Stevenage town centre was unique, even within the New Town movement, because we were, as landlords, in direct relationship with traders. No land had been put out to property companies to develop and every tenant was a lessee of the Corporation and we could, therefore, through leases, control the actual trades and specify what they were permitted to sell ... By and large it worked and it also gave the opportunity to adjust rents according to the profit level on turnover of the individual traders.

Some of the planners' original ideas had had to be changed during the course of construction work: for example, when the architects designed the first phase of the town centre, they planned for a district heating system which would serve all the premises from one boiler house located in the Southgate car park. However, the multiple traders rejected this idea, insisting on having their own heating plants, so the scheme was modified to serve only the southern section of Queensway and Market Place. For the Town Square paving, Ray Gorbing had the idea of incorporating 'a little bit of old London' by using granite setts bought from one of the London boroughs which no longer required them. The setts were laid on a bed of large aggregate around the existing and newly-planted trees.

'Joy Ride' sculpture. (Stevenage Museum P2823)

By July 1958 the Town Square was completed and the clock tower was under construction, but the Corporation felt that something extra was needed, something that would symbolise the birth of a new town. Several ideas were discussed before it was decided to approach a well-known Czech-born sculptor, Franta Belsky, and ask him to create an artwork. The result was a bronze statue of a young mother with a little boy on her back, which he called 'Joy Ride'. It was unveiled by the Hon. David Bowes Lyon, uncle of the Queen and Lord Lieutenant of Hertfordshire, on 30 September 1958. Ray Gorbing was intrigued by the varied reactions of onlookers: 'Ridiculous', 'A downright shame', 'It looks dull and a bit rusty,' 'Very nice indeed' and 'Gives our new Town Centre an air of distinction' were some of the remarks he overheard. Sir Roydon Dash, speaking at the unveiling, said,

> We have tried not merely to build shops and offices but to achieve in the town centre a unity of design which will make it equal, in the modern idiom, to the best building of the past. It seemed desirable to us to place here something which would, as a work of art, reflect the youth and vigour of the new community and give expression to the alliance of beauty and practical need at which we aim.

The statue was to become the symbol of the new towns movement.

Other concerns were still waiting to be addressed. Complaints about the Great North Road continued and one letter in *The Times,* accusing the Corporation of neglecting to improve it, produced a somewhat irate response from McDougall on 23 September 1958. He pointed out that the A1, the Great North Road, was a trunk road, responsibility for which rested with the Minister of Transport, not with the Development Corporation. Furthermore, he added, not only the 'planners' but the whole of Stevenage had been pressing the Minister for a by-pass for many years. He was able to say that construction of this road was scheduled to begin in a few months.

A joyful event took place in the newly-completed Town Square on 14 December 1958, when the Swedish Ambassador, Hr Hagglof, presented a Christmas tree to the town. This was a gift from the people of Vallingby, a suburb of Stockholm, with whom Stevenage had established a link of Friendship. The Ambassador then switched on the illuminations to begin the Festival of Light celebration, something which had never been held in Stevenage before. Several hundred people watched Katrina Ullen, as Queen of Light, lead a procession of white-clad attendants carrying electric candles, after which massed choirs from all the Anglican churches in the town took part in a carol service. In return, the Corporation sent a metal arch made in Stevenage, to be erected in the Vallingby centre, plus sprigs of mistletoe with which to decorate it and suggestions as to its purpose.

But tragedy struck the day before Christmas Eve, when one of the Irish building workers was reported missing after a drinking session with his workmates. His body was found in the Stevenage Brook at Roaring Meg and it was thought that he slipped on the bank, which was sodden with rain and fell in. So the town centre project claimed a second victim.

Monday 20 April 1959 was a day to remember in the development of the new town. It was the day that Her Majesty Queen Elizabeth II first visited Stevenage, to declare the first fully pedestrianised town centre in Europe open. The visit is commemorated by a plaque that she unveiled on the clock tower in Town Square and the naming of the principal pedestrian walkway 'Queensway'. The first 55 shops had opened in time for Christmas 1958. By the time of the Queen's visit four months later, 86 shops were trading, including Boots the chemists, a Co-Operative department store, Fine Fare and Sainsbury Supermarkets, W H Smiths, Woolworth's, a main post office, a public house, two banks and a café. The central bus station, public car parks and public toilets were also open.

The official programme for the Queen's visit contained an up-beat resumé of the new town's progress to date:

> Stevenage today is a thriving community of nearly 35,000 people ... in an area of 6,100 acres, nearly 3 miles from north to south and almost 2 miles from east to west ...
>
> Already the first stage [of the town centre] has been completed and plans are being prepared for the final stage of the shopping area. The inner shopping centre will be ringed by offices and public buildings including the Town Hall, library, clinic, police and fire stations, hospital outpatients' department, swimming pool, dance hall, youth centre and parish church, some of which are already under construction. All this will be in an area of about 100 acres.
>
> The population of the town is increasing at the rate of about 5,000 a year. Day by day, week in, week out, 5 loaded removal vans enter the town. Stevenage's prime purpose is to house London families and most of the newcomers hail from either the densely populated inner boroughs – Lambeth, Hammersmith, St Pancras, Marylebone, Holborn – and from the East End and dockland areas like Poplar, Bow, Mile End and Limehouse, or from the industrial suburbs of Acton, Willesden, Kilburn, Hornsey, Tottenham and Islington. But people also come from Chelsea and Hampstead, Mordern, Twickenham and Wimbledon, Harrow and Barnet and indeed, from all parts of the Greater London area. Londoners get priority for both employment and housing and without having work in the town there is little prospect of a would-be immigrant being able to obtain a house to rent.

> In addition to the constant stream of newcomers, the natural increase of population is already running at the rate of 700 a year, which means that almost every day two babies are born in the town. More than three-quarters of the new residents are young couples ... The birthrate in Stevenage is amongst the highest in the country, being twice the national average ... The death rate is less than half the national figure ... soon there will be as many teenagers in Stevenage as would normally be found in a town of 150,000 people.'
>
> Since building began more than 7,500 houses have been finished and in the last three years houses have been completed and occupied at the rate of about 1,200 a year ... over 80 different types of family houses with gardens, also a few bungalows for old people, maisonettes in the shopping centres and a variety of flats ... as far as possible the Corporation leaves prospective tenants to choose the type ... a measure of the town's prosperity is the large number of car owners. More than 2,600 garages have already been built and nearly 600 more are under construction ... most built in 'compounds'.
>
> Already the industrial area contains factories of varying sizes which employ as few as ten or as many as four thousand people ... also two government laboratories and a Post Office depot ... many bear nationally-known names and some have world-wide reputations ... products include mechanical and electrical engineering equipment, electronic parts and products, woodwork, pens and pencils, plastics, photographic apparatus and food ... Today Stevenage employs in industry and trade about 14,000 men and women in modern and hygienic conditions. Industrial welfare is highly regarded. One factory employing many married women has a day nursery; three have extensive sports grounds ... Stevenage Inter-Works Sports and Social Organisation, with over twenty member clubs promotes competitions in outdoor and indoor sports and games. Footpaths and cycle ways which pass under and over the Great North Road link the Industrial Area with the Town Centre and neighbourhood roads.
>
> The Hertfordshire County Council, as the Local Education Authority, has a high reputation both at home and abroad ... it has already built seven new primary schools, three new secondary modern schools and a grammar school for girls and enlarged Alleyne's Grammar School. These schools provide over 5,000 places but three times that figure will be needed when the town is complete.

Attended by her Lady-in-Waiting, Private Secretary and Equerry, the Queen arrived by car at Town Square, where a large crowd of cheering, flag-waving residents welcomed her, at 2.45 pm. The royal standard was raised on the mast-head above the clock tower by John Austin, who had recently won the Scouts' Gilt Cross for his bravery in rescuing a mother and two children from drowning. The Queen was received by her uncle, the Hon. David Bowes-Lyon, and then

Her Majesty Queen Elizabeth II in the town centre, 1959. (Stevenage Museum 0563)

Her Majesty Queen Elizabeth II visiting a house in Wigram Way, 1959. (Stevenage Museum P8064)

inspected a Guard of Honour from the Hertfordshire Regiment of the Territorial Army. A number of local people were presented to her, including the High Sheriff for Hertfordshire; the Lord Bishop of the Diocese of St Albans; the Rt Hon. Henry Brooke, MP, Minister for Housing and Local Government; Martin Maddan, Member of Parliament for Hitchin; members and officers of Stevenage

Development Corporation, Hertfordshire County Council and Stevenage Urban District Council; representatives of Stevenage and District Industrial Employers' Group, building companies, building workers, town centre traders and local churches. She was then presented with a bouquet by Yvonne Hide, daughter of Councillor Frank Hide, Chairman of Stevenage Urban District Council, and Mrs Anne Hide.

Before leaving the town centre, the Queen visited the butcher's shop of W H Shepherd, in Market Place, then went on to the English Electric Aviation Systems site, in the Gunnels Wood Industrial Area, where a ground-to-air missile system was on show. Representatives of employers and employees of local industrial firms and of trade unions were presented to her there. After leaving the English Electric site with the cheers of employees and their families ringing in her ears, the Queen visited the Caxton Way factory of Fleming Radio (Developments) Ltd. The next stop was Bedwell Community Centre where representatives of the local community, social and welfare organisations, residents and schools were presented. In Wigram Way, Shephall, the Queen was invited into a Development Corporation rented house and at the Oaks Cross shopping centre in Longmeadow, Broadwater, into a Corporation rented bungalow for the elderly and into the 'Pied Piper' public house, where the manager, former professional footballer Wilf Mannion, invited her behind the bar to pull a pint.

During her two hour tour of the town, the Queen was greeted everywhere by enthusiastic adults and children. She then visited Aston House, headquarters of the Development Corporation, where she inspected an exhibition of plans, photographs and models showing the planning and development of the new town, before taking tea and departing for Windsor Castle.

Town Square. (Stevenage Museum)

CHAPTER NINE
Heart of a town

AN ARTICLE BY THE EDITOR, Winifred Fowler, in the January 1955 issue of the *Stevenage Echo* questioned the very basis of the plan for the new town, the neighbourhood concept. It asked, is Stevenage 'one town – or many?'

> Towns which, like Topsy, have 'just growed' usually do so around some social or geographic feature, like a market, a port, a defence point or religious building. They grow organically with the needs of their community ... With time, the town acquires its character and tradition ... security comes from belonging ... New towns start with none of this ready made cohesion ... Architecture and planning make only a frame within which a community can develop ...
>
> Stevenage is at the moment two, perhaps even three towns. The new town, which is far from merged with the old, is divided by a valley ... We want Stevenage, when it has its 60,000 souls, to be one town and not Bedwell plus Broadwater, plus Pin Green and the rest ... Somehow all of the new and the old town must be joined in a single unity.

The article was written before the building of the town centre, where the clock tower and the 'Joy Ride' sculpture have become symbolic of new Stevenage. But the question persisted – where or what is the town's heart? The answer was provided brilliantly in response to a competition initiated by the Urban District Council. At their meeting on 11 February 1957, the Council resolved to ask the Divisional Education Officer to invite local schools to submit ideas for a design and motto for a coat of arms for the town. This was done and subsequently designs submitted by pupils at Heathcote and Barclay Schools were considered by a committee, who recommended that by Michael Keulemans. A suggestion from Richard Ingell, also 15 and a pupil at the Barclay secondary modern school, resulted in the ideal motto for Stevenage: 'The Heart of a Town lies in its People'.

Subject to a few minor amendments, the design was approved by the College of Heralds, which gave the Council a Grant of Arms. The Heralds felt that the motto was too long, but the Council resolved to keep it in its entirety and the motto and coat of arms were adopted in 1958.

When the town adopted its motto 52 years ago, the coat of arms encompassed both the historic old town and the developing new one, where hundreds of young families from London were moving into newly-built houses in the Bedwell and Broadwater neighbourhoods. These became known as the 'pioneers'. Contrary to the fears of old town residents, they were, in the main, young, hard-working citizens. Journalists who interviewed them were impressed by their energy and good humour. They brought to Stevenage something of the wartime London spirit.

In many towns before the Second World War, the leading figures in the community tended to be local business and professional men. Few working-class people were able to offer themselves for election to the local authority, whose meetings were usually held in the afternoon. Most of the councillors were shopkeepers, other self-employed and retired men, with very few women, who had stood for election as 'Independent' candidates. Stevenage was no exception to the general rule.

All that changed in the 1950s with the development of the new town, bringing with it a reversal of Stevenage's former social structure and politics. A large influx of building and factory workers from London replaced most of the business and professional class, leaving almost none of the traditional authority figures to turn to. As a result, the new community had to find leaders from its own ranks and these soon emerged – men and women of high calibre and great ability who, had they remained in their London boroughs, would in all probability never have had an opportunity to realise their potential. Among the first pioneers in the early 1950s were married building workers who, rather than remain on the interminable waiting lists of the London boroughs, got themselves jobs with one of the large building companies, such as Terson's or Carlton's, working on a Stevenage construction site.

Initially, the big building contractors bussed their employees from various pick-up points in London each morning and back again at the end of the working day. However, the Corporation was anxious to build up a large, permanent force of building workers resident in the town where thousands of new houses, shops, offices, factories, schools and other buildings were due to be constructed for some years ahead. Builders were therefore some of the first to be allocated the houses they themselves were building. They had anything from six months to a year to wait before they and their families could move into the first homes of their own, but when they did, it was into brand new houses which they themselves had built with pride and with their own hands.

Among them was Dunkirk Veteran Alf Luhman, a carpenter, from the London borough of Hoxton, who started work in Stevenage in June 1951. He, with his wife, Ann, son, Alan and daughter, Maureen, moved into their allocated house in Broxdell, Stony Hall estate, twelve months later. Thrilled with her new home, Ann told a reporter that for the first day or two she walked around the house, from room to room and into the garden, pinching herself for fear that it was all a dream.

Alf, who quickly became active in the setting up of a tenants' association, was the first new town resident to be elected, as a Labour Party candidate, to the Stevenage Urban District Council. He went on to become chairman of the Council's Parks and Entertainments Committee and then, in 1959, chairman of the Council itself, later becoming, for a year, the town's mayor. Having left the building trade, he was appointed manager of a shirt-making factory in the Gunnels Wood Industrial Area. He also served on the governing body of Alleyne's Grammar School for Boys.

When Alf Luhman was elected to the Urban District council in 1953, it was a small authority with only the one electoral ward. As the town's population grew with the development of new residential areas, so new wards were created and the number of councillors increased. The first residents to be elected to represent the new Bedwell ward in 1956, were Con Carey and Fred Udell, both building workers and Labour Party candidates.

Fred Udell had served in the Royal Navy's Fleet Air Arm, in the perilous convoys that took military supplies to the Soviet Union in the Second World War. He first viewed Stevenage one frosty morning in January 1951 when, 'frozen stiff', after travelling on a motor-cycle from Dagenham, east London, he visited the Development Corporation offices at Aston House to enquire about housing. He was advised that he would be eligible if he was employed by one of the Corporation's building contractors and without more ado he got a job as a bricklayer. For the next eight months he was bussed to Stevenage and back, leaving his in-laws' house in Dagenham at 5 am and walking the one and a half miles to the bus pick-up point at Chadwell Heath. For the return journey the bus left Stevenage at 5.30 pm in convoy with other private buses bound for their own pick-up points in the London area.

In June 1952 Fred and his wife, Vi, moved into their house in Abbots Grove, Bedwell, transferring later to The Dell and soon became involved in local politics. In due course Fred became vice-chairman of the Council, a member of the

Stevenage Housing Association, chairman of Stevenage Labour Party and chairman of the Stevenage-Ingelheim Link Committee.

Another building worker, Labour Party activist and Bedwell resident who became a local councillor was Michael Cotter. Originally from Cork, in the Republic of Ireland, Mick Cotter started work in the new town in June 1951 as an employee of Terson's and was bussed to Stevenage from Stoke Newington each day for eight months. He, with his wife, Anne, and their three young sons, had been living in Hornsey, in grossly overcrowded conditions in Anne's mother's house, facing a seven or eight year wait for council accommodation. They moved into Rockingham Way, Monks Wood estate, in February 1952 and joined the Monks Wood Residents' Association. Mick became its delegate to the Stevenage Residents' Federation, of which he was later chairman. In 1957 he was elected to the Urban District Council, becoming chairman of the Housing Committee for a number of years, then chairman of the Council itself, was elected a member of Hertfordshire County Council, appointed a member of the Board of Stevenage Development Corporation in 1964 and later elected mayor of the Borough of Stevenage.

Bill and Hilda Lawrence, from Leytonstone, moved into Rockingham Way in 1953. Bill was an engineer who had obtained work with W H Saunders (Electronics) Ltd, at their new factory in Gunnels Wood Road. Later he worked for British Aerospace, which was very good in giving its councillor employees reasonable time off to fulfil their civic duties. A Labour Party candidate, Bill was elected to the Urban District Council in 1961 and served continuously until he retired 38 years later. He had served a term as chairman of the Urban District Council and, later, was twice elected mayor of the Borough. After his retirement he was made an Honorary Alderman.

Cllrs Bill and Hilda Lawrence.

Bill's wife, Hilda, is a remarkable woman, a campaigner, who made an enormous contribution to the town and to the wider community for some 45 years. She began her public life as elected secretary first of the Monks Wood Residents' Association and then of the Stevenage Residents' Federation. She was for a time editor of the Federation's newspaper, the *Stevenage Echo*, and was actively involved in the campaigns for a hospital, a traffic-free town centre, nursery school facilities and other needs. Standing as a Labour Party candidate, Hilda was elected to both the Urban District Council and the Hertfordshire County Council.

Connie Rees.
(Stevenage Museum
P13097)

Connie Rees is another outstanding personality, whose contribution to the development of the town and the well-being of many of its residents has been immense. She arrived in Stevenage in September 1952, 'straight from the maternity ward of the Royal London Hospital', with a two-and-a-half week old baby son, Jonathan, and husband, Huw, who had been appointed a senior probation office in the town. In London, Connie had been a housing officer in Holborn, working under Mary Tabor who, in 1951, was appointed Stevenage Development Corporation's Housing Manager. Connie and Huw were living in a requisitioned flat in Hackney when they were allocated a three-bedroomed house in the Stony Hall estate.

Connie soon became active in the new neighbourhood, helping to start the Bedwell Tenants' Association and the Bedwell Community Association. She helped to set up the Town Forum, where representatives of the residents could question representatives of the Development Corporation, the Urban District Council and other bodies. In 1956 she started the Stevenage Citizens Advice Bureau. Despite suffering from multiple sclerosis, which was diagnosed in 1963, she has continued to serve the community in so many ways that it is impossible to list them all, but mention must be made of the two publications which she and Huw compiled to record the early days of the new town. *The History Makers* was published in 1991 and *Stevenage Pioneers* in 2006. They include stories of hardship in post-war London: some families living in two rooms with a shared bathroom, some with only one (cold water) tap, some sharing a lavatory and others living above rat-infested premises. Stevenage, although muddy and unfinished, offered 'fresh air everywhere', a house with a kitchen and 'best of all' – a bathroom. In 2001, Connie was awarded an MBE.

Other early pioneers who became Labour councillors included Stanley Munden, who was active in the Marymead Residents' Federation, became chairman of the Stevenage Residents' Federation and, in 1972 was elected chairman of Stevenage Urban District Council; James Cockerton, John Grice, Les Cummins, Fred Schofield and building worker Fred Millard, after whom a sheltered housing scheme in Bedwell was later named.

Among the many others who made major contributions to their new community were Basil and Maureen Wratten, who moved into the Stony Hall estate in 1950. Maureen was a particualarly conscientious social worker. She became chairman of Stony Hall Residents' Association, first chairman of the Residents' Federation and a member of the Urban District Council. In 1954 she was appointed a Justice of the Peace. Her husband, Basil, was an officer of the Development Corporation.

Mary Tabor. (Stevenage Museum P7091)

There was among the new residents a scattering of intellectuals who were interested in the new town movement. One of the most outstanding was Dr John Morris, who held the chair of ancient history at the University of London and who became president of Stevenage Residents' Federation and 'father' of the Stevenage Museum. His wife, Susan, played a major role in the Stevenage Forum and in other activities on behalf of the community.

Among the most important people in the the life of the new community were the builders. Without them, there would be no new town and they can rightly be included among the pioneers. They were not always happy and not always co-operative. Disputes and strikes on the sites were not uncommon in the 1950s. On occasions, after downing tools, the workers would march *en masse* to the Aston House headquarters of the Development Corporation to put their grievances about the contractors to the general manager of the Corporation. Some became well-known for their trades union activities, including Bert Lowe, Jim Cunningham, Jim Collman and Pat Sullivan. They, and many others, all made their mark on the history of the town.

It is impossible to name everyone who contributed to the life of the new town in its early days. Very many more than those included here gave up time and energy to help form new organisations, to serve on committees and above all, to help each other as good neighbours. One more name must be included, however, that of Mary Tabor, the Development Corporation's housing manager. Since her appointment in 1951 she had interviewed thousands of applicants and was known personally to the majority of people in the new town. Many spoke of her kindness and practical help. She was awarded the MBE in the Queen's Birthday Honours in 1956 and in the same week, was sworn in as a JP at the Hertfordshire Quarter Sessions, to serve on the Stevenage Bench.

Although the pioneers may have felt homesick for families, friends and the urban landscape of London, they had not come to a desert. In the old town were shops, doctors, schools and churches. The people living there might have been overwhelmed by the number of newcomers, their different accent and cultural background, but most were prepared at least to be helpful and some went out of their way to integrate the two communities. Robert McArthur, who came to Stevenage to teach at the Barclay School in its early days, commented, 'Discipline was difficult because we were dealing with two different cultures, but many of the kids were anxious to learn and I don't think the old town people resented the new people coming. I can't remember that feeling at all.' Some newcomers said that old town shop-keepers were unfriendly to them. It is true that the High Street had its share of eccentrics at that time, but they did not differentiate between old and new – they were off-hand with everyone! To redress the balance there were many shop assistants and others who were known throughout the town for their kindness. Notable among these was Betty Game, who worked at Thurlow's drapery shop on the corner of Albert Street and High Street. Her cheerful smile made her many new friends. In an interview for *Stevenage Voices*, she said, 'I think some of the new town people thought we didn't want them to come, so we tried to make them welcome. There was quite a lot in the press about opposition – after all, that makes news.'

As has already been noted, the vast majority of incomers to Stevenage were of one class. At the same time many middle-class residents were leaving the old town. Some were more or less forced out. Their houses in London Road, Bedwell Lane and elsewhere were marked for demolition and they decided to move away rather than accept alternative, modern accommodation which could not compare with their existing dwellings. Others left of their own accord, taking advantage of the scheme whereby the Development Corporation could be required to buy property which suffered from planning blight.

However, some stayed, not all of them entirely happy with events, but prepared to co-operate with the new regime. The former chairman of the Urban District Council, Major Arthur Howard and his family had to leave their large house, The Hermitage in London Road but were enabled to build a new

Stevenage High Street. (Stevenage Museum)

residence in Rectory Lane, on land which the Church Commissioners, Lords of the Manor of Stevenage, had made available for private development. A number of other new houses were built in Rectory Lane, many of which were built for ex-Development Corporation staff . There were some, too, who worked positively to bring people together, whatever their origins, as residents of one town. Dr Deneys Swayne and his wife, Dr Margaret, who lived at High Trees in North Road, made it their mission to integrate the old and new communities, particularly through social activities. Dr Deneys' great enthusiasm was the Lytton Players and the works of Gilbert and Sullivan. He became famous for one of the first questions he asked new patients, 'Can you sing?'

Dr Margaret was much more than a doctor of medicine. She would unhesitatingly respond to a call for help and many people, with problems of all kinds, turned to her in times of trouble, confident that she would be able to suggest a way forward.

One group of people whose way of life came to an end with the development of the new town were the farmers, whose fields became housing estates. At Fairlands, Stan and Sybil Marriott were surrounded by new roads, new houses and new people. The farmhouse is an historically important, timber-framed building dating to the early 1660s. In 1951 the Development Corporation served a compulsory purchase order on the owners, Gonville and Caius College, Cambridge, but allowed the Marriotts to remain as tenants until 1968. Farming in the midst of a developing new town is not easy, as children, and even some adults, rampage through crops; nor is it pleasant to watch your last herd of cattle being sold off and to know that soon you, too, will have to move out. But instead of being bitter Stan and Sybil made friends with the children at nearby Bedwell school and helped educate them in the ways of farming and the countryside. So great was their contribution and their kindness to the children that in 1995, after a rebuilding programme, the school was renamed 'Marriotts' in their honour.

The man most concerned to unite the old and new communities was Philip Ireton, whose name will always be remembered in the history of Stevenage. Born in the old town in 1904, he became interested in town-planning as he watched the development of Letchworth, the first garden city. He was elected to the Stevenage Urban District Council in 1937 and urged his fellow councillors to take a more practical interest in planning matters, hoping that Stevenage, which was in need of more local industry and improved facilities, would one day follow the Letchworth model. At first, his was a lone voice, but he gradually gained support. As a member of the Town and Country Planning Association he became conversant with the ideas that were being discussed by people such as Sir Patrick Abercrombie and he realised the implications for Stevenage of the Greater London Plan.

When the Development Corporation Board was set up Philip Ireton was among the first members to be appointed and the only one to continue for the full life of the Board. Although an enthusiast for the new town, he was at times unhappy with the way the Corporation operated and with some decisions that were made. He felt there would have been less local opposition and more co-operation from the Urban District Council if the Corporation had treated them with respect and listened to their suggestions, some of which were wiser than those of the Corporation. Although he was a member of the Corporation Board, he was also, and foremost, a councillor and put himself at the service of residents, helping many individuals with problems of all kinds.

When he was first elected, Labour supporters were in a minority in Stevenage and he was looked upon with suspicion or worse. As he became known and trusted, even many ardent Conservatives agreed that he was a good man. He was very keen to improve educational opportunities for all. As a pupil at the Letchmore Road Boys' School, he had wanted to go on to Alleyne's Grammar School, but had been persuaded not to by a teacher who thought his future would be in horticulture. He did retain a life-long interest in gardening and won the Royal Horticultural Society's Banksian Medal, but he always regretted missing out on his education and was determined to help other young people. To this end he served on many educational committees and became chairman of the governors of several schools. It is little wonder that he became known as 'Mr Stevenage'.

Not only the residents, but those who worked for the Corporation, planners, architects, engineers and other staff were part of the heart of the town. Much of the work they did was pioneering of a kind and some of them stayed to live in Stevenage for the rest of their lives. Leonard Vincent joined the Corporation in 1949 as an assistant chief architect, later becoming chief architect and planner. Although mainly remembered today for his work on England's first pedestrian town centre, Leonard Vincent did very much more than that, from designing not only some of the first houses and shops, but also a variety of new factory buildings. In 1967 he reflected, 'Of course, being an architect, with hindsight there are a lot of things I would like to have done differently. ... I think this particularly applies to some of the earlier housing – I would like to have seen a higher standard of design concept – but as in all things it is a question of money.' At that time he saw new towns as 'the only answer to overspill and the population explosion'. When he first arrived in Stevenage he and his wife, Evelyn, lived in Corporation housing but in 1965 he designed and built his own house in the old town. He was appointed CBE in the 1960 New Year's Honours.

For a time in 1962 there was a strong possibility that the government would disband the Stevenage Development Corporation. This did not happen, but

Leonard Vincent and his colleagues, Ray Gorbing, decided to set up a private practice that would preserve the expertise they had gained during the development of the new town. They did undertake private commercial and housing work but, for the next 18 years, also acted as consultants to the Stevenage Development Corporation. Both partners continued to live in Stevenage and contribute to the life of the town. Ray Gorbing, having been recruited by Dr Deneys Swayne, became locally famous as one of the stalwarts of the Lytton Players.

Eric Claxton was involved with the planning of the new town of Stevenage from the beginning. On 1 January 1946 he became part of the team at the Ministry of Town and Country Planning in London which, under the leadership of Gordon Stephenson, was drawing up the plan for a new town of 60,000 people. In 1947 he became Deputy Chief Engineer to George Hardy, then Chief Engineer from 1963 to 1972. He spent much time in meticulous research, measuring, analysing and recording the physical features of the designated area, such as water sources, soil, contours; observing traffic flows, calculating measurements needed to produce optimum designs for roundabouts, underpasses and cycle tracks He was particularly interested in the problems being created by the increasing number of motor vehicles and very keen to design a transport system that would reduce accidents and make the new town a safe place to move around. As a cyclist, he studied ways of separating bicycles and pedestrians from other traffic and designed the cycle-ways that became such a feature of New Stevenage. He explained his approach, 'Clearly the most important aim must be to eliminate all vestiges of conflict.'

Eric Claxton. (Stevenage Museum P1153)

Eric Claxton had decided opinions, based largely upon observation, about many things, for example, the place of car drivers, 'Motorists should remember that every one of them becomes a pedestrian when he leaves his vehicle' and, more controversially, 'In a collision between a pedestrian and a cyclist the cyclist comes off worse because he has further to fall'. Not everyone would agree. In 1964, Eric Claxton was awarded the OBE in addition to the MBE he already had for services to the Casualties Union. Fortunately for those who would like to know more of his work on the new town, he described it in some detail in his book *Hidden Stevenage: the Creation of the Sub-Structure of Britain's First New Town,* published in 1992.

James Boyd was the Development Corporation's water engineer from 1947 to

1960, when he and his staff were transferred to the newly established Lee Valley Water Company which had responsibility for supplying water to the Stevenage area. He, his wife, Winifred, and children Margaret and Gavin, made their home in Stevenage, living for many years in Julians Road. Both Boyds were elected as Conservative councillors to the Stevenage Urban District Council, and Winifred also served on the County Council. So greatly had Stevenage politics changed since the influx of Londoners that for most of the time the Conservatives were in a minority on the borough council, but from 1969 to 1971 they took control, with James as chairman. Labour opposition gave them a hard time by using tactics such as deliberately dragging out Council meetings until late at night, with the result that some Conservative councillors refused to stand at the next election.

Francis Cammaerts, headmaster of Alleyne's Grammar School, believed strongly in the importance of travel as an aid to international understanding. In the summer of 1957 he visited the Sebastian-Münster co-educational Gymnasium in Ingelheim-am-Rhine, Germany, to discuss with the headmaster, Walter Ashenbach, the possibility of exchange visits between their two schools. An agreement was reached and in August the following year a group of 11 boys from Alleyne's, under the leadership of their German language teacher, Brian Roberts, made the journey to the 'Red Wine Town' as Ingelheim was known, staying in the homes of their Ingelheim partners.

A reciprocal visit took place at Easter 1959, when Studienrat Ernst Mahr, head of the English department, brought a group of 20 boys and five girls from Ingelheim to Stevenage, so establishing a link also with Stevenage Girls' Grammar School, whose headmistress was Miss Margaret Osborn. The German school group was accompanied by a civic delegation of three, Bürgermeister Heinz Kühn, deputy bürgermeister Wilhelm Fries and Helmut Baumgärtner, a council officer. The visit was curtailed when Herr Fries suffered a heart attack and died.

On Bürgermeister Kühn's return home, Ingelheim Town Council invited a civic delegation from Stevenage to visit them in August. The civic party consisted of Council chairman Alf Luhman; vice-chairman Fred Udell, immediate past chairman Frank Hyde; town clerk Ted Bowers and Development Corporation chairman, Evelyn Denington. During this visit Bürgermeister Kühn proposed an official civic link between the two councils. This suggestion was considered by the full council at its meeting in September, but eventually rejected: one of the grounds for this was a fear that local ratepayers might be opposed to the Council spending their money on a link with a German town. By no means every member of the council agreed with the decision.

It was with disappointment and hurt that the Stevenage Council's decision was received in Ingelheim – and, indeed, in some quarters in Stevenage. Before the year was out, a meeting of representatives of Stevenage town organisations was called to discuss the situation. The result was the formation of a Stevenage–Ingelheim Committee, with Margaret Osborn as chairman and Brian Roberts as secretary, to forge an unofficial link between organisations and people in the two towns.

At the invitation of the committee, Heinz Kühn and Helmut Baumgärtner, accompanied by newspaper reporter Robert Hammer, visited Stevenage at Easter 1960 to discuss the way forward. A series of two-way visits was programmed, under which the first party of Stevenage townspeople travelled by boat and train to Ingelheim in September to attend its annual Red Wine Festival. Several new town members of Stevenage Urban District Council, mostly ex-servicemen with young families, became involved in the annual reciprocal visits in a private capacity, as did the clerk of the Council, Ted Bowers, and his deputy, Don Best.

In 1961 Francois Lachenal, of Ingelheim's major industrial undertaking, the pharmaceutical giant Boehringer, visited Stevenage for discussions with representatives of the committee. His company staged an important Foreign Fortnight in Ingelheim every year and it was intended to stage a British Fortnight in 1962. They would like Stevenage to provide the major contribution. The challenge was accepted and during the two-week period, scores of Stevenage people took part, staying in the homes of Ingelheim hosts. The Lytton Players, with a Gilbert and Sullivan comic operetta, actors, dancers, musicians and singers; the Elizabethans; Stevenage Caledonian Society Scottish dancers; Morris dancers; and a drama group from Alleyne's Grammar School performing Shakespeare all staged performances before large and enthusiastic audiences. Chess, football and table-tennis teams played matches against local opposition.

Stevenage Development Corporation mounted a manned exhibition on the development of Stevenage as Britain's first new town and several Stevenage industries displayed details of their products.

The undertaking was so successful, that the Stevenage–Ingelheim Committee called a public meeting at the town hall in early 1963 to present a report on the link and on Stevenage's contribution to British Fortnight in Ingelheim. The meeting was well-attended and unanimously passed the proposals that a Stevenage–Ingelheim Link Association, free to anyone living, working or studying in the town, without a subscription, be formed and that the Stevenage Urban District Council be called upon, in the name of the people of the town, to enter into a formal link with Ingelheim. As a result, the Council vice-chairman, John Grice, was sent to Ingelheim to sign the official 'twinning' document on behalf of the Council, which was then invited to elect councillor representatives to the association.

Stevenage Day, 18 June, 1965. Miss Valerie Preston, Stevenage Carnival Queen and Miss Ruth Marie Huff, Wine Queen from Ingelheim (second from right) with Susan Ravenscroft, Yvonne Hardy, Bob Potter and the Mayor, Cllr J. Cockerton. (Stevenage Museum)

The link between the two towns became recognised as one of the most active involving a town in England – an example to other towns with links, or considering forging links, with towns overseas, especially on the continent of Europe. So impressive was the link that the Stevenage–Ingelheim Link Association was invited to be represented on the influential national Anglo-German Association.

Reciprocal visits between groups of townspeople and between like organisations, including schools, hockey clubs, ten-pin bowlers and rifle-shooting clubs in the two towns became annual events. Highlights of the activities in Stevenage were a Red Wine Ball at the Mecca Locarno Ballroom and an annual Three Choirs Concert involving Stevenage Male Voice Choir, Stevenage Ladies' Choir and Ingelheim's Schubert Quartette male voice choir. The Stevenage choirs were invited back to Ingelheim. Several marriages between former Stevenage and Ingelheim school pupils took place. Brian Roberts married Fräuline Irmgard Grober, the daughter of Paul Grober, teacher of English at the Sebastian-Münster Gymnasium. She had spent a year as assistant teacher of German at Stevenage Girls' Grammar School. Other young Ingelheim teachers who spent a year in Stevenage as assistant teachers of German at Alleyne's Grammar School were Volker Mathes, who is now chairman of Ingelheim's town-twinning committee and Willi Mahr, elder son of Ernst Mahr. In Stevenage a sheltered housing scheme was named Ingelheim Court, and in Ingelheim there is a road named after Stevenage.

In 2005, Ingelheim honoured Brian Hall, leader of Stevenage Borough Council, by making him 'Ehrenburgerrecht' (Freeman) of Ingelheim, only the second to be appointed.

THE STEVENAGE COAT OF ARMS

ARMS Argent on a Mount in base point Vert an Oak Tree eradicated proper fructed Or transfixed with a Sword in bend sinister point downward also proper hilt and pommel also Or and over all a Fesse Gules charged with six Mullets of six points Gold.

CREST: Out of a Crown Palisado Or a demi Hart proper its sinister fore leg resting upon a Cogwheel Gold, Mantled Vert doubled Argent.

Granted 10th March 1958, to the Stevenage Urban District Council.

Motto 'THE HEART OF A TOWN LIES IN ITS PEOPLE'.

INTERPRETATION

Shield: The oak tree represents the great expanse of woodland in and around Stevenage and the rural charm of the town. The acorns symbolise the steady growth and prosperity of the town. The sword comes from the arms of the Bishops of London, who owned Stevenage during the middle ages. The red horizontal band represents the Great North Road which runs through the centre of the town. The six stars represent the six neighbourhoods of the new town (Old Stevenage, Bedwell, Broadwater, Shephall, Chells and Pin Green).

Crest: Above the shield is the closed helm proper to civic arms, with its crest wreath and mantling in the main colours of the shield, green and silver. Upon the helm is a crown of palisades in gold. This represents a planned area. The crest proper is a figure in half-length of a hart, which comes from the Arms of the County of Hertfordshire in which Stevenage is situated. The hoof of the hart rests on a cogwheel. This symbolises the modern industry carried on in the industrial area of Stevenage.

In the interests of accuracy, it should be recorded that the manor of Stevenage was held by the Abbot of Westminster from 1062 to 1540, by the Bishop of Westminster to 1550, by the Bishop of London from 1550 to 1649, by Thomas Ayres from 1649 to 1660 and again by the Bishop of London from 1660 to 1868, since when it has been held by the Ecclesiastical Commissioners (named changed to Church Commissioners in 1948). Also, since the Arms were designed another neighbourhood, that of Symonds Green, has been added, plus additional housing areas at St Nicholas, the Poplars and Chells Manor.

CHAPTER TEN
Old gives way to new

AFTER THE HIGH POINT of the Queen's visit, life returned to normal. Other matters began to take centre stage, among them the realisation that Stevenage was likely, very soon, to have an unusually large percentage of teenagers in its population. The word 'teenager' itself was relatively new, as was the concept of special provision for this group. Stevenage decided to keep ahead of events. So far the town had no 'youth problem' but there was a realisation that this state of affairs might not last and the Development Corporation took a lead in helping to set up a Youth Advisory Council to co-ordinate the activities of the town's many youth organisations. It also persuaded the Calouste Gulbenkian Foundation to appoint and finance a committee to investigate what provision would be appropriate for young people in Stevenage. Chaired by Brigadier E T Williams, Warden of Rhodes House, Oxford, the committee represented a very wide range of expertise. Among its members was the immensely popular singer, Frankie Vaughan, who had been involved in youth work in London for some time. He made several visits to Stevenage, talking with police, probation officers, teachers, youth workers and the young people themselves. At one meeting, he told a group of youngsters that he preferred small youth clubs, which would resemble families. Everyone who came into contact with him gained a good deal of respect for him. Knowledgeable, from personal experience, on the subject of youth provision, he knew the right questions to ask and his friendly personality put people at their ease. 'Frankie Vaughan was a most charming gentleman', commented one youth worker. He was also a valuable asset to the committee.

The Williams (Gulbenkian) Report, published in October 1959 with the title *The Needs of Youth in Stevenage* found that the proportion of young people, aged between 15 and 20 years, in relation to the total population of Stevenage, was currently below the national average. However, the expected increase, from 2,400 to 9,205 in the next 15 years, made it clear that 'what may be adequate in Stevenage now will rapidly become less and less so with every year that passes'. Recommendations included; the appointment by Hertfordshire County Council of a youth officer for Stevenage as part of a new county youth service; a trust to be set up to administer funds; a site in the town centre to be reserved for a youth centre and the provision of neighbourhood youth centres to be given a high priority. The report ended with the finding that industrialists were showing interest in these recommendations and their power and readiness to help was one of the most encouraging features of the situation.

Members of the Stevenage Development Corporation Board declared themselves 'most anxious to implement the recommendations of the Williams Committee as soon as possible'. Strictly speaking, services for young people were the responsibility of Hertfordshire County Council, as the local education authority, but they were not able to move fast enough to meet the accelerating demand for facilities in Stevenage. The Corporation most creditably stepped in and arranged for the formation of a Stevenage Youth Trust, whose remit was to accumulate and administer funds obtained from public and private sources, to complement the youth provision made by the local authorities. The Ministry of Town and County Planning allowed the Corporation to contribute 10 shillings (50 pence), up to a maximum of £35,000, for every £1 obtained from other sources by the Youth Trust, whose target was £100,000.

Stevenage was fortunate in that the Bowes Lyon family, of St Pauls Waldenbury, were prepared to take an active interest in the town and particularly in its young people. The Hon. David Bowes Lyon, KCVO, agreed to be Chairman of the Trust, with R S (Sedge) McDougall, the Corporation's General Manager, as secretary. The committee was made up of representatives from a cross-section of the local community, including the Corporation, the County Council, the Urban District Council, the Youth Advisory Council, employers, traders and employees. The Corporation also engaged, for a short time, a former tutor of Prince Charles, as a youth officer. His name was Chris Ellis and he had a wide experience of working with, and motivating, young people. By his easy manner, treating youngsters as responsible and trustworthy adults, he got the best out of them. He was based at a bungalow at Bedwell Plash which became a small-scale, unofficial temporary youth centre, and he quickly endeared himself to the young people who flocked to it. Some of them, thanks to Chris Ellis, were fortunate enough to serve on a tall ship, a once-in-a-lifetime, character-building experience.

The Corporation earmarked a site in St George's way for the future Stevenage Youth Centre, but building could not begin until sufficient money was available.

In the meantime, Sishes End, in Pin Green, the large country house and grounds, once the home of Julius Bertram, MP and more recently of Edgar Dennis, was leased to the Youth Trust. Sishes End became home to a variety of activities for young people. It was later taken over by the YMCA for use as a youth hostel and club.

The 1960s have become identified in many people's minds as the 'Swinging Sixties' when young people had more money and more freedom than ever before. For many, social life was dominated by popular music epitomised by the Beatles and by the new 'discos', new 'kitchen sink' plays and films, mini-skirts and Mini cars. Stevenage shared in these manifestations of the new. Convoys of Mods on scooters and Rockers on motor bikes sometimes roared into town, through the High Street, down London Road and into the town centre. The Astonia Cinema showed *A Taste of Honey, Saturday Night and Sunday Morning* and other new films – but the new town centre began to take over from the old High Street as the commercial and civic centre of Stevenage. In 1959, the market, held in the High Street since 1223, had moved to Cutty's Lane and later into the new market place in the town centre. The same year the Quaker Meeting House, in Cutty's Lane opened, replacing the small building at the corner of Stanmore and Basils Road; and the Corporation's Estate Office transferred from the High Street to 13, Town Square, together with the Social Relations Department which was formerly at Aston House.

The Social Relations Officer at this time, who had replaced Charles Madge in 1954, was Tom Hampson, an athlete of international repute. In the 1932 Olympic Games at Los Angeles he won the gold medal for the 800 metres, setting a new world record of 1 minute 49.7 seconds, and a silver medal in the 4 x 400 metres relay. At Stevenage he became known for his willingness to talk to the new residents and speak on their behalf to the Corporation, particularly in respect of sporting and leisure facilities. He also edited the Corporation's quarterly magazine, *Purpose*, which was in itself a means of liaising with the public. One helpful feature was the series of profiles of members and officers of the Board which, it was hoped, would reduce the criticism that the Corporation was a remote, faceless institution. Tom Hampson helped to dispel this

Tom Hampson. (Stevenage Museum P11436)

idea, partly by his personality but, perhaps even more, by living in Stevenage, unlike many of his colleagues. He died, aged 57, in 1965. When the garden and grounds of Highfield, former home of the Poston family and, later, the Keysells, were designated as a park for the Pin Green neighbourhood, it was renamed Hampson Park, in memory of Tom Hampson.

The General Manager of the Corporation from 1957 to 1967, 'Sedge' McDougall, was generally acclaimed as an energetic, efficient and sociable man, who took a keen, personal interest in the town and was responsible for a great deal of progress during his term of office. He also chose to live in Stevenage, at The Priory in Rectory Lane. This Georgian house, built as the Rectory for the parish in the late eighteenth century had recently been the home of Michael Tetley, one of the three leading campaigners who took the fight against the new town to the House of Lords in 1947.

An historic event on 13 June 1959 was the first Stevenage Day, held on the King George V playing field, an appropriate venue at the edge of the old town, facing Fairlands Way and the new town centre. The date was originally chosen to coincide with the Urban District Council's opening of the new pavilion. Organisations of all kinds from the whole of the town took stands to display information about their activities. The programme included athletics, inter-works seven-a-side football, tug-o'-war and other competitons. It was decided not to have a beer tent, as alcohol was both out of place and unnecessary on what should be a family day out. The idea came out of a meeting of representatives of local organisations, held at the Coach and Horses public house. Les Taylor was elected the first chairman of the Stevenage Day Committee, with Eddie Messent as secretary. It was instantly successful and has continued annually ever since.

'Sedge' McDougall. (Stevenage Museum P11501)

STEVENAGE DAY 13 JUNE 1959 PROGRAMME

We take this opportunity to extend a very warm welcome to all who support this, the first 'Stevenage Day'.

Whilst the many Sports Clubs and other voluntary bodies functioning in Stevenage stage their own activities, this event represents a co-ordinated effort by representatives from many sections of the town's educational, cultural, industrial, sporting and social life. The extensive programme being presented has been arranged by a most energetic organising committee, and we trust that, by your generous support, they will be encouraged to make the 'Stevenage Day' an annual event.

We hope that the 'Stevenage Day' will make a further contribution towards creating good fellowship among the town's ever growing population, and we wish you all a most pleasant afternoon.

Alf Luhman Chairman, Stevenage Urban District Council.
Leslie T Taylor Chairman, The 'Stevenage Day' Organisation.

STEVENAGE DAY COMMITTEE

Chairman: L T Taylor Esq. Vice-Chairman: N Thomas Esq.

Secretary: E T Messent Esq. Treasurer: H D Darlow Esq.

Members: Messrs J Avery, D C Brown, WA Brown, K Goldsmith, A. Hammond, D H Hills, J W Howells, C May, A Primett, J F Roberts, D L Rees, S Packhard, B Slade, D Taylor, G Turner, J D Williams.

Stevenage Inter-works Sports and Social Organisation

Stevenage Football Club

Stevenage and District Primary Schools Sports association

St John Ambulance Brigade

Bridgeway Lawn Tennis Club

Womens' Voluntary Service

Stevenage Dramatic Society

Stevenage Cricket Club

Stevenage Caledonian Society

The Stevenage Society for Archaeology, Arts and Natural History

The transfer of institutions from the old town to the new continued apace. The police station, never long in one place, had moved from its Stanmore Road site to Southgate in 1959. Stevenage's first police station had been at 3 North Road but in 1871 it was incorporated into the newly built town hall in Orchard Road. In 1916 it moved again, to purpose-built premises in Stanmore Road. As events turned out, it was not destined to stay long in Southgate.

The Market in its historic site in the High Street, 1950s. (Stevenage Museum P431)

The new church of St George, replacing the ancient church of St Nicholas as the parish church of Stevenage, was consecrated on 28 November 1960 by the Bishop of St Albans, the Right Reverend Dr E M Gresford Jones, in the presence of Queen Elizabeth the Queen Mother. The Bishop, aware of mixed reactions to the architecture, said in his address 'Here is light, grace and dignity. To those of you of an older generation who may find this building puzzling or even repellent, I say reserve your judgement.' The Queen Mother praised the 'lovely feeling of space'. Among gifts from local organisations and schools to the new church was a table for the conference room presented by the Jewish fraternity in Stevenage.

At last, in 1961, the County Council's Health Centre and Library building, designed under the direction of County Architect G C Fardell, opened in Southgate. The official opening of the first phase of the town's new Central Library took place on 18 January 1961. Geoffrey Powell Davies, JP, who had worked long and hard as Chairman of the Stevenage Local Library Committee, made the introductory remarks and welcomed the poet Cecil Day Lewis, who declared the library open. J T Barker, JP, Chairman of the North Herts. Regional Library Committee, proposed a vote of thanks, seconded by County Alderman Philip Ireton, JP. The new Stevenage Librarian, Peter Labdon, was introduced. The old town library in Orchard Road remained in operation with Doris Baker as librarian, and a mobile library service also continued. In the same year, the County Council was able to open the first stage of the Stevenage

Stevenage Central Library. (Stevenage Museum P3957)

College of Further Education, on the site of the former Six Hills Nursery, with George Lighton as its first Principal. The County Council's remaining major building in Stevenage, the Fire and Ambulance Station in St George's Way, would not be ready until 1962.

It was unfortunate that, throughout the whole country, outbreaks of wanton destruction began at this time, usually carried out by youths who found a new pastime in wrecking public property, destroying trees and generally spoiling life for other people. An old word was re-invented to describe their activities – vandalism. This was a national phenomenon, not peculiar to Stevenage, but the press was avid for news about new towns and eagerly followed up stories such as that in *The Times* of 1 May 1961, under the heading, 'Cinema Passports at Stevenage'. No community is without its share of delinquents and, regrettably, a group of these had been slashing seats at the Astonia Cinema, resulting in a ban on teenagers. A national newspaper reporter on the trail of this story made much of it, including persuading a group of youngsters to try to gain admission to the cinema so that they could be photographed as they were turned away. Another group agreed to leave a town centre coffee bar to have their photograph taken under a street lamp on the grounds that the lighting was better there. The caption to the published picture referred to young people hanging about under street lamps because they had nothing else to do.

Previously, another national newspaper reporter had come to the town to write a 'responsible and helpful' article concerning a pregnant schoolgirl. He had not arrived with an open mind. Parents, school teachers, young people and youth workers were interviewed, unaware of the negative nature of the article to be written. The result, given a two page spread, was sensationally headed 'Cloud Over Stevenage'. About every six months or so, it seemed, some sociologist would arrive to see how the town was growing. The findings were hardly meaningful. After all, one does not regularly pull a young growing plant out of the ground and take a look at its roots to see how it is faring.

Another expression popular with reporters in the 1950s and '60s was 'New Town Blues'. It referred not to jazz numbers, nor to drugs, but to a supposed condition existing among young wives who were early residents of new towns. Anyone who did not know differently could be forgiven for believing that new towns in general, and Stevenage in particular, were full of lonely housewives and bored young people. According to reports many young housewives were depressed because they missed the bright lights of London and were homesick for families and friends. With their husbands at work they were alone in the house all day with nothing to do, nowhere to go and knowing no-one. Such stories were irritating not only to the majority of new town residents, but also to those in the old town, who felt that their former rural surroundings and way of life had been destroyed for nothing if the newcomers were not happy here.

In fact, most young housewives could hardly believe their good fortune in moving out of a claustrophobic city environment and into a house of their own, with a garden where young children could play in safety and clean country air to breathe. It is true that they and their husbands missed the parents they had left behind. John Amess, with his wife and baby son, came to Stevenage in 1957. He later recalled, 'Moving from South London to Stevenage in those days was almost like emigrating ... It was a long time before we had a telephone, so letter writing was important. Our parents felt as though we had moved to Australia.'

As a result, there was a period in the early days of the new town when the 'up' platform at Stevenage railway station was packed on Saturday and Sunday mornings with young couples on their way back to the 'Smoke' to visit their parents. Recognising the situation, Stevenage Development Corporation, in co-operation with architects from the Ministry of Housing and Local Government began an experiment of building specially-designed bungalows and flats for the elderly parents of new town residents. They combined independent accommodation with shared facilities such as a common room, and the support of a resident warden. Each flat had its own small kitchen and a bellpush for contacting the warden in emergencies.

The experiment was a great success. One elderly parent told a reporter, 'I have a lovely flat – I wouldn't part with that.' Another commented, 'I wouldn't move back to London for all the tea in China.' and another, 'As we sit at our breakfast table in the morning we can actually wave to our daughter as she cycles past on her way to work.' Stevenage was once again in the news, but this time for a positive reason. 'Flats for the Old in New Town; joint experiment at Stevenage' was the heading in *The Times* for 2 September 1960.

Another housing experiment was taking place in the newest neighbourhoods of the new town, in the Chells and Pin Green neighbourhoods, where Leonard Vincent was determined not only to follow the Radburn theory of pedestrian housing estates, but to improve upon it. The first houses at Elm Green, Chells estate were occupied in 1960. They were sited around paved squares, with pedestrian routes from the front gardens, while access to vehicular roads and garages for cars was from the back. The Pin Green plan was for a self-contained, pedestrianised area of 8,000 houses. By means of underpasses, culs-de-sac and a series of winding minor roads rather than a major ring road, residents would be able to walk safely to shops and schools, with no major road to cross. Ray Gorbing commented, 'The problem encountered here was the one involving house numbering in relation to street names. When the first section of Almond Spring was completed the local postmen nearly went berserk.'

Tuesday 2 October 1961 was Open Day for the Mecca Locarno Ballroom in Danestrete. Ray Gorbing, the architect, had found the project a particularly challenging one, not least because the client tended to make unexpected demands. He sometimes requested the architect to meet him on site 'at some unearthly hour' such as 6.30 am, then immediately to produce a sketch drawing

The Mecca Ballroom. (Stevenage Museum P6825)

of an agreed alteration and give it to the contractor at start of the day's work. Some of the client's instructions were unclear. For example, the design brief called for the walls of the dance hall to be 'in marble'. Fortunately, when this was queried it was found that what was really meant was 'a marble effect', which Mecca had achieved in other dance halls by employing a very skilful elderly man who worked with a feather over a painted surface 'with an absolutely incredible result'. Finally, two days before the official opening, the Mecca boss suddenly decided that he wanted a starlight effect, which could only be achieved by installing one thousand small twinkling ceiling lights. Working non-stop day and night, the electricians just managed to complete the work on time.

The manager, B A Elmer-Smith, told reporters that Mecca ballrooms were usually found in well-established, well-populated towns, so that having one in Stevenage was something of an experiment. However, it proved to be highly successful, beginning with queues of visitors to the Open Day. One of the first events held there was a ball, attended by nearly 500 people, in aid of the Hitchin and District Multiple Sclerosis Society. The cabaret included world professional ballroom dancing champions Bob Burgess and Doreen Freeman and Scottish dancing led by the Stevenage Pipe Band. It is now a Mecca bingo hall.

There was provision for more sporting and recreational facilities in 1962, including the swimming pool on the corner of St George's Way and Fairlands Way, designed by the Corporation's architects but opened under the auspices of the Urban District Council. In Danestrete the Corporation-built Ambassador Lanes Tenpin Bowling Centre was officially opened by the actor Roger Moore. The Stevenage Town Football Club had transferred to its new ground in Broadhall Way the previous year. As yet it was only an idea, but there was enthusiastic talk of a sports hall somewhere near the town centre.

The long-awaited day arrived when the Stevenage by-pass was finally opened, in July 1962. This was a great relief to the many who worked in the industrial area, whose daily journeys could now be accomplished safely: and it was a development which pleased residents of the old town at least as much as those in the new. It was now possible to cross the High Street on foot or to turn into it by car without waiting what seemed a lifetime for a gap in the traffic. Some shopkeepers may have been worried that they would lose trade, but their fears were groundless. In fact, it was not long before traffic began to build up again, although without the juggernaut lorries and other heavy vehicles which formerly dominated the road. No doubt their drivers were equally pleased. But despite the improvement, there was nostalgia for the days when Stevenage could boast that its High Street was part of the country's major highway, the A1 Great North Road.

With grants from the Ministry of Education, the County Council, the Urban District Council, the King George VI Memorial Fund and other donations, the

The Stevenage Swimming Centre. (Stevenage Museum)

Youth Trust was able to begin building the Youth Centre in St George's Way in March 1964. It opened in April the following year as Bowes Lyon House, named after its former chairman who, sadly, had not lived to see the day. At a meeting of the Urban District Council on 3 October 1961, the Chairman, Cllr Mick Cotter, had expressed the Council's regret on the death of Sir David Bowes Lyon and paid tribute to his work for the Stevenage Youth Trust and the interest he had taken in the development of the town. Cllr Ireton said he was a man of great charm and obvious sincerity. The centre became known to its young users simply as 'Bowes'. It was the largest purpose-built youth centre in Europe, capable of taking some 2,000 young people at any one time. Sedge McDougall called it 'the largest street corner in Europe'– perhaps because one

The Tenpin Bowling Centre, Danestrete. (Stevenage Museum P6858)

ground-floor corner of the building was open to the street on two sides for activities such as roller skating. At first the centre was managed by the Trust and later taken over by the County Council. After giving financial help to several other bodies concerned with youth provision in the town, the Youth Trust eventually disbanded in 1976. It had done a magnificent job.

There was a dark side to the 1960s. Inflation was a major problem, along with industrial unrest and strikes. One which made intriguing headlines in *The Times* of Friday 4 March 1960 was 'Moscow Work delayed by Stevenage Strike'. It apppears that a British consortium was building a tyre factory near Moscow and the Stevenage firm of Geo. W King was producing the conveyor system for it. An unofficial strike of about 900 men at Stevenage, in protest against the refusal of six men to join any union, was holding up progress. Relations between Soviet Russia and the West were at a very low ebb at the time, leading to a space race and competition for nuclear missiles. This had a direct impact on Stevenage, where, in 1960, 607,935 people were employed at the British Aircraft Corporation (English Electric) and 2,100 at Hawker Siddeley Dynamics, both companies which were heavily involved in this field.

The space and guided missile industries brought employment to Stevenage, but many people were uneasy about the morality of this. Some had joined the Campaign for Nuclear Disarmament, formed in 1958, or taken part in the first Aldermaston March to 'Ban the Bomb' the same year. Others, in churches, through the letters pages of the *Stevenage Gazette* or informally in pubs and social gatherings, debated the pros and cons. On Friday 3 April 1959 the front page headline in the *Stevenage Gazette* was 'New Town Missile Factories Target for Protest: workers urged to give up their jobs'. A national organisation, the Direct Action Committee Against Nuclear War had come to Stevenage to lead a week-long campaign, in which they appealed to local people to refuse to take part in the manufacture of guided missiles. The Committee distributed a leaflet, in which the following plea was made,

> Stevenage was the first New Town. Let it also be the first town to turn away from H-bombs and rockets and work for a peaceful and prosperous world ... All living in Stevenage share responsibility for the work on weapons of mass destruction carried out here ... [in] a New Town built to house the homeless of World War II.

The leaders of the campaign, Michael Randle and Patricia Arrowsmith, talked to members of the Stevenage Trades Council at their monthly meeting at the Club and Institute, in Stevenage High Street, on 1 April. Among those present was Cllr Stan Munden, an employee of English Electric, who observed that a close-down of the English Electric and De Havilland factories would result in unemployment for over 20,000 people. Miss Arrowsmith replied that no sacrifice was too great to avoid the horrors of nuclear war. Other speakers, including Patrick Sullivan and Mr J Brocklehurst, felt that it was too much to ask people to give up their jobs without alternative employment. Fred Schofield told the visitors that they were in effect calling for a general strike in Stevenage as 'practically every other firm in the town was connected with sub-contract work for English Electric and De Havilland'.

However, one group of workers did respond to the call for action. In his autobiography, *Anchorman*, Bert Lowe described his part in persuading building workers to stage a demonstration. After a discussion with Pat Arrowsmith at his home, he promised her his full support and invited her to address the Stevenage Branch of the AUBTW. Following a successful meeting, he organised further meetings at building sites throughout the new town and, with difficulty, managed to persuade most workers to take part in a demonstration on Friday 10 April 1959. On the day, nearly every construction worker from the Stevenage sites stopped work. As the town centre clock struck four, they downed tools and began moving towards the Town Square. Some were carrying placards with messages such as 'Stop work on the Blue Streak missile', 'No rocket factories for Stevenage' and 'Nuclear weapons threaten your kids' futures'.

Bert Lowe calculated that about one thousand workers took part in the demonstration, which was reported in the national and local press and broadcast on BBC and ITV. He concluded, 'Such was the spirit of the day I believe that it remains the only industrial action taken in this country against nuclear weapons. Another first for Stevenage!'

Although comparatively few people actually responded to the call to give up their work, there were many who worried about it. There was also a general consensus that Stevenage appeared to be in danger of becoming dependent upon the arms industry, and of putting too many eggs into one employment basket. There were calls for English Electric to diversify and manufacture domestic electrical goods, such as washing machines, for which there was a great demand, but to no avail. English Electric (later the British Aircraft Corporation and then British Aerospace) continued successfully to develop guided weapons for the British Army, the Royal Navy and the Royal Air Force and for export markets. The company then won a government contract to develop and manufacture inter-continental ballistic missiles, which they named 'Blue Water' and 'Blue Steel', both of which could be fitted with nuclear warheads.

On a nearby site was a division of the De Havilland Aircraft Company (later Hawker Siddeley Dynamics). They, too, won a government contract to develop and manufacture an inter-continental ballistic missile, which they named 'Blue Streak', and other guided weapons. Stevenage followed closely news of test firings of the missile at the Woomera test site in Australia.

Then came the shock that had been warned about earlier. On 30 April 1960 the government cancelled the missile contracts. The 'brains' of the British rocket industry were located at Stevenage. Once the projects were abandoned there was no other employment for them in this country if they wished to remain in the industry. Many emigrated to the United States of America, where their expertise and knowledge was welcomed by such companies as McDonnell Douglas.

Inevitably job losses followed and in 1962 both the Urban District Council and the Corporation appealed to the government for help. But Stevenage was not alone with its unemployment problems and the request was turned down on the grounds that development areas in other parts of the country were more in need of jobs. However, 16 months later front page headlines in the *Stevenage Gazette* for 11 December 1964, announced; 'Stevenage men in joint project with French Firm. Will build new space satellite. Work should keep team busy for two years'. The report went on,

> Stevenage space project workers at Hawker Siddeley Dynamics may be the spearhead of Britain's first attempt to reach the moon or other planets in the distant future. To the Stevenage men goes this distinction because the company's space projects division, working in collaboration with Engins Matra, of France, has been selected to develop the first research satellite for ESRO (European Space Research Association). This very important development opens up a new era for Stevenage ... This order, for the first co-operative European satellite has been won by Hawker Siddeley Dynamics in the face of very fierce international competition from European countries within ESRO. One estimate is that initially the contract is worth £1,000,000 ...

The indoor market. (Stevenage Museum P3285)

A spokesman explained that the contract would put the company ahead of all other aero-space companies in Europe and, most important of all, it meant that Europe would not be left behind in the space race. By developing their own satellite, Europe would no longer be leaving everything to the Americans and the Russians. Naturally there was relief in Stevenage to think that so many jobs now appeared secure, but also an awareness that it was not wise for the town to be heavily dependent on one industry.

Meanwhile, as more new buildings were completed, the relocation of organisations was still going on. The original Daneshill House in London Road, former home of the Popple family, had been demolished and its name taken for a modern office building in Danestrete. The whole of the Development Corporation staff transferred there in 1961, quitting Aston House and leaving 13, Town Square to be occupied by the Stevenage Council of Social Service and the Family Centre. These two bodies were new concepts in themselves, offering a range of related services under one roof. Then, in 1964, the Urban District Council moved from its long-time home in the Victorian town hall in Orchard Road to temporary premises in Southgate House, while waiting for the new Civic Suite, a superior town hall, to be built in The Forum.

By this time, there were very many voluntary groups in Stevenage. To give just one example, the Stevenage Branch of Amnesty International was extremely active. In December 1964 it turned Human Rights Day into a week of exhibitions, talks and prayers, involving schools, churches and youth clubs. On Wednesday 9 December a small and very successful group met at the Friends' Meeting House to celebrate the Declaration of Human Rights in the UN Charter. Participants included Roger Dinsdale from Alleyne's Grammar School sixth form, Doug Cross of the Stevenage DSIR Laboratory, John Somerville and Mr E Fox. Finally the group listened to Nelson Mandela's speech at his Rivonia trial, read by Peter Finch on a gramophone record.

Christmas festivities were perhaps surprisingly traditional. Children in the rehabilitation class at Pin Green Junior School, all of whom had some kind of emotional problem, performed an interpretation of *The Sleeping Beauty*. They used puppets which they had made themselves, against a brightly painted backdrop of mediaeval figures. Their teacher, Mrs Bennett, explained that most of them were highly intelligent and very enthusiastic about the play. They helped to select the music and ended up with a combination of Ravel, Warlock and Tchaikovsky.

Shephalbury School staged a presentation of Skakespeare's *The Merchant of Venice*. A review, published in the *Stevenage Gazette* for 11 December 1964, was written by sixth form pupil Marion Crawford. She praised several of the actors, particularly Mr Williams, one of the teachers, who stepped in at very short notice to play Shylock. She concluded '*The Merchant of Venice* is not the easiest of plays to perform but I thought our production merited praise'.

As the year ended, there was increasing demand for a sports hall. There was a suggestion that it could be built at Roaring Meg, the old sewage works site in London Road. Stevenage Urban District Council's Parks and Entertainments Committee took up the idea with enthusiasm and pressed for it to be considered as soon as possible. However, once again Stevenage was in the grip of planning mania and nothing could be decided until after a decision had been made as to whether or not the town would expand.

'THE MOVING POLICE STATION'

1841 – 3, North Road
1871 – adjacent to the new town hall in Orchard Road
1916 – Stanmore Road. The Fox twins helped to build it.
1959 – Southgate
1974 – Lytton Way
2007 – enlarged and access changed

Cycling in Stevenage.

CHAPTER ELEVEN
Master Plan Madness

'MASTER PLAN', a term unknown before 1946, had become very familiar to all residents of Stevenage since then. Master Plans ruled people's lives. They determined where new houses would be built; which existing ones would be demolished; which land would be developed; which roads would be built, re-routed or cut off altogether; what, if any, green space would be left. The very words 'Master Plan' emphasised the apparent omnipotence of planners and, particularly in the early days, the powerlessness of those who would have to live with the result. Perhaps even more frustrating was the propensity of 'Master Plan's to change: the modern expression 'moving the goal posts' describes it perfectly. Just as the populace had become used to the pattern of life produced by the 1949 Plan, another was required, then another. In Stevenage both old and new, it seemed that the town would never be able to settle down.

When the new town was first designated in 1946, a provisional plan was drawn up which, with minimal alterations, became the 1949 Master Plan. The two main differences were: the area originally allowed for industry was reduced, thus saving the part of Fairview Road scheduled for demolition, and the primary road planned to cross Fairlands Valley was deleted. By 1955 Stevenage had a population of about 17,500 with new employment in the industrial area for about 1,500. In that year, the Corporation's request to its chief architect and planner, Leonard Vincent, resulted in a revised plan incorporating the alterations already made to the 1949 plan and also showing, at the government's behest, how the housing density could be increased to an average of 50 people per acre.

After 1955 the population of the town increased more rapidly:

30 June 1957	26,560
1959	34,580
1961	43,600
1963	50,270
1965	54,300

New industrial buildings and numbers of employees had kept pace with population growth.

Year	Industrial floor area completed	Industrial floor area under construction	Estimated ultimate total number of employees
1957	933,000 sq ft	315,639 sq ft	6,700
1959	1,500,000	263,677	8,500
1961	2,138,500	171,234	12,750
1963	2,638,850	377,380	15,475
1965	3,187,914	126,624	17,555 In buildings completed or under construction.

By 1961, house building in the Bedwell, Broadwater and Shephall neighbourhoods was almost finished, Chells would be completed between 1959 and 1964, and in 1962 the first houses in Pin Green were under construction. To all intents and purposes the town was nearing completion and residents might reasonably expect to be allowed time to adjust to their new or changed surroundings and to get on with their lives as they would in a more conventional town. This was not to be. For the next 18 years, the Corporation's planning policies were beset by problems as changes of government, and consequent changes of Ministers responsible for new towns, led to changing instructions from Whitehall. In 1958, Henry Brooke, the new Minister for Housing and Local Government, gave as his provisional opinion that the ultimate population of Stevenage should be revised from a figure of 60,000 to 80,000. This would mean a period of rapid growth as more people were brought into the town until the figure of 60,000 was reached, after which the population would grow by natural increase to 80,000, assuming that the children of residents remained in the town.

The Corporations' planners, therefore, worked towards a full revision of the Master Plan and in the interim, in 1960, the Minister approved proposals for the development of the Pin Green neighbourhood, based on the assumption that the greater part of the natural increase in population would be accommodated there. This meant that land initially intended to be left as open space, or Green Belt, within the designated area boundary, would now be built on. The original principle of neighbourhood planning was also modified. Pin Green was to form just one large residential sector of about 20,000 people, rather than the

10,000 first planned, by the addition of the confusingly-named St Nicholas area, with a higher housing density.

In the early sixties, government cuts in expenditure led to the idea of the 'people's house', a method of producing more houses more cheaply. Ray Gorbing, who was having to wrestle with the problem of how to design a house for the minimum cost and still maintain standards, said that he never could understand why the 'people's house' was so-called. He explained,

> The scream in those days was for houses and more houses. Speed of erection was the criterion which led to blind eyes being paid to poor workmanship ... Speed meant new methods of construction and manufacturers wooed the authorities with system building using factory produced components ... I don't think we were very happy with system building during that period. A few years later when circumstances had changed and more traditional materials were on the market, people made comparisons and severely criticised some of the system built areas, forgetting, or not knowing, the difficulties under which we had to work.

As news of the revised plan became public, it all sounded so familiar to those who had been living in Stevenage in 1946. Elizabeth Poston was alarmed to hear of the decision to build on land previously listed as green space in the vicinity of Rooks Nest, E M Forster's childhood home and the original *Howards End* of his famous novel. Supported by many friends, she began a campaign to protect the house and its surroundings. The *Guardian* newspaper took up the cause, publishing an article on 19 October 1960, headed, 'Fate of Forster Country'. On 24 December the same year, a letter signed by, among others, W H Auden, John Betjeman, Arthur Bryant, Lord David Cecil, John G Murray, Harold Nicolson, Max Reinhardt, C V Wedgewood and Vita Sackville-West expressed the hope of 'literate people the world over [that] the Forster Country of *Howards End* ... should be preserved in its rightful setting as one of our great literary landmarks'.

View into Forster Country from St Nicholas' churchyard. (John Hepworth)

While the literary establishment was campaigning on behalf of the Forster Country in the north of Stevenage, another battle was being fought in Fairlands Valley. There are several versions of this story. A paragraph in the first chapter of the 1966 Stevenage Master Plan states:

> In 1961 a preliminary draft Master Plan was prepared. In the event this plan was neither submitted to the Minister nor taken further, but a version was obtained and published in the local press. This resulted in considerable public interest, mainly confined to the supposition that Fairlands Valley was to be completely built over. A petition of protest was signed by about 10,000 persons.

Fred Udell, in *The History Makers,* describes 'the threat by the Stevenage Development Corporation to build on Fairlands Valley. Although they denied that this was so, one of our members, Fred Millard ... got hold of a secret report by the SDC showing and outlining building that was to take place.' A 'Save the Valley Committee' was formed, with Connie Rees as secretary and Gerry Anstock, headmaster of Peartree Spring Junior School, as chairman. He described in *The History Makers* how a copy of the preliminary draft plan was delivered as a 'secret loan' to Fred Millard for two hours on a Sunday night by a member of the Board of the Development Corporation and shown to him in the Red Lion lounge bar, in Shephall. He, with some difficulty, had it copied in a very short time, with the aid of many friends. He then contacted the *Stevenage Gazette,* telling them that he had seen the secret plan. The story was taken up by a friend who worked for the BBC and it featured in a news item, with interviews taking place in Fairlands Valley.

Huw Rees explained that the first anyone in Stevenage knew about the plan was '... an article in *The Times* by their architectural correspondent saying that Stevenage planners had ideas to erect superior housing on the valley, which because of the location and excellent views, would command high prices.' He wrote at once to the *Stevenage Gazette,* as did Susan Morris, whose letter began, 'Sir, Following so closely on the questions raised on your front page last week as to the future of Fairlands Valley, it is profoundly disturbing that *The Times* should report on July 3: "Leonard Vincent at Stevenage proposes to build on most of the wide meadows intended in the Master Plan to separate the neighbourhoods" – almost an accomplished fact before we in Stevenage have had the barest chance to comment.'

Councillors Fred Millard (right), Mick Cotter (centre) and Ken Vale (left)

The Save the Valley Committee decided to hold a public meeting and found a great supporter in George Lighton, Principal of the Stevenage College of Further Education, who allowed the meeting to be held there. It was a 'huge success', packed to the doors with many people standing outside. A petition, organised like a military operation was also successful, achieving 11,000 signatures against building on the valley and none in favour. Among those most upset at the prospect of seeing the farmland disappear under brick and concrete were Stan and Sybil Marriott, at Fairlands Farmhouse. Their friend, Roy Findley, shared their concern and offered his help to the Committee, collecting over 1,000 signatures from the old town. This was handed to the Development Corporation and, after much hard work by the Committee and others, the valley was saved. Gerry Anstock's final comments were, 'Many good persons were involved ... [but] the member of the Board who loaned the copy marked "Secret to the Development Corporation" never slept for weeks in case I divulged whence we obtained this irrefutable evidence.'

These two campaigns, on behalf of the Forster Country and Fairlands Valley, raised important issues. Rooks Nest House itself was never in danger (although the countryside around it was) but those who had seen the destruction of historic buildings, including Highfield and Sishes, could believe the Corporation capable of anything. Assurances had been given that Fairlands Valley was never in danger either and that the feasibility study for its development was an officer exercise and had never been put to the Board for consideration, but those who had seen the draft could only believe what they saw on paper.

In both cases it hardly mattered that the campaigners may have been fighting needlessly. What did matter was the degree of mistrust that existed towards the planning process. The planners themselves, of course, were only doing their jobs and following government directives. They had no choice and were themselves often disappointed when, for example, road widths had to be reduced, housing densities increased or standards lowered to save money. But the planning process involved an almost total lack of communication, let alone consultation, with the people most concerned, those actually living in the town. It appears that no lessons had been learned since 1946.

For some years, the government had been concerned about the serious problems likely to arise from the apparently rapidly increasing population of the country. It had been predicted that the population of the United Kingdom would rise from 52 million in 1961 to 61 million in 1981 and to 72 million by 2000. To help plan for this, the Ministry of Housing and Local Government instituted regional studies, one of which, the *South East Study*, included Hertfordshire. Although the final version was not published until March 1964, research for the study indicated that 3,500,000 more people might have to be accommodated in this region by 1981. The building of more new towns and the expansion of some already in existence was seen as the solution. In July 1962 the Ministry of Housing and Local Government asked the Stevenage Development Corporation to examine the feasibility of expanding Stevenage to within a population of about 150,000 as part of the study of the South East region. As requested, Leonard Vincent prepared a study, *The Expansion of Stevenage – a Technical Appraisal, February 1963*, which the Corporation submitted to the Minister. The Report concluded that a population of 130,000 to 140,000 could be accommodated in the expanded town and that the additional area for expansion should be mainly to the west of the A1(M).

On Monday 4 March 1963 the Development Corporation invited 400 leading townspeople to a meeting at the College of Further Education to discuss the report on the feasibility of expanding the town to a population of 140,000. Those opposed included the Labour-dominated Urban District Council. Sir Arthur Rucker, Chairman of the Development Corporation, reminded the meeting that they were not there to make a decision, or a resolution, since the report only expressed a possibility. Martin Maddan, the Conservative MP for the Hitchin Division, said that it would be entirely wrong for Stevenage to expand outside the designated area, partly because of the bad effect the arrival of so many newcomers in such a short time would have on the development of community spirit and partly because of the effect on neighbouring villages and on farming. The expansion would require more than 3,000 acres of mainly farm land, 2,130 of which was not designated for development and would have to be acquired at its full market value. Expansion to the west of the A1(M) meant that Hertfordshire would become one huge industrial conglomerate.

The Corporation, on the other hand, saw 'considerable advantages' in expanding the population of the new town to 140,000. Stevenage would then become the principal town in an area bounded by Cambridge, Bedford, Watford, Luton and Hatfield.

But another new Minister had a different idea. In 1964, Sir Keith Joseph, asked the Corporation to examine the feasibility of the town's expansion to provide for a population of approximately 150,000. Doing its duty, the Corporation submitted proposals for a town of 130,000 to 160,000 population, mainly by development to the west of the A1(M), between the motorway and the A600 Hitchin–Codicote road. In August 1964 the Ministry published a draft Designation Amendment Order to extend the designated area generally in accordance with the recommendations made in the 1963 expansion report. A public inquiry was to be held in Stevenage in December 1964, but before then, in a new departure, an inquiry 'Open Evening' was held at Stevenage College, under a directive from the inquiry organisers headed 'Let the people speak'. This directive was an interim result of research being carried out for the Ministry of Housing and Local Government, on 'Public Participation in

Planning'. At last the authorities were recognising that the very people to be affected by planning decisions had very little say in their making. The final report, known as the *Skeffington Report*, was not published until 1969, but planning authorities were being urged not to wait for that but to find ways of involving the public in planning matters.

The *Stevenage Gazette* for 11 December 1964 summarised the situation:

> **It is proposed** by the Minister of Housing and Local Government that Stevenage should be expanded –
>
> * from the present target of 80,000 to one of 100,000 by 1979 and then to increase by natural expansion to more than 130,000 by the year 2000;
>
> * from the present designated area of 6,100 acres to 7,650 acres (an extra 1,450 acres to the west of the town, and 100 acres to the north-east).
>
> **In support** of the proposals – the Ministry Housing and Local Government, Stevenage Development Corporation, Stevenage Employers' Association, local trade unions.
>
> **In opposition** – Hertfordshire County Council, Stevenage Urban District Council, Stevenage Trades Council, all adjacent local authorities, the National Farmers' Union, the Hertfordshire Society and other bodies and individuals.
>
> **Holding the Inquiry** – Mr S Lloyd Jones, Town Clerk of Plymouth, appointed by the Minister as an independent Inspector, to hear all the arguments for and against, and submit a report.

Surprisingly, only about 30 members of the public were present in the hall on the evening of Wednesday 9 December 1964 when the Inspector, Mr S Lloyd Jones, arrived to hear personal statements for and against from the general public. Those supporting expansion were allowed to speak first and included Tony Dickens, of ASSET, an organisation affiliated to Stevenage Trades Council, who was concerned with security of employment. He drew attention to the 'imbalance of industry built into the town' which had led to many redundancies. He knew of people who had been made redundant three times in the past five years and felt there was an obvious need to diversify industry and also to provide a wide range of opportunities for school leavers, whose numbers were predicted to rise to 12,000 in 1978.

There was support also from Fred Millard, who had so recently fought to save Fairlands Valley. Described in the *Stevenage Gazette* as 'the well-known trades unionist', he was representing a local committee of the National Federation of Building Trade Operatives. He said, 'Stevenage people are special people and when they are disturbed they do something about it ... If they had been against expansion they would have said so clearly'. He also believed there was an

Cottages and St Nicholas' church at corner of Weston Road and Rectory Lane. (Stevenage Museum 0078)

adequate labour force in the town to tackle expansion and hoped that the building rate could be increased to 1,500 houses per year compared with 1,000 during the 1951–61 period.

Speaking on behalf of the North Hertfordshire Liberal Association, Mrs Elma Dangerfield, prospective Liberal candidate for the Hitchin Division, gave conditional support to the expansion proposals, one proviso being the preservation of Langley Village. She also suggested that the Corporation should be wound up when the town was completed and responsibility handed over to the Stevenage Urban District Council. This was becoming an increasingly common demand, as residents sought the end of rule by the Corporation.

Those opposed to expansion included the Hertfordshire County Council, the Hertfordshire Society, Stevenage Urban District Council and other councils who opposed the extension of the designated area to the west. Local residents, particularly those living in the villages bordering Stevenage, had formed a Campaign Against Stevenage Expansion (CASE), whose main spokeman was S T McCombie. A second organisation, the Campaign Against Unnecessary Stevenage Expansion (CAUSE) was led by Mrs Marion Powell. Both were vociferously opposed to the proposal. The Stevenage Residents' Protection Association, now much reduced since many of its original leaders had moved away or become disillusioned, was represented by Mr H M Sterling. He pleaded for the preservation of the few rural amenities left to old Stevenage, such as The Avenue and the area round St Nicholas' church. He also felt that expansion would put even more pressure on existing amenities. Brian Hall, Chairman of the Stevenage Trades Council, also spoke against the proposed expansion. The town's new Labour Member of Parliament, Mrs Shirley Williams, who had been elected the previous October, was numbered with the objectors. She decided to support her constituents and the Stevenage Council, rather than meekly follow the Ministry's line.

The inquiry proper was described in detail in the *Stevenage Gazette*, which began with the portentous but apt words, 'A town's future hung in the balance this week– and not only the future of the town but of the whole area surrounding it.' There were 86 objectors, one of whom, Mr Raymond Croxson, caused something of a stir when he said that, besides speaking for a number of clients, he was also keeping a watching brief for the Chelsea College of Science and Technology, but he would not be making any comment on their behalf.

Following the inquiry, the Inspector recommended against the major extension but concluded that a population of 91,000 could be accommodated without spoiling the town and that the designated area should be extended by about 100 acres in the north-eastern sector. He then added that on closer study it might be possible to accommodate more than 91,000.

This was a time of much theorising about planning matters. Even as the public inquiry was going on at Stevenage, the eminent town planner Dr R E Pahl was lecturing at Letchworth Library on the topic 'Living in Hertfordshire in 2000 ad', beginning his talk with the words, 'The year is 2000 ad. You are living in Britain's first linear city: the first linear city of North Hertfordshire. You have two cars and two houses, which you accept as a matter of course ...' He thought that 'North Hertfordshire was one of the most likely places for an experimental linear city to be built as it was one of the few parts of the country where a lineal pattern was already building up naturally ... In addition young people from as far away as Tring and Royston travel to Stevenage Bowling Alley ... People had got used to the idea that towns should have a centre which gives a sense of living in a distinct place ...' but he 'wondered if the people of Letchworth really got their sense of place from a corset factory or the people of Stevenage from the offices of the Development Corporation or St George's church.'

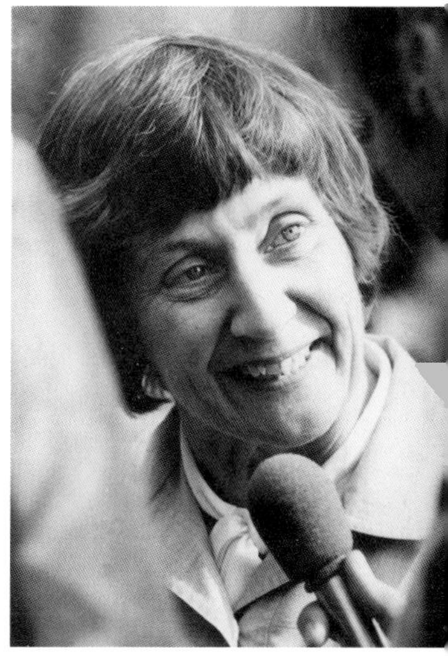
Shirley Williams, MP. (Stevenage Museum P11511)

Meanwhile, back in the real world, another change at the Ministry brought Richard Crossman to the office of Minister of Housing and Local Government. He rejected the Corporation's plans, proposing instead a marginal enlargement of Stevenage by taking into the designated area 100 acres of land in the north-east corner, and invited the Corporation to prepare a new Master Plan to accommodate as large a population (including as many Londoners) as possible as would be compatible with good planning and with facilities comparable to those already achieved.

The Corporation dutifully went to work again and, the following year, produced a revised Master Plan which proposed that the town's population, by then some 50,000, should grow to approximately 105,000 by the end of the century, with in-migration halting at 80,000. Land at Symonds Green in the north-west of the town, which had previously been zoned for future industrial development, would be changed to residential use. It would also be necessary to make improvements to the capacity of the town's main roads system, and more open space land on the periphery of the town would be developed. After that, development would be continued by other bodies including Stevenage Urban District Council and Hertfordshire County Council and private developers.

There was still strong opposition to the plan, which was the subject of yet another public inquiry in January 1967 – and yet another new Minister, Anthony Greenwood, who agreed in the main with the Corporation's proposals but was of the opinion that the ultimate population figure should be left open and reviewed in subsequent revisions of the Master Plan. What that meant and where it left the Corporation, and the people living and working in the town, was unclear.

However, the Corporation was able to go ahead with the new developments in Pin Green. In 1969, the first houses at High Acres, in the St Nicholas' area to the north of Martin's Way, were completed and work began on the Pin Green Industrial Area. Progress was rapid and in 1970 the first Pin Green factory, that of Johnson Gibbons, was in operation. Within a year several new schools were opened. The Giles School, in Durham Road, and Round Diamond School, in Derby Way, were both named after fields now built over. In Webb Rise, Lonsdale and Hilltop Schools were partially residential special schools for handicapped children. The Pin Green Adventure Playground for children, and Hobbs Court, in Vardon Road, another of the Corporation's complexes of specially-designed flatlets and bungalows for the elderly, were completed in 1970.

The St Nicholas shops, in Canterbury Way, were opened in 1973, followed within a year by a pub of the same name and the Borough Council's St Nicholas Park recreation centre and pavilion, which included a scrambling circuit for school-age motor-cycle enthusiasts.

One of the Corporation's responsibilities, as new roads were built was to find suitable names for them. It therefore set up a Street Naming Committee, consisting of representatives from the Post Office, Ambulance, Fire and Police Services, the Urban District Council, the Corporation and a local historian. Initially, much useful work in compiling a 'Stevenage Chronicle' was carried out by Joyce Lenton, the Corporation's Assistant Press Officer from 1956. In the early days, existing names of fields, woods and farms were used and then those of personalities from the history of old Stevenage, such as Richard Bowcock, innkeeper of the Swan Inn in the High Street, who was mentioned in Samuel Pepys' diary for 1667. Bowcock Walk is named after him. New roads in

The Old Bury, formerly Stevenagebury, the mediaeval manor house. (Margaret Ashby)

Lonsdale Road, Pin Green. (Ann Parnell)

Shephall were largely named after former clergy or Lords of the Manor. The Corporation did make great efforts to research and retain the old names, but had the irritating habit of sometimes using a name in the wrong place. Probably the worst example of this is Cleviscroft or Gleviscroft, which was a field near Fishers Green, very well documented in the records of the Hellard Almhouses. The Corporation kept the name alive, which is good, but for some unknown reason used it for a road some two miles away – not so good.

When the Chells and Pin Green neighbourhoods were being developed it became apparent to the Street Naming Committee that they would soon run out of field names. They then invited the help of the town's two new grammar schools, Nobel School and Stevenage Girls' Grammar School. Between them, they had the idea of using themes for groups of roads, so that Chells has roads named after scientists, explorers, engineers, eminent women, poets, military and naval leaders and, of course, in recognition of the Chells coin hoard, people and places of ancient Rome. Pin Green was given the theme of famous sportsmen, with an early emphasis on cricket. Later, roads named after cathedral cities were added and in the Pin Green Industrial Area, names such as Wedgwood Way, commemorating famous industrialists.

The neighbourhood centre for Pin Green was named The Oval, a reference to the famous cricket ground at Lord's, in keeping with the sporting theme. The Corporation had great plans for it, including additional shops, offices, a community centre, a library and a shared church. Unfortunately the offices and the library did not materialise but eventually a dual-purpose building, housing both the community centre and the church, was completed in 1974. On the morning of 21 September that year, the Community Centre was opened by Dame Evelyn Denington, Chairman of the Stevenage Development Corporation. The church, named All Saints, was a new venture, officially termed an ecumenical experiment, as the building was shared between the Church of England, the Roman Catholics and the Methodists. It was dedicated in the afternoon of 21 September, the ceremony conducted by the Bishop of St Albans, the Rt Revd Robert Runcie, the Roman Catholic Archbishop of Westminster and the Chairman of the London North West District of the Methodist Church.

Whether it was a result of the high density housing in parts of Pin Green, against which so many had warned, or the culture of the times or some other

The water tower, Pin Green. (Margaret Ashby)

reason, The Oval later became a target for vandalism and street fights. The problem was overcome in due course, but it was unpleasant while it lasted and gave the town adverse publicity.

For at least 150 years, Highfield House had stood at the top of Pin Green hill, 450 feet above sea-level, set in extensive grounds. It was a Georgian building, enlarged in the 1880s by Charles Poston, father of the composer Elizabeth Poston. He also created a terrace garden and planted an arboretum of fine trees. In accordance with the Master Plan, the Corporation took over the estate, which was to become a public park, demolished the house and put in its place an undistinguished timber and metal pavilion, which has since been taken down by the Borough Council. The one structure which now acts as a landmark for Pin Green is the 85 feet high Stevenage water tower. When water engineer James Boyd and his team were surveying the ground prior to building the tower, they found a very large – 'room-sized' – piece of Hertfordshire puddingstone. It was the largest piece ever found and rather than attempt to move it, they decided to leave it where it was and to build the water tower over it.

The Tom Tiddler public house in Symonds Green. (Margaret Ashby)

As development at Pin Green was nearing completion in 1974, the first houses on the opposite side of the town, in Symonds Green, were being built. Under the first Master Plan, this area had been designated as a possible additional industrial site and not as one of the original neighbourhoods. Ironically, it was in effect a large extension of the little group of roads off Fishers Green Road known before 1946 as 'New Town'. Most of these roads were for some reason named after seaside towns and this theme was continued for the new development. The first and largest new road became 'Scarborough Avenue' but for another reason besides the seaside connection. In the first half of the twentieth century there was a grocery shop on the corner of Fishers Green Road and Nottingham Road, run by Christopher Scarborough. On his death, his daughters carried on the business and one of them, Lilias, was also a greatly loved and respected music teacher. Their name is now perpetuated in Scarborough Avenue.

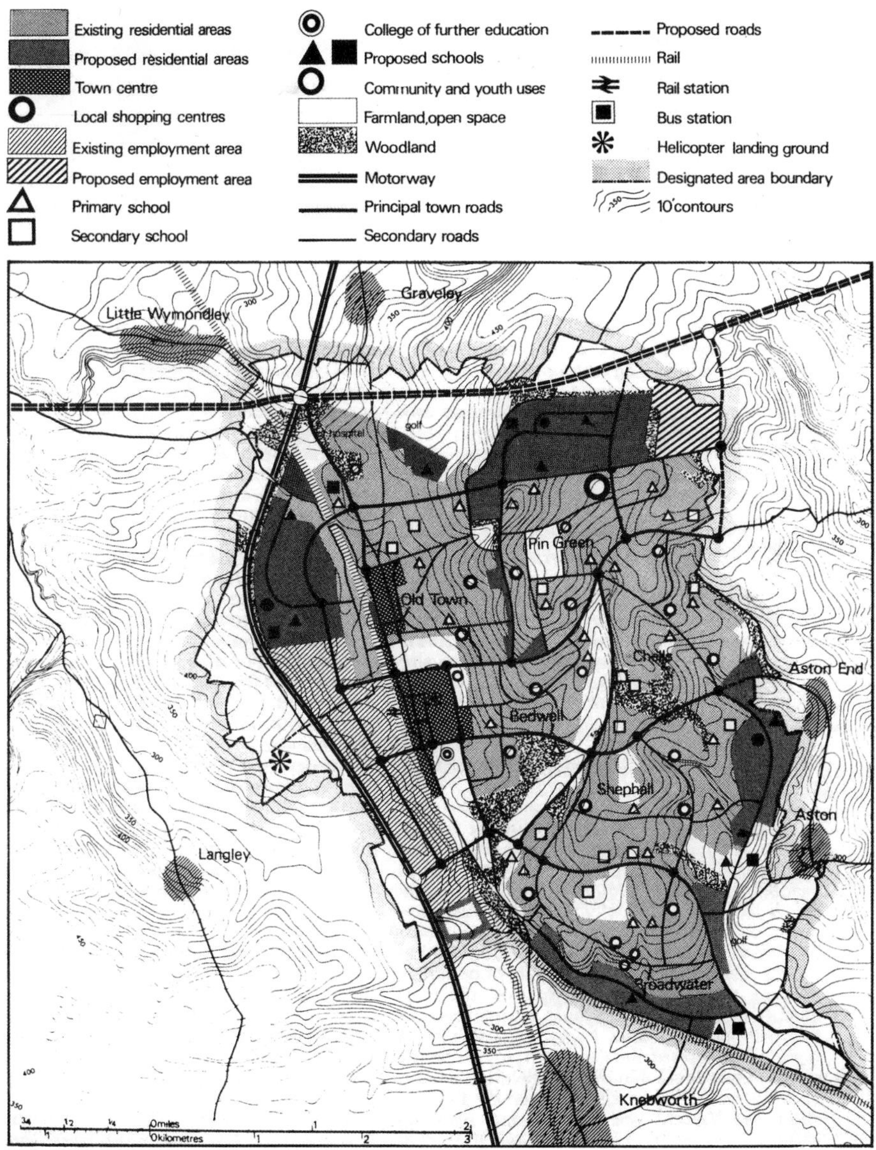

1966 Master Plan

In developing Symonds Green, another old name was brought back to life. This was Woolenwick, which appears in *Domesday Book* as a small manor, with meadow land for grazing animals, hence probably the origin of the name Meadway, the road which led from Fairview Road to Symonds Green. The name Woolenwick fell out of use and the exact whereabouts of the settlement was forgotten over the centuries. However, in 1973, a new junior school was built off Meadway, near the site of the former Oakmead Nursery, and given the name Woolenwick, thus keeping history alive.

The Symonds Green neighbourhood includes several innovative developments. Scarborough House, a specially-designed residential centre for mentally handicapped people, has been very successfully integrated into the community. Bungalows, flats and a community centre for the elderly have proved popular. Symonds Green also has a combined community centre and church complex, which was opened in June 1982. The church part of the building is shared between the Church of England, as part of the old town parish of Holy Trinity, the Roman Catholic Church and the United Reformed Church. The name of the shared church was decided by a committee of representatives from each of the three denominations. Several suggestions were put forward, including that of St Michael and All Angels, but the meeting deferred to the Roman Catholic choice of Christ the King.

One other innovation, this time in human form, was the appointment of a new post of Church and Community Worker, who was paid partly by the Church of England and partly by the Hertfordshire County Council. Anne Haines, who took this job, contributed greatly to the community life of Symonds Green. One of her team of Sunday School teachers at Christ the King was Sharon Taylor, who was later to take a leading role in local politics.

STEVENAGE MPS 1955–70

Until 1974 Stevenage was part of the Hitchin Constituency
20 May 1955
Hitchin: Martin Maddan. Conservative.
8 October 1959
Hitchin: Martin Maddan. Conservative
15 October 1964
Hitchin: Shirley Williams. Labour
31 March 1966
Hitchin: Shirley Williams. Labour
18 June 1970
Hitchin: Shirley Williams Labour

CHAPTER TWELVE
Sixties and Seventies

As the 'Swinging Sixties' merged into the 'Striking Seventies', it seemed as if the whole country, if not the whole world, was at sixes and sevens. There were historic achievements: America won the space race to put a man on the moon; a British man became the first to sail single-handed, non-stop around the world; Britain at last joined the European Economic Community and introduced decimal currency; the country joined in national celebrations for the 25th anniversary of the Queen's accession. On the other hand, there was disaster and muddle: war in Vietnam and the Middle East; continuing fighting in Northern Ireland, with IRA bombing campaigns in England; high inflation; high unemployment; strikes in all sectors of the economy; the three-day week.

Much of the national unrest was echoed in Stevenage. In many ways progress was good, as in Chells where, after a slow start, development proceeded steadily though the sixties. By this time there was no longer a need for the Residents' Associations which had sustained the earliest settlers. Many of the amenities they had fought for had been, or were about to be, provided. The town centre, although not yet complete, had shops, cafes, dance hall, swimming pool, tenpin bowling centre, museum, library and health centre.

At Chells itself, the first houses were occupied in 1960, as Charles and Betty Bush recalled in *Stevenage Pioneers*: 'We were one of the first families to move into the new Chells area and have a lovely three bedroom house. A kitchen, which was modern for those times, and best of all, a bathroom, a big garden, trees and fresh air everywhere.' Their children, David and Kathleen, attended the new Camps Hill School, where Miss Cutler, Head of the Infants', and Mr Shepherd, Head of the Juniors', gave them a good education. There were after school clubs and scout

The Coffee Cabin (Stevenage Museum)

and guide groups as well, all helping members of the new community to establish friendships quickly. During weekdays there was an hourly bus service, but none on Sundays or in the evenings. However, there was a mobile shop and also a lady called Mary who used to call with greengroceries and later opened shops in Austen Paths and Pin Green. The Bushes concluded, 'We have never regretted moving here and have a lot to thank Stevenage for. We attended the church of St Hugh's, situated in four garages in Pankhurst Close. The Revd Arnold Bennett was vicar and his lovely wife, Ruth, ran Young Wives and Mothers' Union.'

In 1963, as the second phase of the town centre shops, including a Littlewoods Store, opened, the Chells neighbourhood centre at the Glebe was almost complete. The shops were finished first, closely followed by Chells Secondary School, then the Community Hall and St John's Methodist church in 1964, St Hugh's church (replacing the garages) and the Swan public house in 1965.

While Chells was still only partially built, development began at Pin Green in 1962. With its areas of high-density housing, experimental Radburn layouts and later an industrial area of its own, it was in many ways different from the original neighbourhood concept. It was also subject to 'cut-the-cost' experimental houses. The Corporation and its architects were under great pressure to meet government house-building targets but within strict budgets. In an effort to achieve the almost impossible, Leonard Vincent and his team arranged with a contractor to develop 'linings' for house interiors, made not of plaster but of a fine concrete of high insulation value and as smooth as plaster. These were made at a depot at Welham Green and delivered to the houses dry and ready for decoration, needing no plastering. Another scheme, to be tried out on 20 houses in Pin Green, was to develop a 'stabilised soil' base for houses. This process made the normal earth foundation rock hard by treatment with chemicals, thus doing away with the traditional concrete foundations. The experiments were not an unqualified success and as as soon as possible a return was made to more conventional methods.

The growth of the Chells and Pin Green neighbourhoods, which are furthest from the Gunnels Wood Industrial Area, coincided with the growth of car ownership, and it was not long before the Corporation began to have serious concerns about road congestion at peak periods. Three possible solutions were proposed: employers were asked to stagger working hours and where this was done it had some beneficial effect; existing primary roads were converted, over a period of years, to dual carriageways; the third solution, to persuade workers to leave their cars at home, was less straightforward. Roy Lenthall, deputy to Eric Claxton, realised that the only way this could be achieved would be by providing a higher standard of public transport – in other words, a better bus service. Between 1970 and 1976, following initial research and consultation, experimental services were introduced, beginning with the Blue Arrow, run by the London Transport Board. This made a financial loss and was withdrawn in 1972. The second scheme, beginning in 1971, was run by London Country Buses, successors to London Transport and became known as Superbus. By 1974 over 23 per cent of Chells residents had changed from car to bus for getting to work. There was, of course, another answer to the problem of congestion during rush-hour periods and that was to provide employment nearer to where people lived, instead of concentrating everything at Gunnels Wood. This was to happen at Pin Green, where a new industrial area was being built. The first company to move in was Johnson Gibbons Ltd, in 1970. No doubt some old town councillors, remembering their own 1946 plan which had been so summarily dismissed, were muttering 'Told you so!'

During the 1964 public inquiry, interest had been aroused at the mention of a possible site in Stevenage for the Chelsea College of Science and Technology. This was later revealed to be a result of the 1963 Robbins Report on Higher Education, which recommended that some regional colleges should join with other institutions and become universities. In 1964 a proposal was made that Hatfield College of Technology should merge with the Chelsea College of Science and Technology to form a University of Hertfordshire. There had also been suggestions a few years earlier that a university could be set up in one of the new towns. The Stevenage Development Corporation had listened with enthusiasm to the idea and discussed several possible sites including, initially, Fairlands Valley. Its chairman, Sir Arthur Rucker, who was also chairman of the University Grants Commission, did his utmost to secure a University of Hertfordshire at Stevenage.

A Radburn housing estate in Chells, 1961. (Stevenage Museum)

In 1964 there came what seemed an ideal solution, to build the university at Knebworth Park, whose owners, Lord and Lady Cobbold, were prepared to sell part of their estate for the purpose. Unfortunately, at this precise time, the energies of both the Stevenage Urban District Council and the Hertfordshire County Council were taken up with the fight against the proposed expansion of Stevenage and perhaps could not give the university plan the attention it deserved. Both were afraid that agreeing to the university might give more weight to the expansion proposals and some members of the Stevenage Council were nervous lest agreeing to a university might extend the Corporation's reign.

The Corporation had persuaded the Ministry of Housing and Local Government to allow it to buy the site from the Cobbolds and give it as a gift to the new university and also to let the Corporation help the university by building student accommodation. It seems that the Corporation had hopes of persuading the Stevenage Council to support these plans, but the County Council was irrevocably against the Knebworth idea because it was promoting a site of its own, near St Albans. So, a magnificent opportunity, which would have brought enormous benefits to Stevenage and north Hertfordshire, was lost. In the words of the poet John Greenleaf Whittier (1807–1892);

For of all sad words of tongue and pen
The saddest are these:
'It might have been.'
(Poem, *Maud Muller*)

The word 'Shock!' was perhaps overused in headlines in Stevenage newspapers of this period, but when it appeared yet again on Thursday 16 November 1967 it was appropriate. The *Stevenage Gazette* announced; 'Demolition shock in Road 10 Plan: 70 properties in High Street area likely to be affected'. This referred to the Corporation's decision to provide a relief road for the High Street by building a dual carriageway extension of Lytton Way from its Fairlands Way junction in the south to a widened and dualled Hitchin Road in the north, on a line between the High Street and the railway. Volume 1 of the *1966 Stevenage Master Plan*, Paragraph 13.28, describes the expected effect on the High Street and adjacent old town landscape; 'Within Old Stevenage there would be two main east–west connections, Orchard Road–Walkern Road to the north, and in the south a new southern link road with Sish Lane. The north end of the High Street around the War Memorial and the southern end by Trinity church would be modified to ensure that the central commercial part is easily accessible to all.' All this was part of the Corporation's High Street Improvement Plan.

To make way for the dual carriageway and attendant roundabouts, it would have been necessary to demolish a number of properties, including 1 Julians

Early twentieth century horse trough placed on the Bowling Green where the A1 Great North Road forked to the right and the Hitchin Road to the left before the introduction of the one-way system. (Stevenage Museum)

Road, an attractive old cottage on the corner of Julians Road and Hitchin Road. As most old town natives knew, this building had previously been three small damp and insanitary dwellings that were in a very poor condition and had been condemned. After being unoccupied for some time, they were bought by a man, skilled in do-it-yourself renovation, who converted the three cottages into one, greatly improving the building both inside and out. He later moved away and the property came into the hands of the Development Corporation, who rented it to actor Derren Nesbitt and his actress wife, Ann Aubrey.

When the Road 10 plans were unveiled, the Nesbitts led a campaign of opposition, attracting a great deal of publicity and enlisting the support of a number of prominent local residents. Unfortunately, because the objectors focussed their energies on saving The Old Cottage, more deserving causes were sidelined. Much more important, historically and architecturally, were the buildings in Trinity Road, formerly called Brick Kiln Lane, at the south of the High Street, where numbers 15 to 19 were listed as being of 'special architectural or historical interest'.

There were protests and public meetings against the route of Road 10. Many people were of the opinion that it was not necessary at all, that clear signs to direct through traffic on the A602 Hitchin–Hertford road away from the High Street would have been perfectly adequate. However, after a local public inquiry, the Corporation gave way to public pressure and drastically amended the plan. The Old Cottage was saved, at the cost of a dangerous and unsightly 'gyratory system' around the Bowling Green, which is still in place today. This turns the northern part of the High Street into a virtual island, requiring a pedestrian underpass to link it with the High Street south of the James Way (formerly Orchard Road) junction. Officially named Lytton Way, Road 10 and its associated destruction, was completed in 1973. It cut through the gardens to the west of the High Street, demolishing part of Orchard Road, including the former

Trinity Road.
(Stevenage Museum PP61)

jewellers' shop on the corner of the High Street, the town hall and the original public library, which then took over the old Northmet premises at 38, High Street.

All the houses in Trinity Road were demolished. From the new roundabout on Lytton Way, a one-way system on the line of the former Trinity Road required another pedestrian underpass to link the High Street with London Road. This, in 1969, was made into a dead end at the point where Fairlands Way cut across it, downgraded and given the name of a little track that joined it from the east, Ditchmore Lane. This clever piece of planning effectively cut off the old town from the new, except for a pedestrian underpass. In 1971, as part of a planned network of high level walkways, a pedestrian bridge across Fairlands Way was opened, hardly a fitting replacement for the famous Great North Road. In 1980, Jack Balchin recorded a walk 'to check on what had happened to the High Street up to that point'. His comment on Ditchmore Lane (formerly London Road) is interesting, 'on the left, the big houses which once graced the entrance to the High Street but now, in their use as guest houses etc offer only a depressed and sometimes neglected facade to a back-water'. No comment was made as to how that backwater was created.

Another proposed road was in the headlines at this time. Road 9, through Fairlands Valley, had been in and out of Master Plans from the early days. It re-appeared in 1966, to the fury of residents. In his autobiography, *Anchorman*, Bert Lowe described it as 'a further attempt by the Stevenage Development Corporation to destroy the Valley by building a major road across the centre of it. The reason given on this occasion was that the existing roads would not be able to cope with the traffic. We all knew that once you built a major road through a green belt site it would only be a matter of time before houses would be built along each side of it.'

Road 9 was opposed by the Shephall Labour Party led by Cllr Tony Dickens and County Councillor Brian Hall. Fred Millard took a leading part in the campaign. At a mass meeting held at Stevenage College, Cllr Les Cummins announced, to enormous applause from the audience, that the road would have to be built over his dead body. A tape of road noise was made and was played via an amplifier wheeled through Fairlands Valley on a perambulator, which shed a wheel on Six Hills Way, resulting in a huge traffic jam.

When the proposal for the road arrived at the County Council Highways Committee, Cllr Hall moved for a five-year postponement to the road, which amendment was carried by the committee. When the five years had elapsed the proposal was once again put to the County Highways Committee, now chaired by Cllr Hall. He proposed its cancellation and Road 9 died at that meeting.

A relic of the preparations for Road 9 is the underpass and roundabout which leads to nowhere opposite the Broadhall Way Football ground. Bert Lowe also points out that the town's building workers 'gave 100% support' to both the campaign to save the Valley and the campaign to scrap Road 9, even though if either project had gone ahead it would have meant more work for their members.

In 1968 Helen Inns, widow of the Stevenage millionaire Jeremiah Inns, died. Her husband had left her Springfield House, at the north end of the High Street, for her lifetime, after which it was to pass to the Stevenage Urban District Council for use as a cottage hospital. Although at this time the whole of Stevenage was still waiting for their new hospital to be built, it was clear that Springfield House could not be used as Jeremiah Inns had intended. Since the passing of the National Health Act, local cottage hospitals were no longer required. The Urban District Council was given two years to decide whether it

London Road c1910, now Ditchmore Lane.

wanted to accept Springfield House and if so, what it would do with it. One suggestion was a rehabilitation centre for patients who had lived at the Fairfield Mental Hospital, near Arlesey, for many years. They would be men and women aged 38–55 years and would be looked after by adequate nursing staff. Councillor Hilda Lawrence, who was much concerned for the welfare of the mentally ill, was enthusiastic, considering this 'a marvellous scheme'.

A public meeting was held at Alleyne's Grammar School on 27 February 1970, at which one person asked about possible violent behaviour by the patients. Dr James Hall, Medical Officer of Health for North Hertfordshire, tried to reassure the audience by telling them that there were many mentally ill people walking around all over North Hertfordshire but, 'You just don't know about them. The type of person we have in mind for Springfield is much less dangerous.' The scheme almost went ahead but fell foul of bureaucracy. After prolonged discussion and negotiation, in 1971 Springfield came into the hands of the Stevenage Development Corporation which, the following year, passed it to the Old Stevenage Community Association for use as a Community Centre, also housing a Royal British Legion office and the Denington Gallery, where members of the Stevenage Artists' Co-operative have their studios and exhibition space. For the previous four years they had met in a house in Green Street.

Also in 1970 the Conservative Government introduced a 'right to buy' policy to allow local authority and Development Corporation sitting tenants to buy their houses. The Corporation had for many years wished to increase the number of owner-occupied houses but had not managed to do very much about it. The government scheme, however, proved very popular, 5,390 Corporation houses were sold in three years, before the Labour Government called a temporary halt to the scheme in 1974. By then, the combined number of owner-occupied houses in Stevenage, including those, mostly in the old town, which were privately-built, was 7,000. This was 35 per cent of all homes, less than the national average of 52 per cent but far more than the 10 per cent it had been before 'right to buy' was introduced. At the time, the Conservatives were in the majority on Stevenage Urban District Council, but Labour councillors fought against the sale of Council houses, of which there were only 1,500 in Stevenage, because sales would reduce the number of dwellings left for rent. In the event, only five were sold.

The principle of owner-occupation was the cause of yet another Master Plan revision in 1972, when Peter Walker, Secretary of State for the Environment, requested the Corporation to submit proposals for an expansion of Stevenage which would include 10,000 houses for owner-occupation. These would be in addition to public-sector housing and other provision as appropriate. It was back to the drawing board once more for the Development Corporation. Then, in

January 1974, Peter Walker was succeeded by Geoffrey Rippon, who told the Corporation that in-migration to the town should cease after 1976 and that only a small-scale expansion would be necessary thereafter for natural growth.

The uncertainty continued, affecting not just the Corporation's professional planners, but also the residents of Stevenage and the adjacent countryside. Two General Elections later, in 1975, Anthony Crossland became the new Secretary of State for the Environment, with John Silkin, son of the late Lord Lewis Silkin, as Minister for Land and Planning with responsibility for new towns. They confirmed Geoffrey Rippon's policy for Stevenage, invited the Corporation to submit plans for a 'mini-expansion' and published a Draft Designation Order enlarging the Designated Area by some 850 acres to the north and east. Following one more public inquiry, in April 1976, the Ministry inspector recommended that the Draft Order be confirmed.

However, by then John Silkin had been replaced by Reg Freeson and Anthony Crossland by Peter Shore, who totally rejected the Inspector's recommendations and the 'mini-expansion' idea. Instead, he decided that the Development Corporation should cease to exist from 1980. Although disappointed, the Corporation now knew exactly where it stood and prepared for its orderly demise and withdrawal from the town. After consultations with the County, Stevenage Borough, North Hertfordshire and East Hertfordshire District Councils and the general public locally, the Corporation presented an updated Master Plan that included private housing provision to the east (Chells Manor Village) and a Pin Green employment area to the north-east. For a while, at least, there was to be a respite from Master Plan revisions.

For the first twenty years or so of the Corporation's existence it dominated life in Stevenage, leaving the Urban District Council to look after housing in the old town and essential but unexciting services such as refuse collection for the town as a whole. One of the Council's first projects in the new town had been the swimming pool in St George's way, but even that had been designed by Corporation architects. The Corporation had also made the site available for a nominal sum, given a financial contribution of £15,000 and supervised the building contract. The state-of-the-art swimming centre opened in 1962, complete with main pool, learners' pool, public gallery, club room and a south-facing side sunbathing area.

The construction of Fairlands Valley Park was a major project, encompassing a large spine of former farmland in the centre of the town, from Fairlands Way in the north to Broadhall Way in the south. In the Development Corporation's 1966 revised Master Plan, the valley was shown as the town's principal area of recreation and open space, with a boating and fishing lake of about 17 acres, between Fairlands Way and Six Hills Way, and large areas for picnics and children's play areas.

Fairlands Valley Park sailing lake. (Ann Parnell)

The Council set about turning the proposal into reality. Mr Vanstone, of Vanstone Park Garden Centre, near Codicote, which had a large artificial lake, was invited to advise the Council on a water feature scheme for the 150–acre park. Mr Vanstone submitted proposals for a linear scheme consisting of a main sailing lake and a smaller fishing and children's boating lake, together amounting to 11 acres, a smaller nature reserve and wildfowl water feature and a settling pond. To ensure that the water did not become stagnant, a pumping system was installed to recirculate the water. The Corporation made the valley land available to the council on satisfactory terms, made a financial contribution of £65,000 towards the cost of the project and organised the accumulation of spoil necessary to raise levels where the lake was constructed. A significant grant was also received from the Hertfordshire County Council. But it was a Stevenage Council project that was formally opened in the summer of 1972 by Sir Alec Rose, famous yachtsman who had become the first to sail single-handed round the world. A children's paddling pool, modernistic band stand, clubhouse, car parks and Continental-style fitness features in a jogging track in adjacent woodland were also provided. The southern part of the valley, off Broadhall Way, is used as a showground, a regular site for circuses and funfairs.

Monks Wood and Whomerley Wood, which form a backdrop to Fairlands Valley, were important wildlife sites. Once the builders had left, the Stevenage Woodlands Conservation Society, which was formed in 1967, established a bird and wildlife sanctuary in Whomerley Wood in 1969. The Hertfordshire Society also became involved some years later, in helping to gain recognition and protection for Monks Wood as one of the county's most beautiful bluebell woods.

Stevenage golf course (SBC)

Concert in Fairlands Valley, 1975. (Stevenage Museum P11417)

Bluebells in Monks Wood (Margaret Ashby)

To a greater or lesser degree there was always tension between the Council and the Corporation. In a contribution to the booklet *Brave New World*, edited by Judith Carruthers and published in 1966, Leonard Vincent expressed his understanding of the Council's point of view,

> It was a bit like 'Big Brother' the Development Corporation with its special powers which the indigenous population of Stevenage as it was then, (I have every sympathy with them), viewed with great suspicion. Being mainly recruited from the Old Town because that's all there was at the time, the Council just didn't like 'Big Brother' telling them what to do with the area. Right from the start it had this sort of basic suspicion but they never fell out with one another, it was almost an uneasy neutrality.

It was not only old town councillors who viewed the Corporation askance. Many of the newcomers, as they became involved in local affairs, were even more anxious to see the time when Stevenage would be run by its elected Council. This was to be true of a Labour councillor first elected in 1967. His name was Brian Hall and his ability and single-minded – some would say ruthless – dedication to Council business was soon recognised and he became leader of the Labour Group in 1969, then leader of the Council in 1971, when Labour took control again after two years of a Conservative majority.

In fact, after the first few years, some of those appointed to the Development Corporation Board were from Stevenage or its immediate vicinity. Of the 36 people appointed to the Board at various times, 12 could be classed as 'locals', the majority being members of the Conservative-controlled Hertfordshire County Council or the Labour-dominated Stevenage Council. Philip Ireton, who began his political career in Stevenage in the 1930s, was the only Board member to serve for the whole of its life.

Other local people appointed to the Board were

W A Winson (1950/52), chairman of the Unilever Transport subsidiary SPW Ltd

Major A G Howard (1952/56), a member and sometime chairman of the Stevenage Urban District Council

Peter Pryor (1956/60), a member of Hertfordshire County Council, gentleman farmer and 'squire' of Weston

Geoffrey Hughes (1956/80) chairman of the Stevenage Industrial Employers' Group, managing director of Shunic Ltd of Stevenage, chairman of the Stevenage Conservative Association

The Revd Eric Cordingly, MBE (1960/62), Rector of Stevenage and Honorary Chaplain to the Queen

Commander Peter Martineau, RN (rtd) (1962/69), a solicitor, who was deputy chairman for a time

Sam Clarke (1962/71), Director of the Government's Warren Spring Laboratory in the Gunnels Wood Industrial Area

Michael Cotter (1964/80), a building worker, a former chairman of Stevenage Residents' Federation and a Labour member of the Hertfordshire County and Stevenage Borough Councils

Mrs Hilda Lawrence (1965/80), campaigner, former secretary of the Stevenage Residents' Federation, a Labour member of both the Hertfordshire County and Stevenage Borough Councils

Denis Crane (1970/80), secretary of Hawker Siddeley Dynamics (later part of British Aerospace) in Stevenage

Ken McKechnie (1970/80), a Conservative member of both the Hertfordshire County and Stevenage Borough Councils

Group Captain Douglas (later Sir Douglas) Bader (1972/73) chairman of the Civil Aviation Authority

Peter Metcalfe (1974/1980) a Labour member of Stevenage Urban District/ Borough Council

After Philip Ireton, the longest serving member of the Board was Evelyn Denington. Appointed in 1950, she was then a member of the St Pancras Metropolitan Borough Council and vice-chairman of the London County Council's Housing Committee. After a remarkable record of service to local government in London she became chairman of the Greater London Council itself. In 1966 she was appointed Chairman of the Stevenage Development Corporation on the retirement of Sir Arthur Rucker, KCMG, CB, CBE, a distinguished civil servant who, at various times, had been Principal Private Secretary to Prime Minister Neville Chamberlain, Deputy Secretary at the Ministry of Health, a member of the wartime government's Security Executive, Deputy Director General of the International Refugee Organisation and Deputy Agent-General of the United Nations Korean Reconstruction Agency. In 1974, Evelyn Denington was created a Dame Commander of the Order of the British Empire. Four years later she was

Dame Evelyn Denington. (Stevenage Museum P12425)

raised to the Peerage, taking the title Baroness Denington of Stevenage. She had come a long way since her first job as a journalist on the *Architect and Building News.* Evelyn Denington was an outstanding chairman of the Corporation and one who was anxious to do all she could to improve relations with the local Council, initiating joint meetings between the two bodies on a regular basis.

One of the most colourful members of the Board was ex-RAF Group Captain and famous 1940s Battle of Britain fighter pilot Douglas Bader. The story of his heroic determination to continue flying, even after losing both legs ion a flying accident in the early 1930s, was told in a 1956 feature film, *Reach for the Sky,* based on the book by Paul Brickhill and starring Kenneth More. He was on the Board for only a year. Bader Close in Pin Green is named after him.

The third phase of the town centre was under construction in 1972 when a national strike of building workers, members of the Union of Construction Allied Trades and Technicians (UCATT) took place, over wages and conditions of work. The strike began on 25 June when UCATT instructed its regional Committees to call out selected sites, one of which was in Stevenage. The strike became national on 14 August and ended on 15 September 1972 with the biggest pay increase ever recorded for building workers in England, although not all their demands were met.

In the same year another new building was opened, probably the most important and certainly the most longed-for of any, the New Lister Hospital in Coreys Mill Lane. It was 28 years from the designation of Stevenage as a new town in November 1946 to the official opening by Queen Elizabeth the Queen Mother in November 1972. There were several changes of authorities responsible for providing local health services during these years. Jack Balchin summarises the delays:

> At the formative period it was the Hospital Board and the County Council that the Corporation with others looked to for action. The Corporation had the land available, whether it was for a hospital or health centre or surgery … Whatever the system, the Corporation could help, but the initiative belonged elsewhere. Ten years after the designation of Stevenage that initiative seemed still to be wholly lacking.

It took another 18 years before work started on the hospital site and yet another four years to complete the first phase. The Maternity Unit remained at Hitchin until 1983. By that time the priorities had changed somewhat. The previously exceptionally high birth-rate was falling, but the number of elderly people in the town was increasing, which meant that a range of new geriatric services would soon be needed.

Another long-promised improvement was the new railway station. Since 1850, the railway station at the top of Julians Road had served the town, initially as part of the Great Northern Railway, then the London and North-Eastern and finally, British Rail. It was in many ways cosy, especially in winter, when there would be a roaring open fire on the staff side of the booking office. It also had many inadequacies, one being the pedestrian bridge, with gaps in the wooden floor, and the other being the very short platform, which meant that passengers intending to alight at Stevenage had to make sure they were in a central carriage, or get carried on to the next station. In 1973, the new station was opened off Lytton Way, with a high-level pedestrian walkway to the town centre. No longer need passengers worry about short platforms, but there was disappointment in other respects. In particular, the stairway access to platforms, with no kind of separation or handrail between those passengers going up and those going down, was not easy to negotiate at busy times. However, the railway service to London, Edinburgh and many other destinations has given Stevenage an important role in the region.

Stevenage New Town certainly had its share of frustration, disappointment and conflict, its bad press and its denigrators, but to many in the outside world, it was an enviable example of twentieth-century planning. When, in May 1946, Lewis Silkin, Minister of Town and Country Planning, told a hostile public meeting in Stevenage that 'Stevenage will, in a short time, become world famous' and that 'people from all over the world will come to Stevenage to see how we in this country are building for the new way of life', some members of the audience laughed. But within 15 years Silkin's prophesy had come true. People were coming from all over the world to see Britain's first new town and to learn from what they saw. It began as a trickle but became a flood, peaking in the early 1970s with more than 7,000 official visitors in one year alone. They came from all the countries in Western Europe, including Scandinavia and from the Soviet Union, North and South America, Japan and elsewhere.

To cope with the increasing number of visitors, the Corporation's public relations officer recruited, at first on a part-time basis, several local residents with foreign languages. They were soon able to give presentations on the development of Stevenage and to conduct guided tours of the town. Many single visitors and small delegations were making a 'Best-of-Britain' tour of the whole country by car, as guests of the Her Majesty's Government. Arrangements were made for them by the Central Office of Information, and invariably their first stop out of London was at Stevenage. The Development Corporation also received requests for visits from larger groups, including whole coach loads, from foreign embassies in London, the Town and Country Planning Association and other bodies.

The majority of the visitors to Britain's first new town were architects, engineers, educationalists, planners, politicians, sociologists, journalists and students. However, the bold experiment in social planning and new style town development also attracted several heads of state, including the Ruler of Abu Dhabi, the President of Chile, who arrived by helicopter, and the King of Tonga, who was a good customer of the town's oldest industry, the school furniture-making Educational Supply Association. Other notable visitors included the Prime Minister of New South Wales, Australia; the Minister of Housing in the government of the Federal Republic of Germany; a former West Indies Test cricketer who was then involved in social and community development in British Guyana, and an African tribal chief who, colourfully dressed in feathers and monkey skins, attracted quite a bit of public attention! George Romney, USA Secretary for Housing in President Eisenhower's administration, was a prominent member of the Church of Jesus Christ of Latter-day Saints. His visit followed shortly after the opening of the church's new chapel which had been built in Buckthorn Avenue by the voluntary labour of church members, under the direction of a building missionary from the USA, and he was taken there to meet the local bishop and church members.

For one head of state, the King of Burundi, his Sunday visit to Stevenage, turned out to be his last day of peaceful relaxation. He particularly enjoyed his first game of ten-pin bowling with his host for the day, the Corporation's public relations officer, but after he flown back to his country that evening, he was overthrown in a military coup, arrested, imprisoned and executed.

In appreciation of the hospitality received in Stevenage, the Ruler of Abu Dhabi invited the Corporation's public relations officer and his wife to a reception in his suite at the Dorchester Hotel in London's Park Lane. It was the first time that they had seen, as centre-pieces on buffet tables, bowls of sheep's eyes – a delicacy whose temptation they managed to resist!

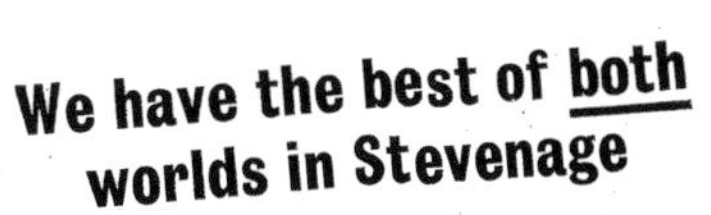

A national newspaper advertisement for Stevenage

CHAPTER THIRTEEN
Borough status

On 1 April 1974 the Local Government Act of 1972 came into force. Its intention was to make local government more efficient. This would be done partly by reforming regulations governing the way local authorities operated, but mainly by reorganising county and district boundaries to reduce the number of local authorities. As a result, all but 10 of the 45 ancient English counties were altered to a greater or lesser extent: for example, the smallest county, Rutland, was absorbed into Leicestershire, Huntingdon became part of Cambridgeshire and parts of Yorkshire and Lincolnshire were joined together to form a new county of Humberside. The changes in Hertfordshire were comparatively small and mainly in the south of the county. Potters Bar, formerly in Middlesex, became part of Hertfordshire but the county lost Barnet, Totteridge and Osidge, which were absorbed into Greater London, itself a new authority set up in 1965.

The 1972 act also made changes in the size and responsibilities of the district councils within counties. Urban and rural district councils were abolished and replaced by district councils, generally covering a larger area than their predecessors, with a population of over 40,000. Thus the former Hitchin Rural and Urban District Councils were merged to create the North Hertfordshire District Council. The Act did, however, retain the ancient and prestigious designation 'borough', which used in mediaeval times to carry with it privileges such as the right to levy certain tolls and the right to send representatives to parliament. It was now open to district councils who wished to apply for the title, which now conveys no advantages save the purely ceremonial one of electing a mayor and creating appropriate chains of office. Stevenage Council decided to pursue this right and in due course, towards the end of 1974, the town was granted borough status.

Elizabeth the Second

by the Grace of God of the United Kingdom of Great Britain and Northern Ireland and of Our other Realms and Territories Queen, Head of the Commonwealth, Defender of the Faith:

To all to whom these presents shall come, Greeting!

WHEREAS certain new local government areas known as districts have been established by the Local Government Act 1972:

AND WHEREAS a petition praying for the grant of a Charter conferring upon the district of Stevenage the status of a borough has been presented unto Us by the Council of the said district:

AND WHEREAS We are pleased by the advice of Our Privy Council to grant a Charter for such purpose.

NOW THEREFORE KNOW YE that We, by virtue of Our Prerogative Royal and in pursuance of the Local Government Act 1972 and of all other powers and authorities enabling Us in that behalf, have granted and declared and by these Presents do grant and declare that the district of Stevenage shall have the status of a borough.

IN WITNESS whereof We have caused these Our Letters to be made Patent.

WITNESS Ourself at Westminster the twenty-seventh day of February in the twenty-third year of Our Reign.

By Warrant under the hands of the Counsellors of State

(*Signed*) DOBSON

Stevenage Borough Charter.

This was not achieved entirely without criticism. There were those who considered it a means of self-glorification for councillors, but others approved, including perhaps the ghost of Richard de Ware, the thirteenth-century Abbot of Westminster and Lord of the Manor of Stevenage, as his dream came true after seven centuries. As the role of mayor became established, people began to appreciate its value in helping to publicise local voluntary and social activities. Each mayor has the opportunity to support chosen charities through an annual concert and donations, and many also focus on a particular theme for his or her year of office.

The first Mayor of Stevenage was Cllr James Cockerton. He was born in a village near Chesterfield, but moved to London in 1952 and thence to Stevenage in 1954, to work at BAC. In 1958 he was elected to the Stevenage Urban District Council, representing Broadwater Ward, and was elected Mayor for the year 1965/66. His contribution to community life included voluntary work as a magistrate, school governor, Chairman of the Citizens' Advice Bureau, President of the Broadwater Division of the St John's Ambulance Brigade cadets, Stevenage Town Band, Stevenage and North Herts Leukaemia Association, the Stevenage Swimming Club and much more.

The Borough of Stevenage was by now the largest town in north Hertfordshire and beginning to take over from Hitchin as the 'capital' of the area, as Philip

Ireton had always wished. Traditionally, people living in the surrounding towns and villages had looked to Hitchin for its market, shops and other services. The North Hertfordshire Hospital, the Lister Hospital, the office of the Registrar of Births, Marriages and Deaths, the Divisional Education Office, the Post Office Sorting Office – all these were at Hitchin and local bus services were largely centred there. As the focus began to shift to Stevenage, it inevitably caused difficulties for some in north Hertfordshire, particularly with transport. For Stevenage residents, in both old and new towns, life was becoming easier as more services were based in their own town.

Ironically, despite its increasing centrality to the area, Stevenage was still largely controlled by the Development Corporation. The Council, regardless of its grand title of 'Borough' had, so far, very little power in the new town, but once the Corporation knew for certain that it would be dissolved or 'wound up' in 1980, it worked closely with the Council to prepare for as smooth a transition as possible. This process was greatly helped by John Silkin, youngest son of Lewis Silkin, who had become Minister for Planning and Local Government, with special responsibility for new towns, in 1974. That year, he visited Stevenage to discuss with borough councillors and members of the Board of the Development Corporation the needs of the town in the years to come. He then

Chain of office for the mayor of Stevenage. (Stevenage Borough Council)

The badge from the mayoral regalia. (Stevenage Borough Council)

set up a working party to report on the implications of transferring housing and related assets from new town development corporations to local authorities. The report would relate to new towns in general, but John Silkin chose Stevenage for a 'model scheme' and the working party became known as the Stevenage Working Party.

Lewis Silkin, known as 'father of the new towns', had died on 11 May 1972 and two years later a ceremony was held in the Town Square, when Prime Minister Harold Wilson, with John Silkin also present, unveiled a plaque in his memory. This was designed and made by Franta Belsky, sculptor of the 'Joy Ride' statue and is mounted on the clock tower.

In March 1976, Philip Ireton was awarded the CBE. A few months later another honour was conferred upon him, as one of the new Borough Council's first actions was to make him a Freeman of the Borough. Although he had been displaced as leader by Brian Hall, he was enormously respected and looked up to by his fellow councillors. The ceremony took place on 6 November, 29 years to the day since Stevenage had been designated as Britain's first post-war new town. It was an impressive occasion. The assembled company stood to receive His Worship the Mayor, wearing the new regalia paid for by British Aerospace. Philip Ireton then made The Freeman's Oath:

> I Philip Thomas Ireton do solemnly and sincerely swear that I will be faithful and bear true allegiance to our Sovereign Lady Queen Elizabeth II, her heirs and successors, according to law, and that I will give due obedience to the Mayor and Council of this Borough and will, as much as lies in my power, contribute and do every act and thing for the good government and safety of the rights and privileges of the Borough and the inhabitants thereof. So help me God.

He was given the Freeman's Scroll and Casket. The Scroll, backed in fine Persian Morocco leather and fully gold tooled, contains an illuminated inscription, and bears the seal of the Borough Council. The casket, of modern design and engraved with the Borough Coat of Arms, has solid silver ends and is mounted on a polished walnut plinth. The citation for Philip Ireton was a summary only of his many activities on behalf of the town:

> Philip Ireton was born in Stevenage in 1904, and can trace his ancestry over two centuries. His early and continuing involvement in political and public life and in community affairs generally is such that no summary can be adequate. He joined the Labour Party at fourteen years old, and entered local government on election as a Member of the former Stevenage Urban District Council in 1937. The record shows that he missed only one Council Meeting in thirty-three years ... He became the first Labour Chairman of the County Council from 1973.

Philip Ireton. (Stevenage Museum P10856)

Philip Ireton's service to education has no equal in human endeavour. He has served on the County Education Committee since 1942. He was the first chairman of the Governors for about a dozen schools in Stevenage; he was a foundation Governor of Hitchin College of Further Education since 1960. He is chairman of the Governors of Alleyne's Secondary School, Woolenwick Primary School and Vice-Chairman of Letchworth College of Technology. He is a Governor of Hatfield Polytechnic and a Member of the Court of Brunel University ... He is the Chairman of the Stevenage Divisional Library Committee and is a member of the Herts Education Foundation Trust and of the East Anglian Regional Council for Higher and Further Education.

It is not surprising that Philip Ireton was appointed to the Board of Stevenage Development Corporation when it was formed in 1946, and he is the longest serving member amongst all the New Towns Development Corporations in the country. He was a Magistrate on the Stevenage Bench from 1942 to 1974 ... He was the longest serving member on the Hertfordshire Commission for the Peace when he retired in 1974.

Despite his commitments relating to local government and kindred bodies ... he has been a perpetual force in local organisations ... How he found time to be a keen gardener and knowledgeable horticulturist remains a mystery. He is a founder of Stevenage Allotment and Gardens Association, Vice-President of the Stevenage Horticultural Society and of the Herts Agricultural Show. This is not a complete picture, but enough to convince anyone that Philip Ireton is indeed a remarkable man and that, in becoming the first Freeman of the Borough of Stevenage, no honour could be more richly deserved.

At this time, the Council were still meeting in their temporary offices in Southgate House. The first Master Plan and all its successors had promised a new civic building to replace the old town hall in Orchard Road. The site allocated for this was in The Forum, the fourth and last phase of the town centre to be built, but the Council waited patiently. Then, in the early 1970s, there were ominous signs that all was not going to plan.

One complication was the difficulty that the Corporation was having in trying to attract a major, traditional department store to the town centre. Although Marks and Spencers, Boots, Woolworths and some 25 other smaller shops built during phase three were now trading successfully in Queensway, there was the wish for something more prestigious. Negotiations with Selfridges almost succeeded but, because of the current economic climate and associated financial constraints, eventually came to nothing. The Corporation was also anxious to fulfil its promise to provide a cinema but, at a time when attendances were dropping, neither of the two big cinema chains were keen to commit themselves to a new building. To these difficulties were added the problems of car parking. The 1966 Master Plan had included six multi-storey car parks, for which charges would be made, although ground level parking was free. With

The Manulife building. (Stevenage Museum)

great difficulty the Corporation at last got permission from the Treasury to begin on the first and most expensive, including a covered market on the ground floor, but only by agreeing to charge for all car parking. It was not an easy project, under construction at a time of unrest in the building industry and with structural problems as well. To make matters worse, without support from the Treasury, the one means by which the Corporation could achieve a department store and more car parking would be to add an office block. Promising negotiations began with a major company just as the government put an embargo on the building of offices.

The Forum's problems were eventually solved when Tesco took over a site on the corner of St George's Way and Fairlands Way, which included a petrol station and a twin-auditoria cinema, seating 400 and 200 people. This complex opened in 1973 and two years later British Home Stores and CA Modes opened on the opposite side of The Forum, facing the Grampian Hotel, opened in the same year. But all this was at the expense of the promised town hall and civic centre. The Council was effectively homeless.

One of the few office blocks which did get built at this time, its construction having begun just before the embargo, was a seven-storey insurance company headquarters named Manulife House, in St George's Way. Internally it incorporated many of the latest technical features: externally, it was depressing. Jack Balchin described it as 'a squat building of medium height that is an ill bedfellow of the church on one side and the fire and ambulance one-storey station on the other'. In the 1966 town centre plan, an L-shaped, relatively unobtrusive building was indicated for this site, but the developers proceeded along quite different lines, partly because of new fire safety regulations relating to offices, but also for economic reasons. To compensate for the unfortunate juxtaposition, the Corporation paid for a large stained-glass east window in St George's church, to obscure the view. Manulife House did have its uses, however, as it was able to rent office space to the Council when there was a shortage of staff accommodation at Southgate House. But it was to be a thorn in the Council's side for the next thirty years.

Another impressive ceremony took place in the Council Offices at Southgate House in 1975. On this occasion, a formal link of friendship was set up between the original twinned towns of Ingelheim and Stevenage and the ancient town of Autun, in the wine-producing Burgundy region of south-east France. Councillor Brian Hall, Mayor of Stevenage, with Ingelheim's Oberbürgermeister, Hans Oehlschlagel, and Senateur Marcel Lucotte, Mayor of Autun, signed a formal tri-partite link document. Similar ceremonies took place in both Ingelheim and Autun at later dates.

The official involvement of the Borough Council, with its generous financial support, breathed new life into the Stevenage-Ingelheim-Autun Link Association.

Later, a project entitled '3 Towns 1 Vision', was established, backed by the councils in all three towns and part funded by the European Union, which recognises its importance. Under this scheme groups of teenagers from the three towns visit each other's areas in turn each year and spend a few days together, learning about the life and culture in each country, discussing matters of common concern, enjoying social and sporting activities and visiting places of interest.

The town's magnificent new Leisure Centre was opened in 1975. It had always been envisaged that Stevenage should one day house an arts centre and a sports centre, albeit on separate sites, in different areas of the town. It was also thought that such provision would have to come through voluntary endeavour, with financial and other support from the County Council, Urban District Council, Development Corporation and the Eastern Regional Arts and Sports Councils.

The Stevenage Arts Guild was formed in the early 1960s and was soon pressing the authorities for a permanent home for the arts in the town. At that time, the Stevenage College of Further Education was the leading venue for the staging of amateur dramatic and musical productions in its well-equipped main hall, to the provision of which the Corporation had made a sizeable financial contribution. The Corporation commissioned Sir William Emrys Ellis, CBE, former Secretary General of the Arts Council of Great Britain, to undertake a survey of the local cultural scene and to produce a report with recommendations on ways in which the needs of the vigorous cultural life developing in the town might best be met. Published in November 1963, the Ellis Report, entitled *The Arts In Stevenage*, recommended the provision of a central building, which would be both a club and an organisational centre, to accommodate as many of the town's dramatic and musical societies, artistic and creative hobby groups as possible. It would also be a meeting place for individuals interested in any form of artistic or cultural activity.

As a result of the Ellis Report, a committee was set up under the chairmanship of Councillor Philip Ireton. In 1966 it was superseded by the Stevenage Arts Trust, modelled on the lines of the Youth Trust. It was chaired at first by Sir William Emrys Ellis, then by Miss Elizabeth Sweeting (nominated by the Arts Council of Great Britain) and finally by Councillor Ireton again. The Trust produced plans for an arts centre on a site in the town centre reserved by the Corporation in its 1966 Master Plan. However, the chairman had reservations in regard to the proposed cost and it was suggested that a smaller, cheaper building should be designed.

By now, a Stevenage Sports Trust had also been established to look into the provision of a sports centre. In 1968, a delegation from Stevenage visited Billingham, in County Durham, to see what was being done there. Councillors came back enthused with the idea of a joint arts/sports centre as a major civic amenity instead of two separate buildings in different areas of the town as was being proposed. The Council realised that all the features planned for the first arts building could be retained, with the added bonus of a larger theatre, which would allow commercial productions in Stevenage. The Arts Trust, which was dominated by representatives of amateur drama, preferred the idea of a small, 400 seat theatre, whereas the Council wanted a 900 seat fully professional theatre. As a compromise, it was agreed to go for 700 seats, although, in the event, 507 seats were provided.

The Council and Development Corporation appointed two advisers, Miss Elizabeth Sweeting and Mr D D Molyneux (nominated by the Central Council of Physical Recreation) to examine the conflicting proposals and to come up with a report containing recommendations. To the surprise of some, their report, published in December 1968, made a strong case for a joint arts and sports centre under the one roof as the Urban District Council had insisted. Not everyone was happy with the idea, particularly the Arts Trust. Some asked whether arts patrons would be willing to mix with 'sweaty' sportsmen. It was estimated that the project, at 1970 prices, would cost well over £1 million. Such a sum could certainly not be found by the Arts and Sports Trusts and the Development Corporation. It was then that the Urban District Council came into its own and took over. Its treasurer, Dick Hughes (later to become its first Chief Executive), made the unorthodox suggestion that a lease-back arrangement with a merchant bank might be entered into by the Council. The plan was successful, the money was forthcoming and building started in 1973. The foundation stone was laid in June the following year by the first Arts Minister, Baroness Jennie Lee of Asheridge, widow of the 1940s Labour Government Health Minister, Aneurin Bevan, who promoted the revolutionary new National Health Service.

Opened in November 1975 the Stevenage Leisure Centre, designed by Vincent Gorbing and Partners, became known as 'The Orange Box' because of its cheerful orange-coloured exterior panels. It incorporated a large sports hall with climbing wall, bowls hall, squash courts, billiards rooms, gymnasium, music, pottery and meeting rooms, restaurant and bars, children's toy library and creche. The theatre is named after the eminent theatre designer, Edward Gordon Craig. He was born in Stevenage in 1872, at 23 Railway Street (later renamed Orchard Road), son of the famous actress, Ellen Terry and the architect, Edward William Godwin. In those days, to have a child out of wedlock brought shame and social ostracism, which may be why Ellen Terry chose the quiet little town of Stevenage for the birth.

Ray Gorbing, who designed the theatre, was concerned about the potential noise problem, given the location of the site near the railway station and beside a main road. Added to that, the town centre was directly under the flight path

The Gordon Craig Theatre, interior. (Stevenage Museum P5910)

The Leisure Centre under construction. (Stevenage Museum P5962)

into Luton Airport. He explained, 'To overcome the noise factor we used cladding and roofing panels of glass reinforced plastic to provide the necessary insulation. I decided that the panels should be in a fairly lively colour to offset the general greyness of most of the buildings in the Town Centre ... Having been to many theatres in London, I had always found myself complaining about the lack of leg room ... I was determined if possible not to have this inconvenience in our theatre and proposed that we should adopt what was known as continental seating, which meant extended leg room along the rows. At the time, I thought our big problem would be to convince our client to agree to this, as it would mean a larger auditorium ... with an increase in cost. However, there was no problem as this was readily agreed.'

Paul Wareham, Sports Manager, was keen to stress the range and flexibility of sports provision. Over twenty different indoor sports were available, suitable 'for every member of the community', for all ages and abilities. Bookings could be made by both individual casual users and by regular groups. Creche facilities and a children's toy library were also provided. A festival of indoor sport was held during the opening week, 3–9 November 1976, including events such as: schools badminton tournament; fencing competition; volleyball; table-tennis; junior five-a-side football; mens' and ladies' hockey; tennis tournament; bowls matches and judo and karate demonstrations.

The complex was completed and opened to the public on 3 November 1975 and four days later the Lytton Players performed on the new stage for the first time in *The Gilbert and Sullivan Story*. Ray Gorbing recalls, 'On November 7 I must confess that I felt a little nervous singing on the stage with the Lytton

Players who had been given the honour of being the first amateur group to perform there. Fortunately all went well and we didn't hear one car, train or plane. Now, 24 years later, I think it can be argued confidently that arts and sports can indeed be combined in one leisure building under one administration'.

The leisure centre cost £3.25 million. It is a highly professional organisation and one of the town's greatest assets, attracting patrons from a wide area. Its outstanding success is largely due to the stand taken by the Stevenage Council, which believed in the viability of a large project combining arts and sports under one roof, when everyone else concerned had envisaged two separate centres on different sites. The local authority was beginning to assert itself.

Also in 1976, the Borough Council bought Stevenage Lodge from the Development Corporation. This was a detached house at Mobbs Hill, Chells, with extensive grounds, which were designated under the 1966 Master Plan as open space and recreational use. The house was probably built in the second half of the nineteenth century, by which time the grounds may have been used for market gardening. Certainly by about 1900 there were fruit trees growing there and the owners, Alfred Young and Thomas Dobinson, were florists and nurserymen. The Borough Council had a similar purpose in mind for the Lodge: it was to become 'a focus for all residents of the town who have an interest in horticulture' and a meeting place for such groups as the Stevenage Allotments and Gardeners' Association, the Stevenage Disabled Gardeners' Association, the newly-formed Stevenage Lodge Horticultural Society and others with related interests. Some of the first special interest groups based at the Lodge were; Floral Art, Fuchsia, Pot plants, Pelargoniums and Geraniums, Primula and Auricula, Chrysanthemums, Herbs, Bonsai, Vegetables, Cacti and Succulents. Under the auspices of the Director of Leisure Services, a programme of talks and demonstrations was scheduled, all of which, like the Lodge itself and its one and a half acres of ground, were arranged to enable disabled gardeners to participate fully. After essential repairs to the house and renovation

Stevenage Lodge Horticultural Centre. (Stevenage Museum)

of the gardens, the first phase of the project was completed in early 1979. It was awarded the prestigious Wilkinson Sword trophy.

In November 1976, the new town of Stevenage was 30 years old. The local press made much of this, with reminiscences, photographs and feature interviews. In the *Midweek Gazette* for 16 November, Leonard Vincent made some frank comments,

> I wish I were younger and could start it again, knowing all I know now, to avoid the mistakes – but then nothing is perfect that is man-made ... A lot of planners have done damn silly things in the past and Stevenage can be criticised with hindsight. But people come from all over the world to see it ... for what it has achieved ... Overall the thing works. This is what matters ... Over the years New Towns have been subject to government mucking about – whichever government has been in power ... If I'd known in 1946 what I know now I shouldn't have said 'More new towns' but 'more slowly'. More to provide the housing needed at the time, more slowly to give welfare and local government time to cope with the situation and people the chance to grow up together.

Stevenage's MP from 1964 was Shirley Williams, daughter of the writer Vera Brittain and an outstandingly able member of the Labour Government. Many political observers thought she would be the first woman prime minister. She had held the posts of Parliamentary Secretary at the Ministry of Labour; Minister of State for Education; junior Minister to the Home Office; Minister for Prices and Consumer Protection, Paymaster General and Secretary for Education. Despite the demands of her ministerial duties, she was an excellent and greatly appreciated constituency MP, spending much time in Stevenage and giving help and support where she could.

Her anniversary greeting included these words,

> Many happy returns to Stevenage on its 30th birthday. The town has had its growing pains but it's a success – people come from all over the world to see and to admire. It's a good-looking town with plenty of trees and green spaces thanks to the wisdom of the Development Corporation. It's a lively town, with excellent services from the Leisure Centre to the holiday hotel for senior citizens, thanks to the enterprise of the Council. It has a wide variety of voluntary organisations so that everyone can develop his or her interests and hobbies ... Strains were acute at one time between the Development Corporation and the Council; but now both work harmoniously on a common housing list and on the smooth transfer of responsibility – indeed, Stevenage is giving a lead to all new towns in this respect ... All in all it is a record to be proud of. May the next 30 years be even better.

Stevenage was very proud if its museum, which began modestly in 1954 in the White Cottage, one of the many houses in London Road scheduled for demolition. It was later relocated further along London Road to Woodstone, which was also awaiting demolition. By 1977, such was the success of the museum that it had outgrown its second home and was hoping for somewhere bigger. In some towns in Hertfordshire, the County Council had taken over responsibility for museums. Letchworth Garden City had its own library and museum building, although the early residents there had had to fight for it. Stevenage residents had begun their own museum with no permanent building but with a great deal of support from both Council and Corporation. Now more help was coming from an unexpected quarter.

St George's church, consecrated in 1960, was built as the civic church for the town, taking over the role of the ancient parish church of St Nicholas. Three years later, as directed by the diocese, it also took over the parish of Bedwell, where a devoted congregation at the modern church of St Andrew had worked hard and loyally since it had opened in 1952. St Andrew's church building ceased to be used for worship from 1963, when its congregation joined St George's. Another reorganisation of the Church of England in Stevenage in 1970 created seven separate parishes, of which St George's was one, responsible for Bedwell, the town centre and the Gunnels Wood Industrial Area. No longer supported financially by the rest of the Anglican parishes in the town, St George's church became an insupportable burden for its congregation. A mutually beneficial solution seemed to be to share the building with the town's museum.

On 2 July 1977, the new museum, in the undercroft of St George's church, opened its doors to the public. The official opening ceremony began at 2.30 when the Bishop of St Albans, the Right Revd Robert Runcie, received the Mayor of Stevenage, Councillor Robert Fowler, at the entrance to the museum, then moved into the lecture room where there were brief speeches by the Bishop, the mayor, Councillor Philip Ireton, Miss Laurel Ball, Director of the Area Museums Service, and Councillor Bill Lawrence, Chairman of the Council's Leisure Services Committee.

The museum was fortunate in having some excellent staff: Curator, Colin Dawes; Assistant Curator, Rosemary Gilmour; Education Officer, Elliott Dalby, all under the direction of Michael Banks, Director of Leisure Services for the Borough Council. A programme of opening events included; Guided tours of the new displays and behind the scenes; open air display and sale of art; demonstrations of rural crafts by members of the Kimpton Arts and Crafts Centre; archaeology film and coffee evening; 'Snakes and other reptiles', a talk by Ron Rees in association with the Stevenage Zoological and Wildlife Preservation Society; a guided tour of Stevenage High Street; 'Saving Britain's Wildlife', a talk by Ken March of the World Wildlife Fund; 'Grandmother's Flower Garden', and an exhibition of American patchwork quilts.

A Street party celebrating the silver jubilee of the Queen's reign. (Stevenage Museum)

During Robert Fowler's mayoral year he made an important contribution to preserving the remaining built heritage of Stevenage. As chairman of the Old Town Civic Committee, he managed to get over 50 buildings in the old town listed by the Department of the Environment. Thirty years later, after several years of research, the Stevenage Society published a book entitled *Historic Buildings of Stevenage*, which gave fuller descriptions and, in some cases, revised grades of Stevenage's listed buildings.

On 1 April 1978, the scheme for the transfer of assets from the Corporation came into operation. Under the New Towns (Amendment) Act of 1976, the Council took over the Corporation's extensive rented housing stock and related assets. The transfer took place in two stages. On 1 April 1978, the transfer included some 14,500 dwellings, some 7,000 car garages, 166 shops (in residential neighbourhood centres), 13 workshops, eight offices, five depots, 14 public house sites, five petrol filling station sites, 17 community and youth buildings and 15 surgeries. Two years later, another 500 dwellings, two shops, a community centre, two blocks of warden-controlled flats for elderly people, the site of a residential care home, a petrol station site and three community buildings were among housing and related assets transferred to the council. At 1980 prices, the value of all these assets was in the order of £300 million. The Council obtained them, on an outstanding debt basis, at a cost of rather less than £60 million. It also took over many of the Corporation's housing staff. The transfer was made with the very active participation of Evelyn Dennington and her Board. In the final years of the Board, relations between it and the Council were extremely harmonious.

The Council, still very conscious of its new status as a borough, now looked forward to the completion of its next big project, the long-awaited municipal golf course. This was achieved on Monday 31 March 1980, when the Mayor of Stevenage, Cllr Les Cummins, and former heavyweight boxing champion Henry Cooper took part in the opening ceremony. As a public course, it was open to everyone, unlike private golf clubs. Such was the enthusiasm of local golfers that, on the first day, some players arrived at 6.30 am and were followed by many more.

Although a golf course had been included in the Master Plan, the Development Corporation had not been able provide one because the Ministry would never allow them to spend sufficient money from the amenity grant. So the Council decided to see what they could do. They asked their newly-appointed Director of Leisure Services, Michael Banks, who later became the Council's Chief Executive Officer, to explore ways and means. The government had introduced a new loan sanction that allowed local authorities a block grant towards their

Signing the transfer of housing stock from the Development Corporation to the Borough Council, 1978.

capital facilities. The Stevenage Council decided that this would provide just enough money for an 18-hole golf course, but not sufficient for a club house and a par 3 course as well. The Development Corporation had made a site available between the A602 Broadhall Way, in the south-east of the town, and the village of Aston a little further to the east. They also made a financial contribution to the project.

Because it could not build a permanent club house, the Council put up a temporary building with changing rooms, four showers and a small bar. It remained in use for several years. Then the Council had the idea of asking brewers Greene King, to enter into a joint venture agreement with them. Negotiations were successful and the brewers agreed to pay for the clubhouse with bar, small restaurant and shop, to pay the wages of a golf professional and to provide a par 3 course, whilst the Council would provide a head greenkeeper and maintenance staff. The profits would be shared jointly between the two partners. When some years, and many thousands of rounds of golf, later, Greene King decided to pull out of their involvement in golf courses and leisure centres, the Council acquired the clubhouse, shop and the par 3 course at a very advantageous price. By then, a driving range had also been added.

As they entered the 1980s, the Borough Council focussed its attention on what promised to be the major event of its short history, the transfer to Council control of the Development Corporation's industrial and commercial assets.

A FIRST AND A LAST

Wishing to mark in some way the letting of a 'milestone' house – one of the last to be let by the Corporation before its housing stock and housing staff were transferred to the Borough Council – the Development Corporation invited a former resident to Stevenage for the day, from Cowes, in the Isle of Wight. He was Geoffrey Gibbons who, 55 years earlier, had moved with his parents into the first Stevenage Council house, in Hellards Road. He now handed over the keys of the new house to the young couple who were to make their home there.

CHAPTER FOURTEEN
The Stevenage Bill

As the government tried desperately to control the economy by announcing a limit of five per cent on pay increases and the unions responded by ever-increasing strikes, from industry to railways to dustmen and many others, 1979 opened to the 'winter of discontent'. On 3 May there was a general election, resulting in a Conservative victory with Margaret Thatcher as Britain's first woman prime minister. In the local parliamentary constituency election, Shirley Williams, who had represented Stevenage for 15 years, lost to the Conservative Bowen Wells. The Council, anxious not to lose connection with Shirley Williams, decided to offer her the Freedom of the Borough, which she accepted.

In both Council and Corporation meetings, attention was now focussed on the coming 'wind-up' of the Corporation and transfer of assets to the Borough Council. Under the original New Towns Act of 1946, the Labour Government had intended that when development was complete, the assets of each new town would be transferred to its elected local authority on financial and other terms that were left vague. However, in 1959, the Conservative Government had passed another Act, which established a Commission for New Towns to hold and manage, on behalf of central government, the assets of development corporations that were being dissolved. Their argument was that the development of new towns had been funded by central government, not by local ratepayers, and, therefore, revenues from sales of a corporation's assets should be returned to central government for the benefit of national taxpayers, not used solely for the benefit of local ratepayers. A further Act, in 1976, provided for the transfer of housing and related properties to local councils while profitable commercial and industrial assets remained with the Commission. In

1979 Stevenage was at the point where the first stage of the transfer of housing had taken place.

During the four years between 1976 and 1980, when the Corporation would be dissolved, the Corporation and Council planned to work together to minimise any adverse effects of the change. This was not as straightforward as had been hoped, because of a difficult economic situation nationally. The Corporation was hampered by government restrictions which prevented it from developing the new Hertford Road and Poplars sites. It therefore encouraged the Council to increase its own building in these two areas, but similar delays and cuts in public expenditure held back the Council's programme as well.

Then, following the 1979 election, Margaret Thatcher's government acted swiftly to implement policies stemming from her political philosophy, including the sale of nationalised industries and the move towards a house-owning democracy. On 16 July 1979, Michael Heseltine, Secretary of State for the Environment, called a meeting of all new town chairmen and general managers of development corporations of the post-war new towns. He told them that money from the National Loans Fund, which had previously supported new town development, would no longer be available. As a result, some of the new towns' assets would have to be sold to pay for future development and he required the corporations, jointly, to raise £100 million from sales of assets during the remaining eight months of that financial year. This idea, for development corporations to sell some assets in order to pay for further development, was not entirely new and was not considered unreasonable. However, when the meeting was persuaded to accept it, Michael Heseltine immediately made a further demand, that one new town would sell its assets to finance expenditure for another. This, said Jack Balchin, the chairmen and general managers agreed 'to swallow reluctantly'.

Inevitably, the new town chosen to be the sacrificial lamb was Stevenage, the oldest and most established of the new towns, with more valuable assets than most. Evelyn Denington, Chairman, and Jack Greenwood, General Manager, of the Stevenage Development Corporation were subsequently told that, although Stevenage only required £3 million to pay for its own future capital expenditure, it must now sell assets worth £20 million. The news was broken to the Board of the Stevenage Development Corporation on 7 August 1979. Unhappily, but seeing no alternative, the Board began the urgent business of finding £20 million in the nine months before 31 March 1980. Jack Balchin explained the difficulties,

> The Corporation's officers advised that the new government's policy, if indiscriminately applied, could pour good money down the drain. There needed to be a careful selection of suitable assets and not a mad rush to achieve an arbitrary target. To sell 'against the clock' was lunacy. The Corporation members thought so too. But they were faced with the fact that the Secretary

of State gave the orders and the Corporation was not, they thought at the time, a free agent in this matter. They could resign of course – as some of the newspaper correspondents urged. But this would achieve nothing – they would be replaced by yes-men and the situation would only become worse. By remaining they could ensure that the government's instructions' were carried out with the least possible harm; after all, that was something the Corporation's present Board and officers could do better than anyone.

The sale of the commercial and industrial premises owned by the Corporation had become the most important and controversial issue that Stevenage had faced since its designation as a new town 33 years earlier. On 13 August, Evelyn Denington wrote to Michael Heseltine expressing the grave concerns of the Board about the impact of the exercise and expressing 'our earnest hope that we will be trusted to meet your requirements in the way we believe to be best suited to Stevenage'. The Minister replied that he had appointed his professional advisers and would take their advice on the suitability of different assets for disposal. Thus were the concerns of Board members ignored, apart from expressing their outrage, there was little they could do.

The Borough Council, equally angry and upset, decided to follow the example of neighbouring Letchworth Garden City which, in 1962 had established the Letchworth Garden City Corporation by means of a private member's bill promoted by its MP, Martin Maddan. It had taken over the estates of the original Garden City Company and was now re-investing the profits for the benefit of residents. Even in its early days, Letchworth had been greatly admired by many, including Philip Ireton, one of its staunchest supporters. By the late twentieth century the first Garden City's success was widely recognised nationally and internationally. Through the Stevenage Development Authority Bill, the Borough Council hoped that the first new town would be able to follow in Letchworth's footsteps.

Jack Balchin.
(Stevenage Museum P11432)

Brian Hall, leader of the Stevenage Borough Council, published a statement of intent, which included the following paragraphs:

> In putting forward the case for the original garden cities, their founder, Ebenezer Howard, was adamant that the towns should belong to the 'municipality' – by which he meant that the inhabitants, by whose efforts the assets had acquired their value, should benefit from their increased values.

The original New Towns Act embodied this fundamental principle and required that, when the new towns had been substantially completed, the outstanding industrial, commercial and housing assets should be transferred to the local authorities in their areas.

It does seem logical that, once the new towns have repaid the capital and income involved in their development, the assets of the towns should be handed to the local inhabitants, This is the case for Stevenage; the town has not only repaid the capital involved in its development but has also made substantial profits for Central Government. Surely the time has now arrived for the future profits to be retained by the local community ...

An added advantage of the Bill would be to allow local councils in new towns to provide all the social facilities which are required by their inhabitants and – as in the case of Letchworth – contributions from the profits of a Development Authority would be readily available to satisfy these needs.

Convincing the Government about the desirability of the Bill will not be easy, and we have a difficult task ahead. But our arguments are sound, well thought out and have stood the test of 70 years from the time they were first formulated. We would point out to the Government that the great need of our country at the present time is for private investment into manufacturing industry and in new technology. It does not require investment in property which does not create wealth for the country as a whole. We would point out to the Government that there is no evidence that the tenants of the industrial

Town Centre, north end, before the Forum was built. (Stevenage Museum PP409)

> and commercial assets are demanding the right to buy their properties or to change to a private landlord. We would point out to the Government that arrangements at Letchworth have proved that it is possible for new towns to grow and develop without the delays and difficulties experienced in other towns – provided they have control of their assets. We would also point out to the Government that the income accruing from the Development Authority would have the potential to free other public agencies from some of their spending commitments for schools, libraries, bus services, recreational facilities etc. and this will help make the town more self-supporting in its social, civic and cultural activities.

The Council was not asking for something for nothing. If the Bill was passed, the Council would borrow the money needed to buy the assets at current market values – estimated to be in the region of £55 million. Also, under the Council's proposals, the Stevenage Development Authority would have a Board of seven people – four to be appointed by the Council, two by the Secretary of State for the Environment and one by Hertfordshire County Council – whose objectives would be to 'manage, turn to account, carry on, develop and extend the undertakings of the Authority as a public service'.

The Bill was drafted, with a preamble including a page of Stevenage statistics:

Population	
0–4 Years	4,530
5–11	8,250
12–16	7,260
17–24	10,620
25–44	19,890
45–59	13,350
60–64	2,850
65+	6,250
Total	73,000
Schools	
Primary, Secondary and Special	60
pupils (All ages)	17,600
Employment (In Stevenage)	
Men	21,800
Women	14,655
Total	36,455

Housing	
Public Sector	16,500
Private Sector	9,150
Total	25,650
Land use	
Total Area (acres)	6,256
Factories, Warehouses and Laboratories (sq ft)	5,500,000
Offices (sq ft)	500,000
Shops (sq ft)	450
Roads (acres)	431
Open Spaces, amenity and recreation (acres)	1,000

Then followed the minutes of the Council meeting at which it was agreed that the Bill should go forward:

At a meeting of the Stevenage Borough Council held on 19 December 1979.

Disposal of the New Town's Assets
It was resolved on the proposition of Councillor B P Hall, seconded by Councillor R W F Fowler, BA

'That the resolution of the Council passed at a special meeting of the Council on November 14 1979 to promote a Bill for certain purposes, which Bill has been duly deposited in both Houses of Parliament intituled "A Bill to constitute the Stevenage Development Authority, to transfer to that Authority the undertaking of the Stevenage Development Corporation; to confer powers upon the Authority; and for other purposes", be and is hereby confirmed.'

In favour (34 members and the Mayor): Councillors G G Balderstone, Mrs B A Beasley, J Boyd, Mrs W Boyd, A G Campbell, R A Clark, J G Clarke, J H Cockerton, Mrs C A Corner, T E Corner, M Cotter, B G Dunnell, R W F Fowler, J F H Graham, S E Greenfield, J B Gotobed, B P Hall, K R Hopkins, I J R Johnson, Mrs H M Lawrence, W L Lawrence, Mrs J E Lloyd, A C Luhman, H Morris, S R Munden, L Robbins, W J Sheaff, R J Smith, Mrs J P Tye, K Vale JP, A J Walker, D G Weston, K Wilkinson and A D Wiltshire.

Against (1 member): Councillor B F Hancock.
The meeting commenced at 7.30 pm and ended at 8.16 pm. Signed
L J A Cummins (Mayor)

The Council promoted the Bill vigorously, both through the press and by distributing copies of a petition throughout the town. Once again there was national interest in what was happening at Stevenage: among supporters of the

Bill were the Town and Country Planning Association, the Parliamentary Labour Party, the Parliamentary Liberal Party and Mrs Shirley Williams, Stevenage's former Member of Parliament, who urged the people of Stevenage to 'Do everything in your power to support the Bill.'

In the 26 February 1980 issue of its magazine, *The Forum*, the Council quoted comments from MPs of several political parties:

> 'I see no reason why I should be opposed to its provisions in any way and hope that it will, indeed, receive all-party support.' Ian Lloyd, Conservative MP for Havant and Waterloo.
>
> 'I do not imagine that there will be anything in the Bill which would cause me not to support it.' Victor Goodhew, Conservative MP for St Albans.
>
> 'Since I am specially interested in New Towns, I think I understand the argument behind the Bill and you can count on my support in the House of Commons.' Terry Davis, Labour MP for Birmingham Stechford.
>
> 'All good luck in your quest to achieve your aims.' Tim Brinton, Conservative MP for Gravesend.
>
> 'Naturally I will support this proposal.' Alfred Dubs, Labour MP for Battersea South.
>
> 'I will support the Stevenage Development Authority Bill.' Cyril Smith, Liberal MP for Rochdale.
>
> 'I intend to support this Bill.' The Rt Hon Dr John Gilbert, Labour MP for Dudley East.
>
> 'The Bill to establish a Stevenage Development Authority is an imaginative scheme which I fully support.' Michael McGuire, Labour MP for Ince.
>
> 'I shall support the Bill when it comes before the House.' The Rt Hon Roland Moyle, Labour MP for Lewisham East.
>
> 'This Bill will have my support when it comes before the House.' Peter Snape, Labour MP for West Bromwich East.
>
> 'I will support your Bill when it comes before the House.' William Wilson, Labour MP for Coventry South East.
>
> 'I am very glad you are taking this initiative and I shall give it whatever help and support I can.' Jack Straw, Labour MP for Blackburn.
>
> 'This is something which has been raised by Labour MPs and which has their backing. I will certainly give it my support.' Ken Woolmer, Labour MP for Batley and Morley.

'I would like you to know that it has my strong support and I shall be happy to do anything I can to assist. It was also discussed in the Labour Party NEC Local Government Sub-Committee when everyone was agreed that the Bill should be supported in every way possible.' John Cartwright, Labour MP for Woolwich East.

Support seemed to be widespread both nationally and locally, where 10,000 residents signed a petition in its favour. But not everyone believed that it was a viable proposal. Stevenage's Conservative MP, Bowen Wells who, it was hoped, would sponsor the Bill in Parliament, had deliberated for several weeks before finally making a decision. Reporter John Adams, writing in the *Stevenage Comet* for 6 February 1980, said

> Mr Wells has given a decisive thumbs-down to the Bill. He says that the measure is a charter for the Borough Council to go into property speculation on a grand scale. It might well lead to a very large increase in rates and by increasing both rents and rates it might create more unemployment in the town. The proposed authority is potentially disastrous for Stevenage.
>
> Wholesale buying up of industrial and commercial assets by public bodies would amount to nationalisation of the town.

Brian Hall responded that Bowen Wells' statement was

> ... arrant nonsense. Mr Wells knows that the properties under question are state-owned assets. How on earth can one nationalise something that was created by and is already owned by the nation? How can Mr Wells justify the sale of these assets to private speculators, thereby putting the nation's profits into the pockets of people who have not contributed one penny piece to the creation of those assets?

Shoppers outside Woolworths in the Town Centre. (Stevenage Museum P1063)

Town Centre Bus Garage canteen. (Stevenage Museum PP288)

The debate continued among Stevenage residents. There was a great deal of support for the aims of the proposal, but doubt about the methods to be employed. Some were sceptical about the financial prospects of the proposed Stevenage Development Authority, doubting whether it would be able to borrow public money at that time and also fearing large increases in rates and rents if things went wrong. Philip Ireton, who was a strong supporter, if not the original instigator, of the Stevenage Development Authority, suggested that the Authority would not necessarily need to borrow from the public sector, but could find private sources. The support of Conservative Councillors, James and Winifred Boyd, encouraged many but by no means all Conservative voters to follow suit. Bowen Wells' decision not to introduce the Bill in Parliament naturally influenced many of his party. Without the support of its own MP, the Council was forced to look elsewhere. It found a willing sponsor in Stan Newens, Labour MP for Harlow and a well-known figure in the new towns movement. He was pleased to be able to say that he had found a great deal of support for the Bill among his fellow MPs.

The debate on the second reading of the Stevenage Development Authority Bill took place on 26 March 1980, which was also budget night. The verbatim account can be read in the *House of Commons Hansard* for that date. Stan Newens gave a full and detailed introduction to the Bill, concluding with the statement,

> The Stevenage Borough Council is a highly progressive authority. It has pioneered many new ideas for its townspeople despite the problems created by the rapid growth that new town development has meant. Its assets have already provided handsome profits to the Exchequer and to the taxpayer over the years. Now that the town must embark on the inevitable process of normalisation, the

> sale of those assets to outside bodies can do nothing but damage to the community there. If Stevenage is left with the unprofitable and unsaleable residue of assets – for example, it will not necessarily be profitable to run car parks – while the profitable assets are sold off, those unprofitable assets will be a burden on the rates of the people of Stevenage in the long term.

Bowen Wells, speaking against the Bill, raised a particular objection to clause five, which provided for four out of seven members of the Authority to be appointed by the Borough Council. Stan Newens explained that the Council would be prepared to modify that clause. Bowen Wells continued,

> The major matter that we should be considering is contained in clause 5. Here we have the authority being controlled by the Borough Council. Four out of seven members are to be appointed by the Borough Council. That is the major cause of our fears. I welcome what the Hon. Member for Harlow said. He pointed out that the Borough Council would be prepared to modify that clause. If it is not modified, the Bill amounts to a major municipalisation, to a Communisation – a Sovietisation, one might say – of Stevenage, because it will be controlled by the political party in power in the Stevenage Borough Council ... The Council has made a major mistake if it wishes to gain any kind of support from Conservative Members in this House, because this aspect of the Bill has led to a great deal of disquiet.

Stan Newens asked Bowen Wells whether, if the clause were satisfactorily amended, he would then either vote in favour of the Bill or abstain, to which there was no direct reply. The debate continued until 10 pm. Up to that time there had been only about 30 MPs in the chamber, since traditionally, budget night is free of Parliamentary business – but not on this occasion. Not unexpectedly, the vote was purely on party political lines. At the request of Bowen Wells, 216 Conservative MPs attended the House that evening to vote against the Stevenage Bill. The result was 158 'Ayes' and 216 'Noes'. The bill was defeated by 58 votes. No Conservative voted in favour, not even those who had apparently pledged their support. Even Prime Minister Margaret Thatcher was there to add her vote to the 'Noes'. Afterwards, Shirley Williams, who had been sitting in the Strangers' Gallery, commented, 'There is no official party whip for a Private Member's Bill. Nevertheless, it was one of the most remarkable turnouts that I have ever seen; it was quite extraordinary.'

And so the sale of the Corporation's wealth-creating commercial and industrial assets went ahead, sold by the Commission for New Towns on the open market to the highest bidders, prominent among whom were pension funds and other financial institutions. Not everything built in Stevenage between 1950 and 1980 was built by the Development Corporation. The larger factories in the industrial areas, the larger shops in the town centre and some office blocks were built by the companies themselves on land obtained from the Corporation. However, many industrial premises, some offices and the majority of the shop premises in the town centre were owned by the Corporation and leased to the occupiers. It was these holdings that were put up for sale. The Council inherited the town centre car parks, service roads, walkways and town centre gardens on the Corporation's departure. Another 566 dwellings, two shops, a community centre, two blocks of warden controlled flats for elderly people, the site of a residential care home, a petrol station site and three community buildings were among the housing and related assets transferred to the Borough Council. It also took over many of the Corporation's housing staff. The Commission for New Towns later changed its name to English Partnerships and changed it again in more recent years to the Homes and Communities Agency.

Three months after the demise of the Bill, *The Stevenage Development Corporation (Transfer of Property and Dissolution) Order 1980* came into effect, on 1 July. As an all-powerful, government-appointed agency, in whose actions the town's ratepayers and residents had no say whatsoever, the Corporation was a very undemocratic organisation. But there can be no denying that it was a highly efficient body – and one that made the town world famous.

The Council now had to face a future far different from what it had hoped. Amid the wreckage of its hopes, at least it was able to acquire Daneshill House for its offices, a far cry from the promised new town hall, but in a good position and providing adequate office space. It did not, however, provide residents with meeting rooms and a natural focus for major events, as the old town hall had done.

The problems of the previous year continued into 1980, and it was not an easy year for anyone involved in national or local government. Unemployment rose from 1.59 million in January to two million by the end of August. In Stevenage, unemployment was rising more rapidly than in the surrounding areas, with over 1,000 jobs lost during the previous twelve months, largely as a result of Bowaters, Kodak, ICI and other companies leaving the town. In response, the Council had pledged itself to create 1,000 more jobs annually.

Shoppers outside Boots in the Town Centre. (Stevenage Museum P11123)

A Council meeting taking place at Daneshill House. (Stevenage Borough Council)

Daneshill House. (Stevenage Museum P3964)

The Labour Party was deeply divided, with a group called the Militant Tendency trying to take control. When James Callaghan resigned as leader in October, the battle for a successor was also a battle between the left and right wings of the party. The left emerged victorious when Michael Foot won the leadership election. Despite the obvious unease many people felt about Labour's divisions, it came as a shock when, on 25 January 1981, four respected former cabinet ministers made their 'Limehouse Declaration' which was a statement severely criticising the Labour Party for moving towards extreme left-wing politics. They proposed setting up a Council for Social Democracy which, could soon become a new party. For the Labour majority group on Stevenage Borough Council the shock was all the greater because the 'Gang of Four', as they came to be known, consisted of Roy Jenkins, William Rodgers, David Owen – and Shirley Williams, who had so recently been made a Freeman of the Borough. Nor was it long before others joined them in forming the Social Democratic Party. Most notable of all the new recruits was Philip Ireton, who had resigned from the Labour Party in 1979, a year after he was presented with a certificate honouring his 60 years of membership. He told a reporter, 'I was warning Labour that there were grim prospects ahead, but they didn't seem to take any notice. At the end of 1979 I didn't renew my membership, and later responded to an advertisement for the SDP shortly before its formation.' However, others were not prepared to change their allegiance and some long-standing friendships were sorely tested. Clearly, the next few years would be interesting for Stevenage.

CHAPTER FIFTEEN
Difficult times

THE BOROUGH COUNCIL was now in charge of the local government of the town. Despite his disappointment over the outcome of the Stevenage Bill, the leader, Brian Hall, had told a *Stevenage Gazette* reporter on 26 June 1980, 'Stevenage will be a model town in 20 to 30 years' time. It's pretty good already. But I really do think that it's going to be a fantastic place to live.' He faced no easy task. By the end of January 1982, unemployment had reached three million and in Stevenage there were 1,800 job losses between 1980 and 1983. British Visqueen, Kodak, Bowater's containers, ICI, Singer Business Machines and Pye Ether were among the companies that had moved out, or were cutting staff. At this difficult time, Stevenage had few resources to fall back on. When the development corporations were in existence, government money was directed towards new towns as a matter of policy. Now there was a change of emphasis, as inner cities and Assisted Areas became the recipients of financial aid instead. Stevenage's problems were also rather obscured because of the town's location in Hertfordshire, a county which generally had low unemployment, although the County Council was beginning to recognise that there were problems which were peculiar to Stevenage.

At that time, Labour was in the majority on the Borough Council but the newly-formed Social Democratic Party (SDP) was gaining strength. An inaugural meeting held at the Leisure Centre in June 1981 had attracted 70 people and since then membership had risen steadily. The new party gained great credibility from the support of Philip Ireton, whose 50 years experience in local politics was unmatchable. Another boost for the new party came when Peter Metcalfe, a highly respected former Labour activist, became Chairman of the Stevenage area SDP. The membership also included former Conservative Party

Brian Hall
(Stevenage Museum)

members, which Peter Metcalfe estimated at about 20 per cent of the total. The Labour Party nationally was in disarray, with the extreme left-wing Militant Tendency trying to take control. To some extent this situation was reflected in Stevenage. Robert Fowler, who was twice mayor of Stevenage, wrote in his memoirs, 'In Stevenage the Young Socialists were all Militants ... They were all expelled by the Stevenage Labour Party in 1986.'

Undeterred by the political situation, Brian Hall focussed single-mindedly on the problems of Stevenage. He was, by this time, being recognised as a strong leader who was determined that the local council was going to play a greater role in shaping the future of the town, and was respected for his ability and his ever-increasing knowledge of many aspects of local government. His aim was to protect Stevenage from the worst effects of the recession that blighted much of the 1980s. As he said, 'If we cannot get employment right in Stevenage we will not get anything right.'

In 1982, as an immediate first step towards helping the unemployed, the Council set up a Business and Technology Centre to help small businesses. Situated in former industrial premises at the corner of Gunnels Wood Road and Bessemer Drive, the centre provided basic but adequate low-cost accommodation for small, start-up businesses. The same year, with a view to longer-term planning the *Stevenage Employment Action Plan* was produced by the Council. It began by stating its rationale:

> The Stevenage Story is largely one of success. The first of eight new towns ringing London ... it is also the first to mature ... Stevenage has attracted a wide range of manufacturing and service businesses in both traditional and, to an increasing degree, the new and developing industries. Stevenage, by its track record, can be seen as an attractive town in which to live and run a business ... However, Stevenage is subject to external forces as much as any other town. An unaccustomed and unacceptable level of unemployment has resulted from the closure of a small number of key plants in a short space of time.
>
> 'Left to themselves, market forces will no doubt reach a point of equilibrium but it may well be at a level far below Stevenage's true potential and the legitimate expectations of its inhabitants. Some control of these market forces is essential. They are, after all, not immutable but rather the result of the conscious decisions and actions of many interested parties. It would be an

abdication of responsibility by the agencies and authorities concerned to allow Stevenage to suffer the consequences of others' actions without attempting to manage the situation to the town's best advantage.

The *Employment Action Plan* was put into effect with some success. As well as the Business and Technology Centre, five small industrial units were being built by the Council at Bedwell and there were plans for similar units at Bolton Road and the old station yard at the top of Julians Road; a Business Advice Centre had been opened and a local enterprise agency, Stevenage Initiative Ltd, established; a local trade directory and a quarterly *Premises Register* were being published. The Council had succeeded in its application for help from the Urban Programme Scheme; Stevenage Information Technology Centre (SITEC) had opened in 1983 and work had also begun on a town promotional campaign.

There is no doubt of the importance of the efforts being made by the Borough Council. At its peak, in September 1982, unemployment in Stevenage was 12.6 per cent of the workforce, compared with 10.5 per cent in the South East, and 13 per cent nationally. Stevenage had become an unemployment blackspot. As far back as 1964, people had been worried about the town's dependence on one major employer and this was still the case. More than 7,000 jobs, that is one fifth of all jobs in Stevenage, had been with British Aerospace. When this company reduced its Stevenage operation to a minimum, selling off half its site, it dealt a heavy blow to the town. Add to this the fact that almost half the total Stevenage unemployed were under 25 and that one in five of the unemployed had been out of work for over a year and the scale of the problem became clear.

Meanwhile, in the wider world, 1982 was to be remembered for the completely unforeseen Falklands War, which erupted at the beginning of April and was over by the beginning of July. At the end of the year, following announcements that the government had agreed to allow the United States to site 96 Cruise Missiles at Greenham Common, some 20,000 women staged a non-violent demonstration against this plan. Of considerable interest to Stevenage was the action of Robert Maxwell, the colourful publisher and businessman, in buying an 85 per cent share of Hollis ESA through his company Pergamon. Some employees at the Fishers Green Road factory had known for a few years that the ESA was struggling to survive, but many in the workforce were unaware of the problems. The takeover by the Maxwell group brought a welcome injection of about £2 million.

On 3 February 1983 it was announced that unemployment had reached an all-time high of 3,224,715. The government, working through the agency of the Manpower Services Commission, was about to set up a Youth Training Scheme (YTS) which would provide a year's training or work experience for all 16-year-old school leavers who could not find a full-time job. Stevenage took up the idea with enthusiasm, the Borough Council, local industry and the unions working together to provide nearly 799 places. The Ridgmond Park Training Centre, opened the same year, was a valuable part of this and other programmes.

The General Election on 10 June was won by the Conservatives with a majority of 144, the largest since 1935. Tim Wood, Conservative, became MP for the new Stevenage constituency, taking 39.4 per cent of votes, closely followed by the SDP candidate B R M Stoneham with 36.1 per cent, leaving Labour trailing with 24 per cent. During this year, new developments in various parts of the town were moving ahead. The first houses were completed in the Poplars area, adjacent to Aston, and a super-store was under consideration there as were retail warehouses at Roaring Meg, site of the former sewage works.

The Council's rented housing stock was greatly increased in the 1970s when it inherited that of the Development Corporation. However, the number of council houses was subsequently depleted under the Conservative Government's 'right to buy' legislation, which enabled tenants to buy their homes at far less than the building costs. The government's attitude was that local councils should not be in the business of building, managing and maintaining houses. Instead, they should make land available to housing societies, to whom they could make nominations from their waiting lists, and also make sites available to private developers for house building, including affordable starter homes, for sale to first-time buyers.

The Council pursued policies that maximised the amount of affordable rented housing within the Borough whilst, at the same time, ensuring that there was a range of housing choices. In the early 1980s it had built some 400 council houses a year, the maximum possible number. It had also created a low-start shared-ownership scheme; provided a tenancy deposit and guarantee scheme to help people to get rented housing in the private sector; introduced a tenant removal scheme to help tenants purchase their own houses in the private sector and repurchased ex-council houses to increase its rented housing stock. In addition, the Council set up a housing advice centre that counselled hundreds of people each year, so preventing homelessness in a large number of cases, and worked with housing associations to provide more than 1,000 social housing units in the Borough. Rent increases were kept to a minimum and a wide range of schemes were introduced to enhance council tenants' homes and keep them up to date.

In 1983, Father Brian Reynolds, parish priest of St. Joseph's Roman Catholic Church, Bedwell, suggested to the Mayor, Michael Cotter that Stevenage Borough Council might now consider forming a link with a town in a third-world or developing country. The idea was put to the Council who accepted it in principle and sent the chief executive, Stephen Catchpole, and the community Services Officer,

John Bentley, to Zimbabwe, formerly Southern Rhodesia, to investigate possibilities. They reported that Kadoma, between Bulawayo and the capital, Harare, seemed the most suitable location because of its similarities with Stevenage – a population of approximately 68,000, a manufacturing-based industry with one dominant company, and surrounded by a rural area. After the necessary preliminaries, a formal twinning arrangement was entered into with the Kadoma Council, and the signing ceremony took place in Kadoma on 20th August 1989.

Among those involved in the early days of the link between the two towns were Leslie Rose, headmaster of Nobel School, teachers Les and Joyce Ransley, David Thompson, Pat Akhurst, Connie Rees and Hilda Lawrence, first chairman of the link committee, all of whom made significant contributions to various aspects of the link. There was genuine heartfelt grief in Kadoma at news of the death of Joyce Ransley, in whose memory a tree was planted in Kadoma town centre gardens.

Adjacent to, and part of, Kadoma is the township of Rimuka where much assistance has been given. Projects have included; help with the Rimuka library, books and computers for schools, school-fees paid for up to 400 pupils, training in aromatherapy to help patients with HIV / AIDS, support for Rimuka's old people's home, equipment for the hospital, partnering schools. A replacement fire engine was delivered to the Rimuka fire brigade by two Stevenage fire fighters, who then trained the firemen in its use.

Support, both financial and practical, has come from individuals and groups, from schools to industry, across Stevenage, but perhaps even more important is the over-riding spirit of friendship. Both towns have benefited from learning more about each other. There has been an amazing range of activities from civic visits and exchanges of council officers to exchange visits by performing arts groups, ecumenical church groups such as Cornerstone, youth groups, teachers and individuals. Cornerstone's co-ordinator, Andrew Hills, has visited Rimuka five times, on three occasions heading groups of Stevenage Christian youth and, together, helped to refurbish a home for elderly people, decorated a special needs school, helped to refurbish a former beer-hall for use as a youth centre and set up the 'Fish Project', a scheme setting up young people in the business of buying and selling fish to help sustain the local economy. When, in 1999, Kadoma sought a visit from a health and safety officer who would inspect premises there and prepare a report on things that might need to be done Tony Hills (Andrew's older brother), Health and Safety Officer with a major national organisation, offered to go.

The Stevenage-Kadoma Link has become widely admired nationally, as well as locally, because it is based on both civic and community organisations. This joint approach has been a great source of strength, enabling the Link to continue its work in difficult times. The Britain Zimbabwe Society and the United Kingdom One World Linking Association, among others, have held conferences in Stevenage.

On 13 July 1983, *The Times* published an article by Sandy McLachlan, entitled *Fall and Rise of Robert Maxwell,* in which he referred to a 1969 Department of Trade and Industry investigation of Maxwell's business methods and said, '... the man the Whitehall inspectors adjudged to be unfit to run a public company is now chairman of two – BPCC and Hollis Bros ESA ...'

1984 did not turn out quite as George Orwell, prophesied in his book 1984, but it had its own problems. The long and bitter miners' strike began on 12 March and on 12 October an IRA bomb blasted the Brighton hotel where the Conservative Party annual conference was being held, killing five and injuring others.

A second edition of *The Stevenage Employment Plan* was published by the Council in January 1984, with an introduction signed by Councillor Reg Smith, chairman of the Economic and Employment Development Committee, and Councillor Robert Clark, chairman of the Planning and Works Committee. They were able to list a number of achievements, including; two successful bids for grant aid for small business training from the European Social Fund; the provision of more small units at several sites across the town; expansion by both the Wine Society and Combustion Engineering. They also ran a successful national media campaign, using the *Daily Telegraph,* the *Financial Times, CBI News* and the *Hertfordshire Businessman,* which led directly to firms such as Marconi, Wiltron and Confederation Life moving to Stevenage. The latter company was to be housed in a new building under construction at the corner of Lytton Way and Chequers Bridge Road.

In addition to encouraging greater employment opportunities in local industry, the Council was planning more retail development, including a new shopping mall, to be known as Westgate, and expansion of The Forum. Environmental improvements to the town centre were also planned, 'to enhance its attractiveness as a shopping and business centre'. Work was continuing at Roaring Meg, where the first retail warehouses were opened during 1984 and a new Technology Park was planned for Meadway, Symonds Green. British Aerospace had built a new Satellite Assembly Integration and Test Facility which was opened on 17 November by Princess Margaret, the Queen's sister. All in all, the Council could feel that much had been achieved by its determined efforts to promote the town as it continued to set targets for growth year by year.

With the pound at an all-time low against the dollar at 0.0765 cents 1985 was another difficult year for the country. There was rioting in several inner-city ones, including Brixton and Tottenham. Fortunately life in Stevenage continued fairly quietly, apart from the continual building work in the newest development areas, Chells Manor Village and the Poplars, where Sainsbury's Superstore was opened the following year. In 1986 the Greater London Council was abolished and its responsibilities delegated to the London boroughs. To ensure co-ordination and 'best practice' in economic development for urban settlements around London, a new body known as the South-East Economic Development Strategy was set up. It became extremely influential. One of its founder members was the Leader of Stevenage Borough Council, Brian Hall. The 40th anniversary of Stevenage New Town was also in 1986, and this was marked by a number of celebrations, including the opening of the Daneshill House Civic Centre by the Mayor, Councillor Stanley Munden.

It seemed that Stevenage could not go for long without being subjected to media scrutiny. A general election was due in 1987 and on 21 March 1986 an article appeared in *The Times* analysing the chances of a win for the Social Democrats in the Stevenage constituency. The writer concluded that the new town, now 40 years old 'seems as dated as only newish things can be'. He believed that Stevenage was the SDP's fourth most marginal seat and there was every chance that the party would win there. The writer considered that 'Stevenage, with its air of classlessness, comes as near to being a classic example of the SDP target seat as any in the country. It is above all a natural for the community politician.' He also pointed out the possible effect of increased home ownership on voting behaviour, 'By 1985 the number of houses in private ownership had risen to 13,151 (47 per cent of the total) from its 1981 figure of 9,660 (33 per cent). In other words, a new town commissioned under Attlee has been partly gentrified under Thatcher.' Finally, he wondered how much voters would be influenced by 'the Shirley factor', the fact that the town's former and highly-respected MP, Shirley Williams, was now President of the Social Democrats. Confidence was high and the SDP candidate, Ben Stoneham, was reported as saying, 'If I don't win then we may as well give up.'

1987 opened with the news that the ESA would close down on 11 February. Many employees were in a state of 'utter shock' and completely failed to understand why this should happen, when 'there was plenty of work about and much overtime was being worked'. Some concluded that the ESA was being made the scapegoat for failures of other companies in the Maxwell Group. Ken Ellis, who had worked his way from shopfloor to management, said, 'Although I had taken it to be inevitable, it was a terrific shock to everybody and a blow to me because I have spent my whole working life there, helping to build the place up and there are a lot of my previous colleagues who have done 40 or 50 years service and I can't see much future for them.' It was a sad and undignified end to a company that had served Stevenage for 104 years. The real reason was revealed later, when the site was sold for housing, producing a large capital sum.

The General Election was held on 12 June 1987. It was won by the Conservatives with a majority of 100. Tim Wood, Conservative, was re-elected

The first ESA building at Holborn Terrace, Fishers Green Road, opposite the Railway Station (Stevenage Musuem)

for Stevenage with 42.1 per cent of votes. Ben Stoneham's share was reduced to 32.5 per cent and the Labour candidate, M R C Withers, achieved 25.4 per cent. On 6 August the SDP agreed to merge with the Liberal Party. As the year progressed, disasters followed one another in rapid succession. On 16 October almost the whole country was swept by 'the Great Storm' which uprooted trees, blew down buildings and caused widespread damage and disruption. In Stevenage it destroyed many of the oldest horse chestnut and lime trees in The Avenue. The Stock Exchange crash known as 'Black Monday' occurred on 19 October. On 18 November there was a disastrous fire at London's Kings Cross station, killing 30 people.

New jobs and trade were brought to Stevenage with the completion of retail warehouses in London Road, and of the Westgate shopping centre, which was opened in 1988 by the Mayor, Councillor Alf Luhman. The changes to the town centre were not universally welcomed. The Westgate development, with its multi-storey car park, resulted in a somewhat claustrophobic appearance at the Swingate approach to Danestrete. A similar problem occurred when the extension to The Forum was completed with no direct throughway for pedestrians.

The Avenue c1980. (Betty Game)

The Avenue after the Great Storm of 1987 (Margaret Ashby)

The Icon, main entrance. (Andrew Hills)

The Confederation Life Insurance Company moved into its new, purpose-built head office in Stevenage in April 1988. This remarkable new building in Lytton Way, officially named the Icon, is a useful landmark, known to many as 'the blue building'. The architects were the Elsworth Sykes Partnership. An information brochure issued at the time listed the many state-of-the art features incorporated within the building; air-conditioning completed by perimeter heating grills, an energy management system, power, data and telephone cabling beneath raised flooring, computers and telephones protected by an uninterruptible power supply, closed-circuit television cameras monitoring the building perimeter and, for staff, a restaurant and showers. Seen from above it has the shape of an eagle with outstreatched wings.

In 1987 a planning application by Richard Daniels Homes and Wheatley Homes to build 2,000 houses on 197 acres of land in the Forster Country was lodged with the Borough Council. To the relief of objectors the Borough Council refused outline planning permission, which the developers appealed against, necessitating a public inquiry. This was held on 20 September 1988 and lasted two weeks, during which there was extensive press coverage. On 7 April 1989 the Secretary of State for the Environment, Nicholas Ridley, announced his decision to uphold the Borough Council's refusal to allow development in the Forster Country and on 21 May a new organisation, the Friends of the Forster Country, was launched with a garden party at Rooks Nest House, E M Forster's childhood home. It was attended by Stevenage MP Tim Wood and the Mayor, Councillor Hilda Lawrence. Dr Malcolm Williamson, Master of the Queen's Music, made the inaugural speech and Dame Iris Murdoch sent the slogan, 'Keep the Green Scene'.

During 1989, among several other new initiatives that year, Councillor Hilda Lawrence suggested that Stevenage should have its own charity, to raise money to help local voluntary organisations, groups or individuals. The idea was well-received and within twelve months the Stevenage Community Trust was formed, an independent local charity. Then, quite unexpectedly, came the opportunity for an additional link town.

Stevenage was already 'twinned' with Ingelheim in Germany, Autun in France and Kadoma in Zimbabwe, when the opportunity presented itself for a fourth link. This came about following a visit by a group of entertainers from a Soviet ship docked on the Thames, in London. The local branch of the British-Soviet Friendship Society invited them to Stevenage, but the only place available at short notice for the dancers, musicians and singers to perform was Town Square. Watched appreciatively by a growing crowd of shoppers, they brought the precinct to a standstill. As a result, a link with a town in the Soviet Union was suggested and the Borough Council wrote to the appropriate Soviet organisation in Moscow expressing their wish to link with a similar-sized town. Their preference was for a new town with a hi-tec industrial base, to the west of Moscow, if this were possible. But this was the period just before the break-up of the Soviet Union in 1989 and it was many months before the Council received any response. When one did arrive, in 1990, it was a communication from the municipality of Shimkent, introducing itself as Stevenage's new link town.

Ten times larger than Stevenage, Shimkent is a city of approximately 850,000 people, in the republic of Kazakhstan, that was formerly part of the Soviet Union. It is situated at a major railroad junction on the Turkestan–Siberia Railway, at the crossroads of two continents, where routes from Europe, China and India meet, on the ancient Silk Road. And so a Stevenage–Shimkent Link Committee was formed and the first of many exchanges followed. A school visit of 24 Stevenage secondary-school students went to Shimkent and shortly afterwards the students' partners came to Stevenage. This visit was notable in that, some years later, one female student stayed in the UK and married an Englishman and one male student subsequently married a Kazakh lady. The link also led to two further marriages. Many other links and friendships have been formed over the years and students from Shimkent are regularly to be seen in Stevenage, studying at the Stevenage College. Students from Shimkent have also enrolled at six English universities and the League of Friends of Kazakhstan, as the Link Committee has become, has arranged exchanges involving dancers, musicians, and business and professional people in addition to students.

Meanwhile, nearer home, alarm bells were ringing. The school which had occupied Shephall Manor for 18 years was about to close and residents could see that there was a strong possibility of the site being sold for development. Richard Holton, a teacher at the school, took the lead in organising a campaign to save it. The story is told in a series of newspaper articles, beginning with the *Stevenage Herald* for 16 September 1988; 'A meeting has been held to discuss the future of Shephall Manor which is due to come up for sale next year ... Richard Holton, a teacher at the school, is leading a campaign to make the manor a listed building and stop any development on the five-acre site'.

On 6 January 1989, the *Herald* reported, 'The building is currently being used as a school by the Inner London Education Authority but that body is to be abolished next year. The Commission for New Towns will become landlords of the house and grounds and are under instructions from the government to sell off their assets to the highest bidder. As it was assumed the Manor would continue being used as a school, no conditions were put in the Borough Council's Local Plan and no preservation orders put on the trees'.

The following week, 13 January 1989, the *Herald* was able to publish some good news; 'Campaigners fighting to save the historic Shephall Manor in Stevenage have won the first round of their battle. With the help of a 4,600 name petition they have persuaded Councillors that the Victorian building is worth saving ... the Planning Committee decided to serve building preservation notices on the property and also a tree preservation order on the grounds. The notices become effective immediately and last six months which should allow enough time for a formal application to the Secretary of State for the Environment to list Shephall Manor as a building of special architectural or historic interest'.

The application was successful and Shephall Manor became a Grade II listed building. In the excellent SMAC (Shephall Manor Action Committee) website, Richard Holton explains:

> 'When it became obvious in about 1988 that Shephall Manor was likely to be closed down by ILEA (Inner London Education Authority) I became worried about what would eventually happen to the building and held a series of meetings that attracted a large number of like minded individuals who eventually formed into a committee that worked for the future preservation of

the building and surrounding park. Although it was a large committee it also contained some very talented and hard working individuals who set about the task with much gusto and I am proud to have been associated with them. We met on a monthly basis at the school with the full blessing and help of Roy Alcock (the Headmaster) and generated a lot of publicity, money and information about the school. It was an early stroke of luck that T Roger Smith, whom not much had been known about, turned out to be a very influential Victorian architect and Shephalbury in 1864 turned out to be virtually his first building.

We also had the full support of Mary Spicer who had done so much to promote Shephall Village and in many ways was custodian of the village history ...'

By government ruling, Shephall Manor still had to be sold, but the Borough Council was able to put strict conditions on its future use. In 1991, on the instructions of the Commission for New Towns, Shephall Manor house and part of the grounds were put up for sale by auction, by auctioneers Hillier Parker May & Rowden, as 'Lot 8, Grade II listed mansion with vacant possession'. It was bought by the Coptic Church, who later themselves built a new cathedral of great architectural interest in the grounds.

Children playing in a Stevenage wood. (SBC)

ALL THE FUN OF THE FAIR

Before Franklin's Field, between Hitchin Road and North Road, was developed as a private housing site, it was the location of the 'overflow' of the centuries-old Stevenage Charter Fair held in the High Street every September. When Franklin's Field was no longer available, the overflow fair moved to a field off Bridge Road, then to Gates' Field off Chequers Bridge Road and finally to the Stevenage Town Football Ground in London Road.

Before the Second World War, small fairs were also held in a field off Sish Lane and circuses erected their 'big top' on the Whitesmead Road recreation ground. During the War, the Fair was suspended, but in the Spring of 1945, the first funfair to be held in the town since 1938 set up in a field off Pound Avenue that is now the site of Fairlands Infants' School.

In 1981, the 700th anniversary of the charter, the Fair was allowed to stay for three days instead of the usual two and the museum put on a special exhibition to mark the occasion.

Stevenage charter fair, High Street, 2003 (Margaret Ashby)

CHAPTER SIXTEEN
The 1990s

Royal visits to Stevenage were quite numerous in 1990. Queen Elizabeth the Queen Mother opened the new Imaging Department at the Lister Hospital; not long afterwards, her granddaughter, the Princess Royal (Princess Anne) opened the hospital's Strathmore Wing for elderly patients, which replaced the original plan to house wounded servicemen from the Gulf War. Then the Duke of Gloucester came, and watched a boxing display by members of the Stevenage Boys' Club. That same year, the new sheltered housing complex, Fred Millard Court, named after the late Stevenage 'pioneer' and Labour councillor, was opened not by a member of the royal family, but by Neil Kinnock, MP, leader of the Labour Party.

The 1991 Census revealed some intriguing information about the county of Hertfordshire and its constituent towns. With regard to modern facilities, Stevenage was usually ahead of other towns. For example, in the county as a whole, 8.6 per cent of households had no central heating in any room, but in Stevenage, partly thanks to the Council's investment in central heating for its housing stock, all but 2.9 per cent of houses in the entire town were centrally heated. Stevenage, as was to be expected in a new town, had the lowest proportion (0.3 per cent) of households which lacked, or had to share, a bath or shower as against 0.7 per cent for the county. On the other hand, in Stevenage 9.6 per cent of men and 4.6 per cent of women aged 16–64 were unemployed as against 6.8 per cent of men and 3.6 per cent of women for Hertfordshire as a whole. This was a big improvement on the 12.6 per cent unemployment figure of 1982, but there was still some way to go.

In response to the loss of jobs at BAE in Hatfield and Stevenage, and the significant reduction in manufacturing, an organisation known as Hertfordshire

Prosperity (HP) was founded in 1991. It was to be the sub-regional economic partnership for Hertfordshire, one of nine sub-regional economic partnerships in the East of England region, set up to encourage various agencies and industries to work together to develop a co-ordinated response to the economic problems of their areas. From now on the Stevenage public would be hearing much more about the East of England Regional Assembly and its planning powers.

At this time, local authorities were being urged by the government to encourage the public to become more involved in local politics. Stevenage was one of the first authorities to set up Joint Local Committees (later called Area Committees) which met regularly in each of the six original neighbourhoods. They are intended to give the residents the opportunity to meet their local councillors and officers, representatives of the police and of the County Council and to raise matters of concern in that particular neighbourhood. Each Area Committee also has a budget to spend on items specific to that neighbourhood. In addition, there are regular presentations on topics of interest, for example, the health service.

On 19 February 1991, a service was held at the old parish church of St Nicholas' to dedicate a tablet in memory of William Allen Jowitt, Viscount Stevenage, son of a former rector of Stevenage, who became Lord Chancellor of England. Without his meticulous work in connection with the Town and Country Planning Act, which became law in 1947, it is possible that the new town might never have come into existence. After his death in 1957, his widow had twice requested permission to erect a plaque in the church in her husband's memory, according to his stated wishes, but the request had been refused on both occasions by the rector, the Revd Eric Cordingly. Now, thirty-four years later, a more generous view prevailed.

In the same year another man was honoured for his service to Stevenage. Michael Cotter had worked long and hard in the cause of prosperity and full employment for the town. In 1991 he was Mayor of Stevenage, Chairman of the Governors of the Barclay School, a former member of the Hertfordshire County Council and previously, for 14 years, a member of the Board of the Development Corporation. His contribution to *The History Makers* ended with the memorable words, 'I think [Stevenage] has become one of the finest towns in Britain. There is less racialism, less community segregation and less ethnic violence than in most other towns ... it is a marvellous place to live and a marvellous community to belong to.' On 24 August 1991 he lay terminally ill and, in a moving ceremony around his hospital bed, the Freedom of the Borough of Stevenage was conferred upon him for his services to the town.

Following the collapse of the former Soviet Union at the end of 1989, the British public were gradually being made aware of some of the horrors of

A Joint Local Committee meeting. (Stevenage Museum)

Stevenage Borough Council Accounts Department staff with their award for service, 1999. (Stevenage Museum)

Michael Cotter. (Stevenage Museum P10857)

poverty and suffering uncovered by Western journalists, particularly the treatment of orphan and unwanted children. Bernie Ross, a reporter for the *Stevenage Herald and Post*, who visited a Romanian orphanage in October 1992, wrote, 'Nothing can prepare you for what you see at the children's orphanage at Siret – the briefest of visits leave you emotionally drained and bewildered. Behind forbidding iron gates stands the old army barracks that has become a prison for some 527 children. Their only crime was to be rejected by a society that judged them handicapped for the slightest defect.' In Britain, a national organisation called Romanian Challenge was co-ordinating donations of money and goods and the Stevenage Rotary Club was one group that was regularly taking desperately needed supplies to Romania and forming relationships with a village community. On 28 October, the *Herald and Post* reported, 'Stevenage Rotarians visited Romania this month bearing early Christmas presents. Patrick Biddulph, of Stevenage Rotary Club, was among the group which went to the village of Laz and a kindergarten at Cluj ... In Laz the Rotarians handed out presents for villagers and aid for the very poor and nursing mothers. The group left aid with the head of the village to alleviate hardship during the winter and also visited the Mayor to check on the progress of a water supply to the village'.

At the same time, Stevenage was rallying to the support of its newest twin town, Shimkent, in Kazakhstan, where help was also needed, though less well-known to the rest of Britain. The Stevenage/Shimkent Association launched an appeal for help in June with a view of helping the orphanage and maternity hospital first. In October, the *Herald* was able to report that,

> The first major delivery of aid has arrived at one of Stevenage's twin towns, Shimkent in Kazakhstan. The industrial city used to be part of the Soviet Union but, since the changes in the USSR, buying baby foods and medicines and equipment has become almost impossible because of currency limitations ... The first half a tonne of aid was sent out by lorry on October 16, accompanied by Bob Clarke of Archer Road, Stevenage, who has been over to the town twice before. The lorry was destined for the worst hit orphanage and contained cot linen, blankets, baby foods, powdered milk, vitamins, nappies and basic medicines.
>
> Brian Underwood, chairman of the Stevenage–Shimkent Association, urged people to support the appeal for aid . He said, 'Dedicated members of the Association have given up their spare time freely for the cause and are now continuing with fund-raising and sponsorship ventures.

Locally, the big concern was still unemployment. The same paper reported,

> Thousands of British Aerospace workers were due to march through London today to call for the Government to save their jobs. Workers travelled from the

> BAe site in Stevenage this morning to join the mass rally at the House of Commons.
>
> They are urging MPs to introduce measures to boost the aerospace industry after last month's announcement of 2,600 job losses at the BAe site in Hatfield. Stevenage representative George Slessor, of the Amalgamated Electrical and Engineering Union, said, 'The theme of the march is about British industry as a whole and what's happened to it' ... He said they would urge the Government to pour more cash into the aerospace industry to give it a quick kick-start. 'My opinion is that we are now into a depression, and the Government must take positive steps to create or save jobs. The engineering industry in particular has taken a real thrashing. No one is left untouched.'

Shadow Chancellor Gordon Brown and Shadow Trade and Industry Secretary Robin Cook were due to speak to them.

In January 1995 a partnership began between Stevenage Borough Council and major local companies, entitled the 'Stevenage Brighter for Business Campaign'. Its purpose was to encourage companies to come to Stevenage, or to expand their existing operations there. The campaign was very effective. One of its successes was the new Glaxo Smith Kline medicines research centre, employing 2,000 scientists, research technicians and support staff, with an investment of over £700 million. It was officially opened by the Queen in April 1995. The Dixons Warehouse Distribution Centre, a major employer based in the Pin Green Industrial Area, had also recently expanded its site and increased its workforce.

Two of the firms relocated to Stevenage in 1995 were IFHR, a ground-breaking communications company, employing 350 staff at its headquarters in Norton Green Road, and UIA (Insurance) Ltd, which moved its head office from Central London. A home contents insurance company, owned by members of the trade union UNISON, it initially brought 65 jobs to the town and subsequently increased staff numbers to 140. The town's main employer continued to be BAe, or Astrium as it had become, a joint venture owned by EADS and BAe Systems. Astrium employed 1,500 people in Stevenage and was continuing to win many contracts related to space infrastructure.

The Stevenage Leisure Park opened in 1996, on the former King's factory site, is directly accessible from the main line railway station and a short walk from the town centre and bus station. Its attractions included a 12 screen Cineworld cinema, a Hollywood tenpin bowling centre, a David Lloyd Fitness Centre and numerous bars, restaurants and nightclubs. The Park brought employment for some 800 people in Stevenage. In its early days it also brought a great deal of anti-social behaviour from home-going patrons, as well as the occasional rumpus at Stevenage railway station from groups of trouble-makers who had arrived by train with the express intention of having a fight.

Standards of behaviour in public places had been deteriorating for many years throughout the country but it seemed to reach a particularly low point in the 1990s. Many towns began to install CCTV cameras as a deterrent and Stevenage, after considering the pros and cons, decided to do the same. The town's CCTV partnership scheme began in 1996 and was gradually extended throughout the Borough.

An odd example of anti-social behaviour occurred on 5 February 1996, when, according to a report in the *Independent* newspaper, a groundsman arrived at the Stevenage Borough Football Club stadium in Broadhall Way to discover that both penalty spots and the centre spot had been stolen. Apparently the thief, armed with a shovel, had climbed over the fence at night and removed them, for what purpose has never been discovered.

The following season, the Football Club was in the news again but for a much more positive reason. Even those who normally had absolutely no interest in football were caught up in the excitement when Stevenage Borough reached the fourth round of the FA cup, where they faced the Premier League club Newcastle United. An additional stand was brought into the Broadhall Way ground, increasing the stadium capacity to 8,040. To the delight of Stevenage supporters and the amazement of expert commentators, Borough held Newcastle to a one-all draw. The replay was to be held at St James Park, Newcastle, and would be broadcast live on television. On the afternoon of the match the whole town went quiet. Everyone, it seemed, was indoors, glued to the screen. Those who just had to go out, perhaps to walk the dog, passed through empty streets but could keep up with the game through the volume and tone of shouts emanating from the assembled viewers. The game ended in an honourable defeat by two goals to one, but as far as most of the Stevenage population was concerned, it was a great achievement.

The new town's 50th anniversary, in 1996, was celebrated with an exhibition at the museum and other events throughout the town. In the same year Brian Hall was made a Freeman of the Borough of Stevenage. He had begun to make his mark from the time he was elected to the Stevenage Urban District Council in 1967. Within two years he was elected leader of the Labour majority group and, in 1971, leader of the council. Apart from his year as mayor, in 1975–1976, he was to serve continually for 40 years, surpassing even Philip Ireton's record to become the country's longest-serving council leader. His influence in the council and, consequently, on matters affecting the town, were unparalleled. It is doubtful that many townspeople were aware of the enormous amount of unstinting background work that the dynamic Brian Hall devoted to the job. His record of local government service in Stevenage is unlikely ever to be matched.

Brian Hall was a strong and determined leader and that made him unpopular at times in some quarters. When a local newspaper reporter asked him, 'What

Stevenage Borough FC v. Newcastle match at Broadhall Way. (*Comet* Newspaper)

Stevenage Borough FC manager, Paul Fairclough, beseiged by the media. (*Comet* newspaper)

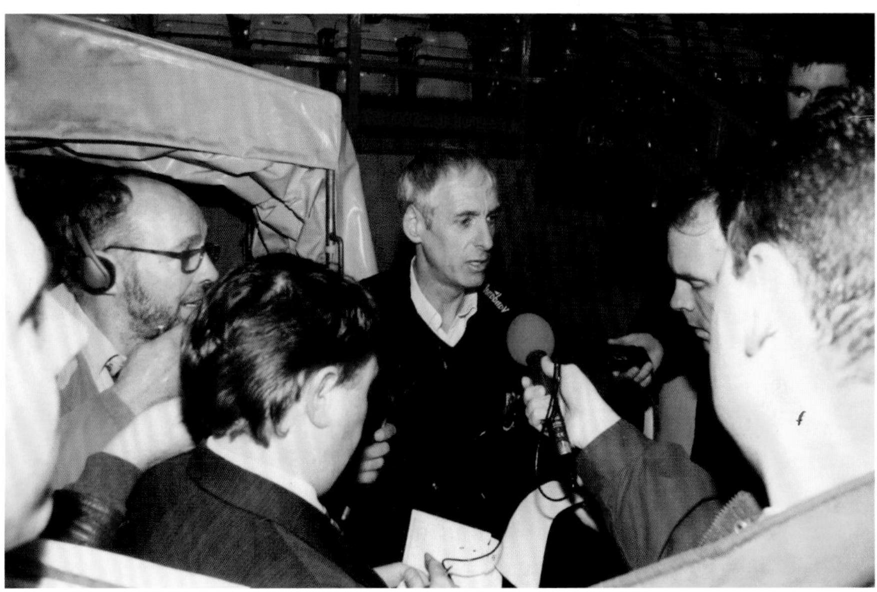

makes a successful Council Leader?' he replied, 'Find out where the group wants to go and lead them there!' It is possible that there were times when Brian Hall had to work hard and patiently on some of his Labour colleagues on the Council before they knew where they wanted to go – which usually was in the direction that he wanted them to go. Nevertheless, his manipulative skill, his tenacity, his foresight, his excellent grasp of finance and his outstanding stature as a local politician can only be admired. There were few Council projects in which the innovative and forceful Council Leader was not closely involved. It can honestly be said that 'He made a difference!'

At the age of 29, Brian Hall became the youngest member of the Hertfordshire County Council and was later elected chairman of its Highways Committee. He served as the representative of Hertfordshire, Bedfordshire and Essex on the Local Government Association's Policy and Strategy Committee, and was a member of the Eastern Region Executive of the Eastern Regional Labour Party and its Working Party on the Future of New Towns. He was later (2006) to be made an honorary citizen of Stevenage's link town of Ingelheim-am-Rhein, an Honorary Borough Alderman (2007), an Honorary Doctor of Laws of the University of Hertfordshire and was also honoured by Stevenage's French link town of Autun.

At this time there was continuing pressure nationally for new house-building programmes. Developers were buying up land wherever they could, including the Forster Country in the north of Stevenage. Despite the 1988 judgement against building in the Forster Country, the developers tried again in 1989 and their application was again refused. In 1992 there was a public inquiry into the Stevenage Borough Council Draft District Plan, at which the Friends of the Forster Country argued that the Green Belt boundary should be revised to include the whole of the Forster Country, thus giving it permanent protection. However, no sooner had that milestone been achieved than planners at national level began to press for building on Green Belt land which, in jargon of the day, equated to 'moving the goalposts'. To make a permanent, visible statement that the Forster Country was in Green Belt specifically to protect it from development, the Friends of the Forster Country, helped by funding from the Borough Council and the County Council, commissioned a sculpture by Angela Godfrey, entitled 'Only Connect' which was erected on the edge of St Nicholas' churchyard, by the footpath into the Forster Country. It was unveiled in November 1997 by Stevenage's new Labour MP, Barbara Follett.

In 1998, as a result of new government directives, there was a change in the way in which the town's leisure facilities were run. Stevenage Leisure Limited (SLL) was established in March 1998 as a company limited by guarantee. SLL was granted 25 year leases by the council to operate four of its leisure facilities: Stevenage Arts and Leisure Centre, Stevenage Swimming Centre, John Henry Newman Leisure Centre and Fairlands Valley Park. The facilities at Ridlins End are managed by Stevenage Borough Council, not by SLL.

Since its inception, SLL has taken over the management of Stevenage Golf Centre and Shephall Leisure Centre. In 2002 it won its first external contract with Mid Beds District Council and since then has won other contracts with North Herts District Council, Herts County Council and East Herts District Council.

Other agreements with neighbouring authorities were also taking place. It was with some surprise that Stevenage residents who happened to be travelling

The unveiling of the 'Only Connect' sculpture, November 1997. L to R – Ian Hamilton, Margaret Ashby, Kenneth Vale (Mayor of Stevenage), Revd John Bainbridge (Vicar of St Nicholas' church), Barbara Follett, MP, John Hepworth, Angela Godfrey (sculptor). (Ann Ward)

between Old Stevenage and Weston in 1998, discovered that a large building site was opening up along the Weston Road, near Botany Bay. They were even more surprised as time went on to discover that it would contain hundreds of new houses as a mainly private development technically within Graveley parish,in North Herts District, but adjoining Stevenage. Those few people who had time and curiosity enough to keep abreast of planning applications in adjacent districts might have known what was happening, but most were unaware. Because the development was in North Hertfordshire, literally a footstep over the Stevenage boundary, it barely featured in Stevenage news reports. It could as well have been in France. In due course it was revealed that services to the new area would be provided by Stevenage but that Stevenage had no powers, for example, to insist upon cycle tracks to link up with the new town cycleways. As the new houses were advertised for sale, they attracted a high proportion of buyers from Stevenage, where private houses were still in short supply.

One more surprise was to come, that of the name for the development – 'Great Ashby'. It took some research before Tony Evenden, of North Herts District Council, found the explanation. It is a made-up name by the developers, who were impressed by the great number of ash trees on the site. To this, they added 'Great' from a modern planning document, source not given, which refers to the building of new areas as 'the great extension'. Finally, they added the suffix 'by' which is Old Norse for 'village' or 'settlement' and common in the midlands and north of England. It is not found in Hertfordshire and is quite inappropriate for this district. 'Great Ashfield' or 'Great Ashworth' would have been a happier choice. As so many road names in old Stevenage have been changed over the years, perhaps one day this name may be changed too.

Perhaps not so much surprise, more a feeling of *deja vu*, was many people's reaction to the Hertfordshire County Council Structure Plan, published in 1998, which included proposals for a development of some 10,000 dwellings in the North Hertfordshire District adjacent to Stevenage. It covered farmland in the Langley Valley between the A1(M) and the B656 Codicote Road – very much as had been proposed and defeated in 1964. The difference was that this time the Stevenage Borough Council was in favour of the development.

The Campaign Against Stevenage Expansion (CASE) and other objectors girded themselves once more for battle, and those in favour marshalled their arguments. Meanwhile, the various authorities concerned were determined that, this time, the public would be fully involved in the planning process and arranged a series of workshops, conferences and research groups as part of a 'citizen participation project ... to ensure sustainable development through community input'. About 250 people took part, many of them finding the experience interesting and informative, although many more were cynical, recognising that they still had no power to prevent the development. A public inquiry was called for, which, including the various stages leading up to it and the wait for a decision afterwards, lasted for the next seven years.

As the decade, and the century, drew to a close, the town centre was looking somewhat neglected. Efforts by the Council to make it more attractive had only partially succeeded. There was general approval of the refurbishment of the pedestrian ways, with seating, planting and signs, all helping greatly to brighten the place up. But a number of shops had closed and were boarded up, particularly at the Queensway end of the town centre and the suggestion was sometimes voiced that perhaps too many shops had been included in the development at The Forum, in the northern end. Change was inevitable, but sometimes painful. Commenting on the refurbishment of the water feature, 'Joy Ride' platform and associated structures, Ray Gorbing, who had designed the Town Square in 1958, wrote sadly in 1999, 'When the public lavatories and water feature had to be refurbished why, oh why, was it found necessary to alter the original conception? The 1959 design principle was for the "Joy Ride" statue on the platform to be in a direct line axis with the most important feature in the square, the clock tower, and viewed from there directly up the steps ...'

In the Council's many questionnaires and other means of public consultation about the town centre, one of the most frequent comments concerned the lack of a department store. This was certainly not for want of trying by either the Development Corporation or the Council. The quest for a prestigious department store had occupied both authorities for years, to their intense frustration as the quarry has, so far, eluded them.

It became clear at the end of the 1990s that Stevenage was not alone with the problem of areas in need of a facelift. Most of the 32 new towns developed between 1946 and 1970 were in much the same position. The matter was being discussed by MPs on the Select Committee on Transport, Local Government and the Regions, who subsequently published a report warning that the new towns were locked into a 'spiral of decline' because of neglect by successive governments. It sounded rather dismal but out of it came a new buzzword, 'Regeneration'. Those who had watched the new town grow from its beginnings

Millennium Wood. (Margaret Ashby)

in 1946, were disappointed to think that, after all the fine promises from the first Master Plan onwards, Stevenage should now contain within it areas of social deprivation. Sadly, Stevenage was ranked as the most deprived district in Hertfordshire and part of Bedwell as one of the most deprived wards in the country. Fortunately, help was now available through a new government grant known as the Single Regeneration Budget, which was a seven-year scheme to provide additional funds to deprived areas and in 1998 Stevenage councillors were delighted to be able to announce that the town had been granted £6.3 million under this scheme. They began immediately to plan the strategies which would rejuvenate the town in the new millennium.

Alongside proposals for the future, a new political structure was being introduced for the Borough Council, in common with many other local authorities. Intended to increase efficiency and speed up decision-making, the new arrangement was comparable to the cabinet system of central government, with individual councillors becoming portfolio holders for specific 'departments' or areas of work.

As the grown-ups talked and planned about the future, children were getting down to practical work. The Steering Committee which had been set up to suggest ways of marking the millennium had suggested that a space, roughly one hectare in size, adjoining Whomerley Wood, could be planted with young tress to create a new Millennium Wood. In November 1999, under the guidance of Richard Arnold, 2,000 children from Stevenage primary schools each planted one sapling of a locally native tree species, mainly hornbeam and oak, to merge with the original woodland, and also ash, crab-apple, wayfaring tree, spindle and other native shrubs. A Millennium Avenue of 100 English Oaks, *Quercus robur*, was planted in the same month along the footpath leading from the Broadhall Way car park towards the Millennium Wood. Over the years all these trees will grow to support wildlife and beautify Fairlands Valley for future generations.

CHAPTER SEVENTEEN
The new millennium

THE SECOND MILLENNIUM DAWNED to find Stevenage in optimistic mood. Most of the projects which the Millennium Committee had chosen would continue into the future, enhancing the town and giving pleasure to its residents for many years to come. As well as the newly-planted wood and avenue in Fairlands Valley, one of the lakes was being cleaned and replenished, to become known as the Millennium Lake. The High Street entrance to the King George V playing fields had been transformed from a dull lawn into a Millennium Garden, incorporating plants used through the ages, from the Roman Empire to modern times. The finishing touch was provided by a wooden sculpture, by Dennis Heath, of a hand holding a dove, entitled 'Friendship and Peace'. Unfortunately the dove's beak has since been broken off, but the message remains.

The museum had benefited from a grant to enable the complete renewal of its galleries telling the history of the town. The new galleries won an 'Interpret Britain' award, which was presented in 2003 to Jo Ward, Cultural Services Manager, at the Royal Horticultural Hall in London, where she received a framed certificate from Lloyd Grossman. Only a few months later the museum was granted a Charter Mark for excellence in customer service. The assessors who visited the museum in December 2002 spent considerable time making an in-depth evaluation. They awarded the Charter Mark because of the excellent quality of displays, the enthusiasm of the staff and the high standing of the museum in the community. Councillor Sue Myson commented, 'The judging panel informed us that this is not an award that is easily won, so it is a true tribute to the museum.'

Prince Charles visiting the 'Wheels' project for young people. (Stevenage Museum)

Stevenage Museum staff Caroline Weldham and Emma Steed taking part in a Tudors Exhibition. (Stevenage Museum)

An intriguing project was the millennium pavement. This involved 'neighbourhood twinning' using public artwork to link outlying neighbourhoods to the town centre, where a large mosaic, incorporating symbols representing each neighbourhood, was inlaid into the pavement. Beginning with Bedwell and Shephall, the neighbourhoods themselves would also have a mosaic with their own symbols. In addition, many of the town's music and arts groups put on a special millennium programme, such as that by the Stevenage Symphony Orchestra.

The year 2000 saw the completion of another of the town centre's refurbishments. When the main Post Office was transferred to its new site in Westgate, the original premises were no longer required and were demolished. In their place came The Plaza, an area of cafes, pubs and restaurants, with a modern fitness centre adjacent to it, in Danestrete. Subsequently the former Langley House, on the corner of Danestrete and Southgate, was also demolished and replaced by the Holiday Express Hotel. The same year the Business and Technology Centre re-opened after a £3 million upgrade.

A Pop in the Park concert. (Stevenage Museum)

But not every building was getting the attention it needed. The empty Manulife House was still standing, derelict and battered, between St Andrew's and St George's church and the fire station. After unsuccessful attempts by arsonists to burn it down, the Council was forced to spend money on protective metal fencing because the owners could not be traced. It was now considered the ugliest building in Stevenage, nearby residents were becoming considerably annoyed and, despite strenuous efforts by the Council, a solution seemed no nearer. Then, in 2001, to mixed reactions, the Council received a planning application for the conversion of the Manulife building into an hotel. Some neighbouring residents were in favour of, at least, getting something done, others thought the design poor. But it all came to nothing and the building continued in a derelict state, with the council powerless to do anything about it for the time being.

Home Office statistics published in July 2000 showed that the North Hertfordshire district was the 11th safest place to live in the country, but Stevenage came 108th out of 315 areas. The figures were based on the number of violent crimes for every 1,000 people. According to a report in the *Comet* for 27 July the divisional Police Commander, Superintendent Terry Ives, explained,

> Stevenage is a very safe place to live, even compared with the quieter parts of Hertfordshire. We have been actively encouraging victims of domestic violence to report these crimes and that is one reason why it appears that we have more violent crimes than any other part of the country. All forms of violent crime ... feature high on our priority action plans. We have a dedicated community team which solves on-going problems and targets trouble hotspots across the town.

Two years later, in March 2003, Stevenage became one of the first towns to have the services of the new Police Community Support Officers. They spend at least 80 per cent of their time outside, in the community, on the watch for anti-social behaviour of all kinds, including shop-lifting, pickpockets and similar unpleasant and unlawful activities. Perhaps most important of all is their high visibility which gives reassurance to the general public and the opposite to those of criminal intent.

During Councillor Hugh Tessier's mayoral year, 2001–2, the 'Pride in Our Town' scheme was launched. This invited the public to nominate places or features of the town that were particularly important to them and which they felt helped to make Stevenage a good place to live. Unsurprisingly, some of the first to be nominated and most highly rated were: the woodlands, Fairlands Valley, the Forster Country, cycleways and the old town High Street. Many people were also very pleased when, in 2001, the swimming pool was re-opened after a £2.9 million refurbishment which had taken longer than anticipated.

In November 2001, over 60 years after the beginning of the Second World War and the Nazi persecutions of the Jews, there was international agreement to designate a Holocaust Memorial Day. Stevenage gave full support to this, with an exhibition of posters in Westgate and a reception in Daneshill House. Other events held in subsequent years have included drama, talks, readings, tree planting and film shows.

A general election was due in 2002 and the government was considering ways of encouraging more people to vote, particularly in local elections where turn-outs had been declining for many years. Eventually, it was agreed to investigate the feasibility of postal voting and in 2000 a pilot scheme was carried out in various parts of the country, including two wards in Stevenage. The results were encouraging, increasing the number of people voting by 17 per cent. The Borough Council was keen to extend it to the whole town, which they were allowed to do in the 2002 election, when Stevenage had postal voting only. Turnout increased to over 50 per cent of the electorate. Subsequently Stevenage used both voting at a polling station and postal voting at elections. However, there could be timing errors, as in the year when the postal voting papers, urging people to return them quickly, were sent out before the political parties had had time to distribute their campaign literature.

Into the hi-tec, hygienic, highly organised second millennium, an old untidy image suddenly presented itself. Gypsies (or travellers, to use the modern term) were back in the town. For centuries there had been an association between gypsies and Stevenage. According to the historian Herbert W Tompkins, one gypsy king, Henry Boswell, was born at Six Hills in about 1690. He died aged 90 in 1786 and was buried in St Katherine's churchyard, Ickleford. Until the building of the new town gypsies, or Romanies, were frequent visitors to the Stevenage district, camping on the many green spaces including the Whitesmead Road Recreation Ground, where, in the 1920s, residents in nearby cottages sold them water from their recently installed mains supply. Gypsy women and children went from house to house selling lace, clothes pegs and 'lucky heather', and the men sometimes found casual work on farms at harvest time. Inevitably, some were on the look-out for chickens or other desirables to make off with.

Fishers Green was a traditional camping ground. The dark-haired, dark-eyed gypsies with their horse-drawn wagons and open fires, made a romantic and colourful scene, but not one which many would envy. Children at the old St Nicholas' School on Burymead who were taught the song about the 'Raggle Taggle Gipsies' did not really wish to leave home for a travelling life of hardship and uncertainty. On the contrary, some gypsies settled in Stevenage, making a home here for themselves and their descendants. Nowadays local authorities are bound by law to provide permanent sites for travellers. The Stevenage site, in Dyes Lane, is near another traditional resting place where the Johnson brothers and their aged mother lived for many years. After the old lady's death, the brothers, now in old age themselves, were subjected to persecution from groups of louts. A number of kindly Stevenage people, notably George and Isobel Ellis, helped them with food and other necessities and eventually rescued them from their caravan when it was attacked. Social worker Muriel Chesterton took over their case and arranged for them to spend the rest of their lives in one of the Hellard Almshouses in Church Lane.

But the travellers who arrived in the twenty-first century were not Romany gypsies. They came in large motor vans, often in convoys, and took over parts of Fairlands Valley and occupied Fishers Green, to the exclusion of other people. Many residents complained bitterly about their behaviour and the filth they left. Council officers tried for many months to resolve the problem so that all parties, gypsies and residents, were treated fairly and in accordance with the law. Eventually the travellers moved on and, to prevent motor vehicles from driving on to it, earth embankments were built up round Fishers Green and planted with spring bulbs. Those with long memories now look at the daffodils at Fishers Green and remember the gypsies.

A new millennium might have arrived, but the same controversial issues remained. Arguments and campaigns for and against the inclusion in the County Council's Structure Plan for the building of up to 10,000 new houses in countryside to the west of Stevenage continued until, in September 2001, they were brought to an unexpected halt. North Herts District Council (NHDC), having taken expert advice, decided to withdraw their own District Plan, which was needed before the County Plan could go ahead. The NHDC based its action on the grounds that the proposed development plans were not consistent with the government's own recent guidelines, which stated that councils must make every effort to use brownfield sites in cities, towns and suburbs before using unspoilt countryside for developments. Peter Lilley, MP for Hitchin and Harpenden, which covered the area in question, was quoted as saying that the planned development would have turned north Hertfordshire into a concrete jungle from Stevenage through Hitchin to Luton. He said, 'In its new Planning Guidance the Government has launched a boomerang which has come back and hit them. The Green Belt has been the biggest single issue since I was elected in this part of the world and this infraction of it causes an uproar.' Tim Akeroyd, chairman of CASE, said, 'This is wonderful news. The position of CASE and its thousands of supporters has been fully vindicated.' CASE had massive backing locally and although nearly 1,500 people supported the proposal, a total of 2,600 had sent in objection forms ...'

The debate raged on for the next few years attracting, as always, much coverage in the national as well as the local press. As decision time drew near, the *Guardian* featured an article, entitled *Water Supply Fears for 500,000 New Homes,* about the planned building in countryside in Hertfordshire, Bedfordshire and Cambridgeshire. It pointed out that, more than anything else, it was the loss of Green Belt land that was causing concern. Interviews with North Herts residents living near Stevenage included the comment, with reference to the Green Belt, 'It's all just going to be swallowed up, isn't it? ... And the wildlife, what's going to happen there? The wildlife is part of our country and if you do away with that out here you have nothing left.' A spokesman for the Campaign for the Protection of Rural England said, 'It will result in urban sprawl over some of our finest countryside, more road congestion, water shortages and a rolling back of rural tranquility.'

Three days later, a letter was published in response from Stevenage Borough Councillor, John Gardner. It said,

> Stevenage's latest housing study shows that we need to build 4,000 affordable homes between now and 2011, but have only enough land in our urban area to build 3,000 homes of all types. The best population projections show we will have over 8,000 new households by 2021: where are they supposed to live?

> The children of existing households in the region cannot find nor afford to buy homes where they were brought up. The children are then forced away, with consequent impacts upon the economy and public service.

Another *Guardian* article, on 15 October, included a classic dilemma voiced by one interviewee who had lived in Stevenage New Town since 1958. He was concerned that the local infrastructure would not be able to cope with the new development, but added, 'But it is a difficult situation, people saying they don't want redevelopment, because if there wasn't any redevelopment in the first place then I wouldn't have my home here ... so in a way it's a bit naughty of us who have homes here to say we don't want others coming in.'

The planning process ground on to September 2005, when the draft *East of England Plan* was debated at an Examination in Public at Ely, moving on to Letchworth during January and March 2006. The *Plan* was finally published later that year by the East of England Assembly, an organisation that at least one person described as 'a distant, unelected regional body which swept aside the concerns of local people'. The 2006 *East of England Plan* gave the go-ahead for 3,600 new houses west of Stevenage, among others in the region. Stevenage was also identified as a Key Centre for Development (Policy SS2), a Regional Interchange Centre (Policy T2), a Priority Area for Regeneration (Policy SS11) and a Regional Retail Centre (Policy E9). Another report, *Prioritisation in the East of England*, identified Stevenage as an area of strong economic performance and high deprivation with two of the region's most disadvantaged wards located in the Borough. 'Growth, bringing with it increased investment and opportunities, needs to be linked to regeneration. The Borough Council has plans for a major regeneration of the Town Centre, which will both benefit from and support the growth of the town stated the Report.

The CPRE and others who objected to the west of Stevenage proposals pointed out something that had not been very obvious when they were first made, viz that plans for a second terminal at Luton Airport would mean building new homes for some 9,000 extra staff, together with more car parks and motorways for the additional passengers. The land requested for these developments is in north Hertfordshire.

For the people involved, the campaigners, the local government officers and others, the convoluted planning process took over their lives. For the rest of the population, the jargon, the time-consuming meetings, the number of documents to be read and responded to, the confusing array of authorities, especially the East of England Regional Authority which seemed to have appeared out of nowhere, were all just too much. In recent years Stevenage Borough Council has made heroic efforts to put its documents into plain English but, even so, the whole system is overwhelming and what is worse, never-ending. So while the *East of England Plan* evolved in the background, most people got on with their everyday lives. They were generally pleased in 2002 when the Council began a weekly collection of glass, tins and newspapers from households, but made rather a song and dance about the brown wheelie bins that were introduced later to collect garden waste. Most were appreciative, some absolutely delighted and others annoyed at the size of the bins which they said they did not want anyway. Letters on this subject, and on the question of putting out black rubbish bags, appeared with monotonous regularity in the *Comet* newspaper until eventually everyone calmed down. As people got used to recycling, the clamour directed at councillors was to recycle more, such as plastic and cardboard. New controversy developed when the part of Great Ashby controlled by North Hertfordshire District Council went over to fortnightly waste collection while the rest of Stevenage retained its weekly collection of black sacks.

On the leisure front, 2002 was a good year. A new leisure centre at Shephall was opened and also the new Community Arts Centre at Roaring Meg to replace the former building. The new one, better placed near London Road, had a good-sized main hall with ancillary rooms and was immediately popular with local arts and recreational groups, administered through the Stevenage Arts Guild. In this year, too, the Council were able to buy the Golf Clubhouse.

In recognition of her 45 years of service to public life, Hilda Lawrence was made a Freeman of the Borough of Stevenage in 2002. During that time she had been a Labour Councillor; Chairman of the Borough Council's Health and Community Services Committee and Vice-Chairman of its Finance and Policy Resources Committee. Elected also to the Hertfordshire County Council, she became Chairman of the Community Care Committee, Vice-chairman of the County Council itself and a County Alderman.

From 1965 to 1980 she was a member of the Board of the Stevenage Development Corporation. This was the first of three government appointments by successive Home Secretaries, the later two appointments being to the Annan Committee on Broadcasting and to a regional mental health tribunal. Her active interest in health matters led to her appointments to the Luton, Dunstable and Hitchin Hospitals Management Committee; the Hertfordshire Area Health Authority; the North Herts Health Authority, of which she was vice-chairman; the local Community Health Council and the local Family Practitioners' Committee. She was also chairman of the North Herts Committee for the Disabled and president of the Stevenage and District Society for Mentally Handicapped Children (Mencap) and was involved in the establishment in Stevenage of sheltered workshops for disabled and handicapped adults and young people.

In addition, Hilda was, at various times, chairman of the local Police Consultative Committee; chairman of the governing bodies of Collenswood

Secondary Modern and Broom Barns Primary Schools and a governor of Nobel School. In her mayoral year she inaugurated the Stevenage Community Trust, which has given many thousands of pounds in grants to local voluntary organisations. Having twice been mayoress when her husband Bill was mayor, Hilda Lawrence became the first woman to be elected Mayor of the Borough of Stevenage and she received a further accolade from her colleagues when they elected her the fourth Freeman of the Borough.

On 11 September 2002, the optimism and hope that had characterised the opening of the new millennium were shattered when two airliners that had been hi-jacked by terrorists smashed into the World Trade Centre in New York, and a third into the Pentagon at Washington, DC. There were fears that this heralded the beginning of a third world war.

The next few months were taken up with debate, discussion and theorising about the previously unheard-of Al-Queida organisation. Western governments talked of a 'war on terrorism', but in March 2003 the talking stopped and people realised with a jolt of horror that the United States, and probably Britain, would invade Iraq. The papers were immediately inundated with letters on the subject, many protesting against military action. It so happened that this was taking place at a time when the Labour Government was trying to honour its

The Stevenage contingent prepare to board coaches for the Peace March in London, to oppose an invasion of Iraq, 2003. (Ray Peters)

pre-election promise to ban foxhunting. One Hertfordshire resident was moved to write to *The Times* on 4 March, questioning why it was now apparently justifiable to kill Iraqis but not foxes. In the short time available anti-invasion groups took to the streets in silent protest. They had strong support in Stevenage and several coachloads of protesters went to London to take part in a peaceful mass demonstration. It was to no avail, the invasion took place and British and American troops have remained in Iraq for over seven years.

In December 2002, a new ASDA store opened on the old Stevenage College site, which had itself been built on the former Six Hills Nursery of renowned alpine plant specialist Clarence Elliott. In an arrangement with the North Hertfordshire College, ASDA provided £20 million towards a new college building, to be known as North Herts College, Stevenage Centre. This was built on open ground previously used as the college playing field. It provided a magnificent further education centre, with inter-active white boards and other state-of-the-art teaching facilities and was largely the inspiration of North Herts College Principal, Roger Gochin, who had master-minded similar new further education buildings in Hitchin and Letchworth. The new development was not without its critics; many regretted yet another infill of green space caused by the loss of the playing fields.

The new college building was opened in 2003 by the Queen and the Duke of Edinburgh, who arrived to find that many in the watching crowd were sporting red noses in aid of Comic Relief's Red Nose Day. The Queen herself entered into the spirit of the occasion by wearing a red coat. This was the first time that the Queen had been to Hertfordshire in five years. She spent some time in touring the college and talking to staff and students before moving on to the arts and leisure centre, where an exhibition entitled 'Innovation – Stevenage 2003' had been organised by a partnership of the Stevenage Chamber of Commerce, Stevenage Borough Council and major local businesses. It was one of the largest trade fairs of its kind in the country and its purpose was to promote Stevenage and its many innovative and world-class businesses.

The annual Stevenage Carnival had, for many years, been raising money for charity and giving enjoyment to the crowds who lined the streets to see it. But times had changed since the early days when horses and carts, assorted lorries and farm vehicles laden with volunteers in fancy dress made their leisurely way through the town, with a few police officers to hold up the traffic for them. In the twenty-first century Health and Safety Legislation, together with fees for road closures and insurance, had made the cost of running a carnival prohibitive in many towns. The Stevenage carnival was the only one left in North Hertfordshire in 2003, thanks to the support of the Borough Council in paying for road closures, but in future the carnival committee of the Rotary Club would also be required by law to pay an independent company to make the necessary

Stevenage Carnival, 1988. Methodist Church float celebrating the 250th anniversary of John Wesley. Huw Rees dressed as John Wesley. (Colin Killick)

risk assessment. The carnival committee chairman, Bryan Cornish, said they were unlikely ever to be able to afford to pay such a company, as the whole purpose of the event was to raise as much money as possible for charity. Fortunately, John Fitzpatrick, of Aquesia Consultants at Pin Green, offered his services free to the committee saying that it would be a great shame for the town if the carnival stopped.

Later in the year more crowds descended on Stevenage on their way to Knebworth House, which had become known as 'the stately home of rock', having hosted many celebrity rock concerts over the years. In 2003, the three-day concert featured the star of the moment, Robbie Williams, and attracted a record number of 350,000 fans. Many walked from Stevenage as the A1 and all minor roads off it had ground to a halt in a monumental traffic jam. Those living in the south of the town had no need to leave home, as the concert was clearly audible for miles around.

The use of Indian call centre and secretarial services was becoming popular with industry and commerce as a means of saving money by reducing staffing levels in England. One example in 2004 was the decision by Norwich Union, Britain's biggest insurer, to cut a total of nearly 1,000 jobs from five of its branches, including Stevenage. A year later, a cost-cutting pilot scheme by managers at the Lister Hospital sent typing to India, with the possible result that a quarter of hospital secretaries could be made redundant. Both patients and doctors were worried to hear of this and consultants at the hospital stressed the value of qualified medical secretaries.

On 2 February 2005 a terrible tragedy occurred at a high rise block of flats, Harrow Court, in Silam Road. Fire broke out at about 3 am on the 14th floor and, through intense heat and thick smoke, two firemen attempted to rescue a resident trapped in the blazing flat. The firemen, Michael Millar and Jeff Wornham, both died and a woman resident also lost her life. The shock of this event was felt not only in Stevenage but throughout the country. Special memorial services were held later for the firemen, they were both subsequently awarded the George Medal and two roads in the redeveloped Stony Hall site off Sish Lane were named after them. Their bravery will not be forgotten.

Work on the town centre improvements was continuing with enhancements to Queensway, which helped attract more businesses to that end of the town centre. There seemed to be a little progress, too, on the Manulife building which by now had been empty for five years. A report by Sarah Tregoning in the *Comet* for 10 July 2003, about the future of the 'decaying six storey Manulife building' stated that Stevenage Borough Council had served a dangerous structures notice on the owners, Bluebirds Holdings, to try to force them to make the building safe by installing steel shutters, replacing broken windows and fencing off the courtyard. The Council had themselves already spent over £4,000 on repair work. The difficulty lay in enforcing the notice because the company was registered outside the United Kingdom. Councillors discovered that the property was owned by a development company registered in the British Virgin Islands. When attempts to contact that company failed, it was suggested that a working party travel to the British Virgin Islands to lobby for the refurbishment of the building. Eventually, however, a more conventional local government solution was employed when the Council agreed to seek a compulsory purchase order for the building to enable a housing development in the area to be funded by money from central government. There was jubilation in March 2004 when John Prescott visited Stevenage and announced that there would be funding for a regeneration project for the town, which would include demolishing the Manulife building and replacing it with much-needed housing for key workers. Many people looked forward with enthusiasm to the day when the demolition team would start work. Then, just weeks before the Council would be empowered to go through with the compulsory purchase, scaffolding and a builders' hut appeared on site and work on a long planned hotel began.

To mark the centenary of the birth of Elizabeth Poston, composer, on 24 October 2005 the Friends of the Forster Country organised a year-long programme to celebrate her life and music. It began on what would have been her 100th birthday with the planting of an apple tree by the entrance to Stevenage Museum, accompanied by the singing of her most well-known carol *Jesus Christ the Apple Tree*. The event was recorded for the BBC Radio 4's *Country File* programme. When it was broadcast nationally the presenter began with a reference to the derelict Manulife building which loomed like Nemesis over the museum. Once again the building's owners had failed to co-operate and councillors were by now almost tearing their hair out in frustration at the lack of progress.

In its Housing Strategy Programme *Good Housing for All, 2005–2010*, the Borough Council published statistics showing that about 45 per cent of households in Stevenage were owner-occupied with a mortgage, 19 per cent were owned outright, 27 per cent were Council rented accommodation, 5 per cent private rented accommodation and 4 per cent in Housing Association homes. There was increasing pressure to find space to build 'affordable homes' and in 2003 a statement from the Office of the Deputy Prime Minister, John Prescott, named four sites in Stevenage which were under the control of English Partnerships (formerly the Commission for New Towns) as available for affordable housing. However, the Borough Council was not in favour of developing sites at Bonfield, off Edmonds Drive, nor land off Hertford Road, which was reserved in the Stevenage District Plan for educational and leisure use. They did give planning permission for the sports field off Fairview Road in the old town, to be used. This was subsequently developed and given the name Silkin's Field. It included a controversial tall block of flats, painted externally in an unusual combination of colours.

In 2004, a government directive required local authorities to take action to ensure that, by 2010, all their housing would meet the Decent Homes Standard. This meant that all council houses must be warm, weatherproof and in a good state of repair, with modern kitchen and bathroom. Stevenage Borough Council set up a Housing Strategy Group to examine four options for the future of council housing in the town. These were; a Private Finance Initiative; retention of the council's housing stock; the establishment of an 'Arms Length' Management Organisation (ALMO) to manage and maintain the housing which would continue to be owned by the council; or a Large Scale Voluntary Transfer scheme (LSVT) to a housing association.

A Housing Options Appraisal carried out by the strategy group found that the Council did not have sufficient funds to meet the standard by itself and would face a shortfall of £20 million if it attempted to do so. In 2005, tenants were consulted as to whether they would prefer to remain with the Council as landlord on the understanding that such a choice would mean an ALMO and a lower level of improvements to their homes, or transfer to a housing association with a higher level of improvement: 87 per cent of tenants said that they would prefer the Council to remain as their landlord, accepted an ALMO, and rejected LSVT.

Thus Stevenage Homes Ltd was set up in 2006 to manage and maintain the houses owned by the Council and to provide housing services, including major improvement works. Stevenage Homes is run by a management board consisting of tenant representatives, Council representatives and independent people with expertise in such areas as finance, law and construction. The Council is involved in setting service standards in a management agreement between the two bodies and monitors the way in which Stevenage Homes Ltd operates. Stevenage Homes Ltd is regularly inspected by government inspectors and has to show that it is providing a good standard of service before it can acquire extra funding to enable it to improve houses to meet the Decent Homes Standard. To ensure that tenants and leaseholders had access to independent and impartial advice throughout the project, the Council, on the recommendation of the Federation of Stevenage Tenants' Associations, appointed a firm of specialised advisers on the Housing Options Appraisal process.

In 2006 Stevenage New Town was sixty years old. An extensive programme of celebratory events was planned and to add to the celebrations, at last the Manulife problem seemed to be solved. On 19 June the Council gave planning permission to Bluebird Holdings to convert the building into a 140 bed hotel. Work began and proceeded rather slowly, with many starts and stops, but eventually, in 2008, to the general relief, it was finished. Meanwhile, the anniversary year got into its stride. A great many people contributed to the Stevenage Tapestry, the brainchild of Julia Taylor. It ended as a huge wall hanging, covering not only aspects of the town's history from Roman times to 2006, but also including wildlife, sport, community groups, churches, schools and industry. The final result, now hanging in the Arts and Leisure Centre, is something any town would be proud of.

JULIA TAYLOR (5 FEBRUARY 1956–20 MAY 2009) AND THE STEVENAGE TAPESTRY

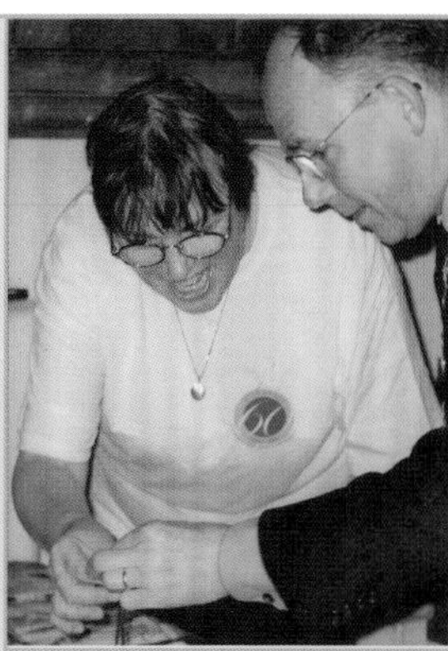

Julia learned to sew from her mother and had a life-long passion for creative processes, principally stitching, but including knitting and drawing. She went on to study design as a mature student. In 2004 she moved to Stevenage from Ware and was told, shortly after, that she had breast cancer. Through her positive attitude she continued to stitch, draw and design right through her treatment.

A meeting with Sharon Taylor, Leader of the Borough Council, led to the idea of sewing a tapestry to commemorate the 60th anniversary of Stevenage New Town. Beginning with the Romans, the tapestry tells the story of the town to the end of the Second World War. Other panels provide information on the schools, the clubs, societies, churches and groups that give the town its heart. Hanging in three large panels and one smaller one, it is a testament to Julia's foresight and planning.

Julia started the project in Spring 2006, little thinking it would take more than two years to stitch the panels. She was keen to get as many people as possible involved and the total number was over 300. The furthest a piece of work travelled to be stitched was to Vanuatu, in the Coral Sea, east of Australia, but most of it was stitched by the people of Stevenage.

Julia designed virtually every piece on the panels, and stitched many of the tricky ones. She would sit in bed on those nights when she couldn't sleep, and sew for an hour or two. She found it therapeutic and was able to lose herself completely in her sewing.

Julia's health deteriorated and she was devastated to learn that the cancer had returned and was working through her body, with the inevitable, final conclusion. She managed to stay positive throughout her last few months, continuing to stitch and enjoy life. Friends felt that it was the tapestry that kept Julia alive for that time, as the panels were completed and then displayed for the world to see.

Julia was immensely proud of the Stevenage Tapestry and the team of stitchers working with her enjoyed her enthusiasm and passion in creating it. The Tapestry is Julia's contribution to the town and we will remember her each time we look at it.

(Words by Jennifer Meek and Marilyn Emerson)

Stevenage was also very proud that, having won the 'best small city' category in the 2006 Britain in Bloom regional competition, it had been chosen to represent the Anglia Region in 2007. On the theme of planting for the future, Connie Rees organised a group of Stevenage 'pioneers' to plant an oak tree and some yellow roses, called 'Simply the Best', in Fairlands Valley.

Mayor for the year was Simon Speller who, on 30 March, represented the town at the consecration of the new Coptic cathedral of St George, built in the grounds of Shephalbury. An impressive number of dignitaries was present, including Sir Simon and Lady Bowes-Lyon, the Duke of Gloucester, who read a message from the Queen, the Egyptian Ambassador, the Archbishop of Canterbury, representatives from the Armenian Orthodox Church, the Roman Catholic Church and many others. Councillor Speller's speech was also impressive, based on the theme of connection and uniting old and new.

Among the numerous events held to mark the anniversary, there was a Family Fun day at Great Ashby, a fancy dress party at Douglas Drive Day Centre, an even-more-brilliant-than-usual Fifth of November firework display at Fairlands Valley Park lakes and a Cyclists' Touring Club 60th anniversary ride over a 100 kilometre course from Stevenage through the neighbouring villages. More than 900 people took part in the 20th Stevenage half-marathon race and a major photographic exhibition of the history of the town was held at the museum. Music was celebrated through concerts, workshops and talks throughout the town, in schools, churches and in the open air. The English Sinfonia put on a magnificent concert at the Gordon Craig Theatre, featuring the renowned concert pianist John Lill, described as the leading British pianist of his generation, who had played with the world's greatest orchestras. He had been awarded the CBE for his services to music the previous year.

The anniversary year culminated in a concert, with a lantern procession by children from Round Diamond, Fairlands, the Leys and St Nicholas Schools. The concert included performances by the local groups Footworks, Fusion, Blessings, Stevenage Ladies' Choir, Stevenage Male Voice Choir, Stevenage Wind Band, Churches Together in Stevenage and solo singer Elaine Simpson. Between performances, the audience was shown short film clips of life in Stevenage during the past 60 years.

Stevenage Borough Football Club gave their supporters a pleasant surprise in 2007 when they reached the final of the Football Association Carlsberg Trophy. The match would be all the more exciting because it would be the first to be played at Wembley Stadium since its £750 million refurbishment. On 12 May, thousands of supporters watched a thrilling match against Kidderminster, which was full of drama and tension. Not until the 88th minute was the winning goal scored – by Stevenage. On their return home, the Borough team toured the town in an open-topped bus through streets lined with cheering fans.

Mayor Lilian Strange with a young Stevenage in Bloom award winner, 2002. (Stevenage Museum)

Also in May 2007, after 40 years of service, Brian Hall stepped down from his role as the longest-serving council leader in the country and was succeeded by Sharon Taylor, the first woman to hold that position. She had been a councillor since 1997.

Sixty years on, the Stony Hall Flats, controversial when they were first built in the early 1950s, were once more in the news. In the 25 years since the Corporation and Council housing lists had been merged, and because of the shortage of council housing following the sale of council houses, the Borough Council had been forced to allocate these flats to some people for whom they were not suitable and who were not suitable to live in them. The environment steadily deteriorated, tennis courts and rose gardens were damaged and life became unpleasant for many who had previously lived amicably together. Eventually, after a period of research, the Council decided to redevelop the area with smaller blocks of dwellings in a more traditional style, through the William Sutton Housing Association. The regeneration scheme cost £15 million and provided a total of 140 affordable, brick-built homes, variously and attractively grouped. Ironically, as the original Stonyhall blocks were being demolished, not one but two new and controversial large blocks of flats, known to some as Casablanca, were under construction on the former Elmes Yard, off Lytton Way, at the entrance to the old town.

For some years the Council had been concerned about the public's perception of the town centre. There was criticism in particular of the range and quality of shops and the lack of a department store. After much debate and research into opportunities and the potential for a dramatically improved town centre, the Council, together with development partners English Partnerships (the former Commission for New Towns) ran a competition to find a developer to undertake a comprehensive redevelopment. Under European law it was necessary to open the competition across the European Union for the opportunity to invest the £500 million needed to carry out the project. Three potential developers were shortlisted and a partnership made up of Stanhope PLC and ING Real Estate was picked on the strength of the ambition of their design and track record of successful mixed-use developments across Europe. Through a complex series of land deals, the partnership, named Stevenage Regeneration Ltd, manages the new elements of the development, whilst the council retains the freeholds and safeguards its existing sources of revenue, such as car parking and some commercial tenants.

Mindful of the need to consult residents about the future of their town, the developers arranged a public exhibition in the spring of 2007 at the former Edward the Confessor public house, which they had bought and transformed into an exhibition centre. Over 6,500 people went to see it and to give their comments. Among the proposals for the town centre were a three-storey department store; variety store; a discovery centre, housing museum and library; new bus station; 2,000 extra parking spaces; 90 new shops and up to 900 new homes. The work would be likely to take four to five years in a number of phases. It would need to be done carefully so as not to disrupt the rest of the town centre and to take account of the fact that Town Square is a conservation area. Part of the Council's requirement was for significant numbers of new affordable housing. Some of the new affordable homes were planned for the town centre and others, such as family homes, elsewhere. Visitors to the exhibition were given a questionnaire, and, in answer to the main question; 'Having now viewed the proposals for the redevelopment are you in favour of the scheme overall?' 88 per cent responded positively.

The 120 acre Fairlands Valley Park was also being improved. An Environment Lake was completed in 2008, providing ideal habitats for birds, mammals and amphibians to thrive. In May 2009 a new Aqua Play area was opened, replacing the old paddling pools which had been a feature at Fairlands Valley Park since 1972. It contains equipment which sprays, squirts, mists or sheets water into the play area, giving fun play for youngsters in a safe and interactive environment. The design of the area allows for features and games to be scaled up or down according to the ages of the children present.

Designed by the Borough Council's Senior Architect, Andrew Hills, and his talented team, a £5.5 million, three-storey, state-of-the-art extension to the successful Business and Technology Centre, with a café on the ground-floor, was opened in 2009.

There was good news, too, in regard to health provision. Since 1972, the Lister Hospital has provided care for local people in the many wards housed in its white tower block that can be seen for miles . Whilst this image will remain, the NHS has begun a programme of investment of over £100 million that will see the Lister hospital become the centre for all acute hospital care for north Hertfordshire and south Bedfordshire.

The redevelopment programme is in several phases and will take a number of years to complete. Work has already begun, the first step in the process being the building of a £47 million Surgicentre at the front of the Lister site. This facility will treat some 15,000 NHS patients a year for common procedures such as hip and knee replacements, hernia repairs and cataracts. As a dedicated facility for patients undergoing non-emergency surgery, the new facility will help to reduce waiting times, as well as the risk of patients' operations being cancelled at short notice. It will also provide NHS patients with increased choice as to where they receive their operation.

The next phases in the redevelopment will be the completion of a new £16.4 million maternity extension and a new multi-storey car park. It is anticipated that these will be operational during 2011.

Stevenage is now looking to the future with hope and enthusiasm. Much more seems possible than ever before. There is even the chance that some Stevenage youngster will reach the UK Olympic team in 2012. But nothing is certain. The current recession may – or may not – be followed by a long depression. Everything changes and Stevenage will change, but as long as it lives up to its motto 'The heart of a town lies in its people' then in years to come we will be proud to say, 'Stevenage is my town'.

CHAPTER EIGHTEEN

Green spaces

When Stevenage was designated a new town in 1946, it was very much a rural community, surrounded by farmland. The concept of a new town had its origins in the Garden City Movement of Ebenezer Howard and others. Central to the movement's policy was the belief that a garden city would combine the best aspects of both town and country, that the two could co-exist as *'Rus in Urbe'* – 'the country in the town'. Before this dream could be realised, however, much of the *'rus'* on which the *'urbs'* was to be built had to be destroyed, and then parts replanted to provide green spaces within the town. This happened at Stevenage, although some existing green features were retained and buildings erected around them. The 1949 Master Plan stated firmly that 'The woods and copses will be preserved, so will the vast majority of single trees and many of the existing hedgelines', although those living here at the time have sad memories of swathes of woodland being demolished in order that the remainder would fit the Plan. But in general the policy of preservation was followed. In fact, through its planting programme, the Development Corporation was able to increase the total area of woodland from the original 252 acres to 277. Then came the landscaping of the new town.

Gordon Patterson, landscape architect for the Development Corporation, described in 1991, in *The History Makers*, the four main aspects of the landscaping programme. These were; the preservation of existing natural features; respect for natural enclosures such as those provided by land form and forestry; the formation of plant communities and new planting within development areas. He explained that the Stevenage landscape was developed as part of an overall pattern.

Annual November the fifth firework display at Fairlands Valley Park (SBC)

Autumn in Martins Way. (Ann Parnell)

Because the budgets for landscaping were very stringent, tree-planting was given priority as the most efficient means of creating a green environment. Each season at least 10,000 trees and shrubs were planted, varying from woodland to single specimens and were mostly native species, although Norway Maple was dominant, chosen because it grew well.

Sixty years later, the result of the tree-planting programme is the glory of Stevenage. Looking down on the town from Knebworth in spring and summer it is almost possible to believe that here is one great forest as, apart from the tower blocks, buildings are hidden under a canopy of green. Later, the maples come into their own with vivid autumn colour comparable, many people have said, with those at Kew. Had the Stevenage landscape designers followed fashion and planted flowering cherries, there would have been a short burst of blossom in spring but not the year-round splendour that the town enjoys today.

All the publicity material inviting people to move into the new town emphasised its open green spaces and access to the countryside. The 1953 brochure distributed in the Greater London area by English Electric included a simplified map of the 1949 Master Plan which encouraged potential new residents to believe that they would be living an almost rural life in Stevenage. A paragraph headed 'Green Fields and Open Spaces' went on to say, 'Notice, too, the abundance of open spaces and green belts (shown in green on the map). Green belts surround and separate the housing areas from one another. Trees, fields and countryside will never be far from you. This feature of New Town life is one of the biggest attractions to Londoners now settling in Stevenage.' With promises such as this is, it no wonder that new town residents reacted so strongly to any

New Town Plan from the 1953 English Electric brochure, showing green spaces.

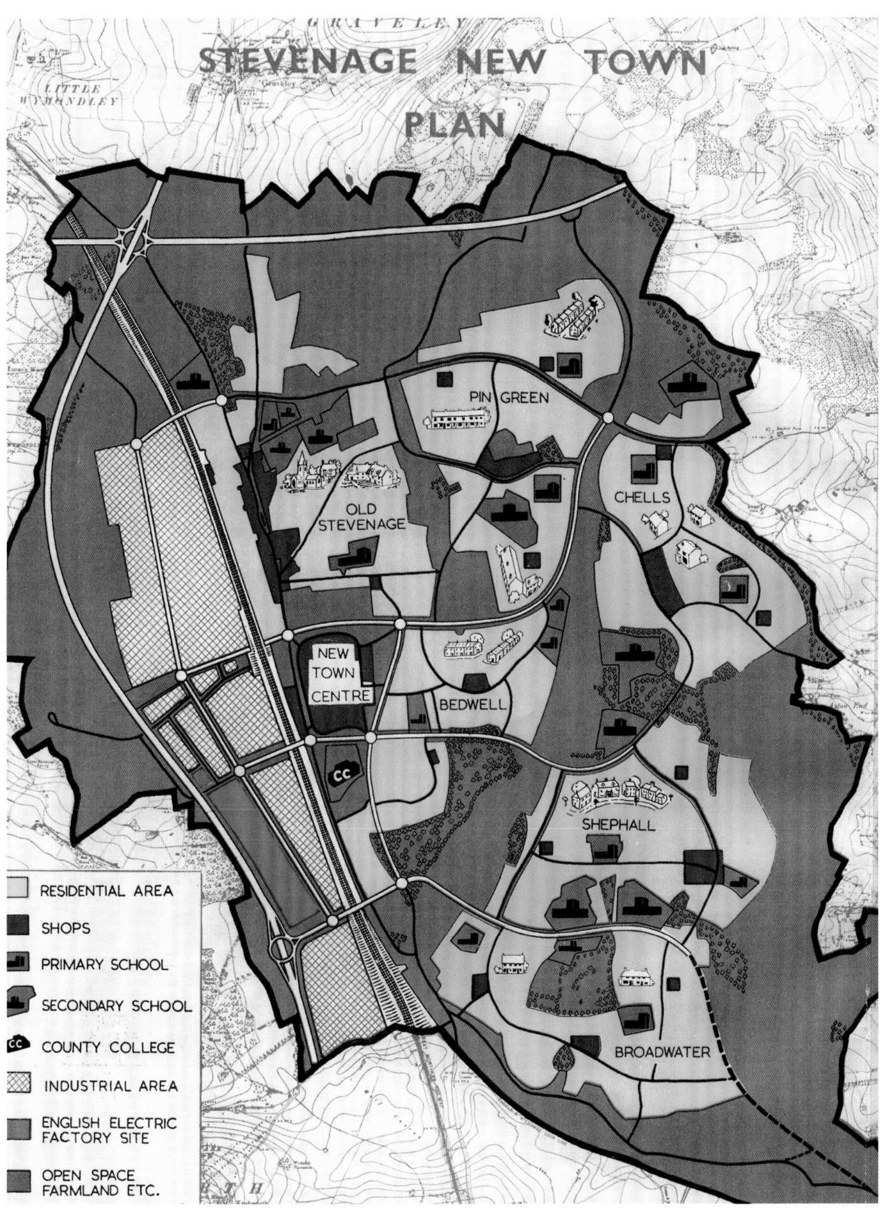

suggestion of a road or any other building in Fairlands Valley. Alf Luhman commented in *The History Makers* that those coming from parts of London where green open spaces were few and far between were particularly keen to have them in Stevenage.

The *Official Guide to Stevenage,* edited by Don Hills and published in 1955, admitted, 'Development has changed the pattern of much of the fair countryside which surrounded Old Stevenage and obliterated some of the footpath walks in whole or in part, but there is still a wealth of countryside around to be enjoyed and explored ... Many of the villages near Stevenage are acclaimed among the most lovely in Hertfordshire, the tiny village of Shephall left intact in the new Shephall neighbourhood, Benington and Ardeley with their thatched cottages, and Ashwell with its well-cared-for fifteenth-century houses.' The prospect of visiting such picturesque places, only a few miles away, no doubt attracted many a new resident but in the 1950s few people had cars, and buses to anywhere except Hitchin or southwards on the Great North Road were few and far between. To get to Ashwell by bus from Stevenage was virtually impossible.

The Development Corporation's quarterly journal, *Purpose,* continued the theme, with a regular feature entitled 'Landscapes'. The summer 1957 issue focussed on farming – 'one of the country's most important industries ... the fields of Fairlands Valley, Aston End, Broadwater and Hertford Road are producing just as much as the factories in the industrial area.' The writer conceded:

> 'Inevitably, with the construction of a new town, the farmer have to suffer considerably. Some farms have to be taken over completely, but this does not prevent a Development Corporation from retaining farmland wherever possible and, as at Stevenage, keeping wedges and belts of country within the town ... .
>
> ... It is unfortunately true that farmers are still having to sacrifice land. Mr T Young at Broadwater Farm is faced with losing nearly half his land to industrial development, his 310-acre dairy farm will dwindle in time to only 120 acres. With the development of the Chells and Pin Green areas, the area farmed from Fairlands Farm will be cut from 300 acres to 160 acres but, like other farmers in the area, Mr R V Marriott and his three sons at Fairlands are determined to continue. To farm in the centre of a town is regarded by many agriculturalists as well-nigh impossible, but the Marriott family have yet to be convinced of this. They are the pioneers of the Corporation's scheme to preserve a wedge of farmland in Fairlands Valley within the new residential neighbourhoods, an experiment which is being watched with interest all over the country. For the Marriotts the reduction of their present holding will mean a change in their farming system, for their herd of over 100 Ayrshire cattle is to be sold in the autumn and they will then concentrate on arable farming. The

Farming in Fairlands Valley, an illustration from *Purpose* 1958.

Ayrshire breed of cattle they favour is highly strung and tends to be disturbed by dogs and boisterous youngsters from the town. It must be hard to give up a fine pedigree herd which has taken years to build.'

One farmer, in the Chells area, did not wait for the Development Corporation to take his land. Well before the Corporation needed it, he exercised his right to force them to buy his land and buildings, then moved his livestock, implements, machinery and vehicles by special train from Stevenage railway station to Wales, where he had bought a replacement farm.

An illustration from *Purpose*, 1957.

In the end, despite all the good intentions, farms and the traditional way of life were overwhelmed by the developing new town. It became impossible to hold on to the original dream of '*rus in urbe*' and the green spaces in Stevenage became parks, not farmland. There is one exception: the Stevenagebury land surrounding the ancient parish church of St Nicholas and the site of the Saxon village of Stigenace is still under cultivation, though now mainly arable. Most of it is within the area known as the Forster Country, which stretches from Rectory Lane and the Weston Road to Chesfield, Graveley and beyond, in the North Herts Rural District.

The change from mixed farming to arable and then to no farming at all, as the bulldozers moved in, had a deleterious effect on wildlife. The absence of cattle and pigs meant an absence of attendant insects and the birds which fed on them. Barn owls, with nowhere to build their nests, also declined as did once common birds of gardens and hedgerows, such as bullfinches, linnets and yellowhammers. As land was drained for building, there were no damp meadows for the winter flocks of lapwings which used regularly to visit the town, some venturing into the King George V playing field. Skylarks also were common, even quite close to the built-up area. As a boy before the Second World War, Walter Marchant used to go with his grandfather to the allotments at the top of Walkern Road where, he said, 'Invariably from Spring the larks used to rise up from the allotment and it was just beautiful.'

Wild flowers, too, were affected, their decline hastened nationally by the widespread, irresponsible use of pesticides and herbicides in the decades following the Second World War. Cornfield flowers, such as cornflowers, scabious and corncockle inevitably disappeared as have poppies, although their seeds lie in the ground, ready to spring to life if the soil is ever turned over again. With the loss of meadows went the formerly common meadow saxifrage, marguerites and lady's smock and the absence of flowers contributed to an absence of butterflies. The wide grass verges of the new town, although green, did not compensate for what they replaced: their closely mown, uniform areas provided nothing for flora and fauna. However, the decline in wildlife cannot be blamed entirely on the development of the new town. It was part of a national trend, which had many causes including the increasing use of chemicals in farming, in gardens and by local authorities.

The increasing urbanisation of the town brought other changes. For many years the veterinary practice at Fairlight House, in London Road (now called Ditchmore Lane), was largely concerned with horses, cattle and other farm stock. Now the emphasis shifted and Stevenage, almost denuded of large animals, became home to countless dogs, cats and assorted small pets. A second veterinary practice opened behind the Roebuck shops, and later a third was established in Maxwell Road. Concern for animals had been evident for many years in Stevenage, from the time of the Band of Mercy, which raised money for a water trough to be placed at the road fork on the Bowling Green for the benefit of passing horses, to the post-war street collections for the RSPCA. This work was also continued by many new town residents, including Mrs Dockerill and Mr and Mrs Tinkler, who all worked hard over the years on behalf of animal welfare. The *Stevenage Echo* for September 1953 reported, 'Mrs Dockerill, who organised collections in the new town for Animals Day thanks all who collected or donated. The total for the new town was £20 17s 7½d [£20.88] and the combined total for the whole of Stevenage was more than £43'. The paragraph ended with the message that 'It will be a very long time before there is an animal clinic in Stevenage', but for some years a weekly RSPCA mobile clinic came to the new town. There have been many changes since that time, but the concern

Lot
35. A ditto
36. A 9 ft. wooden cattle crib
37. A ditto
38. A ditto
39. A timber egg laying unit
40. A ditto
41. A ditto
42. A 23 rung wood ladder
43. A 29 rung ditto
44. Two smaller ditto
45. Three smaller ditto
46. A trailer tilt
47. A ditto
48. A ditto
49. Three 6 ft. 0 ins. chicken feeders
50. Three ditto
51.
52.
53.
54.
55.
56. A steel trough
57. A ditto
58. A cast iron ditto
59. A ditto
60. A ditto
61. Four galvanised troughs
62. Three ditto
63. A large wooden bin
64. Four poultry dry meal feeders
65. Four ditto
66. Four ditto
67. A 6 ft. galvanised water trough
68. A ditto
69. Two timber laying units
70. Two ditto
71. Two steel feeders, various
72. Two sinks
73. A circular iron pig trough
74. A ditto
75. A ditto
76. A ditto
77. A ditto

Lot
78. ~~A ditto~~
79. Two wheel barrows
80.
81.
82.
83.
84.

IMPLEMENTS AND MACHINERY

85. A Ford Ransome three furrow mounted plough
86. A Ransome two furrow mounted plough
87. A set of Ferguson mounted disc harrows
88. A set of three heavy drag harrows and whippletree
89. A set of five seed harrows and whippletree
90. A set of three seed harrows and whippletree
91. A nine tine trailer cultivator
92. A set of mounted Stevenage spring tine harrows with following harrow
93. A Wheatley tipping trailer with corn shoots
94. A two wheel tipping trailer with shoot attachment
95. A two wheel trailer with racks
96.
97.
98.
99.
100.
101. A Massey Harris power driven pick-up baler
102. An International 6 ft. cut power mower
103. A mounted Weedmaster 40 gallon sprayer
104. A Ransome 60 gallon low volume mounted sprayer
105. A Ferguson manure spreader
106. A Massey Harris 15 coulter seed and fertilizer drill
107. A set of Isaac ring rolls
108. A Massey Ferguson 780 Special 8 ft. 6 in. cut combine
109. A Massey Ferguson 65 diesel tractor Reg. No. 3198 UR (First registered December, 1961)
110. A Fordson Super Major tractor Reg. No. 7027 RO with MIL dung loader (First registered July, 1961)
111. A garage about 14 ft. 0 ins. x 9 ft. 0 ins. with sleeper bottom and corrugated asbestos roof.
112.

Farm sale at Fairlands, 1968.

remains. Stevenage Borough Council's magazine, the *Chronicle*, for Spring 2009 reported that following legislation which made local councils, rather than the police, responsible for stray dogs, Stevenage had been awarded the RSPCA's Gold Footprint. 'This makes us one of only 14 councils in the country to receive this prestigious award for looking after stray dogs' welfare from the moment we collect them to the time when they are returned or re-homed.'

There were compensations to balance the loss of wildlife. The craze for egg-collecting and shooting, which had been popular during the first half of the twentieth century, began to die down as public opinion and education helped focus interest on conservation. Subsequently, although almost too late for some species, much wildlife has been protected by law. At the same time, charities such as the Herts and Middlesex Wildlife Trust have been able to acquire, protect and manage some particularly important wildlife sites. For some years Watery Grove, on the border of Stevenage and Knebworth, at Norton Green, was one such site and volunteers from Stevenage helped look after it. Other societies were set up in Stevenage, supported by enthusiasts from both old and new towns. The Stevenage and District Ornithological Society flourished for many years and enjoyed many a visit to, among other places, the old sewage farm at Roaring Meg, an excellent place for birdwatching before it was built over. Two other successful organisations were the Stevenage Zoological and Wildlife Preservation Society and the Stevenage Woodlands Conservation Society, though neither is still in existence today.

Before the development of the new town, Stevenage, although well-supplied with springs and small streams, had no large area of water. The flooding of Fairlands Valley to create the lakes brought to Stevenage water birds that were previously rarely seen there. Now it is quite usual to hear the honking of geese as they fly in to the Valley. The Development Corporation also constructed water meadows in several areas of the town, to prevent flooding in unusually heavy rainfall when the storm water drainage system might overflow. Rainwater would be allowed to collect in these low-lying open spaces, which would remain under water until the storm was over, when the water would be released into the town's drainage system. Despite the amount of publicity given to the scheme, many residents remained unaware of the purpose of the meadows, which became favourite informal play areas for children living nearby. Notices erected there soon disappeared and when the meadows were under water, mothers would telephone the Corporation offices to complain that their children's playground was flooded and demand that something be done about it.

The RSPCA mobile clinic which served the New Town in the 1960s. (Stevenage Museum P3988)

The green spaces of Stevenage owe a great deal to the two men largely responsible for their maintenance, Richard Arnold, known to many as 'the tree man', and Chris Woodard, Animal Services Manager, and their staffs. Chris began working for the Borough Council in 1987 as Pest Control Officer and over the years he has gained enormous specialist knowledge. He and his team have acquired expertise and developed new techniques in such matters as controlling pests without harming other species, and now they advise other local authorities, give lectures and run training sessions for some government departments. But it is the protection of wildlife that most interests Chris and, working closely with Richard Arnold and others, he monitors the ponds in woods and on the periphery of the town, a number of which have good populations of amphibians and dragonflies. He has recorded 10 different species of dragonflies and damselflies. Thanks to Chris, Stevenage has the only site within three counties where the Great Green Bush Cricket resides. It was widespread in Hertfordshire in the nineteenth century but last recorded in the county in 1926. In 1998 Chris rescued 14 from a road through a nature reserve in the south of England and brought them to Shackledell grassland off Fairlands Valley. Now there is a colony of hundreds in this six-acre area of very diverse habitat which houses an interesting variety of plants and insects, including another five species of bush cricket, an unusually high number.

As new town residents settled in, they turned with enthusiasm to gardening and the June 1954 issue of the *Echo* reported '... a surprisingly heavy demand for allotments, ten and a half acres to date'. Many joined the Stevenage Allotments and Gardeners' Association, entered shows and won cups. Others put their gardens forward for awards and the first-ever photograph in the *Echo* was of a prize-winning garden. Allotments and gardens add greatly to the green areas of a town, not only presenting pleasing vistas to passers-by but also providing 'wildlife corridors', especially for birds. Councils are legally required to provide sufficient allotments to meet demand, but may also sell allotment land or give planning permission to owners of private allotment land to develop it. This has happened at least twice in Stevenage in recent times: The road named Pike End was built on former allotments between Pound Avenue and Haycroft Road, and Fresson Road was built on the site of the allotments off Walkern Road, where Walter Marchant used to watch the skylarks.

School playing fields also add to the green spaces of a town in much the same way as allotments and gardens. The 1944 Education Act, which laid down minimum areas for playing fields, resulted in the demolition of a row of cottages in Primrose Hill to make way for a playing field, in order that the new Fairlands Primary School, opened in 1951, would meet the requirements of the Act. In the 1980s the rules changed and education authorities began selling off playing fields: a corner of the Fairlands Infants' School ground was sold for housing.

Stevenage has also seen whole school sites used for housing, including the former Girls' Grammar, St Michael's and Shephalbury Schools. There were strong objections to these developments.

From the early 1970s until the formation of the Stevenage Partnership, various groups who were concerned with aspects of conservation were brought together through the Stevenage Conservation Liaison Committee (SCLC). They included representatives from the Herts and Middlesex Wildlife Trust, the Royal Society for the Protection of Birds, the Friends of the Forster Country, the Stevenage Society, Friends of the Earth and others. A representative from the Borough Council's Planning Department attended meetings and made an invaluable contribution. The SCLC was also responsible for the Ed Sones Award for an outstanding contribution to wildlife conservation, which was given in memory of Ed Sones, a Stevenage conservationist.

Following the 1966 Master Plan, updated in 1978, and the additional developments since then, especially in the north and east of the town, the amount of green space has been reduced and later maps look very different to that publicised in 1953. The old town in particular has been surrounded by new development and choked by the infilling of even the smallest green spaces. Perhaps the most amazing is the building of flats on the tiny area of grass on the edge of Lytton Way behind the old town library. As well as Fairlands Valley, Stevenage has several large green areas, notably Shephalbury Park and Hampson Park, together with very many small green spaces, but of all the neighbourhoods, the old town and north Stevenage are now least well served.

Following the publication in 2002 of the government's *Planning Policy Guidance Note (PPG) 17: Planning for Open Space, Sport and Recreation and assessing Needs and Opportunities,* Stevenage Borough Council appointed PMP

Chells Manor pond. (Stevenage Museum)

Mayor Hugh Tessier presents a 'Pride in our Town' award to Tom McGrath in recognition of his outstanding contribution over many years to the Stevenage Allotments and Gardeners' Association. (Stevenage Museum)

to undertake a study of open space, recreation and sport in the town. This report was published in 2006. It began by identifying eight types of green open space;

Parks and gardens
Natural and semi-natural open spaces
Amenity green spaces
Provision for children and young people
Outdoor sports facilities
Allotments and community gardens
Green corridors
Churchyards and cemeteries. (Para 2.5)

It also emphasised the importance of assessing local needs, rather than simply following national trends (para 2.1). In order to investigate local needs in Stevenage, 5,000 household questionnaires were distributed randomly across the Borough, spread evenly between six areas; Broadwater, Chells, Old Stevenage, Bedwell, St Nicholas and Shephall. There were also other opportunities for the general public to comment or to join consultation groups of various kinds (para 2.11). In addition, those carrying out the study visited 532 sites in Stevenage covering a range of different types of open space (para 2.14).

Based on the questionnaires and consultations, the Study discovered that the types of open space most frequently used by respondents were as follows;

The maze at the Fairlands Way entrance to Fairlands Valley Park. (Ann Parnell)

42% parks and gardens
27% green corridors
16% natural and semi-natural
9% provision for children and young people
4% amenity green space
3% outdoor sports facilities
1% allotments (para 4.41).

The consultation process also invited suggestions for improving open spaces, one of which was that open spaces need to be managed in a way which provides areas for wildlife as well as people and that there is potential for involving schools in the conservation of sites (para 4.48). Concern was also expressed about protecting the existing provision from development (para 4.59). In the section on natural and semi-natural open space, the Report quoted from the draft Local Biodiversity Plan produced for Stevenage by the Hertfordshire and Middlesex Wildlife Trust. This stated that 'The main habitat types found within the Borough are; woodland, grassland, wetlands, hedgerows and urban and artificial habitats. On the whole, the provision of habitats is less than national averages, predominately due to the urban nature of the Borough' (para 6.4) and 'The species identified as priorities for conservation are bats, badgers, great crested newts, reptiles, house sparrow, great green bush cricket and bluebell' (para 6.5).

The Report listed 72 areas of natural and semi-natural open space across the Borough of Stevenage, most of which are fairly small. The following, it suggested, are of 'significant size';

Whomerley Wood – 14.37 hectares
Monks Wood – 10.47 ha
Sound Barrier B – 7.22 ha
Ridlins Wood – 7.02 ha
Wychdell Watermeadow – 6.72 ha
Lanterns Wood 6.35 ha (para 6.12)

The question of how much open space should be allocated to a town the size of Stevenage was also addressed;

> 'The provision of natural and semi-natural open space amounts to 142.11 hectares in total across the Borough. Therefore the current provision ... per 1,000 population is 1.78 ha'. (para 6.14).
>
> 'The only definitive national standards for natural and semi-natural areas is the English Nature Accessible Natural Green Space Standard (ANGSt). This suggests that there should be at least 2 ha of accessible natural green space per 1,000 population ...' (para 6.15).
>
> 'Overall opinion suggests that the current provision [in Stevenage] of 1.78 ha per 1,000 population is "about right" ... however 35% of residents suggested this provision for this type of open space was "not enough". The split in opinion is a cause of some local deficiencies ... Provision in St Nicholas is lowest, with only .74 ha per 1,000 population supporting the 44% of people [living there] who feel that provision is not enough' (para 6.16).

Walking in the Forster Country. (Margaret Ashby)

Ironically, Old Stevenage, once a country town, features in the Report as an area that has a deficiency in natural and semi-natural open space, with only 1.46 ha per 1,000 population. In section 13, under Key Issues, Old Stevenage is listed as 'significantly under-provided in parks and gardens and natural and semi-natural open space.' Only brief extracts of the Report have been included here. It is a very detailed, substantial document, accessible at www. stevenage. gov.uk

Although the Borough of Stevenage is generally adequately provided with open green space, there are many who feel that the town, and north Hertfordshire in general, lack a country park comparable in size to those such as Aldenham or even Ashridge, in the west of the county. The Great Ashby development has helped to confine north and east Stevenage, emphasising the importance of the Forster Country as a green lung for that end of the town. For 20 years, the Friends of the Forster Country had been campaigning to save this historic piece of countryside from development and had been successful in getting that part of the Forster Country which lies within the Stevenage Borough boundary designated as Green Belt. The remainder of the Foster Country is in North Herts District. In 2007, a change of planning procedures came about, whereby Stevenage and North Herts were required to work together under SNAP – the Stevenage and North Herts Action Plan – to try to agree a joint scheme in response to central government demands. The Friends of the Forster Country are working within this framework with the aim of persuading the two authorities to create a Forster Country Park for Stevenage and North Herts, a green open space which would be comparable to a large country park, a place where human life and wildlife could co-exist in peace.

Chris Woodard (left) and Richard Arnold checking wildlife habitats at Monks Wood. (Margaret Ashby)

CHAPTER NINETEEN
The churches

Churches in Stevenage from early days to 1946

THE OLDEST BUILDING IN STEVENAGE is St Nicholas' church on the hilltop which was at the centre of the original Saxon village of Stigenace. It probably began as a wooden structure, but by about 1120 the villagers were collecting flints from the surrounding fields to begin constructing a tower. During Saxon times, England was divided into parishes, each with its church and a rector or vicar to care for the souls of those living there. The boundaries of the parish of Stevenage, as established in about 1100, remained unchanged for the next 850 years, during which time the church building was enlarged and embellished. The parishes themselves were organised into dioceses, each headed by a bishop who was responsible for the clergy within his diocese. Stevenage at that time was in the enormous Diocese of Lincoln, which stretched from the Humber to the Thames. The dioceses themselves were grouped into one of two provinces, the Province of York, with an Archbishop to administer it, and the Province of Canterbury, whose Archbishop was the senior cleric in England, but himself responsible to the Pope in Rome. England was only a small part of the Roman Catholic Church to which the whole of Western Europe belonged.

During the sixteenth century, new ideas about religion resulted in bitter strife between factions with differing beliefs. The emerging Protestant groups were persecuted by the traditionalist Catholics and they in turn persecuted the Catholics. During the height of this religious upheaval, in the reigns of Henry VIII, Edward VI and Mary Tudor, from Henry's break with Rome in 1535 to the death of Mary in 1558, Stevenage was fortunate to have as its rector the Revd Thomas Alleyne, who somehow kept not only his living but also the respect and love of his parishioners, to whom he was a father-figure. Out of these tumultuous years, the Church of England, or the Anglican Church, emerged, as an English version of the Catholic Church, which recognised the reigning monarch as its head, or governor, and not the Pope. Those who still followed the old religion and acknowledged the Pope became known as Papists or Roman Catholics, but were not allowed to practise their religion freely for another 250 years. It is very likely that, during those centuries of repression, some Roman Catholics were living in the Stevenage area and worshipping in secret, but nothing is known of them.

More information is available about the various Protestant sects which dissented from the doctrines of the Anglican Church. During the English Civil War, between 1642 and 1649, and the Commonwealth that followed it, extreme Protestant groups, known as Puritans, were a powerful force, particularly in the East of England. This included Stevenage, though whether the 'ordinary' people were devout Puritans, or just went along with the majority for a quiet life, is questionable. However, the story of one Roman Catholic priest has survived, as told by John Amess;

> On 6th November 1643 Parliamentary soldiers apprehended a man in Stevenage on suspicion of being a spy. Having searched the man, the soldiers asked a local schoolmaster to interpret several religious papers found in the man's bags. The schoolmaster obviously decided that the papers were of a 'suspicious nature' and the man was held overnight. The following morning he was again searched and this time the soldiers discovered a letter addressed to the Spanish Ambassador in London in which it stated that the man was a member of the Order of St Francis. Following further questioning the man was held under suspicion of being a Roman Catholic priest. Father Francis Bell, as he indeed was, was taken from Stevenage for examination by government officials before being committed to Newgate prison in London to await trial. The trial took place on 7 December 1643 and Fr Bell was sentenced to death by the prescribed means (to be hung, dismembered, disembowelled and quartered). Fr Bell was executed at Tyburn on 11 December 1643 aged 54.

Similar brutality, including the burning of heretics, had befallen many, Protestants as well as Catholics, during the years of religious strife.

By 1660, with the restoration of the monarchy in the person of Charles II, the Church of England had survived the unsettled times and was once more the established church. This did not mean that everyone conformed. The Roman Catholics were being kept firmly at bay by a country which feared their allegiance to Rome, but many Protestants would not be silenced. In Stevenage, in 1676, ten parishioners admitted publicly that they dissented from the teachings of the Anglican Church. They, and others like them throughout the country, put so much pressure on the government and the Church, that in 1689 the Toleration Act was passed, permitting Protestant Nonconformists, or Dissenters, to worship as they wished, provided that they registered their meeting place.

The first Stevenage registration under the Act took place on 14 July 1698, when Thomas Packet, Henry Farrow and George Heath declared that they would be meeting for religious worship at the home of Thomas Packet. On 17 May 1709, Edward Crouch and William Bradley registered the use of a barn for Quaker Worship. 'These are to certify that a barn standing in the yard belonging to the dwelling house of William Bradley in Stevenage and also one other barn in Stevenage, aforesaid, which the said Mr Bradley holds of John Langthorne of Ashwell, are respectively appointed as the places of worship for Protestant Dissenters, commonly called Quakers'. On 10 January 1737–38 another registration was made for Quaker worship, at Broomin Green, at the house of Thomas Impey.

Wesleyans, or Methodists as they came to be known, were probably active in Stevenage from as early as 1759. On 7 August that year, John Wesley recorded in his *Journal* that he put up at an inn in the town on his way to Yorkshire. Two more records, for 25 May 1777 and 15 July 1788, show that he again stayed here. On 29 November 1790, at the age of 87, he preached in Stevenage, probably at the house of Mrs Parker, who is mentioned in his *Journal* for that day. In his booklet, *Wesleyan Methodism in Stevenage*, the Revd Leslie Spencer quotes Mr B E L Culpin as saying, 'In those days [mid nineteenth century] the main burden of the work was borne by women.' One woman who was a generous benefactor of the Methodist cause was Ms Harvey, who lived at Hinxworth and paid for the building of several chapels, including one in Stevenage High Street. It is possible that a building near 118 High Street had been in use as a chapel for a while but, in 1835, Ms Harvey's chapel was the first purpose-built Methodist place of worship in Stevenage. It had a gallery, where a small band, including flute, bass viol, clarinet and violin, accompanied the singing. The building is currently numbered 38 High Street and occupied by the public library.

The first purpose-built Baptist chapel in Stevenage was erected in 1814. Surprisingly, so soon after the 1807 Great Fire of Stevenage, it was built of wood rather than brick. It is the black and white building now 63 High Street. In 1857 a Baptist chapel was built in Albert Street, the new road leading from the High Street to Letchmore Road and named after Queen Victoria's consort, Prince Albert. The Albert Street chapel was often referred to as the 'Ebenezer', a term sometimes used by Baptists, Methodists and other dissenters for their chapels. The word means 'stone of the help' from the Biblical reference in the First Book of Samuel, chapter 7, verse 12. One preacher there was Henry Fox, father of the Fox twins, who were born in the same year as the chapel and named after it – Albert Ebenezer and Ebenezer Albert.

Albert Street showing railings in front of the Ebenezer Chapel on the left. (Stevenage Museum)

The Church of England was also expanding. In 1861, when Canon Blomfield was rector, the church of the Holy Trinity was built at the south end of the High Street, on the site of a pond which was part of the manorial waste. It was intended as a chapel-of-ease, to help the growing population at this end of the town who had a long walk up to St Nicholas', often to find the church so full that there were no seats available when they got there. The architect of Holy Trinity was Arthur Blomfield, nephew of the rector and son of his brother, the Bishop of London, who also happened to be Lord of the Manor of Stevenage. This was one of Arthur Blomfield's first commissions: he went on to become a very distinguished architect and was awarded a knighthood. The builders were the local firm of Bates and Warren.

Holy Trinity church was built opposite the Coach and Horses inn, on the far side of which was an open space. There, in 1876, a new, much larger Methodist chapel, with school rooms, was built to cater for the growing congregation which could no longer be accommodated in the existing chapel. The foundation stone was laid on 27 July 1876 and in four months the building was finished. The opening services were held on Thursday 23 November 1876, when two sermons were preached, one at 3.15 pm and one at 6.30 pm. The land for the new chapel had cost £151 18s 6d (£151.93) and the cost of building work was £1237 9s 8d (£1237.48). This money had been raised partly by the sale of the old chapel to Mr Shelford for £177 7s 7d (£177.38) and partly by donations and collections.

Holy Trinity church, built 1861–2, extended 1881. (Stevenage Museum PP541)

High Street Methodist church, built in 1876. (Stevenage Museum PP626)

No sooner had the Methodists built their new chapel than the Anglicans found it necessary to extend Holy Trinity church, which was now too small to cater for all those who wished to worship there. At Easter 1880, Rector William Jowitt, who had succeeded Canon Blomfield, appealed for funds to build an extension. Within a year £1660 10s 6d (£1660.52) had been raised, enough to add a new nave, designed by Messrs Tate and Popplewell of Manchester and built by Bates and Warren. In 1885 a new chancel was built, with a stained glass window by Heaton, Butler and Bayne in memory of Dr Andrew Whyte Barclay, of Whitney Wood.

As the nineteenth century drew to a close, another new church building was being planned, this time for the Baptists. The Baptist Church was strong in North Hertfordshire, partly because of the influence of John Bunyan, who had preached in the district, usually in various outdoor meeting places, such as Wain Wood near Preston. A group of evangelical Baptists began meeting in Stevenage in 1897, their first ten members being Ben, Eliza, Herbert, Annie, Agnes and Wallace Culpin, Charles Thompson, Henry Wheeler and Mr and Mrs Bentinck, but numbers grew rapidly. They bought a plot of land on the Basil's Estate in 1899 for £130 and in 1901 John Marnham paid for the building of the Bunyan Baptist chapel and school room there. It was immediately successful. The Sunday School had 56 children during the first year and 200 by the end of the second. Initially served by students from Regent's Park College, London, the fellowship was able, in 1903, to appoint their first full-time pastor, the Revd R Vernon Bird, from St Albans. It also began to attract members from the Albert Street chapel, whose numbers declined until it was closed in 1953 and demolished in 1965, when Albert Street was rebuilt.

During the later years of the twentieth century, Bunyan church, along with others, engaged in a number of outreach activities such as the Cornerstone project for young people, pioneered by Andrew Hills and Jean O'Neill.

Pastors of Bunyan Baptist church:

R Vernon Bird	1903–1923
Russell Tomlin	1923–1925
A E Phillips	1928–1935
L F Higgs	1936–1951
Alfred G Robins	1952–1964
Stanley Lane	1966–1968
Henry Morton	1972–?
Alan Westwood	1988–1991
Paul Goodliff	1992–2001
Dave Morris	2002–

The Roman Catholics also had plans for a church building. From the late eighteenth century, a number of Catholic Emancipation Acts had gradually allowed them the freedom to build churches and establish a religious hierarchy in England. For the few Roman Catholics living in the Stevenage area

A Christmas service in the Bunyan Baptist church, Basils Road.

at the beginning of the twentieth century, the nearest Mass centre was at Hitchin, where the service was held in St Michael's School, which had been established in 1903. As the Stevenage Roman Catholic community grew, a mission chapel, called St Martin's, was opened in premises in Albert Street. It was quite small, and was sometimes referred to as a shed. In July 1912 a Catholic Motor Mission toured the country in a motor van converted into a mobile chapel. It arrived in Stevenage and parked near the White Lion Hotel. The purpose of the mission was to promote understanding of the Roman Catholic faith, and discussions at the well-attended meetings in the town hall were described as lively but good humoured. However, anti-Roman Catholic protesters outside the hall caused some disruption and, for several weeks afterwards, protests against the visit continued in correspondence to local newspapers. One writer advised readers to 'resist Popery as they would the Devil'. But in general there was growing tolerance, understanding and co-operation between the various Christian denominations as shown by the fact that the previous Christmas a joint carol service, including Roman Catholics, had been held on Bowling Green.

In 1913 the Roman Catholic community bought a narrow strip of land between Basil's Road and Grove Road and on Wednesday 1 October 1913, in the presence of representatives of all the other Stevenage churches, Dr Adrian Fortescue laid the foundation stone for the new church. The architect was

E H Major of London and the building contractors were two local firms, Messrs Austin & Sons and Mr W J Spratt. The new church, named the Transfiguration of Our Lord, was officially opened at a service on Sunday 25 January 1914. Fr Landrin, SSE, was priest-in-charge until August 1914 when Fr Basil Barton took over, serving the parish from Baldock. It was not until 1917, when Fr Oates was appointed, that the town had a resident parish priest. He lived initially at 19 Green Street and later at 119 High Street. The First World War brought an unexpected increase in attendance at the church, when a number of mainly Roman Catholic Belgian refugees were billeted in the town.

The church had been built on the Grove Road half of the land bought by the community, and during 1925–26 a presbytery was built on the Basils Road half. By 1937 the church had become too small for its congregation and work began on an extension. The porch on the east side was closed to make room for the baptistery and the original baptistery area converted to contain a confessional box. The nave was extended and a new and higher box-shape building with an apex roof added to form a larger sanctuary. A sacristy and coke store were added to the north-east corner of the building and a new entrance to the north-west corner.

Churches since 1946

Following the designation of Stevenage as a new town in 1946, most of the Nonconformists and the Roman Catholics declared their wish to build new churches there. This meant asking the Development Corporation to allocate them sites and then raising the money for the building work and staff from their own resources. For the Church of England, it was more complex. The centuries-old pattern of church life within the town would be changed. The rector in 1946 was the Revd John King who, with a curate, the Revd Edward Harper, was responsible for the parish church of St Nicholas and its daughter church, Holy Trinity which, between them served the whole town as one parish. The rector lived in the new rectory, built in 1919 at the top of Rectory Lane, near St Nicholas church. In 1952, the Diocese of St Albans built St Andrew's church for the new Bedwell neighbourhood, within the Parish of Stevenage, with the Revd Edward Harper as priest-in-charge, under the overall care of the rector. Some members of the existing congregations of Holy Trinity and St Nicholas' were asked to transfer to the Bedwell church and help to establish a new congregation there. This they did, rather reluctantly at first, but eventually becoming very attached to St Andrew's.

In 1954, Rector King left to take up a position in Bedford and was succeeded in 1955 by the Revd Eric Cordingly, chaplain to the Queen, who was to lead the development and reorganisation of the Church of England in Stevenage. This, the existing congregations were told, would mean that each neighbourhood of the new town would have a church building and a priest-in-charge of its own, with a new, large, centrally-located church, as the parish church for the town. St Nicholas' and Holy Trinity would become daughter churches. The Parish of St Mary, Shephall, was brought into the parish of Stevenage, which would be run as a team ministry, with the priests-in-charge responsible to the rector, the title which would be attached to the new central church. Although there was general approval of the plan for an Anglican church in each neighbourhood, there was no shortage of sarcastic remarks at the idea of a daughter being older than the mother and some resentment at the way in which the much-loved St Nicholas' church, with 850 years' of service to the town, now appeared to be casually demoted. Worse was to come, however. When the new St George's church was nearing completion in 1960, the choir, organist and choirmaster of St Nicholas' were asked to transfer to the new church. Most felt duty-bound to do as they were bidden, leaving St Nicholas' bereft of musical leadership. The next shock came in 1963, when the Diocese decided that, now St George's was built, St Andrew's was surplus to requirements and would be closed. The unhappiness and annoyance that this caused rankled for many years, until in 1984, the church of St George was renamed St Andrew and St George. After being put to a variety of uses, the former St Andrew's church was demolished in 1993 and the site sold for housing development.

In 1970 the ecclesiastical Parish of Stevenage was divided into seven parishes and a group ministry was formed. Each parish had its own church and vicar; St George's, being parish church at the time of this development, retained the title of rector. The Stevenage Anglican parishes, plus Shephall, are listed below in chronological order of church building, with names of the incumbents who served them.

St Nicholas, Stevenage – building began c1120

Names of Stevenage Rectors

Nicholas Fitz-Simon	1213–?
William de Berkhamsted	?–?
Adam de Boxgrave	?–1255
Henry de Borham	?–?
Gerald de Standon	1276–?
Richard de Gloucester	1314–?
John de Michaeldeane	1328–?
Philip de Westone	1333–?
Robert de Lee	1340–?
Robert atte Brome	1350–?
William Tankerville	1373–?
John Dyne	1382–?

John de Newton	1393–?
John de Belverge	1395–?
John Rowland	1397–?
John Lawrence	1408–?
William Brewster	?–?
John Pygge	1432–?
Stephen Hellard	1472–1500
William Blackwall	1506–?
Thomas Alleyne	?–1558
John Battle	1558–?
John Sterne	1577–?
Robert Pattinson	1578–?
William Pratt	1598–1629
Robert Chester	1633–1664
Stafford Leventhorpe	1664–1678
Richard Shoard	1678–?
Fulke Tudor	1680–1688
Josiah Bentham	1689–1723
Charles Baron	1723–1725
Thomas Stamper	1725–1733
Robert Style	1734–1737
Nicholas Cholwell	1737–1773
Samuel Hemming	1773–1781
Henry Baker	1781–1832
R G Baker	1833–1834
George Becher Blomfield *(Canon of Chester)*	1834–1874
William Jowitt	1874–1912
Henry William Eliot Molony *(Canon of St Albans)*	1912–1918
Charles Morgan Smith *(Canon of St Albans)*	1918–1945
John Humphrey King	1945–1954
Eric William Bradley Cordingly *(Chaplain to the Queen)*	1955–1962
Stanley Seart Hutton	1962–1969

In 1960, with the completion and consecration of the new parish church of St George, St Nicholas' itself became a district church, in the care of a priest-in-charge. The following served in this office;

Eric Arthur Gaskell	1960–1966
John Trevor Scott	1966–1969
Christopher James Weston	1970–1971

When the parish of Stevenage was divided into seven separate parishes in 1970

St Nicholas' regained its status as a parish church, although of a much smaller parish in area than previously. In 1998 the benefice of St Nicholas was united with that of St Mary's, Graveley.

Vicars of St Nicholas' (from 1998, St Nicholas' and St Mary's, Graveley)

Christopher James Weston	1971–1987
John Richard Bainbridge	1987–1998
Donald Dowling	1999–2010

Holy Trinity, Stevenage Old Town – consecrated 1862, extended 1881

Harold Jones	1959–1964
John D Watson *(Canon of St Albans)*	1964–1974
Mervyn D Terrett	1974–1985
Graham H Newton	1986–1995
Christine Hardman	1996–2001
Geoffrey Tickner	2002–

St Andrew, Bedwell – consecrated 1952, demolished 1993

Edward J. Harper	1952–1955
George N Heath	1955–1960
Trevor G Nash	1961–1963

St Peter, Broadwater – consecrated 1955

The church is a brick building built in 1954 and dedicated on 5 November 1955. Designed by N F Cachemaille Day and Partners, it consists of a nave with slender columns and narrow aisles, a large sanctuary to the east end and small transepts to north and south. There is a tower over the east end. The main entrance to the church is through a small porch on the south side of the building.

The church was designed to have a bell hung outside the building but this never took place and the bell sits in the porch! The exact design for the church was used again to build a sister church, St Michaels and All Angels, at Borehamwood but, because of the different designs in windows, decor and furniture, they look quite different. (Extract from a description by the late Janet White).

Incumbents of St Peter's church

Leonard R Moore	1955–1960
John V Stratton	1960–1965
Duncan J E Sladden	1965–1970
Roy Hubbard	1970–1978
Terry Beaumont	1979–1987
Edward Phillipps-Smith	1987–1989

David Brentnall	1990–1996
David H Hague	1996–2009

St Andrew and St George (St George until 1984) – consecrated 1960
Consecrated in 1960 by the Bishop of St Albans, the Rt Revd Michael Gresford Jones, in the presence of Queen Elizabeth the Queen Mother, who had laid the foundation stone in 1956. It is the largest parish church to have been built in England since the Second World War and is listed Grade II. It was designed by Lord Mottistone, then surveyor to the fabric of St Paul's Cathedral, and built by Messrs Rattee and Kett of Cambridge at a cost of £120,000. The frame of the building was constructed by a method of continuously pouring concrete into moulds which were subsequently broken away, thus there are no joints. Among the notable features of the interior are the interlacing arches and the 1966 stained glass window by Brian Thomas. Externally, the walls are clad in panels faced with Normandy pebbles. Since 1977, Stevenage Museum has been housed in the crypt. A fuller description can be found in the pamphlet *The Parish Church of St Andrew and St George Stevenage: Notes for Visitors*, available in the church.

Incumbents of the church of St Andrew and St George

Alan R G Hawkins (Rector from 1971)	1963–1974
John H Growns	1974–1982
Melvyn Barnsley *(Canon of St Albans)*	1982–

St George's church, consecrated 1960. (Stevenage MuseumP151)

Canon Melvyn Barnsley, Rector of the church of St Andrew and St George.

A concert rehearsal in the church of St Andrew and St George. (Margaret Ashby)

Signing the Declaration of Intent at the church of St Hugh and St John, Easter Sunday 1975.
Left to right: Dr Robert Runcie, Bishop of St Albans (Later Archbishop of Canterbury), Revd Geoffrey Marshall, Vicar of St Hugh's Anglican church, Revd John (Jack) Kaye, Chairman of the London North West District of the Methodist Church, Kathleen Richardson, lay worker at St John's Methodist church, who eventually became the first woman President of the Methodist Conference. (Colin Killick)

All Saints', Pin Green.

In the second half of the twentieth century there was a strong impetus towards Christian unity and this resulted in Stevenage having two purpose-built shared churches and one community church, as well as the united Anglican/Methodist congregation of St Hugh and St John, Chells:

St Hugh and St John, Chells – consecrated 1965

Arnold E Bennett	1959–1964
Christopher W Gonin	1964–1970
Geoffrey E Marshall	1970–1978
John Green	1979–1985
Nicholas J C Pigott	1985–1991
J Duncan Campbell	1993–

(For Methodist ministers see St John's Methodist church under 'Methodists' below)

All Saints, Pin Green (Called St Francis from 1966 to 1974) – dedicated 1974

All Saints is a church shared between Anglicans, Methodists and Roman Catholics, and is an integral part of the Oval Community Centre.

The Anglican and Methodist congregations join together for worship each Sunday. The Roman Catholics hold their own services but all denominations join together for occasional shared worship and other joint activities.

Anglican vicars at All Saints

Phillip Swindells	1966–1978
Stephen Purvis	1979–1988
Christopher Futcher	1988–1995
Susan Austin	1996–1999
Michael Leverton	2000–2010

Christ the King, Symonds Green – consecrated June 1982

The church building is part of the same complex as the Symonds Green Community Centre. It is a modern, multi-purpose building owned by Shared Churches in Hertfordshire and operated by the Church of England (Holy Trinity, High Street), the Roman Catholic Church and the United Reformed Church through the Christ the King, Stevenage, Joint Church Council. The Anglican service offers a more informal style of worship than the parish church of Holy Trinity.

The 14 stations of the cross that hang on the plain walls of the church are by Leslie Melton. In 1994 the late Anne Mariner researched the origins of the paintings and wrote an illustrated booklet about them. Having discovered that the artist had been a student of the sculptor, Sir Henry Moore, she managed to track him down in Australia, and corresponded with him for some 18 months. She wrote:

> It seems that the paintings were a thanksgiving for the artist's recovery from a serious illness. We do know that for some time the pictures decorated the walls of the chapel at St Edmund's College, Ware, in Hertfordshire. In the early 1950s the paintings were destined for the USA but for the intervention of a priest, Fr Davis, who arranged for them to be moved to the Roman Catholic Church of the Assumption of Our Lady in Walkern.
>
> That church closed in the early 1980s and the paintings were stored for some time in St Joseph's, Stevenage, until their installation in 1986 at the shared church of Christ the King, Symonds Green. Since that time, those of us who worship there have had the privilege to absorb their spiritual beauty.

Great Ashby Community Church

c/o Great Ashby Community Centre, Whitehorse Lane, Stevenage, SG1 5HA

Formally established in October 2006 as a joint project between Bunyan Baptist Church and St Nicholas' Anglican Church.

St Mary, Shephall – built c1150 or earlier

Clergy of St Mary's

Robert Goderich	1351– ?
John Taylor	?–1405
Thomas atte Hache	1405–?
William Ledys	?–1458
William Warner	?–?
Robert Watson	?–1539
Robert Cowper	1545–?
George Grayme	?–1562
William Lowyn	1562–?
Robert Wood (clerk)	1581–1594
George Aelmer (curate)	1582–?
Robert Flood (curate)	1584–?
John Rudd	1595–1640
Thomas Marten(curate)	1613–?
James Dent	1640–1641
Thomas Knight	1641–1660
Stafford Leventhorpe	1660–1665
Richard Shoard	1665–1679
Peter Fisher	1679–1691
William Milner	1691–1718
William Hawtayne (clerk)	1719–1734
Robert James (clerk)	1734–1742
John Barnwell	1742–1760
Nicholas Cholwell	1760–1767
John Jones	1768–1770
George Baddeley	1770–1792
Thomas Sisson	1792–1806
The Honourable, later Sir, Henry Leslie	1806–1837
Philip Godfrey (curate)	1822–?
Walter Wortham	1837–1877
Duncan Malcolm MacKenzie	1877–1892
William Henry Poland	1893–1902
Francis Fleetwood Buss	1903–1906
Thomas Davenport Warner	1906–1916
Alexander Macrae	1916–1928
*Horace Sturt	1928–1931
*E L Hensley	1931–1934
*John Pugh	1934–1947

*Harry Blowey 1947–1953
±Donald Howells 1954–1957
Derek Price 1957–1963
Clifford Wright 1963–1967
^Ian Busby 1967–1974
^Nicholas Bury 1975–1984
^John Arthur Terry 1984–1990
^Geoffrey Brian White 1991–2006
^Vivienne Hathaway 2007–

* Incumbents of Aston with Shephall
In 1954 the Benefices (Suspension of Presentation) Measure was applied and the Rector of Stevenage, John H.King, was placed in charge of Shephall. In the same year, Donald L Howells was licensed as Special Curate for Shephall.

± Until 1958 Shephall was in the Deanery of Welwyn. In 1959 it was included in the Deanery of Hitchin, as part of the Parish of Stevenage.

^ From 1970, when the Parish of Stevenage was divided into seven, St Mary's regained its former status as the parish church of Shephall, with its own Vicar.

Cardinal Heenan at Blessed Margaret Clitherow School, 1965. (Stevenage Museum)

The Roman Catholic Church

In 1981 the Roman Catholic parishes of All Saints, Christ the King, St Joseph's and the old town parish were amalgamated to form a Team Ministry parish. St Hilda's remained independent. In 1988 the Team Ministry parish was dissolved and the current parish comprising the old town church and Christ the King was formed.

Parish priests

Fr John Athill SSE	1911–1912
Fr R Landrin SSE	1912–1914
Fr Basil Barton	1914–1917
Fr Austin Oates	1917–1921
Fr Arthur W Valentin	1921–1945
Fr Arthur Welland	1945
Fr W H Ormiston MC	1945–1958
Fr Leo Straub	1958–1980
Fr Michael Roberts	1980–1981
Fr John Atkins	1981–1983
Fr Adrian Walker	1981–1987
Fr Brian Reynolds	1981–1989
Fr Saviour Vella	1989–1994
Fr Paul McAleenan	1991–1995
Fr Peter Newby	1995–1996
Fr Donald Graham	1996
Fr Tony Convery	1987–1999
Fr Joseph Carter	1997–2001
Fr Francis Leonard	2001–

Parish Sisters

Sr Helen Carroll OP	1982–1983
Sr Lucia Fitzpatrick OP	1982–1987
Sr Anthony O'Shea OP	1982–1988
Sr Teresa Donavan OP	1988–1993
Sr Bertranda Mullryan OP	1991–1993
Sr Clare Manning OP	1987–1995
Sr Geraldine McGarry OP	1993–1999
Sr Eileen Airey OP	1995–1999
Sr Loretta Dooley OP	2000–

St Hilda's Roman Catholic church. (Andrew Hills)

St Joseph's church, Bedwell Crescent

St Joseph's church began as a temporary building, known as 'the hut' installed on the Bedwell site in 1953. The new church building was opened by the Archbishop of Westminster on 7 July 1957. In the 1980s problems with the fabric of the structure required the high roof to be removed and replaced by a roof at a lower level. Changes were also made to the internal arrangement of the church. The first parish priest at St Joseph's was Fr John Coughlan.

St Hilda's church, Hydean Way

St Hilda's church, in Shephall, was established in 1958. Initially, the congregation used the temporary building that had been moved from St Joseph's church in Bedwell. The foundation stone of the new church was laid in 1961 and the church was completed and opened in 1962. The first parish priest was Fr Francis Donovan.

The Methodist Church

Superintendent Ministers stationed in Stevenage at the High Street Methodist church

Revd Donald J McNeill	1946–1954
Revd H Hector Chick	1958–1965
Revd Alan Washbrook	1976–1981
Revd David Curran	1981–1993

Since 1993, when Stevenage joined with Hitchin, Letchworth and Baldock, the Superintendent Minister has been stationed at Central Methodist church in Letchworth.

The Revd Donald J McNeill, a very enthusiastic minister of the gospel, was responsible for the High Street Methodist church and the Methodist church in Knebworth. In about 1948 he began a church at Broadwater, in a garage belonging to the Smeeton family. After a while a hut was erected nearby in a small field belonging to Mr L V White, followed sometime later by another small building. As the new town developed the Methodist Church acquired a site on the Roebuck Estate and, with considerable help from the Rank Organisation, St Paul's church, a substantial building, was opened there in the spring of 1955. By this time the Revd Donald McNeill had moved on and the Revd Alan Slater was the minister.

By the early 1980s major repair had become necessary on the St Paul's church building. However, the congregation, led by the Revd David Hinson, decided to sell most of the site to the Aldwick Housing Association, to enable them to build sheltered housing accommodation. With the income from the sale, it was then possible to build a new St Paul's church next to it.

St John's Methodist church, Chells (see also St Hugh and St John above)

Revd Christopher Bamber	1960–1965
Revd Edward Bishop	1965–1971
Mr Sydney Richardson	1971–1974
Mrs Kathleen Richardson	1973–1976
Revd Alan Washbrook	1976–1981
Revd David Curran	1981–1982
Revd John Green	1982–1985
Revd John Risby	1986–1988
Revd Julia Everatt	1988–1993
Revd Duncan Campbell	1993–

United Reformed (previously Congregational) Church – opened 1954

In 1946 the Hertfordshire County Congregational Union applied for a site to be made available in the new town for a Congregational church, school and manse. A site in Bedwell was incorporated into the 1950 Master Plan and a Development Committee of representatives of the Congregational Churches at Knebworth and Hitchin and Letchworth Free Church was set up to oversee the progress of the new church. In the meantime services were held at temporary premises in Stevenage.

Building of the Congregational church began in Cuttys Lane in 1954 and the church was officially opened in September of that year. Miss Pat Ashton served as resident leader of Stevenage Congregational Church for a year from 1953–54, but the first minister proper was the Reverend E R Wimpress, who began his ministry at the church in January 1955 and retired in December 1991. He was the longest-serving and one of the best-loved clergy in the town. His successor in 1992 was the Revd John Maitland, followed in 1996 by the Revd Anne Wilson, who retired in 2004 but continued in a part-time capacity until 2007. She was succeeded by the Revd John Steele in 2009.

Coptic Orthodox Cathedral of St George – inaugurated 2006

Set in the grounds of Shephalbury, this is not only the first Coptic cathedral in the UK, but also the country's first purpose-built Coptic place of worship. There is only one other Coptic cathedral in Western Europe.

The cathedral, built in the shape of a crucifix, was inaugurated by His Grace Bishop Angaelos in September 2006 and incorporates traditional Coptic style and decoration. The two main icons were, however, first used the year before at the Westminster Cathedral Memorial Service for Brother Roger of Taizé. The main area of worship seats 350, but the design brief to architects S and C Molina

The Coptic Orthodox cathedral of St George in the grounds of Shephalbury.

was to accommodate congregations of 500–1,000 at least three times a year. The adjoining multi-purpose hall provides the additional floor area by means of a movable wall. Otherwise used for conferences and a variety of social purposes, it can accommodate a five-a-side football pitch with ease. Additional rooms are available for elements of the Ministry's youth work, discussion groups, Bible studies and other smaller scale activities, and there is also an upper floor, serviced by lift.

In terms of design and decoration, the cathedral combines modern functionality and traditional style. From the exterior, this is dominated by the curved, standing seam, zinc roof construction. Zinc was chosen ahead of other metals for its ease of maintenance, colour retention and sustainability. The pre-weathered mid-grey quartz-zinc requires no painting or associated maintenance and will retain its appearance for decades. In addition to the vaulted roof over the length of the structure, other distinctive elements include a traditional Coptic domed bell tower, crowned with a Coptic cross. Dormer style roof windows were also positioned equidistantly along either side of the roof. The interior is decorated with an iconostasis and highly decorative mouldings and altar decoration, and finished with a traditional marble floor. The ceiling is particularly noteworthy as it includes inlaid, hand-made ceiling panels, each around 12 inches square. In addition to the altar screen and other hand-carved woodwork, they were designed and made by skilled craftsmen in Egypt.

Although the Coptic Church is an ancient one, its role within the community very much reflects that of a living church. It is the largest Christian denomination in the Middle East. The contemporary design of the new cathedral reflects the emphasis on youth and the diversity of pastoral, social and individual activities and services.

The Church of Jesus Christ of Latter-day Saints

The Stevenage ward of the church was formed in 1959. Under the supervision of a building missionary from the USA, members built their meeting-house on a site bought from the Stevenage Development Corporation in Buckthorn Avenue. The building, with its distinctive spike-topped separate tower, was opened in 1965. As well as a chapel, the complex houses a baptistry, cultural hall, classrooms, offices, kitchen and a fully-equipped Family History Centre which is open free to anyone wishing to trace a family tree. There is also a satellite television link with the church's world headquarters at Salt Lake City, Utah, USA.

Alphabetical list of Churches and other religious groups in Stevenage as at 2009

All Saints Church (RC, Anglican and Methodist)
The Oval, Vardon Road, Pin Green

Allied Christian Worship Centre
Hertford Road Community Centre
Kenilworth Close, Bragbury End,

Baha'i Group, Redemption Church

Bunyan Baptist Church
Basil's Road, Old Town

Christadelphians, c/o Springfield House, High Street

Church of Christ the King (RC, Anglican and URC)
Filey Close, Symonds Green

Church of Jesus Christ of Latter-day Saints
Buckthorn Avenue, Bedwell

The Church of The Transfiguration (Roman Catholic)
Grove Road, Stevenage Old Town

Coptic Othodox Cathedral of St George
Shephalbury Manor, Broadhall Way, Broadwater

Grace Community Church (formerly Hydean Way Baptist Church)
Hydean Way, Shephall

Great Ashby Community Church
c/o Great Ashby Community Centre, Whitehorse Lane, Stevenage, SG1 5HA

High Street Methodist Church
High Street, Old Town

Holy Trinity Church (Church of England)
High Street, Old Town

Longmeadow Evangelical Church
Oaks Cross, Broadwater

Religious Society of Friends (Quakers)
The Meeting House, Cutty's Lane, Bedwell

St Andrew and St George (Anglican)
St George's Way, Town Centre

St Hilda's (Roman Catholic)
Hydean Way, Shephall

St Hugh and St John (Church of England & Methodist)
Mobbsbury Way, Chells

St Joseph's (Roman Catholic)
Bedwell Crescent, Bedwell

St Mary's (Church of England)
Shephall Green, Hydean Way, Shephall

St Nicholas (Church of England)
Rectory Lane, Old Town

St Paul's (Methodist)
Turpins Rise, Broadwater

St Peter's (Church of England)
Broadwater Crescent, Broadwater

Salvation Army Corps
190 Bedwell Crescent, Bedwell

Seventh-Day Adventist Church
c/o High Street Methodist Church

Stevenage Central Mosque
The Sishes, Vardon Road

Stevenage Vineyard Fellowship
Thomas Alleyne School, Old Town

United Reformed Church
Cuttys Lane, Bedwell

Whomerley Spiritual Church and Centre,
Gladstone Court, Spring Drive, Broadwater

CHAPTER TWENTY
Industry

In 1946 Stevenage already had a few modern industries. These included, in chronological order of their establishment in the town;

1883 – The Educational Supply Association Ltd (ESA), Esavian Works: School furniture & equipment. The major employer in the town, still referred to as 'The Factory' for many years after the new industrial area was built.

1925 – D Wickham & Co. (Stevenage) Ltd, Six Hills Works: Mechanised plant & vehicle components. Formerly Messrs French & Son, High Street.

1926 – Stevenage Knitting Company Ltd, Sish Lane: Knitwear.

1928 – Vincent Engineers Ltd, High Street and Fishers Green Road Works, which later became Harper Engines Ltd, manufacturing internal combustion precision engines and parts. Makers of the famous 1,000 cc 'Black Shadow' and 'Black Knight' motor cycles.

1938 – Geo. W King Ltd, Argyle Works: Cranes, hoists, conveyors & automation machinery. The first factory to be built in what was to become the new town's principal industrial area. Previously occupying a restricted site near Hitchin railway station, the company built a new factory, called Argyle Works, on land to the south of Stevenage Old Town, between what is now Argyle Way and the former Norton Green Road, now called Six Hills Way. The company was later sold to Tube Investments.

1941 – A Ibbetson & Co., Ibco Works, North Road: Manufacturers of disinfectants, germicides, household cleaners and polishes, employing about 120 people. The company came to Stevenage when its Barking factory was bombed.

Interior of Vincent HRD works, 1948. (Stevenage Museum PP142)

> 1945 – Stevenage Printing Works, formerly Matthews Printing Works, established in 1895: General and Commercial Printing.

> Pre-1940 – W H Sanders (Electronics) Ltd, Bedwell Lane. Radar and electronic equipment manufacturers. Heavily engaged on war work during the Second World War.

These factories, together with many small-scale employers such as builders, blacksmiths, wheelwrights and motor engineers, were the basis of the town's industrial employment.

In the 1949 Master Plan, the area between the proposed A1(M) and the main railway line had been zoned for industry. With the prevailing wind blowing from the west, it was essential that Stevenage attract 'clean' industries to ensure that no smoke or fumes were blown over the proposed residential areas to the east. However, in 1951 attracting industry to the town before roads and factories were built proved difficult. The Corporation, therefore, took the initiative and by April 1952 they had let a contract for the building of the first main length of Gunnels Wood Road, a subway under the railway was under construction and a new bridge over the railway was at design stage. They then opened up land where factories could be built. The industrial area was deliberately sited so that when construction was completed, heavy lorries bringing in building materials could get straight on to the site without going along residential roads.

Thus the development of industry, so vital to the town, could now progress. Furthermore, the Corporation decided that, if industrialists could not be persuaded to build the first factories, then the Corporation would itself build them to a standard design and offer them at 'rack' rents; that is, full market value rental that reflects the value of the land on which the building sits and the value of the building itself.

As housing development was getting into its stride in the mid 1950s, increasing numbers of people were moving out of London to the new town and work had to be found for them. For the Corporation's architects, the emphasis had, very quickly, to be put upon the provision of more factories. Ray Gorbing was one who was taken off designing and building houses and commissioned to design one of the first industrial units, for Shunic Ltd, manufacturers of metal castings and office material, who had decided to move out of London. He was later involved in other factory design, including those for British Aerospace, Kodak, Bowaters and Hawker Siddeley. At the time there was a shortage of trained craftsmen in the building industry, and unskilled labour had to be used in many situations. In addition, tight financial targets we were set by the government, but nevertheless enough industrial premises were built to cope with the labour demands of the incoming population.

Leonard Vincent became involved in the design of 'ready-made' factories, which he compared to 'off-the-peg' suits as being a reasonable fit for average needs. In an undated newspaper clipping, found among his papers, he made the observation that

> ... ready-made factories have come to stay, and there is a big future for them, if intelligently planned, particularly if they are flexible and expansion can take

New factories in the Gunnels Wood Industrial Area. (Stevenage Museum P7425)

Shunic factory, Gunnels Wood Road, c1955. (Stevenage Museum P10836)

The Bay Tree Press. (Stevenage Museum P3735)

place in standard units or bays, as required. Small expanding industries need this facility more than most and, therefore, sufficient land must be available for such purposes. On the other hand, site planning must be done carefully to ensure no waste of land. This is one of the biggest problems in factory estate development, but it does appear that a planned industrial area of ready-made factories is the best way of conserving land.

The first of the standard factories was completed in 1953 and let to the Bay Tree Press. Three more standard factories were almost ready for use and also nearing completion on a 14-acre green-field site was the first stage of the De

Havilland factory, for which the company had taken a building lease after their move had been approved by the Ministry of Supply. This amounted to a total of 150,000 sq ft of industrial space. By the end of the decade, this had increased to 1,755,805 sq ft, with a further 137,000 sq ft under construction. The 900 employees working in the industrial area in 1953 had by 1960 risen to 12,000. The De Havilland factory was formally opened in 1954 by the Marquis of Salisbury. Not long afterwards, it changed its name to De Havilland Aircraft (1954), then to De Havilland Propellers (1954), De Havilland Aircraft Company (1960) and Hawker Siddeley Dynamics (1963).

In 1953, English Electric Ltd decided to move to Stevenage. They had hoped to expand their plant at Luton but the Ministry of Defence had advised the firm that they would not get support for that because every Ministry was against it. However, the Ministry of Defence would support a move to Stevenage. This is a reference to the fact that an industry wishing to move or expand had first to obtain an Industrial Development Certificate from the Department of Trade, in accordance with legislation under the Location of Industries Act which was introduced alongside the new towns legislation in the late 1940s. In effect, this

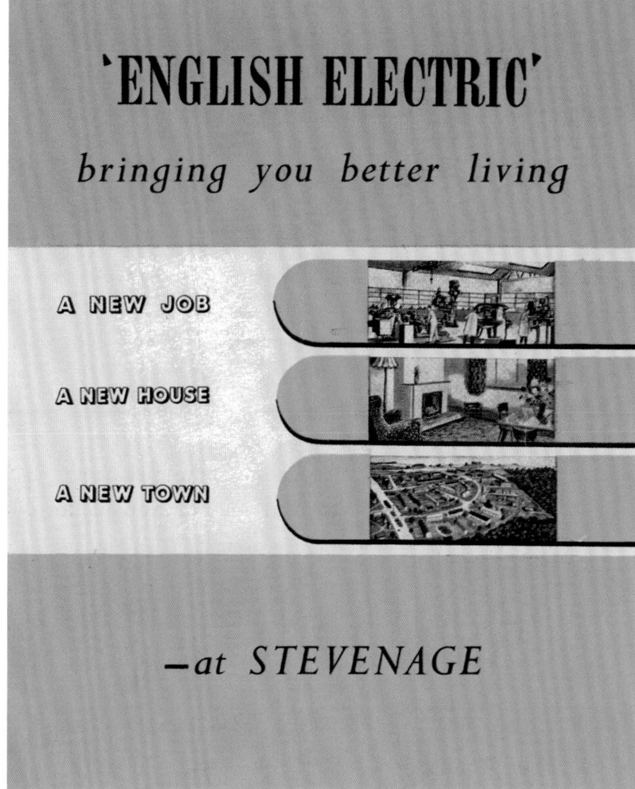

English Electric brochure, 1953.

meant that the government could direct industrial companies which had outgrown their existing sites to specific locations.

The English Electric Guided Weapons Division occupied a standard factory in Caxton Way in 1954 and the Electronic, Control and Airframe Departments moved into the newly erected main buildings in 1955. The following extracts from their publicity brochure *English Electric bringing you better living – at Stevenage,* throw an interesting light on pre-occupations and attitudes in the 1950s;

> The man who joins 'ENGLISH ELECTRIC' becomes a member of a Group of Companies, whose expansion and solid achievements each year make a more vital contribution to the prosperity of Britain and the Commonwealth ... .The work undertaken by the Group is tremendously varied, no firm in the world covering a wider field of electrical and mechanical engineering. Electrical products range from heavy turbines, generators, diesel and locomotive engines ... through the whole field of radar, wireless and telecommunication equipment ... right down to domestic products and appliances, such as the well-known 'ENGLISH ELECTRIC' television sets, washing machines, refrigerators, etc.
>
> Another side is the design and manufacture of aircraft and guided missiles. Work is forging ahead in these most important spheres. That famous product of the Aircraft Division, the 'ENGLISH ELECTRIC' 'Canberra' jet bomber, needs no further recommendation: our employees are proud of the international acclaim it has received.
>
> **Conditions of Work**
>
> You will be employed in a brand new factory, laid out on modern lines. Our site, some 65 acres in extent, is one of the largest and finest sites in the industrial area of the New Town.
>
> Working conditions will be good ... [The factory's] lighting, layout, heating, ventilation and amenities are designed with a view to the betterment of the life one leads during working hours. There will be, among other things, a large modern canteen, a first aid and rest room, and ample cloakroom and toilet facilities.
>
> The Company's working week is the normal 44 hours for operatives and associated work staff; for other staff, 39½ hours.
>
> **Opportunities for your family**
>
> If you have sons, you can be assured that few, if any, firms in this country offer such fine educational and training schemes for young men ... There are schools

> and courses for craft, student and graduate apprentices, trainee draughtsmen and designers. Young men are also trained for commercial work, for management and for other branches or activity ... In the case of your daughter or your wife wishing to find employment, there should be good scope for her within our Division. At Stevenage alone, the Company will need a substantial number of women and girls for secretarial, clerical and general duties.
>
> **A New House**
>
> Once you are engaged by ENGLISH ELECTRIC to work at Stevenage you are then definitely allocated a new house there. The Stevenage Development Corporation builds it and supplies it to you. So it is not in any sense a 'Company' or a 'tied' house. This ensures your security of tenure.

In 1959, the Company announced the first of the many changes of name and organisation that would characterise the aerospace industry in Stevenage, as its newsletter, *Grapevine*, explained;

> **Formation of English Electric Aviation Ltd**
>
> To deal efficiently with the increasing volume of business which we are handling in the aviation field, and to bring together the activities of the Aircraft and Guided Weapons Divisions, a new Company has been formed.
>
> The new wholly-owned £16m subsidiary of the English Electric Company – called English Electric Aviation Ltd, has been formed to take over all the group's existing activities in research, design, development and production of manned aircraft and guided weapons. The new Company will comprise the Aircraft Division of English Electric based at Warton, and the Guided Weapons division based at Stevenage.

The rest of the 1959 newsletter was largely concerned with reports of the wide range of social and sporting activities which were encouraged by English Electric and its successors. These included news that the Foremen's Dinner and Dance was held on 17 April 1959 in the canteen at Stevenage; the Sports and Social Club's Gala Day had been held at Bragbury End on Saturday 20 June; the Production Wing (engineering) Cricket Team had won the Cricket Club's Burgess Cup; the Arts Section of the Sports and Social Club had been invited to stage an 'Artists in Industry' show at the Art Gallery in Letchworth Museum and apprentice Dick Hemmings, winner of the Foreman's Trophy for the second year running, had been presented with the shield by Works Manager, Mr Tom Mason.

In his book, *Good Company; the story of the Guided Weapons Division of the British Aircraft Corporation*, published in 1976, A R Adams describes something of the relationship between English Electric and the Development Corporation and, in particular, the contribution of Peter Russell, who was appointed Commercial Manager and Deputy General Manager of the Guided Weapons Division

> The Stevenage works was, from the start, one of the largest in the New Town, and it is now, with a strength of 6,300, bigger than the next four firms put together. Peter Russell did more than anyone towards its integration into the local community life: as one of the founders of the Stevenage Industrial Employers' Group, and the Company's link-man with the New Town Development Corporation with whom he fought, on the most friendly terms, a running battle on the speed and scale of house-building; as a member of the Stevenage Youth Trust; as the creator of the Company's splendid Sports and Social Club facilities at Bragbury End; and in many other ways – always unobtrusively, but most persistently and effectively.

A brochure for the British Aircraft Corporation, a company of British Aerospace. (MBDA)

The old Stevenage railway station which was in operation 1850–1973. (Stevenage Museum)

Sunblest Bakery. (Stevenage Museum 0221)

In Stevenage itself there was horror and outrage on the part of pacifists, supporters of the Campaign for Nuclear Disarmament and many church people, when they discovered that the English Electric Company in Stevenage was manufacturing not washing machines, but guided weapons that could be fitted with nuclear warheads. This was not what was envisaged by the idealists who planned the brave new town in the aftermath of the Second World War.

Although aware of concerns about the town's dependence on an industry that was making weapons of war, Jack Balchin considered that 'English Electric's coming to Stevenage was one of the most important events in the life of the Corporation ...' He said that many of the smaller firms in Stevenage survived because of the work sub-contracted to them. The economy of the whole town had prospered and stabilised because of English Electric's decision to move from Luton to Stevenage in 1953. As well as English Electric, other companies were now occupying standard factories at rack rents, including International Computers and Tabulators; Kodak (all Kodak cameras made in the UK were made in Stevenage); Electro Methods (scientific and electrical apparatus);

Fleming Radio, makers of electronic equipment; Hilmor (tube bending machinery); Schrieber Wood Industries, makers of radio and television cabinets; J Scott and Co, electrical engineers, and Shunic Ltd.

Between 1953 and 1958, nine companies had taken building sites on ground leases; that is rents reflecting the value of the land before the buildings were put on it, although the presence of buildings might enhance the value of the land. These companies included British Visqueen, a subsidiary of Imperial Chemical Industries, making polythene sheeting; the Mentmore Manufacturing Company, making pens and pencils, and W H Sanders (Electronics) Limited, which had started out in a former cowshed at Bedwell Farm.

By 1967, there were almost 100 companies operating in the Gunnels Wood Industrial Area, many of them household names. Bowater Containers, whose rolling mill produced corrugated cardboard, was the only factory to have railway sidings. Marconi Instruments; John Lewis distribution warehouse; Pye Ether (electronic equipment); Taylor Instrument Companies (Europe) Limited (process control instrumentation); Tatra Plastics; LeRoi Menswear, makers of quality shirts, and the PTP colour processing laboratory were among the well-known companies that made the move to the new town. In 1965, the International Exhibition Co-operative Wine Society arrived. More than a million bottles were transferred, in one weekend, from its ancient cellars in London to the new, above-ground, temperature-controlled bonded warehouse in Stevenage.

Three research laboratories were located in the Gunnels Wood Industrial Area, one for the American Oil Company, one for the Furniture Industry Research Association, one for the Department of Industry and, on a nearby site in Elder Way, the government's Water Pollution Research Laboratory. A block of unit factories, which small starter firms could rent from the Corporation, and a sheltered workshop for disabled and handicapped people, supported and supplied with work by other businesses in the area, were also located in the Gunnels Wood Industrial Area.

At one stage, three out of four workers in the Gunnels Wood Industrial Area were employed by one of the big eight companies located there – English Electric, De Havilland, International Computers, Imperial Chemical Industries (British Visqueen), Kodak, Mentmore, Bowaters and Taylor Instruments. Whilst that brought more worries about the diversification of employment in the town, the fact was that, as Jack Balchin said,

> One may question the wisdom of the Corporation's policy of having so many eggs in such fine baskets, yet without them Stevenage would have struggled along at a much slower rate of development, it would have made a smaller contribution to the London housing problem and there would have been much greater out-commuting for work, making the town more like a dormitory for Luton, London or elsewhere. The eight brought demands for skills of the

> highest order, semi-skills and for unskilled labour, thus maximising for locals as for London people. They also created work opportunities for women who increasingly looked for employment, gave opportunity for sub-contracting firms and stimulated the creation of new firms in the process.

Nevertheless, in 1962 the doubters' fears were realised when Blue Water, English Electric's medium-range guided weapon system, was abruptly cancelled putting many of the Stevenage workforce out of a job. A R Adams described the Company's reaction,

> Blue Water was in the full flood of technical success ... from all accounts it was a most impressive technical achievement and, in a message at the time of cancellation, Lord Portal, BAC's Chairman, referred to '... the brilliant work done, described by the Ministry itself as being of the highest order'. Less than a month before its cancellation the deputy Chief of the Imperial General Staff, together with the Ministry Controller, Guided Weapons, and the Director, Royal Artillery – all the topmost brass concerned – visited Stevenage and said they were delighted with the way the project was going, as it was vital to the Army's future.

Within three months, following a Cabinet re-shuffle, the new Minister of Defence cancelled Blue Water. A R Adams described the decision as '... a cruel blow to English Electric and to Stevenage New Town, where our work-force represented more than a third of the total industrial employment ... at this time there were serious suggestions that the Stevenage works should be closed ...'

In fact the Stevenage factory was not closed, because government officials realised that it possessed probably the main reservoir of specialist knowledge and equipment in the field of guided weapons in the country. Even so, there were large-scale redundancies but great efforts were made to keep the best qualified and most able engineers. This policy was not entirely successful and many left. It was also a difficult time to attract high quality replacement staff, as it was clear that the industry was vulnerable to political changes of mind.

For some years there had been a series of mergers of comparatively small companies in the aircraft and aerospace industry and in 1960, the Aircraft and Guided Weapons Divisions of English Electric had become part of the British Aircraft Corporation. As costs became ever greater and with government encouragement, this trend was accelerated and in 1976 the formation of British Aerospace was announced. A glossy leaflet published at the time stated, 'British Aerospace unites Hawker Siddeley Dynamics, Hawker Siddeley Aviation, British Aircraft Aviation and Scottish Aviation in a powerful new aerospace enterprise which in width of experience and total capability matches any other single organisation in the world aerospace industry'.

Before the merger took effect in 1977, Allen Greenwood, chairman of the British Aircraft Corporation (1976–77) wrote in the final report to employees;

> Last year I was able to initiate a Report to everyone in BAC, describing our results in 1975 as the best ever for our Company. In this year's Report, you will be able to see how the recently-published results for 1976 show that the Company's performance improved even further, to record levels. Even allowing for the effects of inflation in the monetary figures, the results still represent an increase in real terms over our past performance.
>
> The increase in our order book ... clearly shows the confidence in our products shown by customers both at home and overseas and also in our ability to deliver and support them both from Britain and through our overseas management. In 1976 we have made a positive contribution to the country's balance of payments, as exports represent 56% of our total sales. This continues the pattern we have maintained for many years now, of exporting more than half of our annual turnover.
>
> The results described in this Report will be the last achieved wholly under private ownership. We can all be proud of the success which our efforts have brought for the Company over the years since its formation in 1960.

From comparatively small beginnings, the aerospace industry in Stevenage developed into one of the world's foremost space companies, now known as EADS Astrium. It occupies the former De Havilland/Hawker Siddeley Dynamics site, which has seen a number of famous name changes over the years – De Havilland Aircraft Company (1954), De Havilland Propellers (1954), De Havilland Aircraft Company (1960), Hawker Siddeley Dynamics (1963), British

British Aerospace (formerly English Electric), main site looking south before development. (MBDA)

British Aerospace main site, 1980s, looking north. (MBDA)

Aerospace (1977), British Aerospace Dynamics Group (1980), British Aerospace Systems (1990), Matra Marconi Space (1994), Astrium (2000) and EADS Astrium (2003), owned by the European Aeronautic, Defence and Space Company. Astrium built and tested some of the largest satellites in the world, equipped with the most advanced mobile, broadcasting and military communications systems ever flown in space. It became a key player in European and international scientific missions to explore Mars, Venus and the more distant asteroids, and planets – in short, to explore the solar system and unveil the secrets of the universe. Its activities have been regularly reported in the press and on television news programmes.

It is clear that many employees enjoyed working at BAe and its predecessors. Their working conditions were good, social facilities were excellent and pay compared very favourably with that of other industries in the town. There remained the ethical problem: was it right to earn a living by making weapons of war? Some people managed to ignore the question altogether in a 'burying the head in the sand' approach. Others were aware that their work was essential to national security, particularly during the Cold War with Russia, which might at any time have developed into a full-scale conflict. Yet others took the pragmatic approach of accepting whatever employment was available. The opportunity of being at the cutting edge of research and development, of working with the latest technology in an extremely efficient and highly regarded organisation, was a great draw for scientists and engineers of the highest calibre.

Stevenage is also the location for MBDA, the acronym for the merged European missile production company, its full name being Matra BAE Dynamics Alenia. Formed in 2000, it consists of parts of BAE Systems (in the UK),

Finmecannica (in Italy), and EADS (European Aeronautic Defence and Space Company). In 2008, MBDA recorded the memories of some former employees for Stevenage Museum. David Carter, a senior estimator at British Aerospace, described the feeling of uncertainty after Blue Streak was cancelled and then the excitement of being involved with the space Shuttle project, 'When you saw that first Space Shuttle go up and the pictures from space and then you saw that bits of equipment that you had helped to build, to manufacture, were up there – we were was quite proud of our achievement ... that one factory turned out all this equipment that put man in space'.

Janet Liddle, previously a Personal Assistant at Hawker Siddeley, described tense times waiting for news of a launch;

> When we had the actual launches – in the very elementary stages of the launches, that was quite interesting because we would work all through the night, all through the next day and so forth, sometimes, because we had to manually type out all the reports and everything else ... The launch would go and in those days all we had was a ticker-tape thing that came through the telex office and you'd all be huddled up in the telex office, all waiting for the news of whether it had succeeded or not succeeded – so that was quite nice. It was just a general feeling that we all belonged together.

As for being at the cutting edge of technology, Molly Glendinning, remembers being given her specialist tools; 'I got a job with English Electric. It was only a little job, it was soldering, fine work. I always remember they gave us two screwdrivers when we arrive, one to use and one for your pocket – and the one for your pocket was to stir your tea with'.

The list of satellites on the opposite page built at Stevenage by Hawker Siddeley Dynamics, BAe Space Systems, Matra Marconi Space and Astrium was kindly compiled and updated by Astrium Ltd, Gunnels Wood Road, Stevenage.

The European Space Agency's LISA Pathfinder satellite, built at Astrium in Stevenage. (Photo courtesy of Astrium).

Using the experience and expertise it gained from the Beagle 2 Mars lander programme, Astrium in Stevenage is responsible for the development, design and build of the European Space Agency's ExoMars Rover vehicle due for launch in 2016. (Photo courtesy of the European Space Agency)

Three huge, 50m wingspan Inmarsat 4 satellites built by Astrium are already fully operational on geostationary orbit, 36,000 km over the Equator, providing mobile communications and a Broadband Global Area Network(B-GAN) for laptop to laptop communications and Internet access.
(Photo courtesy of Astrium)

No.	Satellite	Launch date
30	Hispasat 1A	11/09/1992
31	Hispasat 1B	23/07/1993
32	Nato IV B	08/12/1993
33	ORION 1	29/11/1994
34	Telecom 2 C	06/12/1995
35	Telecom 2D	09/08/1996
36	HOTBIRD 2	21/11/1996
37	HOTBIRD 3	02/09/1997
38	SKYNET 4D	10/01/1998
39	HOTBIRD 4	27/02/1998
40	Nilesat-101	28/04/1998
41	ST-1A	25/08/1998
42	HOTBIRD 5	09/10/1998
43	Afristar	28/10/1998
44	SKYNET 4E	26/02/1999
45	Asiastar	21/03/2000
46	Nilesat-102	17/08/2000
47	Eutelsat W1	06/09/2000
48	Astra 2B	14/09/2000
49	SKYNET 4F	07/02/2001
50	HOTBIRD 7	11/12/2002
51	Hellas-Sat	13/05/2003
52	Mars Express	03/06/2003
53	Beagle 2	03/06/2003
54	Rosetta	02/03/2004
55	EutelsatW3A	16/03/2004
56	Intelsat 10-02	16/06/2004
57	Amazonas	05/08/2004
58	Inmarsat 1-4F1	11/03/2005
59	ANIK F1R	08/09/2005
60	Inmarsat 1-4F2	08/11/2005
61	Venus Express	09/11/2005
62	Arabsat 4A	28/03/2006
63	HOT BIRD 8	04/08/2006
64	MetOp F2 (A)	19/10/2006
65	Arabsat 4B	08/11/2006
66	Skynet 5A	11/03/2007
67	ANIK F3	09/04/2007
68	Skynet 5B	14/11/2007
69	GIOVE B	26/04/2008
70	Skynet 5C	12/06/2008
71	Badr 6	07/07/2008
72	Inmarsat 1-4F3	18/08/2008
73	NIMIQ 4	19/09/2008
74	HOT BIRD 9	20/12/2008
75	HOT BIRD 10	12-02-2009
76	Ameristar	–
77	Worldstar-4	–
78	MetOp F1	

Pin Green Industrial Area. (Margaret Ashby)

Although guided weapons and aerospace have dominated the Stevenage industrial scene, the town has been home to many other companies. The opening up of the Pin Green Employment Area in the early 1970s brought Johnson Gibbons (London) Limited, Singer (Friden) Progressive Products, British Insulated Callender Cables, Dixon's, with a large distribution warehouse, Sunblest Bakery, Tatra Plastics, Du Pont, the Provident Mutual Life Assurance Association and a number of other companies. In addition, small firms, each providing employment for a few people, exist throughout the town.

The recession of the 1980s saw great changes in the Stevenage industrial scene. Seven of the big eight in the Gunnels Wood Industrial Area closed their Stevenage operations and British Aerospace was greatly reduced. The government's air pollution and water pollution research laboratories and the American Oil Company's research laboratories closed. The three giant insurance companies also left the town and, later on, Dixon's Warehouse moved out.

In the early 1990s, news that the pharmaceutical giant Glaxo (now GlaxoSmithKlein) was coming to Stevenage invoked mixed reactions. Clearly it would bring more employment opportunities, but also animals for use in its laboratories. Many people, especially the young, who were concerned about animal welfare, staged demonstrations and circulated petitions to such effect that the company's large site at the southern end of the Gunnels Wood Industrial Area had to be heavily protected and closely guarded. The company's employees, who would be transferring from other Glaxo premises, were taken to Stevenage, a coach load at a time, on a succession of Saturdays to see the site and to be given a conducted tour of Stevenage and surrounding towns and villages, including housing development sites under construction, in order that they might get some ideas of where they might like to live.

It is not possible to list every firm now existing in Stevenage but the period immediately before the Development Corporation transferred responsibility to the Borough Council was a time of checking and stock-taking. The following list, with accompanying plan, dated 1978, is of particular historic interest as it provides a snapshot of industry in Stevenage, with precise locations, at that time;

Gunnels Wood Industrial Area

1. Tatra Plastics Ltd (Precision moulding and other engineering plastics)
2. Central Electricity Generating Board (Grid sub-station)
3. Hall Co. Ltd (Builders merchants)
4. Spicers Ltd (Paper Distributors)
5. Kalstan Engineering Ltd (Light engineering)
6. Arlun Electronics (Electrical contractor)
7. Cadwell Coachworks (Vehicle spraying)
8. Co-op Dairy (Dairy distribution depot)
9. Acton and Borman Ltd (Abrasive paper s and cloth)
10. Harrow and Besborough (Empress Services)
11. R M Silverstone (Storage and fitting of tyres, batteries and exhaust systems)
12. C C Arthur (Motor repair depot)
13. Peacock and Cortina Construction Ltd (Builders and landscape contractors depot)
14. Freeman Engineering Ltd
15. F T Gearing (Landscape contractor)
16. Vacant
17. G J Pearce and Son (Bakers)
18. J S Clayton and Son (Scrap metal merchant)
19. Howard Organisation Ltd

20. Wm Perring Ltd (Furniture warehouse)
21. Stanley J Murphy (Shopfitters)
22. Berrick Bros Ltd (Stationery warehouse)
23. Stevenage Glass Co. (Glass warehouse)
24. John Lewis Partnership (Warehouse)
25. Warren Point Ltd
26. Contractus (Contract bus hire)
27. British Insulated Callender's Cables Ltd (Distribution warehouse)
28. Vacant
29. International Computers Ltd (electronic computers))
30. CPI Data Peripherals – under-leased from ICL
31. Flexile Metal Co. Ltd (Collapsible metal tubes and containers)
32. GPO District Engineering Depot (Telephone Engineering Depot)
33a. Kodak Ltd (Cameras and photographic supplies)
33b. Kodak Ltd (Cameras and photographic supplies)
34. Printech (Stevenage) Ltd (Printing and paper containers)
35. Hilmor Ltd (Tube bending machinery)
36a. Vacant
36b. Vacant
37. Printech Ltd under-leased.
38. British Aerospace under-leased
39. Fleming Instruments Ltd (Electronic instruments)
40. Mechatron Conversions Ltd (Industrial sewing machines)
41a. ICI
41b. Londonderry Maclaren Holdings
42. Marconi Instruments Ltd (Electronic instruments)
43. British Aerospace
44. Warren Spring Laboratories (Research Laboratories)
45. Taylor Controls Co. Ltd (Process control instruments)
46. Furniture Industry Research Association (Research, development, information and advisory services related to furniture industry)
47. Thermal Syndicate (Industrial ceramics warehouse)
48. PTP Films Ltd (Photographic Film processing)
49. Lee Valley Water Co. Ltd (Water Supply undertaking)
50. ICL
51. Property Reversionary Investments Ltd
52. Voltronic Ltd (Technical writers and electrical engineers)
53. Saxon Press Ltd (General printers, process photographers)
54. DBC Tools Ltd
55. Palmos Engineering
56. New Holland Sheet Metal Co.
57. Fine Fare Ltd (Hardware and textile warehouse)
58. British Aerospace (Hawker Siddeley)

59. Shunic Ltd (Metal castings and pressings, office equipment)

60. Marconi Instruments Ltd (Electronic instruments)

61. Mentmore Manufacturing Co. Ltd (Plastic pressings and "Platignum" pens and propelling pencils)

62. Geo. W King Ltd (Cranes, hoists, conveyors & automation machinery)

63. Vacant

64.
65.
66. } Not Corporation Property: Underleased to various parties.

67. Stevenage Youth Workshop

68. Lawson Computer Centre Ltd (Computer centre)

69. NE Autogas Ltd

70. Express Dairy (Milk distribution depot)

71. Eastern Electricity Board

72. Eastern Electricity Board

73. Associated Tyre Specialists

74. Sybron Taylor (Taylor Controls) (Process control instruments)

75. E C Hodge Ltd (Joinery and general woodwork)

76. British Aerospace (under-leased)

77. D Wickham and Co. Ltd (Mechanised plant & vehicle components)

78. International Exhibition Co-operative Wine Society

79. D Wickham and Co Ltd
80. British Aerospace (under-leased)
81. Eastern Gas Board (Gas Holder)
82. Bowater Packaging Ltd (Corrugated fibre containers)
83. Velux Co. Ltd (Warehouse for glazing units)
84. Ason Electronics (Electronic contractors)
85. Alroy Sheet Metals (Instrument cases, ventilation, ducting and electrical engineering)
86. Alroy Sheet Metals
87. Alroy Sheet Metals
88. Bearing Services Ltd (Bearing distributors)
89. Alroy Sheet Metals
90. Dane Engineering (Light engineering)
91. D G Burton (Spring maker)
92. D G Burton
93. Alroy Sheet Metals
94. J Fuller and Sons Ltd (Sheet metal work)
95. Alroy Sheet Metals
96. Vacant
97. M C Print Co. Ltd (Printing and reprographic work)
98. Adult Training Centre
99. Associated Tyre Specialists Ltd
100. Bulldog Remoulds Ltd
101. Zenith Motors Ltd (Garage)
102. A Gannon Bros (Civil engineering contractors)
103. W and T Avery Ltd (Scale maintenance depot) (Servicing of commercial and industrial weighing equipment)
104. Apex Aerials – D F Worby (TV/FM/aerials, stove enamelling)
105. J V E Brown
106. O C Nye and Sons Ltd (Electrical contractors)
107. Stevens and Barrett Ltd (Joinery and building contractors)
108. Clyne Bros (Decorators and general builders)
109. Harvey, Bradfield and Toyer Ltd (Food warehousing and packaging)
110. Amoco International Laboratories Ltd (Oil and fuel testing laboratory)
111. Contractors Plant Ltd

Pin Green Industrial Area

i Provident Mutual Life Assurance
ii Johnson Gibbons (Wholesale ironmongers)
iii Digico Ltd (Computer manufacturers)
iv Dixons Photographic Ltd (Service warehouse for photographic equipment)
v Sunblest Bakery
vi Craydale Ltd
vii R & D Systems
viii M & F Engineering
ix Servis Domestic Appliances (Servicing and repairing of domestic electrical appliances)

x Propak Ltd (Photographic equipment manufacturers)

xi Technicair Ltd (Development engineers)

xii C & C Appliances Ltd (Servicing and repairing of domestic electrical appliances)

xiii LPR Office Supplies (Herts) Ltd (Office materials wholesalers)

xiv Hertfordshire County Council (Electronics and TV servicing retraining centre)

xv Turners Industrial Cleaning Systems (Office and industrial cleaners)

xvi Advanced Coil Slitters Ltd

xvii Ronston Products (Light engineering)

xviii M H Goldsmith & Sons Ltd (Roofing and fencing contractor)

xix North Herts Scale Service Ltd

xx C E Hodgson

xxi Scott Lawther (Marketing)

xxii Wiremer Ltd

xxiii Buick Photographic

xxiv LPR Office Supplies (Herts) Ltd (Office materials wholesalers)

xxv Flair Electronic Systems

xxvi Flair Electronic Systems

xxvii Welding Tool Supplies Ltd

xxviii Welding Tool Supplies Ltd

xxix Bandfix Tapes Ltd

xxx Bandfix Tapes Ltd

xxxi Multigraphics Ltd

xxxii Propak Photographic Equipment Ltd (Photographic equipment manufacturers)

xxxiii Eastern Electricity Board (Reporting Centre)

xxxiv Car Dump (Botany Bay)

xxxv Unit Factories

xxxvi Unit Factories & Warehouses

xxxvii Propak

xxxviii ICFC Unit Factories

xxxix Du Pont

xxxx Small Service Industries

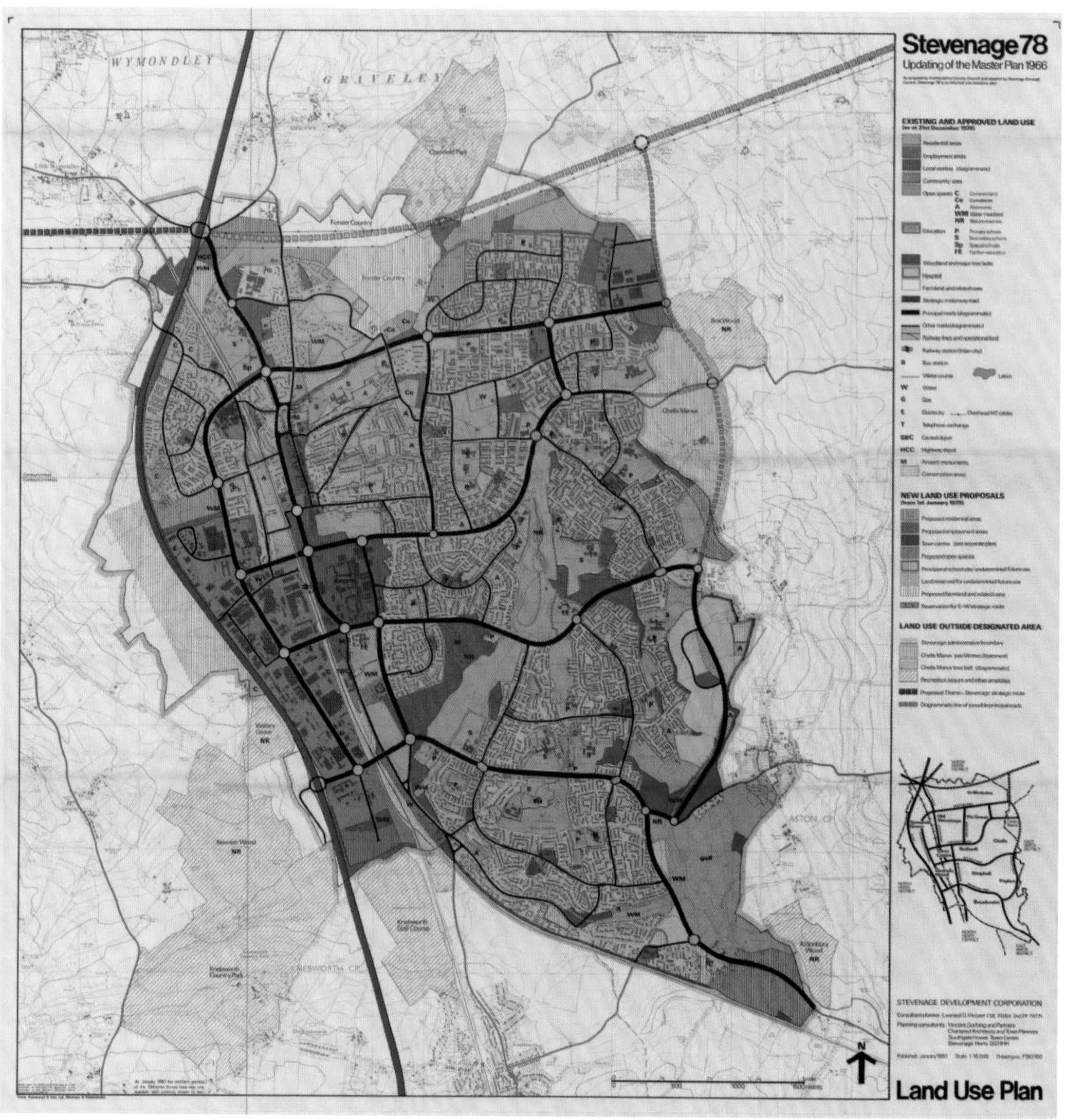

1978 update of the 1966 Master Plan

CHAPTER TWENTY ONE
Sport and leisure

THE STEVENAGE CRICKET CLUB, formed in 1894, is the oldest existing voluntary organisation in the town. It was followed in 1895 by Stevenage Football Club and both clubs played on fields in London Road, where the cricket club still has its ground, although not on the original site. In the 1930s, the cricket club's wicket was said to be the best in Hertfordshire – thanks to the loving care bestowed upon it by groundsman Wally Shelford – and that is why Hertfordshire chose to play some of its Minor Counties League weekday fixtures there. Among the outstanding first team players in the 1930s was wicket-keeper Geoffrey Powell Davis, who was to become a wartime temporary teacher in the early 1940s at Alleyne's Grammar School and, in the 1950s, chairman of the Stevenage Magistrates' Bench. Stevenage also produced an outstanding woman cricketer in Margery Pollard, whose family lived in London Road. In the 1930s she played cricket for the Stevenage, Hertfordshire and England women's cricket teams.

Stevenage had two other football clubs in the 1920s: New Town Rovers and Stevenage Wednesday, formed by local shopkeepers and staff. Its matches were played on Wednesday afternoons because that was the town's early closing day. In the late 1940s, Stevenage United FC was established by Roy Field to compete in the North Herts League. The 1950s saw the formation of Bedwell Rangers FC in the new town and subsequently many other teams were formed in the new neighbourhoods, particularly youth teams.

In 1956, Stevenage Town Football Club joined with Stevenage New Town Rangers Football Club and became known simply as Stevenage Football Club. The word Town was reintroduced to its title in 1960. The following year the club ground was taken by the Stevenage Development Corporation for town

Councillors v. Officers cricket match, 6 August 1978. Geoffrey Powell Davies was the umpire. (Stevenage Museum P1140)

centre development purposes and a replacement ground provided in Broadhall Way. Subsequently, football there, under new club owners, and under different club names, went through some traumatic phases before the establishment of the present successful club.

In 1963, Barclavians and Stevenage Youth Football Club, which was made up of pupils and ex-pupils of Barclay and Heathcote Secondary Modern schools, became the nursery team for the Stevenage Town Club which had now turned semi-professional and joined the Southern League. However, the club found that running a team at that level was financially unviable for them. Supporters were given an option to buy shares at five shillings (25p) each, but the scheme was unsuccessful and the club folded in 1968. It was succeeded by Stevenage Athletic Football Club which, in 1976, also resigned from the Southern League with financial problems. That left the town with a football stadium, in Broadhall Way, owned by the Development Corporation, but no club to play there. Stevenage Football Club was then formed with the hope of playing at Broadhall Way, but its intentions were thwarted when the owner of Athletic had a damaging trench dug across the pitch to prevent its use.

It was not until 1980 that soccer returned to Broadhall Way, the ownership of which had been transferred to Stevenage Borough Council. It then became the home of the present Stevenage Borough Football Club, which had been formed by a group of local football enthusiasts following the closure of Athletic and played in the Chiltern Youth League on the King George V playing fields. At Broadhall Way the club, popularly known as 'Borough', adopted senior status, and from then on made steady improvements. In 1990 it joined the Vauxhall League and, with a 100 per cent home record, romped home with the Division 2 North championship title with an impressive 107 points.

Playing in the Diadora League the following season, Borough won the Division 1 title and went on in the 1993/94 season to win the Premier Division. After just two seasons in the Diadora League – and reaching the quarter-finals of the FA Vase – Borough were promoted to the GM Vauxhall Conference League in 1994. Two years later, under manager Paul Fairclough, the club won the Football Conference, only to be denied promotion to the Football League by the Football Association on the grounds that, at the end of the 1996/97 season, the Broadhall Way stadium had not reached the required standards in its facilities and capacity.

In 1996/97 Borough reached the semi-finals of the Football Association [FA] Trophy and the 3rd round of the FA Cup, having beaten Leyton Orient but then losing to Birmingham City. In 1997/98 it reached the 4th round of the FA Cup with wins against Cambridge United and First Division Swindon before meeting Newcastle United of the Premiership in a 1–1 draw at Broadhall Way, which had a capacity crowd of 8,040 for that game. The replay, held at St James's Park, Newcastle, resulted in a 2–1 victory for Newcastle.

Alleyne's Grammar School football team, 1920–21. (John Allen)

In 2002, Borough reached the final of the FA Trophy, losing to Yeovil at Villa Park, and 2004/05 saw Borough reach the Nationwide Conference play-offs, losing in the final and failing to gain promotion to the Football League. Two seasons later (2006/07) Borough reached the final of the FA Trophy that was played at the new Wembley Stadium. 26,000 tickets were sold by the Borough in less than two weeks. It was a magnificent come-back in front of 53,000 fans, with Borough, 2–0 down at half-time, winning the FA Trophy by three goals to two for the first time. It repeated the performance at Wembley in 2009, beating York City FC, but was unsuccessful in the play-offs in the Blue Square Premier Division of the Conference League.

By beating Kidderminster Harriers two–nil on 17 April 2010 Stevenage Borough FC were assured of promotion from the Blue Square Premier Division of the Conference League to League Two of the Football League in the 2010/2011 season. For the third successive year they had already won their way to the final, to be played at Wembley Stadium on 8 May 2010, of the FA Trophy, of which they were the holders and which they were determined to retain under manager Graham Westley.

No account of football in Stevenage would be complete without mention of Vic Folbigg who did so much to promote youth football at both town and county levels. He died in 2007. Borough also has an army of loyal supporters and one worthy of special mention is Jim Bristow, who worked hard for the Club for many years. On 25 January 2009, Stevenage Borough announced that they had signed a six-figure sponsorship deal with the Lamex Food Group, resulting in the renaming of the Broadhall Way stadium to the Lamex Stadium.

Rugby football came to Stevenage in the 1950s. Dr Denys Swayne, a former Cambridge Blue, and Bill Howells, a former Welsh international, thought it time that Stevenage had a town rugby club, but where were the future players to come from? They discussed the matter with Francis Cammaerts, the new headmaster of Alleyne's Grammar School for Boys and, somewhat controversially, the school dropped soccer in favour of rugger. The town rugby club played on rented pitches and eventually acquired a ground of its own in North Road. Another rugby club, the Bacavians, was established by employees of the British Aircraft Corporation (later British Aerospace) and became very successful.

The game of tennis had been a long-time favourite in Stevenage. Private clubs had grass courts from the 1930s to the 1950s, at the rear of the White Lion Hotel in the High Street and off London Road. Stevenage also had a croquet club before the Second World War. Hard-surface tennis courts and green bowls rinks were later provided at King George V playing fields by the Urban District Council and, in more recent years, the town rugby club became Stevenage Rugby and Tennis Club. Also well-established was Stevenage Bowls Club.

In the late 1940s, Stevenage Hockey Club was restarted by some ex-pupils of Alleyne's Grammar School, led by Alan Primett, playing on the Stevenage Cricket Club ground in the winter season. The club currently has six men's and five ladies' teams as well as junior teams for different age groups. Stevenage table-tennis and darts leagues were also formed in the late 1940s.

The Educational Supply Association in Fairview Road had had its own playing fields and sports clubs long before the formation, in the 1950s, of the Stevenage Inter-works Sports and Social Organisation that arose as a result of the development of new factories in the new town's Gunnels Wood Industrial Area. De Havilland had playing fields in Fairview Road, Kodak opened sports facilities at Roebuck, and British Aerospace had first class and comprehensive sports and social facilities, including those for archery, Association football, bowls, cricket, rifle shooting, rugby and tennis, at Bragbury End. The cricket wicket was probably the finest in the county.

Formed in the 1930s, the Stevenage Six Hills Motor-Cycle Club was 'laid up' during the Second World War, when petrol was rationed for essential users only and many of its members were drafted into the armed forces, but was re-formed in the late 1940s. A Falcon Car Club was formed by the Tucker-Peake brothers, who had taken over the former Shelford and Crowe garage in the High Street. In an interview for the *Daily Telegraph* in 2002, John Surtees, the seven-times world motorcycle champion, said he bought his first car, a secondhand Jowett Javelin, when he was working as an apprentice at the Vincent HRD motorcycle works in Stevenage. He remembered that it cost him about £250 or £300.

Stevenage Hockey Club men's XI. (Stevenage Museum P3866)

Stevenage Amateur Boxing Club, 1957. (Stevenage Museum P6147)

With the development of the new town, a host of new sports clubs sprang up throughout the town and new sports facilities, including those for badminton, five-a-side football, ice-hockey, indoor bowls, swimming and ten-pin bowling were provided by the public and private sectors. Among facilities provided by private investors were an ice-rink at Roaring Meg in London Road, and ten-pin bowling centres in the town centre and at Roaring Meg, but none of these were to survive. Later, a ten-pin bowling centre was built at the Stevenage Leisure Park, which was developed privately on the site of the former George W King factory.

The editor of the April 1955 edition of the *Stevenage Echo* was no doubt delighted to include the headline 'New Town Boy makes Albert Hall' and to report that 13-year-old John P Haggerty, a pupil at Hatfield Technical School, had won through to compete at the Albert Hall as one of the 68 best boxers out of 30,000 entrants in the *Star* boxing competition. Described as 'obviously tough and a good deal more mature than his 13 years', John was runner-up in the Junior 'A', 7st 12lbs class. His father, John P Haggerty senior, was secretary of the Stevenage Amateur Boxing Club, which he had founded with Frank Petty and Stan Gammans. In the 1950s, young Ken Woollard started the Stevenage Harts Cycle-Speedway Club.

There are now many sports clubs in Stevenage for all interests and ages, including a large number of youth football teams and Stevenage and North Herts Athletics Club, whose home is the Borough Council's superb Ridlins End Athletics Centre.

We are indebted to Eddie Messent for the following account, which was written shortly before his death in 2008.

A Summary of Sport from 1950 by Eddie Messent

Prior to the end of the Second World War, the two largest employers – Geo. W King and the Educational Supply Association (ESA) – played an annual football match. The trophy was a Cup, the bowl of teak was made by ESA, whilst the base and lid of solid brass was by Geo. W King, the winner's name being engraved on the lid. This was eventually the first trophy presented to the Stevenage Inter Works Sports and Social Organisation (SIWSSO).

In 1950, two Directors of the companies – Harry King and Miss Dorothy Tear – contacted other companies through the Employers' Group suggesting the formation of a Sports and Social Organisation. Such an organisation would help employees of the new firms locating in the New Town to settle and participate in sports and enjoy a social life in completely new surroundings. Original members included ESA, Geo. W. King, Vincent HRD, Ibco, Wickham French and the North Met. The first newcomer was the Bay Tree Press. The first AGM was in 1952 under its President, Harry King. His advice and support in the early days were terrific, as was also the support from management of all member clubs. The presidency – a year's office – rotated between directors of member clubs, who invariably attended the monthly meetings.

As new companies opened, they and their employees were encouraged to join the organisation and the membership grew rapidly as did the diversity of sports including also sections for ladies. The range of activities was considerable from the conventional sports to indoor rifle shooting, cycling and bowls. Trophies were donated by various companies. A welcome addition was a Dancing Section. Dances were held three or four times a year in either King's or ESA's canteen. Other than the District Council's main hall in the Town Hall, Orchard Road, there were no facilities available. Competitions were held in tango, foxtrot and waltz and professional judges from London were paid five guineas to adjudicate!! Eventually, with the coming of the Mecca, the section folded as competition became too great, although a few dances were held in the new Mecca Dance Hall.

In the 1960s children were taken fishing by unreliable motor coaches to Wyboston, Tempsford, Buckingham Lakes or St. Neots, with the considerable help of anglers from the Stevenage Angling Club. The journey, drink, food and prizes cost half a crown (12½p.) An adults' competition was held later and was extremely competitive and well supported by the local press. Whilst there was a Stevenage Angling Club, SIWSSO held adult competitions which included non-members. When Fairlands Valley was opened in 1972, with its fishing beach, angling competitions became a regular event on the calendar. Fishing was restricted to a certain area and, on the advice of the Sports Council, a

Archery became a popular summer activity in the grounds of Geo. W King. (Stevenage Museum EM3)

special area for disabled fisher folk, with safety railings, was provided. The annual fishing competitions for children and adults, which had been arranged outside Stevenage, were immediately transferred and naturally resulted in many more competitors.

Archery became a popular summer activity in the grounds of Geo. W King, catering for both sexes. Many husband and wife couples enjoyed the sport. By July 1958 membership had reached 24 clubs, of which only four had their own sports fields – Geo. W King, ESA, De Havilland and English Electric.

In 1962 the Stevenage Swimming Pool was opened, the only covered pool for many miles. After lengthy negotiations SIWSSO were allocated a two-hour session once a week from 8 pm. From the opening day it enjoyed maximum usage and quickly the Stevenage Swimming Club found a home there. Later a club for the disabled was formed with allocated pool time on Sunday mornings. A hoist was installed to raise and lower swimmers in and out of the pool. The dedication of the club helpers at the pool-side was fantastic, and swimmers and helpers came from a very wide area.

Athletics was a struggling sport due to the lack of facilities, but around the mid 1950s a sports day was held on the ESA sports ground in Fairview Road and was a happy family affair. By 1958 support was declining and while there was no local athletics club enthusiasts joined the Icknield Harriers, based at Hitchin. The general committee of SIWSSO suggested that an investigation take place to see whether a Town Sports Day would be viable. Under the

ESA women's netball team c1965. (Stevenage Museum P14251)

guidance of the then President, Les Taylor, Director of WH Sanders (Electronics) Ltd, a public meeting was called in the Coach and Horses public house in the High Street. This was a terrific success and, as a consequence, Stevenage Day was born.

The early events were financially self-supporting. Over 100 clubs, in addition to sports clubs, organisations from the neighbourhood centres, churches, voluntary organisations and companies, paid a small fee for the hire of tables. Some clubs and organisations gave demonstrations of their activities in the main area. This invariably increased their membership. One year, at little cost, there was a sheep-dog demonstration. This was very successful until one of the sheep decided she did not like the crowd and bolted up Ditchmore Lane. A small fair for children, held in the southwest corner, supplied a very welcome donation to the funds. For many years an officer of the Stevenage Police organised a ladies' tug-of-war competition, inviting clubs from many parts of the country to participate. This was a very successful attraction. The Council underwrote Stevenage Day against financial loss up to £25. It was not permitted to charge an entrance fee and the many thousands who attended each year well supported the exhibitors. The money raised helped clubs finance their many activities for the following year.

In later years it became very difficult to run Stevenage Day as a self-supporting organisation and eventually the Urban District Council took over the organisation and allocated finances in its annual budget. Member clubs still elected the committee and the Council supplied officers to represent its interests.

As the town grew, new sports fields, including bowling greens and pavilions were constructed,. The major impact was the huge increase in the number of football clubs, especially juniors. At the time, the North Herts. Football League catered for their fixtures. In cricket, an evening league was formed under the guidance of SIWSSO. Bowling received a great boost when additional rinks were laid, and many of the clubs exist today. Thanks to the dedication of the various secretaries in submitting weekly reports, their activities were well covered in the local press.

Several new recreational areas were built. Infilling of land in the Ridlins Wood area in the 1960s led to the building of an ash athletics track in 1962, which became the home of the Stevenage and North Herts. Athletics Club. In October 1996 a start was made on the laying of an all-weather track and this was completed in time for the 1997 season. The building of improved changing facilities and a stand followed in 2003.

In the 1960s the national sports body through its Eastern Region office in Bedford approached SIWSSO and asked if they were prepared to admit outside clubs. The organisation was made up of companies in the Stevenage Urban District area and did not admit private clubs, as it was partially financed by the companies through their individual sports clubs. The answer was therefore, 'No'. By 1965 there were 32 member clubs with 31 sporting sections. SIWSSO was a very successful organisation and sporting friendships between 'old' and 'new' town families were formed, highlighted by the dances at Kings

Dancing display at Stevenage Day 1966. (Stevenage Museum)

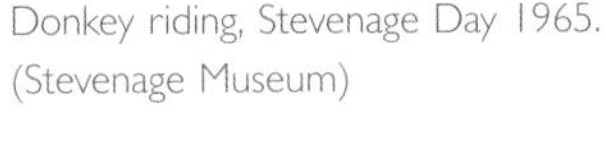

Donkey riding, Stevenage Day 1965. (Stevenage Museum)

and ESA. All sections were well supported and there was keen rivalry for the numerous trophies which had been donated by the many companies.

Indoor rifle shooting was under the strict supervision of the local Superintendent of Police and took place in the ESA Sports Pavilion. Ladies were not forgotten and there was stiff competition for netball and tennis trophies. The satisfaction of taking part was the best reward. Netball has maintained its attraction through various organisation changes and still is enjoyed by many today.

There was stiff competition for Netball and Tennis trophies. (Stevenage Museum EM4)

In late 1964 and early 1965 the Eastern Region Sports Council instigated talks with the local authorities of new towns, including Stevenage, Harlow, Welwyn Garden City, Hemel Hempstead, Crawley and Basildon, to discuss holding a joint sports meeting. Whilst Stevenage Urban District Council was among the prime movers, they could not hold the first event because of the lack of facilities. Harlow hosted the first New Towns' Festival of Sport.

The second Festival was hosted by Stevenage the following year, using eight different locations for the numerous events – public playing fields, school halls and fields, private sports facilities. After every town had hosted the event, the cost to local authorities and to clubs and individuals travelling to the events (over 200 in Stevenage and they had to pay their own travelling expenses and food) became prohibitive and the Festival was discontinued. In addition, many clubs were already competing against each other in inter-county or national events.

The Interworks Sports Association had grown quickly thanks to the enthusiasm of all participants. Most sports were catered for and, where possible, had their ladies' sections. Local companies were very supportive and initially allowed the use of their facilities free. It was a great help in the early days in overcoming the Old Town/New Town syndrome. I resigned as founder chairman of the Interworks Association early in 1965 in order to help in the foundation of the Stevenage Sports Council under the auspices of the Eastern Region Sports

New Towns Festival of Sport.
(Stevenage Museum)

Council. A committee was formed which included members of SIWSSO and members of private clubs. The latter had to have a constitution and the small joining fee was eventually cancelled. The Urban District Council assisted financially and audited accounts were submitted to them annually. The Sports Council was invited to nominate two of its members to sit on a sub-committee of the Stevenage Council's Leisure Services Committee.

In the meantime the work of the Sports Council increased greatly. Throughout all the many competitions organised initially by the Interworks Association and subsequently by the Sports Council, the support given by individuals in the organisation and in stewarding was fantastic; the town can be rightly proud of those early days.

June 1972 saw the first Kermesse cycling race, organised jointly by the Stevenage Cycling Club and the Sports Council, with police consent. The starting point was the junction of Argyle Way and Fairlands Way, then Gunnels Wood Road, Six Hills Way, Lytton Way and Fairlands Way. For many years it attracted a first-class field from across the United Kingdom. Finally it was discontinued because of police objections to traffic disruption.

A considerable amount of time had been spent with a special committee of the Borough Council discussing the location and contents of the proposed Sports Hall. The Sports Council always encouraged the disabled to participate in sport and had a disabled member on its committee. To test arrangements for disabled access, it arranged for a member in a wheelchair to be wheeled or carried through all doors liable to be used by any disabled person. The centre was opened in 1975 and the usage was overwhelming. As was to be expected, there were a few complaints; maybe the most serious was ventilation in the Sports Hall. The theatre had its own cooling system. The main hall hosted many prestigious sporting and commercial events, amongst which was a regular wrestling programme.

In those days there was always a major sports project under discussion. Also in 1975, the Borough Council issued an outline scheme for an 18-hole golf course at Aston, formerly the headquarters of the Stevenage Development

Corporation. In that year I was honoured to be named in the local press as the 'Father of Sport'.

A Sports Scholarship Scheme was launched in 1977 and clubs were invited to submit applications for monetary awards. The award of money to players was very difficult, as in those days amateurs still had to obey the rules of their national governing bodies, which were interpreted rigorously. No payment could be made directly to applicants for fear of jeopardising their amateur status, but money could be paid to the parent, club or national body.

Stevenage was invited by the BBC in 1978 to participate in its popular programme 'It's a Knockout' and eventually won the national final against Hemel Hempstead, at Milton Keynes, after an extra event. The team represented the UK in Arosa, Switzerland, on 9 August of that year but was unplaced. In 1979 details of a Sports Award scheme were announced, inviting nominations of a member who had contributed significantly to his/her club.

Meanwhile, the Borough Council, with the support of the Sports Council, called a meeting at the Girls' Grammar School, Valley Way, to discuss the formation of a golf club. The meeting was very well supported and an initial committee was formed to prepare a constitution. Over 200 people registered as potential members that night. I was invited to be the honorary secretary until the inaugural meeting.

Although it was recognised as having one of the finest municipal golf courses in the country, the amenities at Stevenage were poor. The changing facilities were minimal, the bar held 20 or so people – providing they all stood. Nevertheless, the spirit was strong and the keenness of members to improve their game was encouraging. The Stevenage Golf Club joined the National Association of Public Golf Courses (NAPGC) and the PGA. Thus members could hold an official handicap. Through the NAPGC , the club entered many competitions and enjoyed playing other clubs on a friendly basis. Initially players retired to a local pub for food. It was not until Greene King built a clubhouse that they were able to entertain visitors 'at home.' Membership grew regularly and at one time 803 members were registered, the highest in the country for a municipal club. The three sections – men, ladies and juniors – all ran their own competitions, with many of the trophies being donated by members. Each had its own very hard-working committee. Top honours escaped the club, although national finals were reached on several occasions.

Members did represent the NPGC in many events and the club hosted several NAPGC finals, an indication that the course was considered as one of the best. The junior section, originally under the watchful eye of Stan Horwood, who was

Stevenage Golf Centre, main entrance. (Andrew Hills)

for many years club chairman, flourished and eventually was accepted by the Hertfordshire Junior League, up until then the preserve of private clubs. One junior who progressed to the top flight was Ian Poulter, who plays in worldwide competition against the best and is listed in the Order of Merit (2001/2).

Despite the lack of clubhouse facilities, the club organised an annual Pro-Am competition in the late 1980s. Prize money for professionals was £2,000 and the value of amateur prizes £1,200 – small amounts in comparison to similar events elsewhere, but nevertheless it attracted a good entry. As sponsorship became more difficult the event was eventually dropped. The building of a clubhouse by the brewers, Greene King, was welcomed by members, who were kept informed of the plans. The club were offered, and signed, an agreement with Greene King for the use of a room for the Hon. Secretary free of rent.

The men's section was eventually accepted by the Association of Herts County Golf Clubs to participate in their league. The elitism of golf clubs was gradually being eroded thanks to the quality of the golfers and facilities offered by municipal clubs. The golf club has always enjoyed a healthy bank account thanks to the vigilance of its treasurer, Keith Molyneux. Eventually, in 1993, he and I resigned our positions, having served the club since its inception in 1980.

After serving as chairman of the Sports Council since its formation in 1965, I retired in 1986, handing the reins over to Grahame Bowles who had been vice-chairman for many years and who still remains in office.

The success of sport in Stevenage has been due to a large extent to the dedication of the players who have obviously enjoyed their sport and to the officials – far too numerous to mention – who have given so much of their time. ET Messent 7/21/2003

The first Stevenage Mini Olympics event was held in November 2003 and since then almost 6,000 young people have been given the chance to have a go at sports like badminton, basketball, cricket, football, golf, athletics, gymnastics, netball, lacrosse, tennis, rugby, sailing and kayaking.

In 2006, following government encouragement of, and funding opportunities for, sport in the regions, the Stevenage Sports Council was superseded by Sport Stevenage. This body brings together a number of organisations in the borough which represent or have an interest in sport, including Stevenage Leisure Limited. It acts as a community sports network, a key element in the delivery system for community sport and the link between Hertfordshire Sports Partnership and sport within Stevenage. It is closely aligned to the strategy and priorities of the Partnership, which whom it works closely to ensure that both bodies benefit from the joint resources in support of each other.

Sport Stevenage promotes and highlights the work of local clubs in providing opportunities for young people to become involved in sport on a regular basis, offers support to clubs that develop junior sections and promotes good liaison between Stevenage Schools Sports Partnership, physical education staff at the schools, Stevenage Borough Council sports development and Sport England. Each year, awards are made by the Borough Council to local young people who have achieved international standards or have shown promise at more moderate

Interworks sports annual presentation, 1959. Eddie Messent (seated second left) with president Les Taylor (seated centre). (Stevenage Museum)

Fairlands Valley Park boating lake. (Stevenage Museum)

levels in the sports and arts. The grants may be used to aid their further development and progress or for coaching fees, equipment or travel costs to events in which they are participating.

Stevenage Sports Hall of Fame (www.sportstevenage.co.uk).
Formula 1 driver LEWIS HAMILTON and motorcycle ace GEORGE BROWN are among more than a score of well-known sports personalities with Stevenage associations who are featured on this web-site.

LEWIS HAMILTON was born in Stevenage and attended Peartree Junior and John Henry Newman Secondary schools. At the age of 15 he was the European Kart-Racing Champion. Two years previously he had joined the McClaren Young Driver Support Programme, in which he showed great skill and potential and graduated by winning in Formula 3 and the GP2 World Championships before winning a deserved place in McClaren's Formula 1 racing team in 2007. In the same year he gained four Grand Prix victories, came second twice and third three times. Lewis achieved a personal ambition on a wet 6 July 2008 when, despite starting fourth on the grid, he won his first British Grand Prix before a wildly enthusiastic capacity crowd at Silverstone. He went on to win the drivers' world championship and was awarded an MBE in the Queen's 2009 New Year Honours.

George Brown (l) and Paul Richardson, wearing goggles (r) on Vincent HRD trials bikes, 1950–60. (Stevenage Museum PP822)

As far as many Stevenage fans of sport on wheels are concerned, what Stevenage-born Lewis Hamilton is to Formula One motor-racing, George Brown was to motor-cycle sprint racing and deserves to be officially honoured in the town in which he lived, worked and died. George Brown joined the Vincent-HRD motor-cycle works in Stevenage in the mid-1930s and became the company's chief test rider. In a successful racing career, with brother Cliff as his skilled mechanic, he competed in the Isle of Man Tourist Trophy road races and, on his own, rebuilt and modified Vincent superbikes, 'Nero' and 'Super Nero', on which he set up several sprint records, including the world's fastest run of 236 mph and the world standing start speed record for 1 km of 108.7 mph. He left Vincent's in 1955 to open a successful motor-cycle sales and service business in Stevenage High Street and was much sought out for his expertise by motor-cycle enthusiasts from a wide area.

Another Stevenage man of speed on wheels was successful local garage proprietor Peter Harper, who made a name for himself competing for Rootes Group in specially-prepared Sunbeam works cars in events such as the Alpine Rally.

Lewis Hamilton signing copies of his autobiography at Waterstone's bookshop, Stevenage, 2007. (Stevenage Borough Council)

IAN ALLINSON attended Burydale Junior and the Thomas Alleyne Secondary schools and played for Bedwell Rangers FC before joining Colchester United as a schoolboy in 1974, playing for nine years as a striker and scoring 69 goals in 308 appearances. In 1983 he signed for Arsenal, scoring 23 goals in 106 appearances and was in the team that won the Division I league cup in 1987, after which he joined Stoke before moving on to Luton and then rejoining Colchester.

MARTIN BROWN, who attended Broom Barns Junior and Bedwell Secondary schools, represented England in diving events at the Commonwealth Games at Christchurch, New Zealand, in 1973. He competed in two Commonwealth Games, three World Championships and two Olympic Games. He is now a national coach for British Diving.

ROLAND BUTCHER attended Shephalbury Secondary School, joined Stevenage Cricket Club in 1967 and, seven years later, joined Middlesex CCC as a professional. He was the first black West Indian-born Barbadian to play for England (versus Australia in 1980), toured the West Indies with the England team, played in 277 first-class matches, scored 12,021 runs (including 197 against Yorkshire) and made the fastest century of the 1987 season in 96 minutes off 73 balls.

STEVE DARLOW, who attended Alleyne's Secondary School, gained 16 England caps at basketball. He was a member of the Commonwealth Championship Gold Medal-winning team at Edinburgh in 1991 and, whilst at Loughborough University, was a member of the team that won the Universities Championship. He captained English Universities and British Universities teams and led Stevenage Rebels to the Division I league title in 1997.

FRANK DUFFICY attended St Michael's School for Boys (later John Henry Newman School). He joined the Derek Beaumont Diving Academy, became British Champion at the 10-metre high board in 1972 and 1973, was chosen to represent Great Britain at the Munich Olympic Games in 1974, gained sixth place in the European Championships and represented Great Britain from 1969 to 1975.

JIMMY GILLIGAN, professional footballer from 1981 until 1991, attended Longmeadow Junior and Barnwell Secondary schools. He played for Longmeadow Athletic FC, Hertfordshire Schools and then for England at Under-19 level. He was a striker for Watford FC, scoring the club's first-ever goal in European competition. He moved on to coaching and management with Nottingham

Forest, Wimbledon and Milton Keynes Dons and talent scouting for the England Under-21 squad.

TOM HAMPSON, Stevenage Development Corporation's popular Social Relations Officer from early 1954 until his untimely death in mid-1966, won a gold medal in the 800 metres final and a silver medal in the 4 x 400 metres final at the 1932 Olympic Games in Los Angeles, USA.

MARION HENTHORN attended Roebuck Junior and Stevenage Girls' Grammar schools, enrolled in the Beaumont Diving Academy, represented Great Britain in the Junior European Championship at Oslo, Norway, and England at Commonwealth, European, World and Olympic Games.

KIM LAMBDEN signed up for the Stevenage Open Netball team when she was 15, was selected for the adult team and for the Under-16 Hertfordshire County team as centre, and then for the England Under-18 team as WA. She enjoyed 11 years of international netball, representing England at the World Championships in Singapore in 1983 and the World Games in Australia in 1985.

NEIL McCLELLAN, javelin thrower, attended St Nicholas Junior and Collenswood Secondary schools, joined Stevenage and North Herts Athletic Club, represented Hertfordshire in four English Schools Athletics Championships, was Hertfordshire Champion eight times, South of England Champion three times, came second in the French championships and, in 2007, second in the Amateur Athletics Association National Championships and World Championship Trials. He represented England twice and, in 2007, won an international match in Hungary and represented Great Britain in matches against the USA, China and Russia. His personal best was 74.92 metres. Also in 2007 he was ranked third in Great Britain.

ALAN MUNRO, jockey, grew up in Stevenage and after leaving Barnwell Secondary School obtained an apprenticeship with racehorse trainer Barry Hills in Berkshire. His most famous win was on 'Generous' in the Derby.

SARAH PAVELEY attended Stevenage Girls' Grammar School and regularly won county and regional age-group fencing championships, including the Under-14, Under-16 and Under-18 Hertfordshire County titles. She represented Great Britain at the World Youth Championships at the age of 19 and, at many other events over the years, represented Scotland in two Commonwealth Games, winning two silver medals, and fenced in most European countries as well as in Canada, Malaysia and South America.

KEVIN PHILLIPS, who attended Burydale Junior and Collenswood Secondary schools, joined Southampton FC as a youth player in 1991, was with Baldock FC from 1992 to 1994, Watford from 1994 to 1997 and Sunderland from 1997 to 2003, for whom he made 209 appearances and scored 115 goals. He was a leading scorer and European Golden Boot Award winner in the 1999–2000 season, when he was a member of the full England squad on ten occasions, returned to Southampton for two seasons and then moved to Aston Villa before transferring to West Bromwich Albion in 2006, later joining Birmingham City.

GRAHAM POLL, football referee, born in 1963, who attended Ashtree Junior and Alleyne's schools, was appointed a Premiership referee in 1993, was appointed to FIFA in 1996, refereed the FA Cup Final and in the European Championships in 2000, officiated in the World Cup competitions in Korea and Japan in 2002 and in Germany in 2006, and refereed the European Cup Final in 2005.

IAN POULTER, golf professional, attended Wellfield Wood Junior and Barclay Secondary schools, played golf at the Stevenage Golf Centre and Chesfield Downs Golf Club, obtained a job as an assistant at Leighton Buzzard Golf Club and played – and won – in amateur competitions before turning professional. He was 'Rookie of the Year' in 2000, won a tournament on the world stage every year but one for several years, played in the USA Masters at Augusta in 2004, won the Volvo Masters at Valderama, was a member of the European Ryder Cup team that achieved a record winning score when beating the United States on their home ground by 18.5 to 9.5 points, won the Dunlop Phoenix tournament in Japan in 2007 and represented England with Justin Rose in the World Cup, when they achieved fourth place.

SUZANNE RAYAPPAN, born in 1981, attended the Giles Junior and the Thomas Alleyne Secondary schools, started playing badminton when she was nine, later moved to Milton Keynes to play at the National Badminton Centre, won titles at every age group from 14 to 19, and was selected to play for England against China in 2001. As a mixed-doubles player she was ranked third nationally and 11th internationally.

SANDRA REED won the District Schools 100 metres in her first year at Hitchin Girls' School, joined the Stevenage and North Herts Athletics Club, won a number of county championships over 100 and 200 metres, achieved fifth place in the Inter-Girls 200 metres at the English Schools Championships in Birmingham, was second in the South of England Championships 200 metres in a time of 25.6 seconds, and finished third in the Senior Women's South of England championships 400 metres, being ranked 16th in the UK with a time of 55.21 seconds, in 1989. The following year she represented Great Britain at Gateshead against Canada and the German Democratic Republic. She also won the South of England Championship, being ranked ninth in the UK 400 metres. She represented Hertfordshire more than 15 times. In 1991 she came first in the UK Championships Senior Women's 400 metres in Cardiff and was ranked seventh in the UK over that distance.

JASON SHACKELL, who attended Round Diamond Junior and Barclay Secondary schools and played for Symonds Green Minors FC was offered a one-year trial by Norwich FC, after which he gained a three-year contract at the Norwich City Youth Academy before making his debut with the Norwich first team in April 2003 in a league match at Derby. His first game in the Premiership was against Manchester City in February 2005, playing in the centre of defence. The 2007/08 season saw him as captain of the Norwich first team, for whom, by then, he had made more than 100 appearances.

MATTHEW SMITH, who attended Barclay Secondary School and won the Under-11 category in the annual Stevenage Fun Run went on to win the North Herts Schools District cross-country run in 1987 before joining Stevenage and North Herts Athletic Club. He represented Hertfordshire in eight English Schools Championships and in 1993 was selected to run for Great Britain in a junior cross-country international event in Belgium. He later represented Great Britain and England as a senior at European and World Championships on track and road and at cross-country events. In 2003 he won the English National Senior Cross-Country Championships and was the British first finisher in the World Cross-Country. He finished seventh in the Great North Run half-marathon in 2004, 16th in the 2005 London Marathon and ran his personal best of 2 hours 14 minutes in the 2006 Dublin Marathon.

MOLLY SMITH, who attended Lodge Farm Junior School, Marriotts Gymnastic Club and Marriotts Sports College, competed in her first senior international competition in 2007 when she represented Scotland in the Northern European Championships in Dublin, where the team won a bronze medal. In 2007 she became Scottish National Junior Champion on vault and took Silver on floor, bars and beam.

TIM SPEARS, who attended Barnwell Secondary School, took up sand-yachting at an early age and went on to win the British Junior Championships twice before his 18th birthday and then qualified for the British team at 18. In

1992 he came sixth in the European Championships, gaining two third places in the race series. The following year he competed in his first World Championships in Germany. After taking a break from the sport to go to university and establishing himself in a career, he again qualified for the World Championships in 2004, finished third in the 2005 British Championships, became British Champion in 2006, was runner-up in 2007 and finished in ninth place in the European Championships that same year.

TONY WRIGHT, who was born in 1962, attended Pin Green Junior and Thomas Alleyne Secondary schools, joined Stevenage Cricket Club at the age of 13 and played for the local side for a number of seasons. In 1980 he was signed as a professional by Gloucester County Cricket Club, spent the following 18 years with them and was captain from 1990 to 1993. He played in 287 first-class matches, scoring 13,440 runs, including 18 centuries and 67 half-centuries.

ASHLEY YOUNG, who was born in 1983, attended both Barclay and John Henry Newman Secondary schools and played for Stevenage Colts in local junior league football. He was part of the Watford Youth set-up between the ages of 15 and 17 before signing as a professional. In the 2004–05 season, at the age of 18, he played in 34 of Watford's matches and won their Young Player of the Season award. In 2005–06 he played in 41 league games and scored 15 goals, helping Watford to win promotion to the Premiership. In 2007 he was transferred to Premiership Aston Villa. He played on ten occasions for the England Under-21 squad, including matches in the European Championships, and in 2007 won his first full England place in the team that beat Austria.

CHAPTER TWENTY TWO
Music and the arts

IN THE LATE NINETEENTH and early twentieth centuries there were living in Stevenage a number of outstandingly gifted, creative people. One was Harry Bates, born in 1850, the son of prosperous builder Joseph Bates and his wife, Anne, who lived at the house that is now numbered 7 High Street. He was the fifth of eight children and attended Alleyne's Grammar School in the 1860s before being apprenticed to a stonemason, in the expectation that he would go into the family business. But his artistic talent led him to the Lambeth School of Art and then to the Royal Academy Schools. In 1883 he went to Paris and studied for a time with Rodin. From 1885, he exhibited regularly at the Royal Academy. His particular interest and talent was for relief work, mainly of classical subjects but, to prove that he could work in the round, he produced a remarkable life-size statue called 'Hounds in Leash', after which he was elected an Associate of the Royal Academy in 1892. The plaster casts of two of his reliefs, 'Springtime' and 'Harvest' and the bronze cast of 'Socrates Teaching the People in the Agora', for which he won a Royal Academy Gold Medal, were given to Alleyne's Grammar School (now Thomas Alleyne School). He died in 1899 and is buried in St Nicholas' churchyard.

Rooks Nest House (not to be confused with Rooks Nest Farm next door) was a farmhouse known as Howards for some 300 years until 1882, when the last of the Howard family moved out. The young Edward Morgan Forster and his widowed mother lived there from 1883 to 1893 and his memories of the house and surrounding countryside inspired him to write his famous novel *Howards End*, published in 1910. Twenty-one years later, in 1914, another widow, Clementine Poston, moved in with her children Elizabeth and Ralph. Elizabeth grew up to become a composer, musicologist and broadcaster, with a

Rooks Nest House, home of E M Forster from 1883–1893 and of Elizabeth Poston from 1914–1987. (Margaret Ashby)

wide interest in the arts. She welcomed musicians, writers and artists to the house, including E M Forster, who became a good friend and returned many times to his old home. After Elizabeth Poston's death in 1987, Malcolm Williamson, Master of the Queen's Music, lived at Rooks Nest for five years until August 1992.

Music-making and acting were by no means limited to professionals. Stevenage had its fair share of talented amateur performers who delighted local audiences. During the Second World War, employees of the Educational Supply Association formed a concert party that gave performances at the factory canteen in Fairview Road. Among the cast was an attractive young singer named Nell Gwynne, whose lovely voice enraptured audiences. The pianist was Douglas Fletcher, who also ran a local dance band that was in great demand. Soon after the end of the war, plays and variety shows were put on at the town hall in Orchard Road by the Stevenage Entertainments Society. The society's producers included Freddy Weiss and A A Harrison.

At the Lytton Club in Pound Avenue in 1949, Dr Deneys Swayne formed the Lytton Players. Their first production was a review titled *We Can't Use That!* with mostly original material which he had written himself. The Players' next production, in January 1950, was *Little Red Riding Hood* which, written by Deneys Swayne, bank manager Stanley Bunting and solicitor Morris Williams, ran for a week. It was the first of the Players' popular annual pantomimes and, with a revised script, was repeated several years later. The part of Principal Boy was played by the 'Stevenage nightingale', Nell Gwynne. Home-grown productions of *Jack and the Beanstalk, Babes in the Wood* (repeated another year) and *Dick Whittington* followed. Deneys Swayne then turned his attention to producing an annual *Old Time Music Hall,* in which Ray Gorbing and Stan Taplin put over with professionalism Victorian and Edwardian comedy songs that became their own, with audiences calling for them every year. The presentations were well presided over by Chairman John Austin. The Players also produced regular Gilbert and Sullivan comic operettas. In between all these musical and comedy productions there were straight plays. Stan Bunting, Morris Williams, Freddy Weiss, Teddy Wheeler, Stan Taplin and 'Nonny' Holmes were among the Players' producers.

When the Lytton Club premises were taken over by the County Council for educational purposes in the 1960s and were no longer available to the Players, the company staged productions, particularly the annual *Music Hall*, at the new Stevenage College of Further Education in Monkswood Way. Later, they obtained a site at Sishes End, Pin Green, from the Development Corporation and built their own headquarters, incorporating a small theatre. In the late

Stevenage Male Voice Choir, 1969. (Stevenage Museum P10048)

Stevenage Ladies' Choir winning the Cheltenham cup. (Stevenage Museum P10040)

1940s and early '50s, variety entertainment was also presented by an ad hoc group organised by Ted Wheeler and John and Denis Boorman. Their sketches and quick-fire skits were hilarious. The singers included Eva Davis, John Archer and, of course, Nell Gwynne, and they borrowed the Lytton Players young female dancers.

In the new town at about the same time, the Satellite Players were formed. They put on the pantomime *Aladdin* but did not stay together for very long – unlike the successful Broadhall Players who, well directed by Mavis Stannard, took their music hall (with pit band) far afield, including Stevenage's link towns of Ingelheim in Germany and Autun in France, where they were hugely popular. During its long existence, the group helped to raise many thousands of pounds for worthwhile causes.

On the choral side, two choirs that were well travelled, including concerts in Ingelheim, were Stevenage Male Voice Choir and Stevenage Ladies' Choir, both of which are going strong today. The Male Voice Choir appeared twice on Hughie Green's highly successful television talent show, *Opportunity Knocks*, the first time as contestants, the second as honoured guests.

When Stevenage Girls' Grammar School transferred to new premises, their vacated building in Six Hills Way became the Stevenage Music Centre, where Roger Judd formed and trained an orchestra of young people. The Anglican church of St George (now St Andrew and St George), opened in 1960, with its good acoustics and cathedral-like spaciousness, became an ideal town centre venue for choral and orchestral concerts, including well-attended performances by the Stevenage Choral Society and Stevenage Symphony Orchestra. Professional theatre came to Stevenage in 1975 with the opening of the Borough Council's West End-standard Gordon Craig Theatre, which is also used for amateur productions. The Lytton Players and Hitchin Thespians regularly stage performances there.

A number of Stevenage people with acting and singing talents joined non-Stevenage-based amateur companies, including Hitchin Thespians, the Garden City Players, a Letchworth-based drama festival group, and 'The Elizabethans' a company of actors, musicians, singers and dancers which was formed in 1961. It was directed by Sheila Graham, of nearby Datchworth, who had worked on costume design in the professional theatre and film industry. She took this unique brand of entertainment to cathedrals, festivals, stately homes, theatres and universities the length and breadth of the country, including London's South Bank, for some 30 years.

There have been music societies in Stevenage for 60 years or more, but the present Society has a history dating from 1950 when it was founded as Stevenage Musical Society by Peter Boorman and Elizabeth Poston, who remained as president for the rest of her life. During the 1950s the Society

Orchestra rehearsal in the church of St Andrew and St George, 2006. (Margaret Ashby)
Concert rehearsal in the church of St Andrew and St George, 2006. (Margaret Ashby)

presented concerts, both by its own choral and orchestral groups and by professional performers, many of whom were friends of the president.

By the mid 1960s the Music Society orchestra was flourishing under the baton of Peter Wigfield but the choir had become a small chamber group. However, in 1968 a new independent choir, the Stevenage Choral Society, gave its first concert, and soon invited Peter Wigfield to become its Musical Director. Subsequently the Choral Society merged with the Music Society but kept its name for performing while the Music Society remained the promoting organisation. When Peter Wigfield left the area in 1984 the society suffered a brief downturn in its fortunes and, as a result, the orchestra became independent of the Music Society and now performs as Stevenage Symphony Orchestra. However the choir, for ten years under the batons of Trevor Hughes and, for a short while, of Douglas Coombes, was rejuvenated and continues to thrive.

Recently the choir has become the dominant part of the society's activities and so the name of the society was formally changed to the Stevenage Choral Society. The Choral Society continues to promote performances by other groups, often as part of a shared concert. In recent years these groups have included Hitchin Symphony Orchestra, Hertfordshire Philharmonia, London Pro Arte Orchestra, Phoenix Concert Band, Stevenage Youth Choir, and Kingshott School Chamber Choir.

A particular feature of the repertoire is the performance of music by living composers. The Society has been privileged to give a number of first performances, including *The Selfish Giant* by Paul Adrian Rooke and *Lauda* by Douglas Coombes. As part of the Breakout scheme funded by Arts Council England through Making Music Eastern, they were able to work with local composer Richard Sisson and premiere *Battledore,* his piece for adult and children's choir, band and percussion. In April 2005 they gave a performance of *The Kestrel Road,* with its composer, Peter Maxwell Davies, in the audience.

The Choir has participated in four concerts in the Royal Albert Hall in London, together with other Hertfordshire choirs, performing Britten's *War Requiem* in 1994, Mahler's *Symphony No. 8* in 1999 and Verdi's *Requiem* in 2003. In 2007 they were involved in the most recent Joint Hertfordshire Choirs event, the *Grande Messe des Morts,* by Hector Berlioz. They have also undertaken concert tours, the first in 1990 to the Salzburg region of Austria. This was followed, in May 1992, by a tour of the Moselle region of Germany and, in April 1996, by a 12-day tour in the USA, visiting Maryland, Pennsylvania, and New Jersey, staying with host families at each venue. In May 1999 the Choir spent five days in Prague, in the Czech Republic, giving concerts in three different churches in the city centre.

Stevenage also has a poetry group, 'Parnassus', and a community media project called 'Rewind', which aims to offer hands-on skills in a variety of media, particularly to young people and those at risk of social exclusion.

As for the visual arts, Stevenage has a good heritage from pre-1946 and a flourishing arts scene today. In the mid-nineteenth century, the talented amateur artist Sidney Massie often visited her relations at the Rectory. Whilst staying in the town she executed some very skilful paintings of scenes of Stevenage. Some 70 years later, Mabel Culley, who studied at the Slade School of Art, was capturing the Stevenage scene in watercolour. Then Peter Blagg, who had come to Stevenage with his family in 1958 and was recorded in the Barclay School register as the first pupil from the new town, began his career as an artist with paintings of the locality. German-born Heinz Bosowitz, who came to Stevenage new town as a bricklayer in the early 1950s, was one of a number of successful local artists.

The Stevenage Artists' Co-operative was conceived by a group of Stevenage painters and formed in 1968 with the stated aim of 'Fostering the Arts in Stevenage'. A totally amateur, non-political and democratic organisation, it is run by an executive committee which is elected each year at the annual general meeting. For financial protection, the Society recently formed Stevenage Arts Society Ltd, a non-profit company limited by guarantee. Stevenage Arts Society considers itself to be 'probably the most active amateur art society in the country', with at least three exhibitions each year and working groups meeting on most days of the week. Since 1972 the Society's headquarters have been in Springfield House, in Stevenage High Street, where it has its own galleries, pottery, workshop and private studios.

Since 1993 Stevenage Borough Council has leased Fairlands Farmhouse, a Grade II listed building, to the Digswell Arts Trust, a charity which supports artists who wish to become professionals. The house and outbuildings provide 13 studios for artists working in a variety of media. These include a blacksmith's workshop, a woodturner's workshop, a ceramic studio and a workshop for a chainsaw artist. The large garden is currently being developed as a Community Heritage Garden in partnership with Fairlands Valley Park and North Herts College.

Cinema going has been popular in Stevenage since well before the First World War, when soundless film shows were part of Thurston's travelling funfairs. In 1913, a temporary structure in a meadow behind the White Lion Hotel became the 'Castle' cinema until the removal of the building less than a year later. No doubt the reason for its closure was the opening, the previous month, of the 'Tudor' cinema in a hall next to Tooley's restaurant on Bowling Green Road. It had seating for 300 in the stalls and small balcony. It closed in late 1916 or early 1917, apparently for the want of a projectionist to replace the one called into the Forces. After some alterations and improvements, it reopened

Publix Cinema.
(Stevenage Museum P1428))

in January 1919 and put on variety shows as well as silent feature films. That may explain the reason why part of a drum kit was found in a storage area behind the screen when the cinema closed for good at the end of 1960.

In April 1935, the 'Tudor' Cinema changed its name to the 'Publix'. At the end of the Second World War it had 316 seats – 218 in the stalls and 98 in the circle. It was the first local cinema to install double seats (called 'love seats') for courting couples. Its roof was of corrugated tin, which meant that in heavy rain the loud drumming of rain almost obliterated the sound track. The toilets were in a yard outside. At one time, the lamp in the ancient projector had a carbon 'wick' which, if allowed to burn too low, caused the screen to become darker and darker, resulting in cat-calls and whistles from younger members of the audience. Some patrons alleged that they had seen rats in the auditorium. All this resulted in the cinema being dubbed the 'flea pit' by some patrons.

A few months before the end of the Second World War, the Publix became part of the small London and Provincial circuit. But it could not compete with the modern 'Astonia', at the junction of Pound Avenue and Letchmore Road. Named after its owner, Mr Noel Aston Ayres, the 'Astonia' opened its doors in the same month that the 'Tudor' changed its name to the 'Publix' in 1935. With artificial palm trees in the foyer, a kiosk selling confectionery and cigarettes and concealed lighting in its art deco auditorium, the 'Astonia' quickly became very popular among picture-goers who had watched its building with interest and looked forward to the completion. There were 750 seats in the raked auditorium

The Astonia Cinema. (Stevenage Museum P4115)

but no balcony. In an effort to be different, the 'Publix' screened Continental films with adult-only X certificates, but the end came on 31 December 1960, the building was demolished in October 1965 and the site sold for housing.

The advent of television in nearly every home during the 1960s and '70s had a tremendous impact on cinema-going, which had reached a peak of popularity in an austere, blacked-out and rationed Britain in the Second World War. The war-weary citizens sought an escape for an hour or two from drabness and harsh reality to the escapist entertainment offered by the glitz and glamour of Hollywood comedies and musicals in their local cinemas. With cinema audiences declining, vandalism of seats by young hooligans and plans announced for a new cinema in the new town centre, a decision was taken in 1968 to transform the Astonia into a bingo and social club and it closed as a cinema on 1 March 1969. In 1982, when Mecca changed its Locarno ballroom in the town centre into a well-patronised bingo hall, it became the Stevenage Snooker Club.

A picture house did not materialise in the town centre until 18 November 1973, when a twin-auditoria cinema was opened by the ABC chain above a Tesco supermarket at the St George's Way end of Market Place. The entrance, with pay-box and a kiosk, was on the ground floor and the twin auditoria, one seating 340 patrons, the other with 182 seats, were on the first floor. In 1986, ABC cinemas were acquired by Cannon. For financial reasons, it was said, the cinema closed eight years later, on 7 April 1994. It probably would have been forced to close in 1996 anyway because of the opening in July of that year of a Cine-UK Cineworld The Movies multiplex with twelve screens and a total of 1,914 seats, on the former George W King factory site in the new Stevenage Leisure Park. Bob Monkhouse was a celebrity guest at its launch. Four additional screens were opened at the end of 2002, in what had been part of a failed bingo club next door, taking the total seating capacity to approximately 3,000. Feature films are also shown at the Gordon Craig Theatre.

As well as a location for picture houses, Stevenage has also been a location for picture making. In 1959 an Alva film crew was in the High Street to shoot scenes for *Serious Charge*, the story of a small-town troublemaker (Andrew Ray) who, accused by his priest (Anthony Quayle) of being responsible for the death of a young girl, amuses himself by accusing the priest of making homosexual advances. Directed by Terence Young, this 99-minute film in black and white, also had a young Cliff Richard in the cast. In the film, Springfield House was the home of the priest. *Halliwell's Film Guide* described the film as 'dull, despite earnest performances'.

An American-directed television film crew came to Stevenage in 1961 to make a documentary about a major post-war achievement in England – the establishment of new towns. Stevenage was chosen as the new town location and the documentary was shown on television in America. Entitled *Postscript to*

Empire, it was an excellent film about a brave social experiment that was providing housing and a new and better way of life for young London families in a good country environment.

In 1967, the UA/Giant 96-minute comedy *Here We Go Round the Mulberry Bush*, directed by Clive Donner, was shot entirely on location in Stevenage. And how clean, colourful and new the new town looked in Technicolor! The film dealt in an amusing way with a young bus conductor (Barry Evens) who, obsessed with sex, determined to lose his virginity. Also in the cast were Judy Geeson and Denholm Elliott. Comments in *Halliwell's Film Guide* read, 'Repetitive comedy which certainly opened new avenues in British humour and seemed pretty permissive at the time. In itself, however, more modish than sympathetic' and 'The only incongruity is that it should have been made by adults, so completely does it enter into the teenager's view of himself!'

The umbrella organisation for the arts in Stevenage is the Arts Guild, whose current membership includes;

Stevenage Ladies Choir
Stevenage Family History Society
Stevenage Arts Society (formerly Artists Co-operative)
Stevenage Floral Arts Society
Stevenage Fuchsia Society
Stevenage Male Voice choir
Stevenage Choral Society
Stevenage Photographic Society
Stevenage Underwater Photographers
Stevenage and Knebworth Arts Group
Stevenage Locomotive Society
Stevenage Festival
Stevenage Symphony Orchestra
South Stevenage Flower Club
Rock in the Park
Fusion
Lytton Players
Stevenage University of the Third Age
Friends of Stevenage Music Centre
Extravaganza
Parnassus
The Friends of the Forster Country
Stevenage Knitting Group
Starbound Music
Boozer Daddy (rock group)
Dark Cell (rock group)

The biennial Stevenage Festival of the Arts was started in 1992 by Ron Walker, Roy Mugridge, Jane Tobitt and other members of the Arts Guild. The festival has become increasingly sophisticated over the years, now incorporating Fringe events in addition to its lively programme of local amateur fine art, photography, poetry, theatre and music. It provides a showcase for the wealth of local artistic and performing talent within the Stevenage district.

'One Book for Stevenage', a scheme now in its fifth year, has become increasingly popular. The idea originated when the writer Ken Follett was on tour in the United States. He noticed that several of the cities he visited had community books, one title a year that everyone was encouraged to read and discuss. On his return, he suggested to the Mayor and the Leader of the Council that this could work well in Stevenage and received their support. The dual aim of the project was agreed as promoting literacy and a community spirit through enjoyment of the same book.

Books selected for the scheme must have a wide appeal and be suitable for readers from 14 years to adult. The event requires publicity and information campaigns and, as well as the Borough Council's input, involvement of the County Library, Stevenage Museum, local schools, North Hertfordshire College, the *Comet* newspaper, Hertfordshire County Council and, of course, the general public. Library events, a community launch event, author's visits, events at the

Henry Moore sculpture 'Family Group' at the Barclay School. (Stevenage Museum P3516)

'Urban elephant' by Andrew Burton. (Ann Parnell)

'Only Connect' sculpture by Angela Godfrey, sited in St Nicholas' churchyard beside the footpath into the Forster Country. (John Hepworth)

museum, a fun run, quizzes and competitions are held regularly. One year's book, *Q & A*, by Vikas Swarup, was subsequently made into the Oscar winning film, *Slumdog Millionaire*.

Of all the arts in Stevenage, the most visible are the pieces of sculpture placed throughout the town. The first of these, Henry Moore's 'Family Group' installed at the Barclay school in 1949, set a high standard for the others to follow. There are now so many public art works in the town that probably most residents have not seen all of them. The following list, which may be incomplete, is in chronological order and has been compiled with the help of Stevenage Museum's *Stevenage Sculpture Trail* and the 'List of Artwork and Sculpture in Stevenage' in the *BEAMS Review of Stevenage Conservation Areas, 2005*.

Location	Date installed	Title	Artist
Barclay School	1945	Family Group	Henry Moore
Fairlands Junior School	1951	Adventure	Mary Spencer Watson
Town Square	c1958	Ceramic mural	G Bajio CWS Arch. Dept
(symbolises the Co-operative Movement)			
Town Square	1958	Joy Ride	Franta Belsky (1921–2000)
Grade II listed sculpture in the 'populist' style. Has become the symbol for Stevenage and the new towns).			
Town Square	c1958	Clock Tower	Unknown
The Towers	1963	Seated Figures	David Noble
Bronte/Austen Paths	1963	The Three Geese	David Noble
Chertsey Rise	c1963	Monster	Mark Harvey
Bus Station	1964	Wall Sculpture	Peter Lyon
(This unusually shaped sculpture is made of welded aluminium plate. An original model of this can be found in Stevenage Museum. It is interesting in that at different times of the day, peculiar shaped shadows are created).			
The Glebe, Chells Way	1964	Polar Bear	Mark Harvey
(The artist's previous work was in wood and no longer survives. eg. 'The Fish' (1961) at Elm Green and 'The Donkey' (1969) at Bandley Hill Park).			
Webb Rise/Archer Rd/ Lonsdale Rd	1965	Dancing Figures	Dick Fowler
Archer Road, Pin Green	1965	King Pin	Unknown
(This sculpture, by an unknown artist, stands in the Pin Green community area in Archer Road. It is made of reinforced concrete and colourful glass mosaic).			
Bowes Lyon Centre	1965	Abstract	
Bandley Hill Park	1969	Abstract	Mark Harvey
The Forum	1972	Nameless Abstract	Jose de Alberdi
(The Basque sculptor was reported in *Stevenage Gazette* of 29 March 1972 as: 'cheerfully admitting that he didn't have a clue as to what it was or what it meant!' It cost £3,000. Unveiled by Nigel Abercrombie of the Arts Council in 1972. Moved from its original position in 2000).			
St George's Way underpasses	1973	Reliefs	William Mitchell
(Scenes from Contemporary Life & Abstract).			
Town Square	1974	Lewis Silkin	Franta Belsky
Manulife	1975	Mother & Child	Kuwak
Symonds Green	c1975	Sand Pit	Simon Harvey
Symonds Green	c1975	Clock	Simon Jones
Leisure Centre	1976	Logo	Donald Smith
Town Centre Gardens	1981	Women & Doves	David Norris
(Stands in the middle of the Town Centre Gardens lake and was given to the town by Stevenage Development Corporation).			

Location	Date installed	Title	Artist
Gunnels Wood Way	No date	Robot Family Clock	
(Robots. These cute little fellows made from reinforced concrete were created by an unknown sculptor and stand in between a row of houses off Gunnells Wood Road).			
St Nicholas School	No date	School Gateway	
Stevenage Museum	1991	Urban Elephant	Andrew Burton
(Andrew Burton was the winner of a competition set by the museum. The tower represents the Clock tower and the hooks symbolise local industry).			
Fairlands Valley Farmhouse garden	1995	Two Swans	Dennis Heath
St Nicholas churchyard	1997	Only Connect	Angela Godfrey
(This is a monument to novelist E M Forster, commissioned by the Friends of the Forster Country. Beyond the gate is the Forster Country which inspired his writing).			
St George's Way	No date	Mosaic Fish pavement	
Longmeadow School	c1998	Footballer	Dennis Heath
The Forum	1999	Sun Dial	David Harber
(The sundial bears the words from William Blake's poem *Auguries of Innocence*: 'To see the world in a grain of sand and heaven in a wild flower. To hold infinity in the palm of your hand and eternity in an hour').			
Peartree Park	1999	Totem Pole	Dennis Heath
Millennium Garden, King George V Park	1999	Planet Map	Astrium sponsored
Millennium Garden, King George V Park	2000	Friendship and Peace	Dennis Heath
(The hands represent the two world wars, holding the dove of peace. Carved from sweet chestnut).			
Towers Pond, Six Hills Way	c2000	Millennium milepost	Jon Mills
(Part of the national cycle network, This fish sculpture was unveiled in celebration of the millennium longest cycle event).			
The Forum	2000	Two Mosaics	Peter Dunn, Janette Ireland, Anji Archer, Helen Durrant

CHAPTER TWENTY THREE
Education

STEVENAGE IN 1946, with a population of some 6,500, was served by Alleyne's Grammar School for boys of secondary school age and the Letchmore Road Elementary School for boys aged 7 to 14. For infants aged five to seven years and girls up to 14 there was the St Nicholas' Church of England School on Burymead. Just seven boys and five girls a year might win scholarships to Alleyne's, or Hitchin Girls', Grammar Schools, otherwise they remained at Letchmore Road or St Nicholas'. Until shortly before the Second World War there had also been the Grange Preparatory School at the former Swan Inn in the High Street and, earlier in the century a few very small private schools such as that run by the Misses Beaver in a succession of premises, including 35 High Street. Westover School for Girls, on the corner of Julians Road and Hitchin Road was run by Miss Ruth Culley and her sister, Mabel, who had studied at the Slade School of Art and whose watercolours of Stevenage have left a valuable record of the town in the first half of the twentieth century. A small private school for boys and girls aged up to seven years was held at a hall in Grove Road, run by Miss Symonds, and in London Road a small private school for young girls was run by Miss Woolley.

Even before Stevenage was designated a new town it was clear that there was an urgent need for a secondary school, particularly for girls, and this was given added impetus by the 1944 Education Act which raised the school leaving age to 15 and promised secondary education for all. Unfortunately, this act also sounded a death-knell for St Nicholas' School on its traditional site. Councillors and school managers had long been planning improvements and repairs, but they could not meet all the requirements of the 1944 Act, which included a fenced-off playground and more space for outdoor physical activity.

The former school house and bell tower is all that now remains of the old St Nicholas' School building on Bury Mead. (Margaret Ashby)

The playground for St Nicholas' School was a small tarmac area: the Burymead itself was public open space. There was nowhere for the school to expand. There is no denying that the buildings were somewhat dilapidated and in need of upgrading, but they had served the town for 110 years and were part of its heritage. The last headmistress, Miss Florence Lawrence, her deputy, Miss Doris Ferguson, and their staff gave unstinting time and energy to the school, the standard of teaching was generally excellent and the setting, beside The Avenue, was much loved. But the 1944 Education Act insisted on a minimum site of 1.375 acres and St Nicholas' occupied only .85 of an acre. As it was bounded on one side by the Great North Road and on the other by Burymead, which was held in trust by the Rector of Stevenage and the church wardens as a recreation ground for the residents of the town, it was not possible to extend the site. The school was forced to close in 1963 and was later demolished, apart from the School House. Two new houses were built on the site, one for the Vicar of St Nicholas' church, following reorganisation of Church of England parishes in the town; the other for Eric Claxton, former Chief Engineer to the Development Corporation.

A similar fate almost befell Alleyne's Grammar School, but it managed to cling on to the historic site which had been its home for 400 years, as described in the School Song, written in 1922 by headmaster Hubert Thorne and set to music by Thomas Hassard. There are various versions of the words and that quoted below is taken from the official history, *'An Innings Well Played'*.

Fifteen hundred and fifty eight,
Ere Bess to the throne ascended!
'What shall I do,' quoth his Reverence true,
'For my fame when life is ended?'
Alleyne, Alleyne,
Quoth the Reverend Thomas Alleyne.

'Stevenage, Stone and Uxeter too –
'Schools at them all will I found, sir!
'But Stevenage ever's the home that I love,
'I'll be buried in Stevenage ground, Sir!'
'Stevenage, Stevenage,
'I'll be buried in Stevenage ground, Sir!'

Tudor, Stuart and Hanover men,
Carving an Empire's renown O –
Scions of Alleyne's have watched them pass
Rolling north from London Town O –
Mail coach, rail coach,
Rolling north from London Town O.

Years roll onward and youth has fled
And you're facing life's battle for fame, lad;
Think of the school by the king's highway
That taught you to play the game, lad.
Alleyne's! Alleyne's!
That taught you to play the game, lad!

So come let us sing till the rafters ring
To the praise of all honest endeavour
For Honour and Truth and an Innings well played –
'Nisi Dominus Frustra' for ever
'Dominus, Dominus,
'Nisi Dominus Frustra' for ever!

Alleynes Grammar School memorial gates, erected in 1930 'in memory of the Alleynians who fell in the Great War, 1914–1918'. (Margaret Ashby)

But it seems that Alleyne's school was not, after all, destined to remain in its original site for ever. Currently there are plans for a new, purpose-built school on the outskirts of the town at Great Ashby.

When people arrived from London to the new neighbourhoods of Stevenage, they naturally expected that schools would be available for their children, as promised in the new town publicity material. The Development Corporation's booklet, *The New Town of Stevenage*, published in 1949, recognised that there would be 'a relatively young initial population in the early years and a high proportion of small children, which will place a heavy strain initially on the primary schools and later on the secondary schools.' It added that these characteristics had also been a feature of inter-war housing estates, but went on reassuringly, 'However, with the help of statistical predictions and by close co-ordination with the County Education Authority, it will be possible to overcome the difficulties of providing adequate school facilities.'

Unfortunately, this optimistic forecast did not work out quite as planned. By early 1953 it was clear that there were not enough school places for the hundreds of children now living in the town. In the April 1953 issue of the *Stevenage Echo*, the editor reported:

> When the town of Stevenage was roused to action last January ... a deputation went to the Ministry of Education with full facts and figures to make a case for 'more schools for Stevenage' ... Roebuck School, due to start in late autumn and postponed to March is not yet begun. Bedwell East Junior School due to start July 1953 is now put back to September ... even more alarming is the shortage of school places ... if the building programme keeps to schedule there will be 608 children in 1954 without a place.

School Building Programme for Stevenage

These figures have been agreed by the County Council and the Deputation, which was elected at the meeting in the Town Hall.

Primary Schools

Date (Dec)	Pupils	School places exist/approved	New places planned	Total	Shortage
1953	1,650	1,160	–	1,160	490
1954	2,968	2,360	–	2,360	608
1955	4,413	2,360	1,680	4,040	373
1956	6,035	2,360	1,680	5,720	315

Secondary Schools

Date (Dec)	Pupils	School places exist/approved	New places planned	Total	Shortage
1953	673	600	–	600	73
1954	1,079	600	–	600	479
1955	1,536	1,200	–	1,200	336
1956	2,018	1,200	680	1,800	138

A further comment in the September 1953 issue pointed out that some children due to start school in September would be refused admission, as there would be no room for them. By July 1954 the focus was moving to secondary education, as the following extract makes clear;

> There is now concern about insufficient secondary grammar school places, especially for girls. There seems to be foundation for the belief often expressed locally that girls stand less chance of grammar school places than boys of similar attainment. Hertfordshire County Council Education Committee recommends the building of a grammar school in Stevenage in its 1955–56 building programme. Without such a school it was calculated that only 6.7% of our children would have grammar school tuition in a few years time. Assuming that the Ministry sanction the school it could hardly be ready before late 1957 or more probably 1958. What is to happen in the meantime?
>
> Plans have been made to enlarge Alleyne's Grammar School and for it temporarily to take girls but not a brick has been laid so far and any extra

Peartree Junior School pupils with their model of the Town Square, 1964. (Stevenage Museum P7348)

The music room at Shephalbury School in Lodge Way in 1958. (Stevenage Museum P6572)

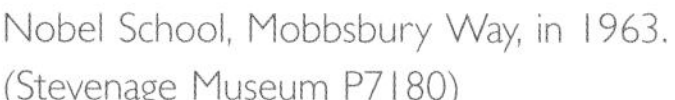

Nobel School, Mobbsbury Way, in 1963. (Stevenage Museum P7180)

accommodation will not be ready for at least a year. By next summer there will be five full primary schools operating in Stevenage and probably an extra one at Peartree, six in all. Compare this with the [one] that used to feed Alleyne's.

Eventually the schools did get built, though there was much sharing of premises in the early days. Leslie Rose, Headmaster of The Nobel School, a technical grammar school for boys and girls, commented in *The History Makers;*

> There was a great deal of co-operation between schools in Stevenage in the sixties; new schools receiving a great deal of help from those already established ... From the start Stevenage schools' governing bodies were very supportive and representative of the town as a whole. There always seemed to be a sympathetic member of the old town as well as many from the new, the Development Corporation was always there and representatives of old and new industries and at least one representative of further and higher education.

However, it comes as a surprise, when studying the history of education in modern Stevenage, to discover how many schools have been built and then closed, or demolished, within the 50 years since 1946. This is particularly true of secondary schools, where five out of 14 have come and gone in that short space of time. Shephalbury School, built in 1958, was closed in the early 1980s, used for a while as an annexe to Stevenage College and finally demolished, after which Grenville Road was built on the site. The Nobel School opened in 1962, was temporarily accommodated in the new Stevenage Girls' Grammar School building before moving into its purpose-built site in Telford Avenue, then, in the early 1980s, it moved to the Chells School site in Mobbsbury Way, the two schools having merged. Collenswood School, opened in 1963, was closed in 2006, becoming part of Barnwell School. St Michael's Roman Catholic Boys' School moved in 1968 from its former home in Hitchin to a purpose-built school in Sandown Road, then closed in 1987 to merge with St Angela's Girls' School in Hitchin Road, to form the John Henry Newman School.

Of all the new Stevenage schools, the Girls' Grammar School had the most disrupted history, as a former pupil, Valerie Lines, recalls;

> Born in 1945 to parents living in Old Stevenage, I attended St Nicholas' Church of England Primary School at the bottom of the Avenue in the Old Town. Passing the 11-plus examination I went to the newly formed Girls' Grammar School, Stevenage (GGSS) with only one year of pupils above me. For my first year we were in borrowed rooms in Heathcote School, Shephall; the second year saw us in borrowed rooms at Alleyne's Grammar School, opposite St Nicholas' Primary School and then for my third and subsequent years I was in the newly-built Girls' Grammar School, in Six Hills Way. After five years and 'O' level examinations I left to attend Letchworth College of Technology for a two year full-time secretarial course.
>
> The GGSS subsequently moved to a new site at Valley Way/Broadhall Way but vacated those buildings when it amalgamated with Alleyne's Grammar School in 1989, to form the Thomas Alleyne Comprehensive School.

Stevenage Girls' Grammar School pupils at school in 1961. Back row left to right, Valerie Lines, Janet Elmes; middle row left to right, Valerie Armstrong, Linda Newton; front row left to right, Sandra Hadley, Jo Mills, Sheila Brightwell. (Valerie Lines)

> I regret to say that since then all my permanent primary, secondary and college buildings have been demolished. A fellow pupil in my year at the GGSS had moved with her parents from London to Bedwell in the early 1950s and spent the remainder of her primary school days moving amongst the New Town primary schools, only one of which remains. The school she left in London is still standing!

The following is, as far as is known, a comprehensive list of all the state schools in Stevenage as at 2009, with date of opening, name of current head teacher and a summary of any changes of name, site or function.

Primary Schools
Almond Hill Junior School, Weston Road. (Head; Judith Lovelock). Opened 1957.

Ashtree Primary School & Nursery, Chertsey Rise. (Head; Beth Kirwan). Formerly Ashtree Junior Mixed, opened 1958 and Ashtree Infants', opened 1958.

Bedwell Primary School & Nursery, Bedwell Crescent. (Head; Judith Moore). Formerly Bedwell Junior Mixed and Bedwell Infants', both opened in 1955. The two schools merged in 1982.

Broom Barns Community Primary School, Homestead Moat. (Head; Tina Jarman). Formerly Broom Barns Infants School, opened 20 April 1953 and Broom Barns Junior Mixed, opened in 1955.

Camps Hill Community Primary School,Chells Way. (Head; Hilary Cliff) Formerly Camp's Hill Junior Mixed, opened 1959 and Camp's Hill Infants', opened 1959. The two schools merged in the late 1970s.

Fairlands Primary School and Nursery, Pound Avenue. (Head; Robert Staples). Formerly Fairlands Junior School, opened 8 January 1951. First Head teacher was Mr. W H Roach, transferred from Letchmore Road Elementary School for Boys. Fairlands Infants' School opened in 1957.

Featherstone Wood Primary School and Nursery, Featherstone Road. (Head; Margaret Conlon). First Head Teacher was Pat Brown. Formerly Bandley Hill Junior Mixed. It opened in 1958. First head teacher was Mr K W Koram. Bandley Hill Infants' opened in 1958. The two schools merged in 1998.

Giles Junior School, Durham Road. (Head; Sue Mitchell). Opened 1970.

Giles Nursery and Infants', Durham Road. (Head; Janice Bonnici). Opened 1970.

Letchmore Infants' and Nursery, Letchmore Road. (Acting head; Roma Mars). Formerly Letchmore Road Boys' Elementary School, opened in 1910, and converted to a Mixed Infants' School in 1950. The last headmaster of the elementary school for boys was Mr W H Roach.

The Leys Primary & Nursery School, Ripon Road. (Head; Cheryl Salmon). Formerly Wellfield Wood Junior Mixed, opened in 1973 and Wellfield Wood Infants', opened in 1973. The two schools merged in 1993.

Almond Hill Junior School harvest festival, 1965. (Stevenage Museum P10079)

Lodge Farm Infants' School pupils with their new play car, 1964. (Stevenage Museum P10943)

Longmeadow School, 1958. (Stevenage Museum P10099)

Lodge Farm Primary, Mobbsbury Way. (Head; Helen Turner). Formerly Lodge Farm Junior Mixed, opened 1962 and Lodge Farm Infants', opened 1962. The two schools merged in 2000.

Longmeadow Primary, Oaks Cross. (Head; Laraine Hodgson)
Formerly Longmeadow Infants, Oaks Cross, opened 16 April 1956. First Head teacher was Miss K Dews and Longmeadow Junior Mixed, opened 10 September 1956. First Head Teacher was Mr Norman Thomas. The two schools merged in 2005.

Martins Wood Primary School, Mildmay Road. (Head; T W Evans). Formerly Martins Wood Junior Mixed, opened 1968 and Martins Wood Infants', opened 1968.

Moss Bury Primary School & Nursery, Webb Rise. (Head; David Morton). Formerly Moss Bury Junior Mixed, opened 1966 and Moss Bury Infants', opened 1966.

Peartree Spring Junior, Hydean Way. (Head: Sarah Vince). Opened in 1955 First Head Teacher was Mr G H Anstock, who retired in 1980 on the school's 25th Anniversary.

Peartree Spring Infants', Hydean Way. (Head; Julie Mary Legg). Opened in 1955.

Mossbury Primary School pupils, Webb Rise, 1960. (Stevenage Museum P7349)

Peartree Junior School in 1958. (Stevenage Museum P6534)

Blessed Margaret Clitherow School, 1965. (Stevenage Museum P10098)

Roebuck Primary School and Nursery,St. Margarets. (Head; Jennifer Phelps). Formerly Roebuck Junior Mixed, and Roebuck Infants, both opened in 1955. The two schools merged in 2001.

Round Diamond Junior Mixed Infants', Whitehorse Lane, Great Ashby Way. Opened at this site in 2003, but originally at Mildmay Road from 1970–2002.

St Margaret Clitherow Roman Catholic Primary School, Broadhall Way. (Head; Geraldine Cartwright). Formerly Blessed Margaret Clitherow Roman Catholic Junior Mixed Infants' School, opened January 1965. First Head Teacher was Mr J D Flanagan. The school was destroyed by fire in 1998 and reopened in new building on the same site in September 2000. The nursery was added in 2005.

St Nicholas Church of England Primary School and Nursery, Six Hills Way. (Acting head; Jackie Roberts). Opened in 1834 on the Burymead, at the bottom of The Avenue in the Old Town. Closed in 1963 and moved to a new site in Six Hills Way. The last headmistress of the old school was Miss Florence Lawrence. She was succeeded by James Arnold, who took over on the old site until the school could move into its new building in September 1963.

St Vincent de Paul Roman Catholic School, Bedwell Crescent, opened September 1990. Formerly Blessed John Southworth Roman Catholic Junior Mixed School, opened 1959. First head teacher was Sister M Padraig Williams, and Blessed John Southworth Roman Catholic Infants', opened 1959. First head teacher was Sister Philomena, and Pope Pius XII Roman Catholic Junior Mixed Infants', Raleigh Crescent, Chells Way, opened 1966. All three schools merged in 1990.

Shephalbury Park Primary School. (Head; Jackie Ashley). Formerly Shephall Green Infants, opened 1961 and Burydale Junior Mixed, opened 13 September 1960. The two schools merged in 2005.

Trotts Hill Primary School and Nursery, Wisden Road. (Head; S. Butterworth). Formerly Trotts Hill Junior Mixed, opened 1968 and Trotts Hill Infants', opened 1968.

Woolenwick Junior Mixed, Bridge Road West. (Head; Michael Crabtree). Opened in 1974.

Woolenwick Infants' and Nursery, Bridge Road West. (Head; Usha Dhorajiwala). Opened in 1974.

Secondary Schools

Barclay School, Walkern Road. (Head; Janet Beacom). Opened 1949. First Head, Peter Osmund.

Barnwell Business & Enterprise School, Barnwell. (Head; R Westergreen-Thorne). Formerly Barnwell School, opened 1960. First head was Mrs Reece.

Heathcote School & Specialist Engineering College, Shephall Green. (Head; Edward Gaynor). Formerly Heathcote School, opened 1955, official opening 15 March 1956. First head was Mr J W Lewis.

John Henry Newman Roman Catholic School, Hitchin Road. (Head; M J Kelly). Formed in 1987 by merger of St Angela's Roman Catholic Girls' School, Hitchin Road and St Michael's Roman Catholic Boys' School, Sandown Road, both opened 1968.

Marriotts School, Telford Avenue. (Head; Patrick Marshall). Formerly Bedwell Secondary School on the same site. Renamed and relaunched in honour of Stanley and Sybil Marriott of Fairlands Farm, in 1994.

Nobel School, Mobbsbury Way. (Head; Alastair Craig). Opened in 1962 in temporary premises at the Girls' Grammar School until its site in Telford Avenue was ready. Merged in early 1980s with Chells Secondary School and moved into their site in Mobbsbury Way. First head was Leslie Rose. Since 2001 Nobel School has been a training school for teacher training and since 2005 a combined Science and Performing Arts Specialist College.

Thomas Alleyne School, High Street. (Head; Jonathan Block). Founded in 1558 in the will of the Revd Thomas Alleyne, Rector of Stevenage. First headmaster was Marcus Dauné, from 1558–1563. The school was known as Alleyne's Grammar School for Boys until 1989, when it merged with the Stevenage Girls' School and the name was changed to The Thomas Alleyne School.

Special Schools
Greenside School, Shephall Green. (Head; David Victor). Formerly known as Homefield School, opened 1977.

Larwood School, Webb Rise. (Head; Alan Whitaker) Formerly known as Hilltop School, opened in 1965. Name changed to Larwood in 1996

Lonsdale School, Webb Rise. (Head; Maria White). Opened in 1971.

Valley School, Valley Way, opened in 1991 on the site of the former Stevenage Girls' School which closed in 1989. (Head; David Harrison).

Schools that have changed their names or are no longer in existence
Alleyne's Grammar school *see* The Thomas Alleyne School.

Bandley Hill Junior School *see* Featherstone Wood Primary School.

Bandley Hill School playground, 1958. (Stevenage Museum P10072

Bedwell Secondary School *see* Marriotts School.

Chells Secondary School *see* The Nobel School.

Collenswood School *see* Barnwell Business & Enterprise School.

Hilltop School, Webb Rise *see* Larwood School.

Homefield School, Shephall Green *see* Greenside School.

Longfield School, Hitchin Road *see* Whitney Wood School.

Pin Green Junior Mixed, Lonsdale Road, opened 1964, closed August 2005.

Pin Green Infants, Lonsdale Road, opened 1964, closed August 2005.

St Angela's Roman Catholic Girls' School *see* John Henry Newman School.

St Michael's Roman Catholic Boys' School *see* John Henry Newman School.

Shephalbury Secondary School, opened 1958. First Head was Mr R G Earnshaw. Closed early 1980s.

Shephall Manor School, Shephalbury. A residential school for orphaned Polish children aged 5 to 11, from 1949 to 1954. From 1971 to 1989 it was a school for children with behavioural problems. Closed 1989.

Stevenage Girls' [Grammar] School *see* The Thomas Alleyne School.

Whitney Wood School, Hitchin Road, opened in 1962. Its name was changed to Longfield School in 1968. Closed in 1991.

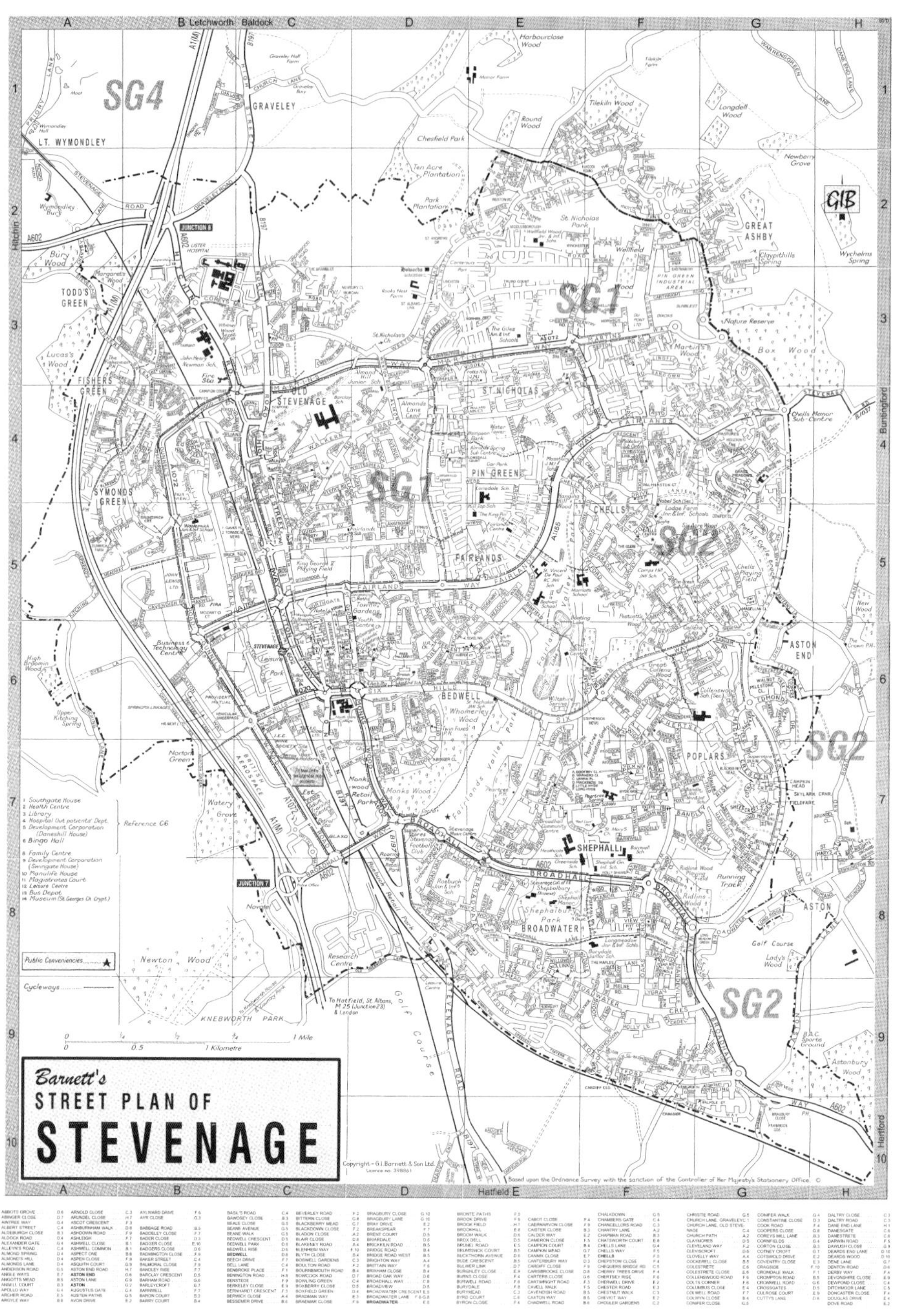

Barnett's Street Plan of Stevenage (Reproduced with permission of G I Barnett & Son Ltd)

APPENDIX I

Members of Parliament for Stevenage, 1945–2005

The following list gives the dates of elections, title of constituency, name and political party of the elected candidate and the percentage of the electorate which voted at that election.

Until 1974 Stevenage was part of the Hitchin Constituency. Subsequently, with the growth of the new town, a separate constituency of Stevenage was established, although its boundaries were redrawn several times to take in parts of the surrounding rural district.

Date	*Constituency*	*Candidate*	*Party*	*Turnout*
5 July 1945	Hitchin	Philip Asterley Jones	Labour	72.44%
23 February 1950	Hitchin	Nigel Fisher	Conservative	85.78%
25 October 1951	Hitchin	Nigel Fisher	Conservative	84.98%
26 May 1955	Hitchin	Martin Maddan	Conservative	83.17%
8 October 1959	Hitchin	Martin Maddan	Conservative	85.43%
15 October 1964	Hitchin	Shirley Williams	Labour	84.54%
31 March 1966	Hitchin	Shirley Williams	Labour	82.21%
18 June 1970	Hitchin	Shirley Williams	Labour	76.88%
28 February 1974	Hertford & Stevenage	Shirley Williams	Labour	83.58%
10 October 1974	Hertford & Stevenage	Shirley Williams	Labour	76.26%
3 May 1979	Hertford & Stevenage	P Bowen Wells	Conservative	80.37%
9 June 1983	Stevenage	Tim Wood	Conservative	77.88%
11 June 1987	Stevenage	Tim Wood	Conservative	80.50%
9 April 1992	Stevenage	Tim Wood	Conservative	83.03%
1 May 1997	Stevenage	Barbara Follett	Labour	76.60%
7 June 2001	Stevenage	Barbara Follett	Labour	60.7%
5 May 2005	Stevenage	Barbara Follett	Labour	63.02%
6 May 2010	Stevenage	Stephen McPartland	Conservative	64.77%

(*Source:* UK General Elections since 1832. www.psr.keele.ac.uk/)

Government Ministers with Responsibility for New Towns

Minister of Local Government and Planning

Hugh Dalton	1951

Minister of Housing and Local Government

Harold Macmillan	1951–54
Duncan Sandys	1954–57
Henry Brooke	1957–61
Charles Hill	1961–62
Keith Joseph	1962–64
Richard Crossman	1964–66
Robert Mellish	1970
Peter Walker	1970

Department of the Environment

Secretary of State and Minister responsible for New Towns

Peter Walker and Julian Amery	1970–72
Geoffrey Rippon and Paul Channon	1972–74
Anthony Crosland and John Silkin	1974–76
Peter Shore and Reg Freeson	1976–79
Michael Heseltine and John Stanley	1979

APPENDIX 2
Stevenage' Local Government

Chairmen of the Stevenage Urban District Council 1938–1974

James A M Popple, MA (Oxon)	1938–1946
William E Conlin	1946–1947
Arthur G Howard, MBE	1947–1952
Philip T Ireton JP, CC	1952–1955
Frederick Newberry	1955–1956
Stanley Ellis	1956–1957
Halcombe H Warren	1957–1958
Frank Hide	1958–1959
Alfred C Luhman, CC	1959–1960
Michael Cotter	1960–1962
Stanley R Munden	1962–1963
Kenneth B Ellis	1963–1964
John G Grice	1964–1965
James H Cockerton JP	1965–1966
Philip T Ireton JP, CA	1966–1967
Gordon G Balderstone	1967–1968
William L Lawrence	1968–1969
James Boyd BSc, MICE	1969–1970
Michael Cotter	1971–1922
Dennis C Burr	1972–1973
Stanley R Munden	1973–1974

Chairman of the Stevenage District Council

Stanley R Munden	1973–1974

Mayors of the Borough of Stevenage, 1974–2009

James H Cockerton, JP	1974/75
Brian P Hall, CC	1975/76
Robert A Clark	1976/77 & 1993/94
Robert W Fowler	1977/78 & 1991/92
John G Clarke	1978/79
Leslie J A Cummins	1979/80
Kenneth Vale	1980/81 & 1997/98

William L Lawrence	1981/82 & 1998/99
Ian J R Johnson	1982/83
Michael Cotter	1983/84
Kenneth R Hopkins	1984/85
Stanley E Greenfield	1985/86
Stanley R Munden, CC	1986/87
Albert C Campbell	1987/88
Alfred C Luhman	1988/89
Hilda M Lawrence	1989/90
Joan E Lloyd	1990/91
Robert V Woodward	1992/93
Reginald J Smith, MBE DL CC	1994/95
David G Weston	1995/96
Brian G Dunnell	1996/97
Eddie Webb	1999/00
David Kissane	2000/01
Hugh Tessier	2001/02
Pam Stuart	2002/03
Lilian Strange	2003/04
David Royall	2004/05
Brian Underwood	2005/06
Simon Speller	2006/07
Graham Clark	2007/08
Michael Patston	2008/09
Susan Myson	2009/10

Local government in Stevenage

Local government in Britain is structured in two contrasting ways. In Scotland, Wales and parts of England, a single tier 'all purpose council' is responsible for all local authority functions (Unitary, Metropolitan or London Borough). The remainder of England has a two-tier system, in which two separate elected councils divide responsibilities between district and county councils. Hertfordshire has a two tier system.

Hertfordshire County Council provides many services, such as caring for the elderly and vulnerable people, children and families; it provides schools, libraries and the Fire and Rescue Service; it enhances the countryside, plans future transport and housing developments and maintains roads in the whole of Hertfordshire.

Stevenage Borough Council provides services such as Council housing, Council Tax and Housing benefits, local services for elderly and vulnerable people such as meals on wheels and sheltered accommodation, free bus passes, environmental health and licensing, play services for children, economic development, provision of community facilities such as community centres, car parking, markets, planning and development, regeneration, neighbourhood services, refuse collection, environmental maintenance and cleansing.

Stevenage Borough Council comprises 39 elected councillors, three for each of the town's thirteen wards. Each councillor is elected for a four year term. One third of the seats, one per ward, are elected in three years out of four.

Hertfordshire County Council has six elected county councillors representing Stevenage who are elected in the fourth year.

Stevenage Borough Council's constitutional arrangements were revised to comply with the Local Government Act 2000, This Act reformed local government in England and Wales, including giving councils new wider powers to promote economic, social and environmental well-being within their boundaries.

Stevenage has an Executive comprising portfolio holders selected from the 39 elected councillors and responsible for specific areas of work such as housing or resources. The Executive is lead by the Leader of the Council and makes most of its major decisions based on advice in detailed written reports from the Council's Chief Executive and other officers. Some decisions, such as setting the budget, setting rents and decisions about the Council's policy framework, are reserved to the Council.

Full Council meetings are attended by all 39 councillors and meets to debate issues of concern to the community and make decisions. Meetings of the Council are chaired by the Mayor. Separate scrutiny arrangements involving non-executive councillors are in place to review areas of the Council's work and scrutinise the decisions of the Executive.

The Mayor

The Mayor of Stevenage is not directly elected. The Mayor is a serving councillor elected annually by the members of the council.

The office of Mayor has both a symbolic and practical importance and as the First Citizen of the Town the Mayor is the recognised representative and spokesperson of the Council on all civic and ceremonial occasions.

The Leader

The Leader is elected by the majority group of the Council and is responsible for:

the executive functions of the Council , including the arrangements for executive responsibilities

appointing a Deputy Leader of the Council

determining the size and membership of the Executive

acting as a chairperson of meetings of the Executive

providing political leadership for the Council

acting as the leader of the majority political party group

proposing the Council's policy framework and setting priorities and objectives

overseeing the implementation of policies and strategies to achieve the priorities and objectives

proposing the Council's budget to achieve its objectives

ensuring the Council achieves its statutory duties.

creating strategic frameworks for effective partnership working

ensuring continuous improvement in service standards and monitoring performance

communicating and advocating the Council's priorities, objectives and decisions

The Leader is provided with the appropriate advice and information to be enabled to take informed decisions by the Council's Chief Executive.

Stevenage Councillors in the Council Chamber, 2009:
Front Row L to R – David Cullen, Carol Latif, Liz Harrington, Ann Webb, Simon Speller, Sharon Taylor, Mick Patston, Richard Henry, Jack Pickerskill, David Kissane, Matthew Hurst, Margaret Notley, Dilys Clark.
Back row L to R – Lis Knight, Lilian Strange, Jacqueline Hollywell, Pam Stuart, Graham Snell, Robin Parker, John Gardner, Bruce Jackson, John Lloyd, Ralph Raynor, Joan Lloyd, Howard Buffell, Graham Clark.
(Councillors not present: Sherma Batson MBE, Monika Cherney-Craw, Laurie Chester, Bob Clark, Michael Downing, James Fraser, Pam Gallagher, Lin Martin-Haugh, Marion Mason, Sue Myson, Jeannette Thomas, Brian Underwood, Vickie Warwick.)

APPENDIX 3

The Stevenage Development Corporation

Chairmen of the Board of the Corporation

Clough Williams Ellis, CBE, MC, JP, FRIBA	1946–1947
Sir Thomas Gardiner, GCB, GBE	1947–1948
The Reverend Charles Jenkinson, MA, LLB	1948–1949
John Corina	
Mrs Monica Felton, Ph.D.	1949–1951
Sir Thomas Bennett, KBE, FRIBA	1951–1953
Sir Roydon Dash, DFC, LL.D, FTICS, FAI	1953–1962
Sir Arthur Rucker, KCMG, CB, CBE	1962–1966
Evelyn Denington, CBE (later Dame Evelyn Denington and subsequently Baroness Denington of Stevenage, DBE)	1966–1980

General managers

Major General Alan Duff, CB OBE MC	1947–1957
R S McDougall, CBE FCA	1957–1967
Kenneth Gale, FIMTA	1967–1969
Jack Balchin, DPA DMA FCIS FIH	1969–1976
Jack Greenwood, IPFA	1976–1980

In the last months of the Corporation's life, in the absence of Jack Greenwood, Roy Lenthall was acting general manager.

Bibliography

Documents

Gorbing, Ray *My Life*, unpublished manuscript (Stevenage, 1999).

Hertfordshire Archives and Local Studies catalogue, *Notes on Administrative History*.

North Herts Joint Planning Committee minutes, Hitchin Rural District Council, HALS, HCP3.

Stevenage Borough Council, *Stevenage Development Authority Bill* (1980).

Stevenage Urban District Council minutes, 1900–1945 [File in Stevenage Museum].

Stevenage Urban District Council, *Planning Scheme, map, 1942*, HALS HCP 3/1/24.

Books

Ackroyd, Sally ed., *Aspects of Stevenage 1700–1945* (Stevenage Museum, 2001).

Adams, A R, *Good Company; the story of the Guided Weapons Division of the British Aircraft Corporation* (British Aircraft Corporation Ltd Guided Weapons Division, Stevenage, Herts. 1976).

Arts In Stevenage [the Ellis Report] (November 1963).

Ashby, Margaret ed., *Stevenage Voices* (Tempus, 1999).

Ashby, Margaret, *A New History of Holy Trinity Church, Stevenage* (Holy Trinity church, High Street, Stevenage, SG1 3HT, 2006).

Ashby, Margaret, *The Hellard Almshouses and other Stevenage charities* (Hertfordshire Record Society, 2005).

Ashby, Margaret, Cudmore, Alan and Killick, Colin, *Historic Buildings of Stevenage* (The Stevenage Society, Stevenage Museum, 2008).

Balchin, Jack, *First New Town* (Stevenage Development Corporation, 1980).

Bostock, Brian, ed., *Aston in Your Pocket* (Aston Village Society, 1997).

Brickhill, Paul, *Reach for the Sky* (Cassell, 1954).

Bressey, Sir Charles and Lutyens, Sir Edwin, *Highway Development Survey for Greater London, 1937* (HMSO, 1938 [known as the 'Bressey Report'])

Carruthers, Judith, ed., *Brave New World* (Stevenage Museum, 1966).

Claxton, Eric, *Hidden Stevenage: the Creation of the Sub-Structure of Britain's First New Town* (The Book Guild Ltd, 1992).

Committee on Land Utilisation in Rural Areas (London, 1942) *Report*, Cmnd 6378 (HMSO, 1942 [known as the 'Scott Report']).

Davies, K Rutherford, *Britons and Saxons; the Chiltern region 400–700* (Phillimore, 1982).

De Salis, Dorothy and Stephens, Richard, *'An Innings Well Played' the story of Alleyne's School Stevenage 1558–1989* (Alleyne's, Stevenage, Old Boys' Association, 1989).

East of England Assembly, *East of England Plan* (2006).

Education Act 1944 (HMSO, 1944).

English Electric Bringing You Better living – a new job, a new house, a new town – at Stevenage (English Electric, 1953).

Expert Committee on Compensation and Betterment (1942) *Report* Cmnd 6386 (HMSO, 1942 [known as the 'Uthwatt Report']).

Eyles, Allen and Stone, Keith, *Cinemas of Hertfordshire*, Hertfordshire Publications (University of Hertfordshire Press, 1985).

Forster, E M, *Howards End* (Edward Arnold, 1910).

Forster, E M, *Two cheers for democracy* (Edward Arnold, 1951).

Fowler, Robert, *My Biography* (Stevenage, 2004).

Gover, E B, Mawer, Allen and Stenton, F M, *The Place-Names of Hertfordshire* (English Place-name Society, 1995 [1938]).

Greenwood, Allen, *Annual Report to Employees*, 1976–77 (British Aircraft Corporation, 1977).

Hansard Reports on Parliamentary Proceedings (House of Commons, 1980)

Harrisson, Tom and Madge, Charles, *Britain by Mass Observation* (Century Hutchinson Ltd, 1939).

Jenkins, Revd Charles, *Our housing objectives* (1943).

Jolliffe, Graham and Jones, Arthur, *Hertfordshire Inns and Public Houses, an Historical Gazetteer* (Hertfordshire Publications, 1995).

Knight, Martin, *Bunyan – the first hundred years; Centenary 1898–1998, Bunyan Baptist church, Stevenage* (Stevenage, 2009).

'List of Artwork and Sculpture in Stevenage', *BEAMS Review of Stevenage Conservation Areas, 2005.*

Lowe, Bert *Anchorman! Autobiography of Bert Lowe, Socialist, Trade-Unionist, Bricklayer and Stevenage Pioneer* (Stevenage, 1996).

Mariner, Anne, *Stations of the Cross* (13, Church Lane, Stevenage, SG1 3QS, 1994).

Methold, E V, *Notes on Stevenage* (Stevenage, 1902).

Ministry of Housing and Local Government, *People and Planning: Report of the Committee on Public Participation in Planning* (HMSO, 1969 [known as the 'Skeffington Report']).

Ministry of Housing and Local Government, *The South East Study* (HMSO, 1964).

Morris, J , ed., *Domesday Book, Hertfordshire* (Phillimore, 1974).

Orlans, Harold, *Stevenage: a sociological study of a new town* (Routledge, 1952).

Page, W B, ed., *The Victoria History of the Counties of England, Hertfordshire* , Vol. 2 (Clarendon Press, 1902).

The Parish Church of St Andrew and St George Stevenage Notes for Visitors.

Parker, David, *Hertfordshire children in war and peace, 1914–1939* (University of Hertfordshire Press, 2007).

Planning Policy Guidance Note (PPG) 17: Planning for Open Space, Sport and Recreation and assessing Needs and Opportunities (2002).

Rackham, Oliver, *The History of the Countryside*, 2ed. (Weidenfeld and Nicolson, 1995).

Rees, Connie and Huw, *Commemorative Trees in Stevenage* (Huw and Connie Rees, Stevenage, 1999).

Rees, Connie and Huw, *Stevenage Pioneers* (Huw and Connie Rees, Stevenage, 2006).

Rees, Connie and Huw, *The History Makers* (Huw and Connie Rees, Stevenage, 1991).

Spencer, Leslie F, *Wesleyan Methodism in Stevenage* (Stevenage, 1927).

Spicer, Mary, *Tyme out of mind* (Stevenage, 1984).

Stevenage Borough Council, Department of Leisure and Community Services, *Stevenage Lodge Horticultural Centre* (Stevenage, 1979).

Stevenage Borough Council, *Open Space, Recreation and Sport Study, a Final Report* by PMP (Stevenage, 2006).

Stevenage Borough Council, *Stevenage Development Authority Bill* (Stevenage, 1980).

Stevenage Borough Council, *Stevenage Employment Action Plan*, 2ed. (Stevenage, 1984).

Stevenage Chamber of Trade, Official Town Guide, ed. Don Hills (1955).

Stevenage Development Corporation, *Master Plan* (Stevenage, 1949).

Stevenage Development Corporation, *The New Town of Stevenage* (1949).

Stevenage Development Corporation, *Stevenage Master Plan* (1966).

Stevenage Museum, *Stevenage Sculpture Trail* (Stevenage, 2008).

Stevenage Urban District Council, *Official Handbook* (Stevenage, 1947).

Swarup, Vikas, *Q & A* (Penguin, 2006).

Tompkins, Herbert W, *Highways and Byways in Hertfordshire* (1902).

Trow-Smith, Robert, *The History of Stevenage* (The Stevenage Society, 1958).

Turner, Des, *Aston: Jack Pallett's Memories and the Village History* (Des Turner, Richmond House, 2, Benington Road, Aston, Stevenage, SG2 7DX, 2007).

Urwick, William, *Nonconformity in Hertfordshire* (1884).

Vincent, Leonard, *The Expansion of Stevenage – a Technical Appraisal* (Stevenage Development Corporation, February 1963).

Walker, John, ed., *Halliwell's Film Guide*, 2ed. (Harper Collins, 1995))
Wallis, David, *If I were a blackbird ... Recollections of Old Stevenage* (Fern House, 2005).
Whittier, John Greenleaf, *Maud Matter* [poem].
Williams, E T, chairman, *Report on the Needs of Youth in Stevenage* (Calouste Gulbenkian Foundation, 1959).
Wood, Michael, *Domesday: a Search for the Roots of England* (BBC Publications, 1986).
Your Town – Stevenage: the Official Guide, edited by Don Hills (Stevenage Chamber of Trade, [1955]).

Newspapers

Hertfordshire Express, 1900–1952 [File at Hitchin Museum].
Purpose, Quarterly Journal of Stevenage Development Corporation, Winter 1958.
Stevenage Comet, 6 February 1980 [File in Stevenage Central Library].
Stevenage Echo, 1953–56 [File in Stevenage Central Library].
Stevenage Gazette, 16 November 1967 [File in Stevenage Central Library].

Newspaper and Journal articles

Adams, John, 'Victory is in sight over 10,000 homes plan', *Stevenage Comet*, 20 July 2000, p. 13.
Adams, John, 'Area is one of the safest in the county', *Stevenage Comet*, 27 July 2000, p. 14.
'Aid reaches twin town destination', *Stevenage Herald and Post* , 28 October 1992.
'Backstage to a Town's Big Day', *The Daily Sketch*, 20 April 1959.
'BAe workers on March for Jobs', *Stevenage Herald and Post*, 28 October 1992.
'Better Youth Services', *The Times*, 14 October 1959.
Culley, Jon and White, Clive, 'That was the weekend that was', *The Independent*, Monday 5 February 1996.
'Fate of Forster Country', *The Guardian*, 19 October 1960.
'First Factory, Macmillan visit', *The Times*, 2 July 1952.
'Flats for the old in new town; joint experiment at Stevenage', *The Times*, 2 September 1960.
'Forster Country', Letter from W H Auden and others, *The Guardian*, 24 December 1960.
Hall, David, 'Town expansion – constructive participation,' *Town and Country Planning*, May 1999.
Iraq Invasion. Letter from Mr Harry Bott, *The Times*, 4 March 2003.
'"Joyride" Expresses New Town's Youth', *The Times*, 30 September 1958.
'Leonard Vincent', *Stevenage Midweek Gazette*, 16 November 1976.
McCarthy, Michael, 'Prescott-backed scheme to build 10,000 Green Belt houses is halted', *The Independent*, 13 January 2001.
'Moscow work delayed by Stevenage strike', The *Times*, Friday 4 March 1960.
'New Towns in 1953', *Town and Country Planning*, January 1954.
'Planner's Dream', *The Times*, 23 May 1958.
'Profile of Mary Tabor', *Stevenage Echo*, June 1956.
Purpose, Quarterly Journal of Stevenage Development Corporation, Summer and Autumn 1957.
'Resignation as residents face crowded future: townsfolk and villagers regret threat to Green Belt posed by Prescott's housing development plans', *The Guardian*, 15 October 2004.
Ross, Bernie, 'A long struggle against despair', *Stevenage Herald and Post*, 14 October 1992.
Selby, Dave, 'Auto Biography John Surtees; The 1964 F1 world champion and seven times world motorcycle champion is one of those rare sorts who's never owned a dodgy motor.' *Daily Telegraph* (London, 13 July 2002): 11. InfoTrac National Newspapers Database.
'Spectrum: The rising tide of moderation; Focus on the Social Democratic Party,' *The Times*, 21 March 1986.
Stevenage Comet, 6 February 1980.
Stevenage Herald, 16 September 1988.
Stevenage Herald, 6 January 1989.
Stevenage Herald, 13 January 1989.
'Stevenage men in joint project with French firm. Will build new space satellite', *Stevenage Gazette*, 11 December 1964.
'Stevenage New Town's Festival of Light', *The Times*, 15 December 1958.

'The day Frankie Vaughan dropped in for tea', *Stevenage Gazette*, Friday 30 January 1959.
The Forum, Magazine of Stevenage Borough Council, edited by Don Hills 26 February 1980.
'The Road North', *The Times*, 23 September 1958.
'This is Your Life', *The Times*, 24 May 1958.
Tregoning, Sarah, 'Work to start on run-down offices, by Stevenage Borough Council, Housing Strategy 2005–2010 "Good Housing for All"', *Stevenage Comet*, 10 July 2003, p. 39.
Walker, David, 'Postal voting increases turnout by 28%', *Guardian Home Pages*, 3 May 2002, p. 9.
'Want sports hall idea taken up now: Site suggested', *Stevenage Gazette*, 11 December 1964.
'Water supply fear for 500,000 new homes', *The Times*, 16 October 2004.
'Where are our children to live?' Letter, *The Guardian*, 19 October 2004.

Websites

Centre for Metropolitan History, *Gazetteer of Markets and Fairs in England and Wales to 1516* . Dr Samantha Letters, 2005, URL: http://www.british-history.ac.uk/report.aspx?compid=40419. Date accessed: 31 May 2008.
www.civicheraldry.co.uk/herts.ht
Website for Shephall – www.shephallmanor.net/SMAC.htm
Stevenage Borough Football Club www.stevenageborofc.com
www.stevenage.gov.uk/leisureandculture/artsentertainment/artsinstevenage
Stevenage Sports Hall of Fame www.sportstevenage.co.uk
www.stevenage.gov.uk/planningandregeneration

Audio-visual sources

Ken Ellis, Stevenage Oral Heritage Project tape recording, Stevenage Museum.
MBDA, *1950s and 1960s; Industry and 999* (2008) [CD audio recording].

Sources for Chapter 1

Books

K Rutherford Davies, *Britons and Saxons; the Chiltern region 400–700* (Phillimore, 1982).
E B Gover, Allen Mawer and F M Stenton, *The Place-Names of Hertfordshire* (1995 edn, first published 1938).
E V Methold, *Notes on Stevenage* (1902).
John Morris, ed., *Domesday Book Hertfordshire* (1976).
Oliver Rackham, *The History of the Countryside*, 2ed. (1995).
Robert Trow-Smith, *The History of Stevenage* (1958).
Michael Wood, *Domesday: a search for the Roots of England* (1986).

Web pages

Centre for Metropolitan History, *Gazetteer of Markets and Fairs in England and Wales to 1516*. Dr Samantha Letters, 2005, URL: http://www.british-history.ac.uk/report.aspx?compid=40419. Date accessed: 31 May 2008.

Sources for Chapter 2

Books

Dorothy De Salis and Richard Stephens, *'An Innings Well Played' the story of Alleyne's School Stevenage 1558–1989* (1989).
Graham Jolliffe and Arthur Jones, *Hertfordshire Inns and Public Houses, an Historical Gazetteer* (1995).
E V Methold, *Notes on Stevenage* (1902).
Robert Trow-Smith, *The History of Stevenage* (1958).

Sources for Chapter 3

Documents

Stevenage Urban District Council, *Minutes 1900–1945* [File in Stevenage Museum].

Stevenage Urban District Council, *Planning Scheme, map, 1942*, HALS HCP 3/1/24.

Books and Reports

Sir C H Bressey and E Lutyens, *The Highway Development Survey for Greater London, 1937* (1938) also known as 'The Bressey Report'.

Committee on Land Utilisation in Rural Areas, Cmnd 6378, *Report, 1942* also known as 'The Scott Report'.

Expert Committee on Compensation and Betterment, Cmnd 6386, *Report, 1942* also known as 'The Uthwatt Report'.

E M Forster, *Howards End* (1910).

David Parker, *Hertfordshire children in war and peace, 1914–1939* (2007).

Lorna N Poole, 'Number Please! The arrival of the telephone service in Stevenage', in Sally Ackroyd, ed., *Aspects of Stevenage* (2001), pp. 64–69.

Newspapers

'Profile of Mary Tabor', *Stevenage Echo*, June 1956.

Sources for Chapter 4

Documents

Stevenage Urban District Council, *Minutes, 26 July 1943–1, December 1947* [File in Stevenage Museum].

Books and Pamphlets

E M Forster, *Two cheers for democracy* (1951).

Tom Harrisson and Charles Madge, *Britain by Mass Observation* (1939).

Harold Orlans, *Stevenage; a Sociological Study of a New Town* (1952).

Stevenage Urban District Council, *Official Handbook* (1947).

Newspapers

Hertfordshire Express, 1946–48 [File at Hitchin Museum].

Sources for Chapter 5

Books and Pamphlets

Jack Balchin, *First New Town* (1980).

Revd Charles Jenkins, *Our housing objectives* (1943).

Harold Orlans, *Stevenage: a sociological study of a new town* (1952).

Stevenage Development Corporation, *The New town of Stevenage* (1949).

Sources for Chapter 6

Books

Jack Balchin, *First New Town* (1980).

Lily Glazebrook, Judith Carruthers, eds, *Brave New World* (1996), p. 8.

Stella Kestin, 'Acres of Mud', in Margaret Ashby, ed. *Stevenage Voices* (1999), p. 103.

Newspapers and Journals

'First Factory, Macmillan visit', *The Times*, 2 July 1952.

Hertfordshire Express, 1952 [File in Hitchin Museum].

'New Towns in 1953', *Town and Country Planning*, January 1954.

Stevenage Echo, 1953 [File in Stevenage Central Library].

Sources for Chapter 7

Documents

North Herts Joint Planning Committee minutes, Hitchin Rural District Council, HALS, HCP3.

Books

Margaret Ashby, *The Hellard Almshouses and other Stevenage charities* (Hertfordshire Record Society, 2005).

Brian Bostock, ed., *Aston in Your Pocket* (Aston Village Society, 1997).

Grace Drackford, in Huw and Connie Rees, *The History Makers* (1991), p. 93.

W Page, ed., *The Victoria Histories of the Counties of England, Hertfordshire*, Vol. 2 (1908).

Mary Spicer, *Tyme out of mind* (1984).

Des Turner, *Aston: Jack Pallett's Memories and the Village History* (2007).

Fred Udell, in Huw and Connie Rees, *The History Makers* (1991), p. 15.

Journals

Purpose, Quarterly Journal of Stevenage Development Corporation, Winter 1958.

Sources for Chapter 9

Books

Margaret Ashby, ed., *Stevenage Voices* (1999).

Eric Claxton, *Hidden Stevenage: the Creation of the Sub-Structure of Britain's First New Town* (1992).

Connie and Huw Rees, *Commemorative Trees in Stevenage* (1999).

Connie and Huw Rees, *The History Makers* (1991).

Connie and Huw Rees, *Stevenage Pioneers* (2006).

Newspapers

Stevenage Echo, January (1955) [File at Stevenage Central Library].

Website

www.civicheraldry.co.uk/herts.ht

Sources for Chapter 10

Documents

Ray Gorbing, *My Life*, unpublished manuscript (1999).

Books and Reports

John Amess, 'No Regrets', in Margaret Ashby, ed., *Stevenage Voices* (1999), p. 113.

Bert Lowe, *Anchorman! Autobiography of Bert Lowe, Socialist, Trade-Unionist, Bricklayer and Stevenage Pioneer* (1996).

E T Williams, chairman, *Report on the Needs of Youth in Stevenage*, Calouste Gulbenkian Foundation (1959).

Newspapers

'Better Youth Services', *The Times*, 14 October 1959.

'Flats for the old in new town; joint experiment at Stevenage', *The Times*, 2 September 1960.

'Moscow work delayed by Stevenage strike', *The Times*, Friday 4 March 1960.

'Stevenage men in joint project with French firm. Will build new space satellite', *Stevenage Gazette*, 11 December 1964.

'The day Frankie Vaughan dropped in for tea', *Stevenage Gazette*, Friday 30 January 1959.

'Want sports hall idea taken up now: Site suggested', *Stevenage Gazette*, 11 December 1964.

Sources for Chapter 11:

Documents
Ray Gorbing, *My Life*, unpublished manuscript (1999).

Books and Reports
Ministry of Housing and Local Government, *People and Planning: Report of the Committee on Public Participation in Planning*, [Skeffington Report], London: HMSO (1969).
Ministry of Housing and Local Government, *The South East Study*, HMSO (1964).
Huw Rees, 'The Valley 1961 and Road 9 1966', *The History Makers* (1991), pp. 126–129.
Fred Udell, in Connie and Huw Rees, *The History Makers* (1991), p. 22.
Leonard Vincent, *The Expansion of Stevenage – a Technical Appraisal* (February 1963).

Newspapers
'Fate of Forster Country', *The Guardian*, 19 October 1960.
'Forster Country', Letter from W H Auden and others, *The Guardian*, 24 December 1960.
Stevenage Gazette, issue 5763, Second Section, 11 December 1964, pp. 21–28.

Sources for Chapter 12

Books and Reports
Jack Balchin, *First New Town* (1980).
Paul Brickhill, *Reach for the Sky* (1954).
Charles and Betty Bush, in Huw and Connie Rees, eds, *Stevenage Pioneers* (2006), p. 21.
Judith Carruthers, *Brave New World* (1966).
Bert Lowe, *Anchorman*, Stevenage (1996).
Stevenage Master Plan, 1966, Vol. 1, para. 13.28.
John Greenleaf Whittier, *Maud Muller* (1856).

Newspapers
Stevenage Gazette, 16 November 1967 [File in Stevenage Central Library].

Sources for Chapter 13

Documents
Ray Gorbing, *My Life*, unpublished manuscript (1999).

Books, Reports and Pamphlets
William Emrys Ellis, *The Arts in Stevenage*, Stevenage Development Corporation (November 1963).
Margaret Ashby, Alan Cudmore and Colin Killick, *Historic Buildings of Stevenage* (2008).
Stevenage Borough Council, Department of Leisure and Community Services, *Stevenage Lodge Horticultural Centre* [1979].

Newspapers
'Leonard Vincent', *Stevenage Midweek Gazette*, 16 November 1976 [File in Stevenage Central Library].

Sources for Chapter 14:

Documents
Stevenage Borough Council, *Minutes, 19 December, 1979* [File in Stevenage Museum].
Stevenage Borough Council, *Stevenage Development Authority Bill* (1980).
The Stevenage Development Corporation (Transfer of Property and Dissolution) Order 1980.

Books
Jack Balchin, *First New Town* (1980).

Newspapers and Journals
House of Commons Hansard, 26 March 1980.
Stevenage Comet, 6 February 1980 [File in Stevenage Museum].
The Forum, Magazine of Stevenage Borough Council, edited by Don Hills, 26 February 1980.

Sources for Chapter 15

Books and Reports
Robert Fowler, *My Biography* (2004).
Stevenage Borough Council, *Stevenage Employment Action Plan*, 2ed. (1984).

Newspapers
'Spectrum: The rising tide of moderation; Focus on the Social Democratic Party,' *The Times*, 21 March 1986.
Stevenage Herald, 16 September 1988 [File in Stevenage Central Library].
Stevenage Herald, 6 January 1989 [File in Stevenage Central Library].
Stevenage Herald, 13 January 1989 [File in Stevenage Central Library].

Websites and audio-visual sources
Website for Shephall – www.shephallmanor.net/SMAC.htm
Ken Ellis, Stevenage Oral Heritage Project tape recording, Stevenage Museum.

Sources for Chapter 16

Documents
Ray Gorbing, *My Life*, unpublished manuscript (1999).

Books
Huw and Connie Rees, eds, *The History Makers* (1991).

Newspapers and Journals
'BAe workers on march for jobs', *Stevenage Herald and Post*, 28 October 1992.
'Aid reaches twin town destination', *Stevenage Herald and Post*, 28 October 1992.
Jon Culley and Clive White, 'That was the weekend that was', *The Independent*, Monday 5 February 1996.
Bernie Ross, 'A long struggle against despair', *Stevenage Herald and Post*, 14 October 1992.

Websites
www.stevenage.gov.uk/planningandregeneration

Sources for Chapter 17

Books and Reports
East of England Assembly, *East of England Plan* (2006).
Herbert W Tompkins, *Highways and Byways in Hertfordshire* (1902), p. 8.

Newspapers
John Adams, 'Area is one of the safest in the county', *Stevenage Comet*, 27 July 2000, p. 14.
John Adams, 'Victory is in sight over 10,000 homes plan', *Stevenage Comet*, 20 July 2000, p. 13.
Iraq Invasion. Letter from Mr Harry Bott, *The Times*, 4 March 2003.
Michael McCarthy, 'Prescott-backed scheme to build 10,000 Green Belt houses is halted', *The Independent*, 13 January 2001.
'Resignation as residents face crowded future: townsfolk and villagers regret threat to Green Belt posed by Prescott's housing development plans', *The Guardian*, 15 October 2004.

Herbert W Tompkins, *Highways and Byways in Hertfordshire* (1902), p. 8.
Sarah Tregoning, 'Work to start on run-down offices, by Stevenage Borough Council, Housing Strategy 2005–2010 "Good Housing for All", *Stevenage Comet*, 10 July 2003, p. 39.
David Walker, 'Postal voting increases turnout by 28%', *Guardian Home Pages*, 3 May 2002, p. 9.
'Water supply fear for 500,000 new homes', *The Times*, 16 October 2004.
'Where are our children to live?' Letter, *The Guardian*, 19 October 2004.

Websites
Stevenage regeneration website – www.stevenageregeneration.org

Sources for Chapter 18

Books, Reports and Pamphlets
English Electric Bringing You Better Living – a new job, a new house, a new town – at Stevenage, English Electric (1953).
Walter Marchant, 'The Skylark's Song', in Margaret Ashby, *Stevenage Voices* (1999), p. 70.
Gordon Patterson, 'Landscaping', in Huw & Connie Rees, eds, *The History Makers* (1991), p. 66.
Planning Policy Guidance Note (PPG) 17: Planning for Open Space, Sport and Recreation and assessing Needs and Opportunities (2002).
Stevenage Borough Council, *Open Space, Recreation and Sport Study, a Final Report* by PMP (2006).
David Wallis, *If I were a blackbird ... Recollections of Old Stevenage* (2005).
Your Town – Stevenage: the Official Guide, edited by Don Hills, Stevenage Chamber of Trade [1955].

Newspapers and Journals
Purpose, Quarterly Journal of Stevenage Development Corporation, Summer 1957.
Purpose, Quarterly Journal of Stevenage Development Corporation, Autumn 1957.

Sources for Chapter 19

Books and Pamphlets
John Amess, 'The Roman Catholic Church in Grove Road', in Sally Ackroyd, ed., *Aspects of Stevenage, 1700–1945* (2001), pp. 60–63.
Margaret Ashby, A New History of Holy Trinity Church, Stevenage (2006).
Anne Mariner, *Stations of the Cross* (1994).
Martin Knight, *Bunyan – the first hundred years; Centenary 1898–1998* [2009].
The Parish Church of St Andrew and St George Stevenage Notes for Visitors.
Leslie F Spencer, *Wesleyan Methodism in Stevenage*, Stevenage, pamphlet, 12pp. (1927).
Robert Trow-Smith, *The History of Stevenage* (1958).
William Urwick, *Nonconformity in Hertfordshire* (1884).
David Wallis, *If I were a blackbird ... Recollections of Old Stevenage* (2005).
Most Stevenage churches have websites, which supplied much of the information for this chapter.

Sources for Chapter 20

Documents
Ray Gorbing, *My Life*, unpublished manuscript (1999).

Books, Reports and Pamphlets
A R Adams, *Good Company; the story of the Guided Weapons Division of the British Aircraft Corporation* (1976).
Jack Balchin, *First New Town* (1980).
English Electric bringing you better living – at Stevenage [1955].
Grapevine, Newsletter of the English Electric Company (1959).
Allen Greenwood, *Annual Report to Employees*, British Aircraft Corporation (1976–77).

Stevenage Development Corporation, *Master Plan* (1949).

Newspapers and Journals
Leonard Vincent [ready made factories, undated newspaper clipping].

Audio-visual sources
MBDA, *1950s and 1960s; Industry and* 999 (2008) [CD audio recording].

Sources for Chapter 21

Newspapers
Dave Selby, 'Auto Biography of John Surtees; The 1964 F1 world champion and seven times world motorcycle champion is one of those rare sorts who's never owned a dodgy motor.' *Daily Telegraph* (London, England) (13 July 2002): 11. InfoTrac National Newspapers Database.
Stevenage Echo, April 1955 [File in Stevenage Central Library].

Websites
Stevenage Borough Football Club website – www.stevenageborofc.com
Stevenage Sports Hall of Fame website – www.sportstevenage.co.uk

Sources for Chapter 22

Books, Reports and Pamphlets
Dorothy De Salis and Richard Stephens, *'An Innings Well Played': the Story of Alleyne's School, Stevenage, 1558–1989* (1989).
Allen Eyles and Keith Stone, *Cinemas of Hertfordshire* (1985).
E M Forster, *Howards End* (1910).
John Walker, ed., *Halliwell's Film Guide*, 2ed. (Harper Collins, 1995).
'List of Artwork and Sculpture in Stevenage', *BEAMS Review of Stevenage Conservation Areas, 2005.*
Stevenage Museum, *Stevenage Sculpture Trail.*
Vikas Swarup, *Q & A* (2006).

Websites
Website for the Stevenage arts scene
www.stevenage.gov.uk/leisureandculture/artsentertainment/artsinstevenage

Sources for Chapter 23

Books and Pamphlets
Dorothy De Salis and Richard Stephens, *'An Innings Well Played': the Story of Alleyne's School, Stevenage, 1558–1989* (1989).
Education Act 1944.
Leslie Rose, 'Stevenage Education', in Huw and Connie Rees, *The History Makers* (1991), pp. 194–200.
Stevenage Development Corporation, *The New Town of Stevenage* (1949).

Newspapers
The Stevenage Echo, April and September 1953 [File in Stevenage Central Library].

Index